GAYS/JUSTICE

Between Men ~ Between Women
Lesbian and Gay Studies

Between Men ~ Between Women publishes current scholarship of lesbian and gay culture in the Humanities and Social Sciences. The series includes both books which rest within specific traditional disciplines and are substantially about gay men or lesbians and books which are interdisciplinary in ways which reveal new insights into gay and lesbian experience, transform traditional disciplinary methods in consequence of the perspectives that experience provides, or begin to establish lesbian and gay studies as a freestanding inquiry. Established to contribute to increased understanding of lesbians and gay men, the Series also aims to provide through that understanding a wider comprehension of culture in general.

General Editor: Richard D. Mohr

Advisory Board of Editors:

GAYS/JUSTICE

A Study of Ethics, Society, and Law

Richard D. Mohr

COLUMBIA UNIVERSITY PRESS

NEW YORK

by the same author:
The Platonic Cosmology

Columbia University Press
New York   Guildford, Surrey

Copyright © 1988 Richard D. Mohr

Library of Congress
Library of Congress Cataloging-in-Publication Data
Mohr, Richard D.
Gays/justice : a study of ethics, society, and law / Richard D. Mohr.
p. cm.
Includes bibliographical references and index.
ISBN 0-231-06734-8
ISBN 0-231-06735-6 (pbk)
1. Gays—United States.   2. Gays—Civil rights—United States.
3. Homosexuality—Law and legislation—United States.   4. AIDS
(Disease)—Social aspects—United States.   5. Homosexuality—United
States—Moral and ethical aspects.   I. Title.
HQ76.3.U5M64 1988
306.7'66'0973—dc 19   88-9688
CIP

c 10 9 8 7 6 5 4 3 2
p 10 9 8 7 6 5 4 3 2 1
Casebound editions of Columbia University Press books are
Smyth-sewn and printed on permanent and durable acid-free paper

Book design by Ken Venezio

for
Robert W. Switzer

Contents

Introduction

Society at large does not know what to think about gays. Social taboos on discussing sexuality, especially gay sexuality, have left a void in society's understanding of gays. This void in understanding, though, has been filled to overflowing with stereotypes, prejudices, and unexamined fears, which in concert have largely governed the development of social policy toward gays. Conversely, because of the socially and legally enforced invisibility of gay people, gays themselves have not been able to develop to any significant degree a public discourse about themselves. Save through the beginnings of a gay literature in the last decade and a half, gays have little sense of the significance of their own experience for themselves; still less do they have a sense of what the significance of their experience might be for society; and they are, in any case, little able to defend themselves or advance their distinctive interests in the forums of social policy. Both social policy on gay issues and the gay rights movement itself have been nearly empty of ideas and so too of their concatenations into arguments. The moral, social, and legal inquiries and arguments of this book are aimed at remedying these two gaps in social knowledge—that of gays and nongays alike.

The book aims to inform the general audience of gay experience, about which it is likely to know little. It is my hope, though not my expectation, that for nongays the annotated essays that make up this volume might have an effect similar to Gunnar Myrdal's masterwork of moral sociology, *An American Dilemma*. That book, written by a foreigner, forced white America in the 1940s to confront the evils of its racism and formed the intellectual backdrop which emboldened the Supreme Court in the 1950s to begin dismantling government sponsored segregation. Even if nongays ultimately find some of the arguments in this book unpersuasive, it will at least introduce them to some of the daily indignity and not infrequent brutality which they inflict upon gays but of which, due to their willful ignorance and the thickly layered social veils that hang around gays, they are largely unaware. Much in the book aims to enlighten. Some enlightenment is unpleasant. Yet, should nongays learn from and act upon some of the book's recommendations, they might find that someone upon whom they now unwittingly tread, but who might then be spared their marks, is someone they love. A recurring theme of the book is that gay rights are, in diverse ways, good for everyone.

For the gay reader, the book aims to help dignify him or her by giving voice to gay experience and expressing for gays social thoughts that have existed only in inchoate form. It is my hope, though not my expectation, that for gay readers the book might have the same effect that, upon first hearing, the trio from Elgar's First Pomp and Circumstance March had on the English, presenting, as it did, not a mere image of the English soul but an exemplar of it. The piece, in a way, is England. But in any case, the point is that at least sometimes character and vision are best captured in distillations having abstract formulation, rather than in pictures of particulars. For gays, my aim is to articulate in distilled abstract form that about gay experience which has been left fragmented or has gotten lost between the back of the mind and the tip of the tongue—that which has been sensed but unsaid. My aim in part then is through argument to generate philosophical myths for gays—myths which will ring true and yet which will be innocent as myths because they are true. The first spoken thing may appear larger than life simply because it is the only thing on the field. (In *Rubyfruit Jungle,* Rita Mae Brown's foursquare lesbian protagonist Molly Bolt appeared so because so.)

Beyond this rarified hope, I have another—that some people will find in my arguments useful knowledge. One of the most remarkable features of the black civil rights movement, as now made clear by subsequent profound social confusion over affirmative action programs, was that its legal successes were achieved without anything remotely resembling an articulated, ramified pattern of reason and argument, let alone a political theory. In practice, it turned out that theory and argument were not needed. There was no articulated, substantive, argumentative opposition to that movement, and religious sentiment and appeal filled in where words failed or were lacking altogether. For the gay movement, such a fortuitous configuration of props and fissures will not be forthcoming— something more is needed. Perhaps nothing will work, but rational argument may have some positive effect in some areas. It is at least worth a go in areas where prejudice is merely a powerful social force but has not risen to the level of a social lens through which all is categorized, interpreted, and assessed. At that level, where reality, meaning, and value are preconfigured in society's hardwiring, argument will not work.

Such necessary failures of argument are explored in a number of the essays on AIDS, the Supreme Court, and, most discouragingly to this academic, academe. The failure of reason in these areas has led me to lose my once-large faith in America. It took social architect Myrdal a lifetime to become disillusioned with his own hopes and blueprints for social progress. It took Martin Luther King Jr. only four quick years from 1964 to 1968. I have followed King rather than Myrdal in this pattern. Yet, for those who have not lost faith, my recommendations for social policies, based on a belief that the best argument should win, will perhaps be of some help in their quest, by offering models for what might be said generally and in offering particular reasoned arguments on a number of specific, live legislative issues.

Part of the problem in arguing for social change, at least on civil rights issues, is that one's opponent usually does not debate in good faith. For the bigot, "arguments" are simply filler for the print media—he has to have something to say. Bigots in America are doing so well now in part because on television and radio one does not need to have anything to say. And on those occasions when connected ideas are called for, it turns out that the bigot's herd of stalking horses is large beyond counting and self-perpetuating. For the bigot, "reason" and "reasons" are pretexts. There is no hope that he will be caught out. The most that can be hoped for is that an impartial person would observe the bigot shifting ground so many times that eventually the bigot can hardly help but appear disingenuous.

To date, gay studies, such as it is, has been the nearly exclusive preserve of historians, sociologists, and anthropologists, who are able to wrap their subjects in the intellectual safety of tales of the past, the numerology of statistics, and the exotics of distance. A book of philosophical essays might run a similarly safe danger, by dealing with gays as mere abstractions and so again as, in a way, dismissible. I have taken pains to avoid such mere abstraction in the book's content, approach, and style. True, the essays appeal to general moral and political principles developed in and precipitated from our civilization, its institutions, culture, and history. But at least equally often, the political discussion is governed by appeal to the ways gays live their everyday lives. The essays are about here and now, and are informed by an insider's perspective.

In content, the political orientation of the book is of a piece with classical liberalism—the belief that the focus of value in society is the individual, rather than groups, classes, or society as a whole, and that the coercive power of the state exists primarily to enhance prospects for individual flourishing and choice—the individual's creating for herself a plan of life and carrying it out in ways compatible with the ability of others to do the same. Usually this ideal will be realized by the state blocking coerced interactions between individuals, and simply withdrawing from the field of those that are voluntary. Government in this view is not, as in socialist countries, to serve paternalistic ends—caring for, but also coercing, its citizens in the way parents look after and coerce their child for its own good as they in their wisdom see it. If on occasion, however, state coercion of voluntary interactions can promote the general background conditions in and through which people come to be in a position to make up their own minds and seek out, in harmonious tolerance of each other, each their own end, as the state does in the case of compulsory, tax-financed education, then a more robust role for government is warranted than merely the provision of civil defense and the enforcement of civic right—the right to the equitable enforcement of protections for persons and property. In this view, then, the state is not purely libertarian. The proper power of the state is not limited merely to enforcing contracts and protecting the right to contract. The book cleaves between socialism and libertarianism.

In method, though, the book does not attempt to deduce the proper nature and powers of the state from axioms and first principles of political philosophy, and then in turn attempt to apply these derived verities to particular circumstances in the world. Such principles, deductions, and verities would likely be, as indeed they have so far proven in philosophical practice to be, vague and disputable, and such applications would likely be mechanical to the point of missing the nature of their objects, all the more so in the case of gays, since their social circumstances so far have, on their own, tended at least to chill, if not also completely arrest, thought on gay issues. Rather than relying on grand theory, the book proceeds in a more moderate, less controversial, admittedly piecemeal, yet, it is to be hoped, more persuasive manner. The book takes a "good reasons" approach to social policy. It gives good reasons to believe that classical liberalism is right in various local contexts, on diverse particular issues. In turn, the book contributes to liberalism generally, by showing this perspective to have an explanatory power rich enough to reveal new and interesting ideas in the previously unexplored areas of political thought raised by gay issues. Liberalism makes moral sense of gay issues; gay issues make moral sense of liberalism.

As a result of the book's general approach to its subject, the specific philosophical styles and techniques used in the book have no common algorism. No single technique generates all or even the most important results. Different points made have required different modes of argumentation. Frequently, the book proceeds by appeal to fairness or moral consistency—the treating of similar cases similarly. It shows that some moral idea worked out and widely accepted in one area of moral experience also holds true of gay experience because the two are relevantly similar. Many comparisons are made between the circumstances of gays and our culture's developed views on religion and race. Beyond consistency, many other styles and techniques are used. There is, here and there, old-fashioned conceptual analysis, which tries to sort out the various possible senses of a term to avoid ambiguity and which tries to trace a term's conceptual network to get clear on what sense and force the term might legitimately carry. At one point—an analysis of the role of the body in the possession of rights—very old-fashioned Aristotelian metaphysics is even brought into play. There is textual interpretation and analysis of basic documents of our civilization and of lesser law. There is moral rummaging in the normative dimensions of law, religion, and the social sciences. There is cultural critique. Here and there the argument advances through a phenomenological analysis of human activities, like having sex. There is the use of telling examples and story telling. Where an area is totally new, I have resorted to those tried and true, ancient and modern, philosophical methods of personal reflection, meditation, and intellectual autobiography as sources and vehicles for ideas.

The book consists of fourteen essays arranged in six groups. The first, single-member, group—"Gay Basics"—is an introductory essay on the current social status of gays and on current social attitudes about gays. It was originally sketched to fulfill a commission from an anthology editor who requested a piece on gay issues for an audience of what he termed "bonehead bigots." Others too may usefully read it. It gives the reader basic information, analyzes and assesses stereotypes, and discusses and rejects some of the most common and deeply held criticisms of gays. The chapter sets themes for the whole and tries to sweep away moral confusion about and social misperceptions of gays, so that subsequent positive arguments about gays can proceed on a field cleared of irrelevant, misleading, or needlessly arresting cultural impediments.

The next three chapters, taken together with an appendix on privacy caselaw and collectively titled "Mr. Justice Douglas at Sodom: Gays and Privacy," address what in a liberal view the state ought not to be doing, indeed ought to be barred from doing: the state ought not to be able to invade the activities of life which can be reasonably argued are private —including gay sex acts. The first chapter in the set argues that even though sodomy laws are virtually never enforced against gays, their mere presence is an assault on the dignity of gays. It is in this rather than in harms which they may indirectly generate that the evil of unenforced sodomy laws lies. The second chapter in the set offers a methodology for broadly interpreting fundamental constitutional immunities against state coercion. The method I call equality-based coherence. It generates a right to privacy which is broad and substantive, but not so broad as to be equivalent to a right protecting all voluntary agreements—a right to independence or a right to contract. The final chapter in the set gives four separately sufficient arguments for why—if there is a general, substantive right to privacy—gay sex should be seen as falling under it. The arguments turn, one each, on the cultural obligations surrounding sex acts, the inherently world-excluding nature of sex acts, the importance of sex in life, and the role of the body in the possession of rights in the first place. An appendix sets out reasons why the Supreme Court's ruling in 1986 that gays have no privacy rights does not even square with its own development of the scope of the right to privacy in its past cases. Over all, I argue that the Court's holdings on gay issues are so far off the mark morally and in every other intellectually respectable way that gays should be having grave doubts—layered with justified bitterness as America marks the Constitution's bicentennial—that the rule of law applies to them.

The third part, consisting of three essays—"The State as Civil Shield" —turns from a discussion of the proper scope of immunities against government to a discussion of the proper ways in which government ought to deploy its powers. The part addresses the most persistent gay social issue of the times: whether gays are to be afforded the same civil protections against discrimination in private sector employment, housing, and public accommodations as have been afforded other groups traditionally subject to discrimination in these areas.

The set begins with an essay that suggests civil rights legislation is one of the few areas in which the deployment of state coercion contributes to rather than squelches independence. Such legislation promotes independence in a variety of ways—by making possible and enhancing individual dignity, self-reliance, individual flourishing, and general prosperity understood as the aggregated happiness of individuals. The arguments are those to which any traditionally downtrodden group might well appeal. This essay attempts to remedy for all groups the curious gap in the history of social thought left by the black civil rights movement and its argument-free successes. The essay shows that the arguments which justify civil rights legislation for groups currently covered by the 1964 Civil Rights Act also justify the extension of civil rights protections to gays—sometimes with special force.

The second essay focuses on arguments for civil rights legislation that are peculiar to gays as an invisible minority. It argues that civil rights protections in the private sector are necessary if gays are to have reasonably guaranteed access to an array of fundamental rights—both civic and political—which virtually everyone would agree are supposed to pertain equally to all persons. The principles appealed to in this essay are so broad that its argument should be persuasive even to conservatives who find themselves unpersuaded by the ideas of the prior essay.

The third essay examines arguments by which opponents of gay rights attempt to show that discrimination against gays is, in general, discrimination in good faith—attempt to show that traditional discrimination against gays in areas otherwise reasonably protected by civil rights is indeed justified. The essay shows that, on examination, the presumptions behind such attempts fall into general patterns of thought all of which have been widely rejected by society as foundations of social policy or which are morally flawed in other ways.

The fourth part consists of four pieces, two long, two short, on the AIDS crisis. Gays may be dismayed to find that I treat AIDS as a gay disease. I do so in the same way that it makes sense to speak of sickle cell anemia as a black disease. Not all blacks get it, not only blacks get it; but the overwhelming number of cases of it do involve blacks and this fact has determined how society has responded to the disease—*pari passu* gay men and AIDS. The first two essays reintroduce in a new context the twin themes of the previous two parts: what the state ought not to be allowed to do and what the state should do. They recommend what the immunities from state coercion and what the proper deployments of state power should be in trying to stem the spread of the disease and in attending to those with it. All too frequently, the use of the vague concept "public health" to justify this or that state action has been the night in which socialism and fascism are one and the same. I argue that the mode of transmission of the disease ought to void the use of state coercion of the means of its possible transmission as a way of trying to stop the spread of the disease. I offer diverse arguments, which avoid socialist premises, principles, and conclusions, to justify state funding for patient care and medical research, and state regulation of the insurance industry.

The second pair of essays turns from brave to brooding. Through sociological analysis and telling stories, the essays suggest that the AIDS crisis has raised a configuration of social forces and perceptions that will defeat any positive role that reason might play in the development of social policy on AIDS. The first indeed suggests that arguments from the medical and public policy communities which show that various coercive measures being tried in the crisis are irrational, since socially inefficient, actually contribute to social evil, by clearly marking the coercive acts as what they really are—not means of stopping the spread of disease but purification rituals and self-sacrifices which reaffirm heterosexuality as society's central sacred value.

The second piece examines a philosopher with AIDS, a doctor with AIDS, and a university with AIDS, and draws a skeptical conclusion on the probable effectiveness of reason in changing individual and collective behavior. Progress, if it occurs, will be in spurts and starts, marred with setback, tangled and messy.

The fifth set of essays—"A Liberal's Education"—is more personal and portrays thought in action, the life of the mind as embedded in the cussedness of culture. The pair of essays too shifts from brave to brooding, and does so along the same lines as the AIDS papers. The pair shifts from guarded optimism on the role of reason in effectuating justice to a recognition that at present, American education is part of the problem of injustice, not part of its solution, and indeed helps defeat the role of reason in public policy.

The first essay is an adventure. It describes the first time I taught a gay studies course. The second essay, considerably more weathered than the first and written after the AIDS crisis had killed off my gay studies course, is a critique of American higher education from the political center. It draws its bead on several structural features of academe which perpetuate social injustices, especially antigay discrimination.

The final, single-member part of the volume addresses the issue of what is to be done when reasoned persuasion makes no progress and justice decisively fails. It suggests that in such circumstances, dignity rather than hoped-for happiness should serve as one's moral guide and that civil disobedience is sometimes justified as a means of establishing dignity even in the face of assured political failure. I would like to think of the essay as a humble counterpart to Martin Luther King Jr.'s "Letter from Birmingham Jail." There are differences.

King scribbled on the margins of newsprint in a barren isolation cell; I on a computer surrounded by mission oak furniture, American art glass shades, and whiskered paperweights. That contrast cannot but engender doubts for me that perhaps what I say is hypocritical or at least facile, though for now I continue to think it true. In his piece, King invokes the authority of six philosophers, Augustine, Aquinas, Buber, Tillich, Niebuhr, and Socrates, three times; I none. King's justification for the moral acceptability of his breaking the laws of man also appeals to authority: he is obeying a higher law, one which he sees revealed in the words of God and the Supreme Court. As far as the Court goes, King confuses immunities and powers. Apparently King, like many conservatives, mistakenly thought that the Supreme Court functions to write laws which deploy powers—such as laws barring private sector lunch counters from refusing to serve blacks—rather than functions merely to dispense immunities *against* laws and their powers. So King thought he could morally obey the Court's law until man's law caught up.

To my mind, a better strategy for justifying civil disobedience—better than appealing to supramundane laws, which will appear as various as their observers' desires—can be found in the recognition that when the very institutions that are structurally designed to promote justice not simply reach a wrong decision but also go about reaching it in ways that contribute to injustice and the degradation of a group—as the Supreme Court has done with gays by holding them unworthy of serious attention and equal respect—then, along the very dimensions of injustice which are thus incorrectable within the system of institutions for justice, a group is not bound to respect the law. For the group cannot be conceived of as having voluntarily agreed to a system of justice which treats its members systematically unjustly, treats them as lesser beings. The legitimate respect generally owed to law cannot be thought binding on those whom the law treats morally like slaves. On my account, the Supreme Court, far from being an oracle of higher law and so a source for justifying civil disobedience as obedience to higher law, is a chief agent of the systematic injustice against gays which justifies civil disobedience as a legitimate response to society casting gays beyond membership in the social contract. When society systematically erases the possibility of gays achieving individual dignity in society, gays are free to achieve some of that dignity denied, by putting their interests and happiness on the line as a means of valuing and respecting themselves—even if the specific political goals of disobedience do not, as King's did, succeed. In morally warranted, gay civil disobedience, the bigot's stalking horses are finally dispersed; here the reason-defeating social lens of heterosexuality is broken; here academe's moral degeneracy is rendered irrelevant. King's letter was written for a specific audience, moderate Southern ministers; others have usefully eavesdropped. My piece is written specifically with the gay political activist in mind; I hope others may usefully audit.

Even in espousing civil disobedience, the book is squarely in the American tradition. When Congress debated whether King should have his birthday marked as a national holiday, his detractors worried publicly only over his possible communist affiliations and sympathies. No one in dissent pointed out that King was, in that very activity by which he was best known and most effective, a common criminal regularly given over to the disruption of the legitimate and legal flow of persons and commerce in America. Civil disobedience may be rarer and so less American than apple pie, but apparently it is as American as George Washington, Abraham Lincoln, Christopher Columbus, and Jesus Christ.

The aim of the book as a whole, and its main intellectual strategy as well, is to dilate one strand already present, though sometimes lost among others, in the diverse strands of American culture—one in fact marked in the nation's remembrance of King—the valorizing of individual dignity. Current gays should be so lucky as to see even a glimmer of it in their lifetimes. If the book sometimes seems harsh in its critique of its country, remember, though, that the greatest oppressors of gays around the world are not Americans but the fraternal twins Catholicism and communism.

In both rhetorical force and literary style the book extends more widely than is usual for books carrying an academic impress. The bulk of the writing is matt discursive and argumentative prose—nothing unusual. But the book is meant not simply to be true, but to be persuasive; and more than simply trying to convince, it also aims to motivate. And where, in the making of public policy, argument is shown to have failed entirely—as I think at least sometimes it has on gay issues—I have been willing to cross swords in kind. These goals collectively mean, though, that the book ranges in rhetoric from lyricism to invective and in tone from comedy to despair, from the teasing to the acerbic, from the dulcet to the cranky. There is even hyperbole—that trope at which an author cashes in his accumulated literary chips. It is at least my intention, though, that in no case—and this also holds for the occasional use of words some might find obscene—should a literary conceit be gratuitous, meretricious, showy for show's sake. I have tried to keep technical jargon to a minimum and have tried to write with a zest that might lead the general reader into new territory otherwise perhaps a bit scary. The book is intended to be an entertaining, if sometimes sobering, read.

Even so, I recognize that given the diverse aims of the book, it must resort to literary triage: some readers will of necessity be lost and so at some point must be literarily written off, lest the whole sink to a moral and literary common denominator which on gay issues is below the threshold of taboo and so would permit nothing. Some of the pieces intentionally keep the reader slightly off center, in turns seducing and prodding him. I hope though that all readers, perhaps especially gay readers, may find in the essays a challenge to conscience.

I have occasionally used slang expressions. If well-embedded in the language, slang terms can have clear denotations, and since they are steeped in the bustle of ordinary life, they have more discriminating connotative weights than most other words. Properly used, they can

simultaneously be clear and pointed. I have, however, avoided a number
of fashionable coinages and barbarisms current in gay political argot
(and elsewhere as well), words like "empowerment," and "network"
used as a verb. More controversially perhaps, I have avoided using the
term "homophobia." Since this term has come to have currency even in
nongay media, it is too late in the day to hope for linguistic counterrefor-
mation, but it is worth noting the problems with the term's adoption. At
a minimum, it is vague. If it just means "fear of gays," modeled, say, on
"xenophobia," why not just say so and save two syllables? More importantly, the coinage is morally misleading. Its use makes it sound as
though bigotry is a mental illness, like agoraphobia, or a physical illness,
like hydrophobia. But the bigot's problem is not disease, whether mental
or physical. The bigot is not sick; he is immoral. So, on the one hand,
the usage of this term unwarrantedly lets the bigot off the hook, and on
the other hand, blurs the distinction between medical and moral categories—an unfortunate conceptual confusion in the best of times and one
of the last things gays should be encouraging now. If antigay bigotry
needs an abstract noun, "heterosexism," though awkward, at least sets
the concept in the correct moral constellation, by placing it along side
"racism" and "sexism."

I have also consciously avoided the phrase "gay community." In
evaluative usages, "community" both depends upon norms and in turn
invokes or prescribes them. I do not think gay life, at least now, fulfills
the norms on which an evaluative sense of the term depend. There is, for
instance, no such thing currently as a gay traitor. Gays let anything pass,
no matter how harmful or insulting one gay's actions may be to other
gays as gays. But, the lack of gay community in a normative sense may
well be for the best. For the norms which community in turn prescribes,
when pressed by a minority upon itself, simply substitute new local
tyrannies for old global ones—and the local variety is likely to be the
more intrusive and pervasive in its manipulations of individuals. A community is a structure of conventions—rules for social coordination which
one violates only when one desires to destroy the rules. Gays should be
hoping for fewer, not more, of such restraints. Further investigation is
needed, but my hunch is that gays, in looking for a positive term for
their group and social identification, should explore the more flexible
and delightfully unwieldy notion of a people. This notion allows for
pockets of convention among group members, but does not require

group-wide conventions to operate as the group's architechtonic. It seems to me that the varieties of Jewishness in contemporary America might be taken as a useful analogue for gauging a desirable, open-textured unity among gays.

The earliest sketches for any of the essays here were written in late 1980. The final revisions of all the essays took place in September 1987. This date must serve as the index for "current," "recent" and "now" and as the *terminus ad quem* for extended discussions of developments in law, medicine, and society. [Some matters addressed in the notes reach into March 1988.] The first, eleventh and thirteenth chapters appear here for the first time. The chapters two through four originally appeared, somewhat bowdlerized, as an article in *Columbia Human Rights Law Review* (1986–87), 18(1). A sketch that became chapter five appeared under the title "Gays and the Civil Rights Act" in *QQ: Report from the Center for Philosophy and Public Policy* (1984), 4(2). Chapter six originally appeared in *Philosophical Forum* (1985), 16(1). The stem for chapter seven was an article "Gay Rights," which originally appeared in *Social Theory and Practice* (1982), 8(1). Chapter eight blends two articles, one from *Raritan: A Quarterly Review* (1986), 6(1), the other from *Bioethics* (1987), 1(1). Chapter nine originally appeared in *Gay Community News* [Boston] (1986), 14(10). A shortened version of chapter ten appeared in *Law, Medicine and Health Care* (1987), 15(4). Chapter twelve originally appeared in *Teaching Philosophy* (1984), 7(2). And chapter fourteen originally appeared in *Christopher Street* [New York] (1986), 9(9).

The book may be read in several different ways. Read collectively and in order the essays systematically survey the major areas of gay liberty. However, each essay and each cluster of essays forming a part also stand on their own, and so may usefully be read locally for topical interest, say, on AIDS or education or sex. In a few places, however, one and the same argument has had to serve double duty. In these cases, I have briefly summarized the argument at its second sounding and have referred the reader back to the earlier full-dress version, thinking this preferable to the wear of repetition on the reader of the whole. Forward looking references simply direct the reader to points of possible further, related interest. Those who wish to read something of the whole, but not everything, may usefully read the first chapter of each section, plus perhaps chapter 4, the author's favorite. The chapters within each part are not arranged as theme and variations, but the argumentation of the first chapters is more straightforward and less likely to appeal to the byways of legal thinking than later chapters, though I believe that the law is not so opaque that it cannot be discussed with grace, charm and wit. Nevertheless, reader, be warned: the tenth and eleventh chapters are, in mood, jetblack and are intended to be depressing. The thirteenth chapter is bitterly cynical. If cynicism and depression are not one's cups of tea, one will easily find other tones elsewhere in the book.

Two other caveats: First, the book chiefly focuses on the relation between state and citizen, rather than on the relation between society and its members. This focus means that two important topics on which one might have otherwise reasonably expected enlightenment have been given only slight attention. One: I do not extensively discuss the mechanisms by which society as opposed to government oppress gay people. Such relative silence should not be taken as an indication that the author believes that such mechanisms do not exist or that on gay issues only governmental reform is needed. Indeed, I believe that an examination of the various modes of the social oppression of gays would reveal that whether gays are or are not objectively like an ethnic minority, it is as an ethnic minority that society treats gays. Further it is in the modes of treatment rather than in the nature of their objects that the inequalities and other iniquities inflicted on minorities chiefly reside. Thus, for instance, slavery is not an evil that could be remedied by redirecting that social institution from blacks to, say, blondes. Slavery is an unjust treatment, whomever it treats. If gays are treated socially as ethnic minorities are treated, there are major issues of equality both social and constitutional that are raised by the treatment. There is another book to be written, one on gays and equality; this book deals chiefly with gays and liberty.

Two: I do not discuss more than in passing what has become the chief debate in gay studies: whether homosexuality is socially constructed. The question, put crudely, is whether social forces do more than simply channel the expression of an abiding natural category of homosexuality. Are they, rather, part of the very meaning of homosexuality? Do social forces stand, as social constructivists claim, to homosexuality as iron stands to hemoglobin—as an essential constitutive part and chief determinant of its properties and behavior—such that without social forces there are no categories of sexuality at all? Though the constructivist's thesis was originally propounded by a philosopher, Michel Foucault, and has had a considerable influence in other disciplines, it has had virtually no impact on studies of sexuality within philosophy. Perhaps this oddity is simply the result of struggles over turf: if the constructivist's thesis is true, there is little a philosopher might add to the discussion of sexuality: there are no eternal verities in sexuality, nor even any interesting generalities to be stated about it; everything becomes social custom and its study, social history. Though a recovering Platonist, I still have little sympathy for the social constructivist's thesis. My hunch is that once the issue is clearly defined, there will be no issue left. But in any case, I think that coming down on one side or the other of the issue does not affect any of the major theses of this book.

Second, I speak more about gay men than lesbians; I know more about them than about lesbians. The correct path for a male to take in writing on issues bearing on lesbians is not clear: silence might appear as willful ignorance or negligence, speaking as impudence or condescension. The first time at a professional conference I read a gay paper, an early sketch of chapter 7, my self-namedly radical lesbian commentator castigated me for discussing lesbian child custody cases—even though I was complaining about judicial abuse of lesbians. The problem was one of standing: as a male, I could not possibly (so it was claimed) understand lesbian issues and so was not to speak on them. Silly me, to think that, given the magnitude of injustice against lesbians, it was substantive issues that mattered. The session devolved into a hissing match. That was 1981. Things are better now.

The lowering of hostilities between lesbians and gay men perhaps has resulted in part from an enhanced or reawakened sense in this neo-American era that common enemies present gays and lesbians graver problems than gays and lesbians present each other. But I think something more is involved, at least within philosophy. Lesbians have been developing their own voice in the discipline. In 1984, the distinguished women's studies journal *Signs* published an issue devoted entirely to lesbian issues. It contained no work either by a lesbian philosopher or on philosophy. When the issue was expanded and reprinted as a book, its editors announced that "the subject of lesbianism seems most highly developed in the fields of literature and history," and after bemoaning the lack of ethnic diversity in lesbian studies, claimed: "More significant, however, is the vacuum in theory [on lesbian issues]." Well, this was not quite true then and is certainly not true now. The second half of Marilyn Frye's *The Politics of Reality: Essays in Feminist Theory* (1983), Jeffner Allen's *Lesbian Philosophy: Explorations* (1986), and recent important essays by Claudia Card, Sarah Lucia Hoagland, and Joyce Trebilcot all attest to a lively and expanding field of lesbian philosophy.

I continue to feel uncomfortable, though, in trying to decide what the right course is in dealing with lesbian issues. I have declined the invitation of my commentator to be entirely silent, but I have not attempted in any substantial way to address feminist lesbian issues where they differ from those of gay men. I think most of what I have to say, save for the AIDS essays, holds equally of gay men and lesbians. And even there, the careful reader will note that in the second long AIDS essay— chapter 10, the last essay in the collection to be written—all of the heroes are women. Maybe I am deceived in my belief in the essays' equal applicability to lesbians and gay men. That lesbians are now speaking for themselves, though, reassures me that if I err in discussing lesbian issues, I shall soon enough hear about it. This is as it should be.

The book has, in the main, been the product of individual initiative and craft. Its ideas arose and were developed chiefly from the author working in isolation. Nevertheless much thanks is due others. The palm for institutional support in the book's creation goes not to my home university, which I thank for sporadic material research support, but rather to the University of Maryland's Center for Philosophy and Public Policy, which had the good taste and inventiveness to give me a Rockefeller Foundation Fellowship in the Humanities over the 1985–86 academic year for the purpose of writing on gay sex. That transferred gift would be reason enough for my admiration and thanks, but what is more, the Center itself provided a materially strong, emotionally supportive, intellectually rousing, and fun place to write. It has proven a source of continued support through friendships begun there. During my year at the Center, I wrote the first, second, third, fourth, eighth, ninth and thirteenth chapters.

Chapters ten, eleven, and fourteen were written and revisions of the whole carried out during the 1986–87 academic year, which my home institution, the University of Illinois, gave me off from teaching on a College of Liberal Arts and Sciences Faculty Study Fellowship. Not a few paragraphs in the book had their origins in letters to administrators, chancellors, and trustees of the University urging civil protections for its gay members. The arguments have fallen on ears deafened by, at best, unthinking minds and numb souls. I have been unable even to get my department chairman to suggest to aged faculty that it is immoral to use departmental memos as vehicles for fag jokes. The absence of moral leadership in what has been misphrased "the marketplace of ideas" ought to give one pause more generally on the prospects for moral reform through reason, or perhaps it is just that academe is structurally such that it attracts more than the usual number of moral weaklings to its administration. That would not surprise me.

Thanks go to a number of individuals for their support and kindnesses. Prof. Lee C. Rice of Marquette University first nobly suggested to me that I try my hand at publishing gay ideas, even though he disagreed with the specific ones I had. Prof. John M. Littlewood, government documents librarian at the University of Illinois, has without credit, adequate budget, or official status developed one of the best gay library collections in the country here. He has kept me posted on more sources and helped me track down more references than I should guess he cares to remember. The reference librarians of the College of Law here, especially Prof. Jane M. Williams, have also been helpful beyond duty.

My greatest debt of gratitude is owed my—if you allow a hendiadys —lover and husband, Robert W. Switzer. Over the years he has spent numerous unremunerated weeks as an underlaborer in the project. He is mentioned here and there, but is more evidently present immediately behind large stretches of the text. It was our relation that set me to wondering and thinking about a number of topics covered in the essays and intimated answers to a number of my queries. This wonder and intimation is most strongly present in the passages on love and sex and couples and bodies, but also is there in the discussions of work (we met when we were both unemployed bums), of intimidation and violence (people throw things at us from cars), and on the generation of value. The book would be better if it had a chapter on gay marriage, a topic broached at several spots. I have examined family law a bit and found it a legal box containing even fewer ideas than others. So the chapter would have had to be autobiographical, and for now I am not up again to the soul-bearing contained even in the current autobiographical chapters, let alone to try to bear for two. But this may be said.

The sanctifications that descend instantly through custom and ritual on current marriages, descend gradually over and through time on gay ones—and in a way they are better for it. For the sacred values and loyal intimacies contained in a gay marriage are products of the relation itself, are truly the couple's own. Marriages are patens for value. In this, though, they vary like patinas. Customary heterosexual marriages with their ceremonial trappings are like copper dunked in sulphates and chlorides—you get quick results, occasionally lasting, occasionally not tacky. Gay marriages, in contrast, are like the development of a patina on wood. The warming, the enriching, the surface that is depth, the depth that is sheen are a result of necessary age. The passage of time and a use that is patient tendance, jointly and solely, produce it. And so, after a decade together, we feel and to many puzzled others appear more married than the married.

All the more strange and enraging is it then that in the eyes of the law we are necessarily strangers to each other, people who had as well never met. In Illinois, one cannot will one's body. By statute, it goes to next of kin. That which was most one's own—the substrate for personality—which was most one's own for another—that in which and by which one loves and makes love—is, for gays, not one's at all. The lover is barred from the lover's funeral. The compulsory intervention of heterosexuality at death is the final degradation worked by The People on gay people. To me, this is unforgivable. For even if only faintly, in the scritching sound from the press of our greying beards, one hears the graze of bones, of death, and the decades are not so few between now and justice that we shall count them.

The University of Illinois–Urbana, October 1, 1987

PART ONE

Optimistic Voices, A Beginning

1. Gay Basics: Some Questions, Facts, and Values

"These are so similar that you are out to skin us alive."
—a psychiatrist to an experimenter testing his ability to
distinguish gay from nongay Rorschach responses (1957).

I. Who Are Gays Anyway?
II. Ignorance, Stereotypes, and Morality.
III. Are Gays Discriminated Against? Does it Matter?
IV. But Aren't They Immoral?
V. But Aren't They Unnatural?
VI. But Aren't Gays Willfully the Way They Are?
VII. How Would Society at Large Be Changed If
Homosexual Acts were Decriminalized and Gays
Socially Tolerated or Even Accepted?

I. WHO ARE GAYS ANYWAY?

A recent Gallup poll found that only one in five Americans reports
having a gay acquaintance.[1] This finding is extraordinary given the
number of practicing homosexuals in America. Alfred Kinsey's 1948
study of the sex lives of 5000 white males shocked the nation: 37 percent
had at least one homosexual experience to orgasm in their adult lives;
an additional 13 percent had homosexual fantasies to orgasm; 4 percent
were exclusively homosexual in their practices; another 5 percent had
virtually no heterosexual experience, and nearly 20 percent had at least
as many homosexual as heterosexual experiences.[2] With only slight
variations, these figures held across all social categories: region, religion,
political belief, class, income, occupation, and education.

1. "Public Fears—And Sympathies," *Newsweek*, August 12, 1985, p. 23.
2. Alfred C. Kinsey, et al., *Sexual Behavior in the Human Male* (Philadelphia: Saunders,
1948), pp. 650–51. On the somewhat lower incidences of lesbianism, see Alfred C. Kinsey,
et al., *Sexual Behavior in the Human Female* (Philadelphia: Saunders, 1953), pp. 472–75.

Two out of five men one passes on the street have had orgasmic sex with men. Every second family in the country has a member who is essentially homosexual, and many more people regularly have homosexual experiences. Who are homosexuals? They are your friends, your minister, your teacher, your bankteller, your doctor, your mailcarrier, your secretary, your congressional representative, your sibling, parent, and spouse. They are everywhere, virtually all ordinary, virtually all unknown.

What follows? First, the country is profoundly ignorant of the actual experience of gay people. Second, social attitudes and practices that are harmful to gays have a much greater overall negative impact on society than is usually realized. Third, most gay people live in hiding—in the closet—making the "coming out" experience the central fixture of gay consciousness and invisibility the chief social characteristic of gays.

II. IGNORANCE, STEREOTYPE, AND MORALITY

Society's ignorance of gay people is, however, not limited to individuals' lack of personal acquaintance with gays. Stigma against gay people is so strong that even discussions of homosexuality are taboo. This taboo is particularly strong in academe, where it is reinforced by the added fear of the teacher as molester. So even within the hearth of reason irrational forces have held virtually unchallenged and largely unchallengeable sway. The usual sort of clarifying research that might be done on a stigmatized minority has with gays only just begun—haltingly—in history, literature, sociology, and the sciences.

Yet ignorance about gays has not stopped people from having strong opinions about them. The void which ignorance leaves has been filled with stereotypes. Society holds chiefly two groups of antigay stereotypes; the two are an oddly contradictory lot. One set of stereotypes revolves around alleged mistakes in an individual's gender identity: lesbians are women that want to be, or at least look and act like, men—bulldykes, diesel dykes; while gay men are those who want to be, or at least look and act like, women—queens, fairies, limp-wrists, nellies. Gays are "queer," which, remember, means at root not merely weird but chiefly counterfeit—"he's as queer as a three dollar bill." These stereotypes of mismatched or fraudulent genders provide the materials through which gays and lesbians become the butts of ethnic-like jokes. These stereotypes and jokes, though derisive, basically view gays and lesbians as ridiculous.

Another set of stereotypes revolves around gays as a pervasive, sinister, conspiratorial, and corruptive threat. The core stereotype here is the gay person as child molester and, more generally, as sex-crazed maniac. These stereotypes carry with them fears of the very destruction of family and civilization itself. Now, that which is essentially ridiculous can hardly have such a staggering effect. Something must be afoot in this incoherent amalgam.

Sense can be made of this incoherence if the nature of stereotypes is clarified. Stereotypes are not *simply* false generalizations from a skewed sample of cases examined. Admittedly, false generalizing plays a part in most stereotypes a society holds. If, for instance, one takes as one's sample homosexuals who are in psychiatric hospitals or prisons, as was done in nearly all early investigations, not surprisingly one will probably find homosexuals to be of a crazed and criminal cast. Such false generalizations, though, simply confirm beliefs already held on independent grounds, ones that likely led the investigator to the prison and psychiatric ward to begin with. Evelyn Hooker, who in the mid-fifties carried out the first rigorous studies to use nonclinical gays, found that psychiatrists, when presented with results of standard psychological diagnostic tests—but with indications of sexual orientation omitted—were able to do no better than if they had guessed randomly in their attempts to distinguish gay files from nongay ones, even though the psychiatrists believed gays to be crazy and supposed themselves to be experts in detecting craziness.[3] These studies proved a profound embarrassment to the psychiatric establishment, the financial well-being of which was substantially enhanced by 'curing' allegedly insane gays. Eventually the studies contributed to the American Psychiatric Association's dropping homosexuality from its registry of mental illnesses in 1973.[4] Nevertheless, the stereotype of gays as sick continues apace in the mind of America.

False generalizations *help maintain* stereotypes; they do not *form*

3. Evelyn Hooker, "The Adjustment of the Male Overt Homosexual," *Journal of Projective Techniques* (1957) 21:18–31, reprinted in Hendrik M. Ruitenbeek, ed., *The Problem of Homosexuality*, pp. 141–61, epigram quote from p. 149 (New York: Dutton, 1963).

4. See Ronald Bayer, *Homosexuality and American Psychiatry* (New York: Basic Books, 1981).

them. As the history of Hooker's discoveries shows, stereotypes have a life beyond facts. Their origin lies in a culture's ideology—the general system of beliefs by which it lives—and they are sustained across generations by diverse cultural transmissions, hardly any of which, including slang and jokes, even purport to have a scientific basis. Stereotypes, then, are not the products of bad science, but are social constructions that perform central functions in maintaining society's conception of itself.

On this understanding, it is easy to see that the antigay stereotypes surrounding gender identification are chiefly means of reinforcing still powerful gender roles in society. If, as this stereotype presumes (and condemns), one is free to choose one's social roles independently of gender, many guiding social divisions, both domestic and commercial, might be threatened. The socially gender-linked distinctions would blur between breadwinner and homemaker, protector and protected, boss and secretary, doctor and nurse, priest and nun, hero and whore, saint and siren, lord and helpmate, and God and his world. The accusations "fag" and "dyke" (which recent philology has indeed shown to be rooted in slang referring to gender-bending, especially cross-dressing)[5] exist in significant part to keep women in their place and to prevent men from breaking ranks and ceding away theirs.

The stereotypes of gays as child molesters, sex-crazed maniacs, and civilization destroyers function to displace (socially irresolvable) problems from their actual source to a foreign (and so, it is thought, manageable) one. Thus, the stereotype of child molester functions to give the family unit a false sheen of absolute innocence. It keeps the unit from being examined too closely for incest, child abuse, wife-battering, and the terrorism of constant threats. The stereotype teaches that the problems of the family are not internal to it, but external.

Because this stereotype has this central social function, it could not be dislodged even by empirical studies, paralleling Hooker's efforts, that showed heterosexuals to be child molesters to a far greater extent than the actual occurrence of heterosexuals in the general population.[6] But

5. See Wayne Dynes, *Homolexis: A Historical and Cultural Lexicon of Homosexuality* (New York: Gay Academic Union, Gai Saber Monograph No. 4, 1985), s.v. dyke, faggot.

6. For studies showing that gay men are no more likely—indeed, are less likely—than heterosexuals to be child molesters and that the most widespread and persistent sexual abusers of children are the children's fathers, stepfathers or mother's boyfriends, see Vincent De Francis, *Protecting the Child Victim of Sex Crimes Committed by Adults* (Denver: The American Humane Association, 1969), pp. vii, 38, 69–70; A. Nicholas

one need not even be aware of such debunking empirical studies in order to see the same cultural forces at work in the social belief that gays are molesters as in its belief that they are crazy. For one can see them now in society's and the media's treatment of current reports of violence, especially domestic violence. When a mother kills her child or a father rapes his daughter—regular Section B fare even in major urbane papers —this is never taken by reporters, columnists, or pundits as evidence that there is something wrong with heterosexuality or with traditional families. These issues are not even raised.

But when a homosexual child molestation is reported it is taken as confirming evidence of the way homosexuals are. One never hears of heterosexual murders, but one regularly reads of "homosexual" ones. Compare the social treatment of Richard Speck's sexually motivated mass murder in 1966 of Chicago nurses with that of John Wayne Gacy's serial murders of Chicago youths. Gacy was in the culture's mind taken as symbolic of gay men in general. To prevent the possibility that The Family was viewed as anything but an innocent victim in this affair, the mainstream press knowingly failed to mention that most of Gacy's adolescent victims were homeless hustlers, even though this was made obvious at his trial.[7] That knowledge would be too much for the six o'clock news and for cherished beliefs.

The stereotype of gays as sex-crazed maniacs functions socially to keep individuals' sexuality contained. For this stereotype makes it look as though the problem of how to address one's considerable sexual drives can and should be answered with repression, for it gives the impression that the cyclone of dangerous psychic forces is *out there* where the fags are, not within one's own breast. With the decline of the stereotype of the black man as raping pillaging marauder (found in such works as *Birth of a Nation, Gone with the Wind,* and *Soul on Ice*), the stereotype of gay men as sex-crazed maniacs has become more aggravated. The stereotype of the sex-crazed threat seems one that society desperately needs to have somewhere in its sexual cosmology.

Groth, "Adult Sexual Orientation and Attraction to Underage Persons," *Archives of Sexual Behavior* (1978) 7:175–81; Mary J. Spencer, "Sexual Abuse of Boys," *Pediatrics* (July 1986) 78(1):133–38.

7. See Lawrence Mass, "Sanity in Chicago: The Trial of John Wayne Gacy and American Psychiatry," *Christopher Street* [New York] (June 1980) 4(7):26. See also Terry Sullivan, *Killer Clown* (New York: Grosset & Dunlap, 1983), pp. 219–25, 315–16; Tim Cahill, *Buried Dreams* (Toronto: Bantam Books, 1986), pp. 318, 352–53, 368–69.

For the repressed homosexual, this stereotype has an especially powerful allure—by hating it consciously, he subconsciously appears to save himself from himself, at least as long as the ruse does not exhaust the considerable psychic energies required to maintain it, or until, like ultraconservative Congressmen Robert E. Bauman (R-Md.) and Jon C. Hinson (R-Miss.), he is caught importuning hustlers or gentlemen in washrooms.[8] If, as Freud and some of his followers thought, everyone feels an urge for sex partners of both genders, then the fear of gays works to show us that we have not "met the enemy and he is us."[9]

By directly invoking sex acts, this second set of stereotypes is the more severe and serious of the two—one never hears child-molester jokes. These stereotypes are aimed chiefly against men, as in turn stereotypically the more sexed of the genders. They are particularly divisive for they create a very strong division between those conceived as "us" and those conceived as "them." This divide is not so strong in the case of the stereotype of gay men as effeminate. For women (and so the woman-like) after all do have their place. Nonstrident, nonuppity useful ones can even be part of "us," indeed, belong, like "our children," to "us." Thus, in many cultures with overweening gender-identified social roles (like prisons, truckstops, the armed forces, Latin America, and the Islamic world) only passive partners in male couplings are derided as homosexual.[10]

Because "the facts" largely do not matter when it comes to the generation and maintenance of stereotypes, the effects of scientific and academic research and of enlightenment generally will be, at best, slight and gradual in the changing fortunes of gays. If this account of stereotypes holds, society has been profoundly immoral. For its treatment of gays is a grand scale rationalization and moral sleight-of-hand. The problem is not that society's usual standards of evidence and procedure in coming to judgments of social policy have been misapplied to gays, rather when

8. For Robert Bauman's account of his undoing, see his autobiography, *The Gentleman from Maryland* (New York: Arbor House, 1986).

9. On Freud, see Timothy F. Murphy, "Freud Reconsidered: Bisexuality, Homosexuality, and Moral Judgment," *Journal of Homosexuality* (1984) 9(2–3):65–77.

10. On prisons, see Wayne Wooden and Jay Parker, *Men Behind Bars: Sexual Exploitation in Prison* (New York: Plenum, 1982). On the armed forces, see George Chauncey Jr., "Christian Brotherhood or Sexual Perversion? Homosexual Identities and the Construction of Sexual Boundaries in the World War One Era," *Journal of Social History* (1985) 19:189–211.

it comes to gays, the standards themselves have simply been ruled out of court and disregarded in favor of mechanisms that encourage unexamined fear and hatred.

III. ARE GAYS DISCRIMINATED AGAINST? DOES IT MATTER?

Partly because lots of people suppose they do not know a gay person and partly through their willful ignorance of society's workings, people are largely unaware of the many ways in which gays are subject to discrimination in consequence of widespread fear and hatred. Contributing to this social ignorance of discrimination is the difficulty for gay people, as an invisible minority, even to complain of discrimination. For if one is gay, to register a complaint would suddenly target one as a stigmatized person, and so, in the absence of any protections against discrimination, would in turn invite additional discrimination.

Further, many people, especially those who are persistently downtrodden and so lack a firm sense of self to begin with, tend either to blame themselves for their troubles or to view their troubles as a matter of bad luck or as the result of an innocent mistake by others—as anything but an injustice indicating something wrong with society. Alfred Dreyfus went to his grave believing his imprisonment for treason and his degradation from the French military, in which he was the highest ranking Jewish officer, had all just been a sort of clerical error, merely requiring recomputation, rather than what it was—lightning striking a promontory from out of a storm of national bigotry.[11] The recognition of injustice requires doing something to rectify wrong; the recognition of systematic injustices requires doing something about the system, and most people, especially the already beleaguered, simply are not up to the former, let alone the latter.

For a number of reasons, then, discrimination against gays, like rape, goes seriously underreported. What do they experience? First, gays are subject to violence and harassment based simply on their perceived status rather than because of any actions they have performed. A recent extensive study by the National Gay and Lesbian Task Force found that over 90 percent of gays and lesbians had been victimized in some form

11. See Jean-Denis Bredin, *The Affair: The Case of Alfred Dreyfus*, trans. Jeffrey Mehlman (1983; New York: George Braziller, 1986), pp. 486–96.

on the basis of their sexual orientation.[12] Greater than one in five gay men and nearly one in ten lesbians had been punched, hit, or kicked; a quarter of all gays had had objects thrown at them; a third had been chased; a third had been sexually harassed and 14 percent had been spit on—all just for being perceived to be gay.

The most extreme form of antigay violence is queerbashing—where groups of young men target another man who they suppose is gay and beat and kick him unconscious and sometimes to death amid a torrent of taunts and slurs. Such seemingly random but in reality socially encouraged violence has the same social origin and function as lynchings of blacks—to keep a whole stigmatized group in line. As with lynchings of the recent past, the police and courts have routinely averted their eyes, giving their implicit approval to the practice.

Few such cases with gay victims reach the courts. Those that do are marked by inequitable procedures and results. Frequently judges will describe queerbashers as "just All-American Boys." In 1984, a District of Columbia judge handed suspended sentences to queerbashers whose victim had been stalked, beaten, stripped at knife point, slashed, kicked, threatened with castration, and pissed on, because the judge thought the bashers were good boys at heart—after all they went to a religious prep school.[13]

In the summer of 1984, three teenagers hurled a gay man to his death from a bridge in Bangor, Maine. Though the youths could have been tried as adults and normally would have been, given the extreme violence of their crime, they were tried rather as children and will be back on the streets again automatically when they turn twenty-one.[14]

Further, police and juries simply discount testimony from gays.[15] They

12. National Gay and Lesbian Task Force, *Anti-Gay/Lesbian Victimization* (New York: National Gay and Lesbian Task Force, 1984). See also, "Anti-Gay Violence," Subcommittee on Criminal Justice, Committee on the Judiciary, House of Representatives, 99th Congress, 2nd Session, October 9, 1986, serial no. 132.

13. "Two St. John's Students Given Probation in Assault on Gay," *The Washington Post,* May 15, 1984, p. 1.
The 1980 Mariel boatlift, which included thousands of gays escaping Cuban internment camps, inspired U.S. Federal District Judge A. Andrew Hauk in open court to comment of a Mexican illegal alien caught while visiting his resident alien daughter: "And he isn't even a fag like all these faggots we're letting in." *The Advocate* [Los Angeles], November 27, 1980, no. 306, p. 15. Cf. "Gay Refugees Tell of Torture, Oppression in Cuba," *The Advocate,* August 21, 1980, no. 299, pp. 15–16.

14. See *The New York Times,* September 17, 1984, p. D17 and October 6, 1984, p. 6.
15. John D'Emilio writes of the trial of seven police officers caught in a gay bar shake-

typically construe assaults on and murders of gays as "justified" self-defense—the killer need only claim his act was a panicked response to a sexual overture.[16] Alternatively, when guilt seems patent, juries will accept highly implausible insanity or other "diminished capacity" defenses. In 1981 a former New York City Transit Authority policeman, later claiming he was just doing the work of God, machine-gunned down nine people, killing two, in two Greenwich Village gay bars. His jury found him innocent due to mental illness.[17] The best known example of a successful "diminished capacity" defense is Dan White's voluntary manslaughter conviction for the 1978 assassination of openly gay San Francisco city councilman Harvey Milk—Hostess Twinkies, his lawyer successfully argued, made him do it.[18]

These inequitable procedures and results collectively show that the life and liberty of gays, like those of blacks, simply count for less than the life and liberty of members of the dominant culture.

The equitable rule of law is the heart of an orderly society. The collapse of the rule of law for gays shows that society is willing to perpetrate the worst possible injustices against them. Conceptually there is a difference only in degree between the collapse of the rule of law and systematic extermination of members of a population simply for having some group status independent of any act an individual has performed. In the Nazi concentration camps, gays were forced to wear pink triangles as identifying badges, just as Jews were forced to wear yellow stars. In remembrance of that collapse of the rule of law, the pink triangle has become the chief symbol of the gay rights movement.[19]

---

down racket: "The defense lawyer cast aspersions on the credibility of the prosecution witnesses . . . and deplored a legal system in which 'the most notorious homosexual may testify against a policeman.' Persuaded by this line of argument, the jury acquitted all of the defendants." *Sexual Politics, Sexual Communities: The Making of a Homosexual Minority in the United States, 1940–1970* (Chicago: University of Chicago Press, 1983), p. 183.

16. See for discussion and examples, Pat Califia, " 'Justifiable' Homicide?" *The Advocate*, May 12, 1983, no. 367, p. 12 and Robert G. Bagnall, et al., "Burdens on Gay Litigants and Bias in the Court System: Homosexual Panic, Child Custody, and Anonymous Parties," *Harvard Civil Rights-Civil Liberties Law Review* (1984) 19:498–515.

17. *The New York Times*, July 25, 1981, p. 27, and July 26, 1981, p. 25.

18. See Randy Shilts, *The Mayor of Castro Street: The Life and Times of Harvey Milk* (New York: St. Martin's, 1982), pp. 308–25.

19. See Richard Plant, *The Pink Triangle: The Nazi War Against Homosexuals* (New York: Holt, 1986). For a moving and insightful first-person account of a concentration camp survivor who was interned for being gay, see Heinz Heger [pseud.], *The Men with the Pink Triangle* (Boston: Alyson, 1980).

Gays have been widely subject to discrimination in employment—the very means by which one puts bread on one's table and one of the chief means by which a person identifies himself to himself and achieves individual dignity. Governments are leading offenders here. They do a lot of discriminating themselves. They require that others, like government contractors, do it, and they set precedents and establish models favoring discrimination in the private sector. The federal government explicitly discriminates against gays in the armed forces, the CIA, the FBI, the National Security Agency, and the state department. The federal government refuses to give security clearances to gays and so forces the country's considerable private-sector military and aerospace contractors to fire known gay employees.[20] State and local governments regularly fire gay teachers, police and fire personnel, social workers, and anyone who has contact with the public. Further, states through licensing laws officially bar gays from a vast array of occupations and professions— everything from doctors, lawyers, accountants, and nurses to hairdressers, morticians, and used car dealers. The American Civil Liberties Union's handbook *The Rights of Gay People* (1975) lists 307 such prohibited occupations.[21]

Gays are subject to discrimination in a wide variety of other ways, including private-sector employment, public accommodations, housing, immigration and naturalization, insurance of all types, custody and adoption, and zoning regulations that bar "singles" or "non-related" couples. All of these discriminations affect central components of a meaningful life; some even reach to the means by which life itself is sustained. In half the states, where gay sex is illegal, the central role of sex to meaningful life is officially denied to gays.[22]

All these sorts of discriminations also affect the ability of people to have significant intimate relations. It is difficult for people to live to-

20. On antigay discrimination in government agencies, see Rhonda R. Rivera, "Queer Law: Sexual Orientation Law in the Mid-eighties: Parts I and II," *University of Dayton Law Review* (1985) 10:483–540, and (1986) 11:275–324.

21. E. C. Boggan, M. G. Haft, C. Lister, and J. P. Rupp, *The Rights of Gay People: The Basic ACLU Guide to a Gay Person's Rights,* 1st ed. (New York: Avon, 1975), pp. 211–35.

22. For an extensive examination of criminal and civil gay law, see National Lawyers Guild Anti-Sexism Committee of San Francisco Bay Area Chapter, Roberta Achtenberg, ed., *Sexual Orientation and the Law* (New York: Clark Boardman, 1985).

gether as couples without having their sexual orientation perceived in the public realm and so becoming targets for discrimination. Illegality, discrimination, and the absorption by gays of society's hatred of them— all interact to impede or block altogether the ability of gays and lesbians to create and maintain significant personal relations with loved ones. So every facet of life is affected by discrimination. Only the most compelling reasons could justify it.

IV. BUT AREN'T THEY IMMORAL?

Many people think society's treatment of gays is justified because gays are extremely immoral. To evaluate this claim, different senses of "moral" must be distinguished. Sometimes by "morality" is meant the overall beliefs affecting behavior in a society—its current mores, norms, and customs. On this understanding, gays certainly are not moral: lots of people hate them and social customs are designed to register widespread disapproval of gays. The problem here is that this sense of morality is merely a *descriptive* one. On this understanding of what morality is, *every* society has a morality—even Nazi society, which had racism and mob rule as central features of its popular "morality." What is needed in order to use the notion of morality to praise or condemn behavior is a sense of morality that is *prescriptive* or *normative*—what is needed is a sense of morality whereby, for instance, the descriptive morality of the Nazis is found wanting.

Moral thinking that carries a prescriptive or normative force has certain basic ground rules to which all people consent when attention is drawn to them. First, normative moral beliefs are not merely expressions of feelings. Rather we—normatively moral agents—both expect and are expected to be able to give reasons or justifications for them. We suspect that beliefs, especially strongly held ones, for which no reasons or justifications can be tendered, are mere expressions of phobias and neuroses. Second, moral thinking must be consistent and fair—we must recognize that our specific moral beliefs commit us to general moral principles in light of which we must be willing to treat relevantly similar cases similarly. Third, we must avoid prejudice and rationalization: we must be willing to apply to ourselves the same rules and standards of evidence and argument that we apply to others. And we must avoid being so peculiar and particular in the scope of our principles that we stand accused of being whimsical and arbitrary in picking them.[23]

Even from this sketch of minimum requirements of a critical or normative morality, it should be clear that something's being descriptively moral or immoral is nowhere near enough to make it normatively moral or immoral. For one of our principles itself is that simply a lot of people's saying something is good, even over eons, does not make it so. Our rejection of the long history of socially approved and state-enforced slavery is a good example of this principle at work. Slavery would be wrong even if nearly everyone liked it. So consistency and fairness requires that the culture abandon the belief that gays are immoral simply because most people dislike or disapprove of gays or gay acts, or even because gay sex acts are illegal.

Further, recent historical and anthropological research has shown that opinion about gays has been by no means universally negative. Historically, it has varied widely even within the larger part of the Christian era and even within the Church itself.[24] There are even societies—current ones—where homosexuality is not only tolerated but even a universal and compulsory part of social maturation.[25] Society holds its current descriptive morality of gays not because it has to, but because it chooses to. Within the last thirty years, American society has undergone a grand turnabout from deeply ingrained, near total condemnation to near total acceptance on two emotionally charged "moral" or "family" issues: adult contraception and divorce. America could do the same with homosexuality if it thought to.

If popular opinion and custom are not enough to ground moral condemnation of homosexuality, perhaps religion can. Such argument proceeds along two lines. One claims that the condemnation is a direct revelation of God, usually through the Bible; the other claims to be able to detect condemnation in God's plan as manifested in nature.

One of the more remarkable discoveries of recent gay research is that

23. For elaboration see, Ronald Dworkin, *Taking Rights Seriously* (Cambridge: Harvard University Press, 1977), pp. 248–54.

24. John Boswell, *Christianity, Social Tolerance and Homosexuality: Gay People in Western Europe from the Beginning of the Christian Era to the Fourteenth Century* (Chicago: The University of Chicago Press, 1980).

25. See Gilbert Herdt, *Guardians of the Flute: Idioms of Masculinity* (New York: McGraw-Hill, 1981), pp. 232–39, 284–88, and see generally Gilbert Herdt, ed., *Ritualized Homosexuality in Melanesia* (Berkeley: University of California Press, 1984).

the Bible may not be as univocal in its condemnation of homosexuality as has been usually believed.[26] Christ never mentions homosexuality. Recent interpreters of the Old Testament have pointed out that the story of Lot at Sodom is probably intended to condemn inhospitality rather than homosexuality. Further, some of the Old Testament condemnations of homosexuality seem simply to be ways of tarring those of the Israelites' opponents who happen to accept homosexual practices when the Israelites themselves did not. If so, the condemnation is merely a quirk of history and rhetoric rather than a moral precept. All of this is hotly contested, and the debate continues.

What does seem clear, though, is that those who regularly cite the Bible to condemn an activity like homosexuality do so by reading it selectively. Do ministers who cite what they take to be condemnations of homosexuality in Leviticus maintain in their lives all the hygienic and dietary laws of Leviticus? If they cite the story of Lot at Sodom to condemn homosexuality, do they also cite the story of Lot in the Cave to praise incestuous rape?[27] If not, they may be hypocrites (against whom Christ frequently riles), but more importantly they violate the normatively moral notions of consistency and fairness—unless of course they can cite some higher principle which generates exceptions to the (now) lower level principle: obey the Bible. But what could that be? It seems then not that the Bible is being used to ground condemnations of homosexuality as much as society's dislike of homosexuality is being used to interpret the Bible.

Even if a consistent portrait of condemnation could be gleaned from the Bible, what social significance should it be given? One of the guiding principles of society, enshrined in the Constitution as a check against the government, is that decisions affecting social policy are not made on religious grounds. If the real ground of the alleged immorality invoked by governments to discriminate against gays is religious, then one of the major commitments of our nation is violated. But this principle is widely accepted as holding even beyond government. Usually one does not pick one's friends and acquaintances according to their religious beliefs or

26. See especially, Boswell, *Christianity,* chapter 4.

27. For Old Testament condemnations of homosexual acts, see Leviticus 18:22, 21:3. For hygienic and dietary codes, see for example, Leviticus 15:19–27 (on the uncleanliness of women) and Leviticus 11:1–47 (on not eating rabbits, pigs, bats, finless water creatures, legless creeping creatures, etc.). For Lot at Sodom, see Genesis 19:1–25. For Lot in the Cave, see Genesis 19:30–38.

their accidental conformity to one's own religious tenets. And this is so because in America people deeply believe that one's religious life is a private matter. Indeed, one has to have built up a relationship of friendly trust with another for the question of religious beliefs even to be broached. No one (other than someone who is despicable on other grounds) points out with pride one's membership in a club that excludes Jews or Catholics—even where the exclusion is legal. People recognize that holding others accountable for religious beliefs is properly a source of shame, even if they go ahead and do it anyway. In respecting religious privacy, then, one does not hold others accountable to the beliefs one holds *solely* on religious grounds. Those who invoke religious sentiments for their attitudes toward gays, then, need to examine whether their religious beliefs are here not really a disguise for some animus for which they have no reasons.

V. BUT AREN'T THEY UNNATURAL?

The most noteworthy feature of the accusation of something being unnatural (where a moral rather than an advertising point is being made) is that the plaint is being made so infrequently. One used to hear the charge leveled against abortion, but it has dropped from public discourse as anti-abortionists have come to lay their chips on the hope that people in general will come to view abortion as murder. Incest used to be considered unnatural but discourse now usually assimilates it to the moral machinery of rape and violated trust. The charge comes up now in ordinary discourse only against homosexuality. This social pattern suggests that the charge is highly idiosyncratic and has little, if any, explanatory force. It fails to put homosexuality in a class with anything else so that one can learn by comparison with clear cases of the class just what exactly it is that is allegedly wrong with it. Nor is homosexuality even a paradigm case for a class of unnatural acts. In popular morality, the charge that homosexuality is immoral because unnatural appeals to a principle so narrow as to be arbitrary.

What the charge of unnaturalness lacks in moral content is compensated for by the emotional thrust with which it is delivered. In ordinary discourse, when the accusation of unnaturalness is applied to homosexuality, it is usually delivered with venom of forethought. It carries a high emotional charge, usually expressing disgust and evincing queasiness.[28] Probably it has no content other than its expression of emotional aversion. For people get equally disgusted and queasy at all sorts of things that are perfectly natural—to be expected in nature apart from artifice —and that could hardly be fit subjects for moral condemnation. Two examples from current American culture are some people's responses to mothers suckling in public and to women who do not shave body hair. When people have strong emotional reactions, as they do in these cases, without being able to give good reasons for the reactions, one thinks of them not as operating morally and certainly not as grounding a morality for others, but rather as being obsessed and manic. So the feelings of disgust that some people have to gays will hardly ground a charge of immorality. People fling the term "unnatural" against gays in the same breath and with the same force as calling gays "sick" and "gross," and when they do this, they give every appearance of being neurotically fearful, while at the same time violating the moral principle that one needs justifying reasons for moral beliefs.

When "nature" is taken in *technical* rather than ordinary usages, it looks like the notion also will not ground a charge of homosexual immorality. When unnatural means "by artifice" or "made by man," one need only point out that virtually everything that is good about life is unnatural in this sense, that one feature that distinguishes people from most other animals is people's ability to make over the world to meet their needs and desires, and that people's well-being depends upon these departures from nature. On this understanding of the natural and people's nature, homosexuality is perfectly unobjectionable.

Another technical sense of natural is that something is natural, and so good, if it fulfills some function in nature. Homosexuality in this view is

28. I have suggested elsewhere that it is the narrowing of the scope of unnaturalness as an accusation in ordinary morality taken together with people's highly emotional response to homosexuality that explains why the Catholic Church has recently pulled out all the stops in its opposition to gays. Since the thirteenth century, naturalness had been the ethical engine of Catholic doctrine. If strong popular objections to homosexuality were allowed to fade, Catholic doctrine would lose any link with ordinary morality and so would, as a mode of thought, become no more than an intellectual oddity of, at most, historical interest. See Richard Mohr, "Why the Catholic Church Can't Give Up Its Antigay Position," *The Advocate*, January 20, 1987, no. 464, p. 9, criticizing *Doctrinal Congregation's Letter to Bishops: The Pastoral Care of Homosexual Persons* (Rome, October 1, 1986). The Vatican's English translation of its pastoral letter is published in full in *Origins: NC Documentary Service* (1986) 16(22):377–82.

unnatural because it allegedly violates the function of genitals, which is to produce babies. One problem with this view is that lots of bodily parts have lots of functions and just because some one activity can be fulfilled by only one organ (say, the mouth for eating) this activity does not condemn other functions of the organ to immortality (say, the mouth for talking, licking stamps, blowing bubbles, or having sex). So the possible use of the genitals to produce children does not, without more, condemn the use of the genitals for other purposes, say, achieving ecstasy and intimacy.

The functional view of nature will provide a morally condemnatory sense to the unnatural only if a thing which might have many uses has but one proper function to the exclusion of all other possible functions. But whether this is so cannot be established simply by looking at the thing. For what is seen is all its possible functions: "it's a stamp-licker," "no, its a talker," "no, it's a bubble-blower," "no, it's a sex organ." It was thought that the notion of function might ground moral authority, but instead it turns out that moral authority is needed to define proper function.

Some people try to fill in this moral authority by appeal to the "design" or "order" of an organ, saying, for instance, that the genitals are designed for the purpose of procreation. But these people intellectually cheat if they fail to make explicit *who* the designer and orderer is. If it is God, the discussion is back to square one—they are holding others accountable for religious beliefs.

Further, ordinary moral attitudes about childrearing will not provide the needed supplement which in conjunction with the natural-function view of bodily parts would produce a positive obligation to use the genitals for procreation. Society's attitude toward a childless couple is that of pity, not censure—even if the couple could have children. The pity may be an unsympathetic one—that is, not registering a course one would choose *for oneself*—but this does not make it a course one would *require* of others. The couple who discovers they cannot have children are viewed not as having thereby had a debt canceled, but rather as having to forgo some of the richness of life, just as a quadriplegic is not viewed as absolved from some moral obligation to hop, skip, and jump, but is viewed as missing some of the richness of life. Consistency requires, then, that, at most, gays who do not or cannot have children are to be pitied rather than condemned. What *is* immoral is the willful preventing of people from achieving the richness of life. Immorality in this regard lies with those social customs, regulations, and statutes that prevent lesbians and gay men from establishing blood or adoptive families, not with gays themselves.

Sometimes people attempt to establish authority for a moral obligation to use certain bodily parts in only one way simply by claiming that moral laws are natural laws and vice versa. On this account, inanimate objects and plants are good in that they follow natural laws by necessity, animals by instinct, and persons by a rational will. People are special in that they must first discover the laws that govern the species. Now, even if one believes the view—dubious in the post-Newtonian, post-Darwinian world—that natural laws in the usual sense ($e = mc^2$, for instance) have some moral content, it is not at all clear how one is to discover the laws in nature that apply to people.

If, on the one hand, one looks to people themselves for a model—and looks hard enough—one finds amazing variety, including homosexual behavior as a social ideal (upper-class fifth-century B.C. Athenians) and even as socially mandatory (Melanesia today). When one looks to people, one is simply unable to strip away the layers of social custom, history, and taboo in order to see what's really there to any degree more specific than that people are the creatures which make over their world and are capable of abstract thought.

Most people, though, do not even try to see *what's there* but instead simply and by default end up projecting the peculiarities of their culture into the universe as cosmic principles. Anthropology has shown that each and every society—however much it may differ from the next—thinks that its own central norms are dictated by and conform with nature writ large.[29] That this is so should raise doubts that neutral principles are to be found in man's nature that will condemn homosexuality.[30] Man may very well be, as Hannah Arendt claimed,

29. For striking examples of a culture incorporating homosexuality into its cosmology, see Walter L. Williams, *The Spirit and the Flesh: Sexual Diversity in American Indian Culture* (Boston: Beacon, 1986), pp. 18–22.

30. The British philosopher John M. Finnis has offered a somewhat more sophisticated account of unnaturalness as a ground for considering homosexuality immoral, in "Natural Law and Unnatural Acts," *Heythrop Journal* (1970) 11:365–87. He holds that nature contains a fixed constellation of basic values, which are heterogeneous in such ways that a person cannot in his or her actions maximize them. Immorality consists therefore not in failing to maximize instantiations of the values, but in knowingly "turning away" from

the creature whose nature it is to have no nature. It is by virtue of this human condition that people can be creative and make moral progress.

On the other hand, if for models one looks to nature apart from people, the possibilities are staggering. There are fish that change gender over their lifetimes: should people "follow nature" and be operative transsexuals? Orangutans, genetically our next of kin, live completely solitary lives without social organization of any kind: ought people to "follow nature" and be hermits? There are many species where only two members per generation reproduce: shall we be bees? The search in nature for people's purpose, far from finding sure models for action, is likely to leave people morally rudderless.[31]

---

any one of them. These values are knowledge, beauty, play, friendship, practical reasonableness, religion and life—or its production. Homosexual acts are therefore supposed to be unnatural and immoral as a turning away from the production of life. Even assuming that this is a coherent position, it has two problems.

First, it is not clear that these values, any or all, are in fact what one would legitimately call *moral* values, that is, values which one might legitimately impose upon others (if not through law, at least through private censure). Indeed, at least the bulk of these values look like goods which are not the concern of anyone or any group other than the individual who does or does not act in accordance with them. If I turn from my contemplation of a beautiful sunset or of dynamic recursion theory to watch an unbeautiful, unintelligent television program, it is a personal failing—not one for which others may legitimately chide or shame, let alone, arrest me. Finnis' values do not have enough oomph, enough *Schwung*, to generate a public morality. If he claims there is no difference between public and private morality, he will simply have revised our understanding of morality beyond recognition.

Second, it cannot convincingly be claimed that homosexual acts are a turning away from (the production of) life. Finnis has to hold that homosexual acts are like the use of contraceptives, where the use of a condom or the pill or a diaphragm is a conscious, planned attempt to interrupt a course of action that would otherwise likely produce human life. But homosexual acts entail no conscious or even unconscious attempt to interrupt what would otherwise produce human life—any more so than does eating a sandwich or reading a book. The argument could go through only if it had as a hidden premise that sex can legitimately exist only for the sake of reproduction, so that homosexuality must be at least a subconscious turning away from what sex is for. But this premise simply collapses the theory back into older, unacceptable forms of natural law ethics.

31. For homosexuality among nonhuman animals, see R. H. Denniston, "Ambisexuality in Animals," in Judd Marmor, ed., *Homosexual Behavior: A Modern Reappraisal*, pp. 25–40 (New York: Basic Books, 1980).

VI. BUT AREN'T GAYS WILLFULLY
THE WAY THEY ARE?

It is generally conceded that if sexual orientation is something over which an individual—for whatever reason—has virtually no control, then discrimination against gays is deplorable, as it is against racial and ethnic classes, because it holds people accountable without regard for anything they themselves have done. And to hold a person accountable for that over which the person has no control is a central form of prejudice.

Attempts to answer the question whether or not sexual orientation is something that is reasonably thought to be within one's own control usually appeal simply to various claims of the biological or "mental" sciences. But the ensuing debate over genes, hormones, twins, early childhood development, and the like—though now pointing in lopsided preponderance toward the conclusion that homosexuality is either genetically determined or a permanent result of early childhood familial configurations[32]—need not be firmly or finally settled beyond doubt in order to answer the morally and socially relevant questions over responsibility, choice, and necessity. One need only look at the social record to answer the question. All that is needed to answer the question is to look at the actual experience of gays in current society and it becomes fairly clear that sexual orientation is not likely a matter of choice. For coming to have a homosexual identity simply does not have the same sort of structure that decision-making has.

On the one hand, the 'choice' of the gender of a sexual partner does not seem to express a trivial desire which might as easily be fulfilled by a simple substitution of the desired object: picking the gender of a sex partner is decidedly dissimilar to picking a flavor of ice cream. If an ice-cream parlor is out of one's flavor, one simply picks another. And if

32. See the Kinsey Institute's retrospective path-analysis study by Alan P. Bell, Martin S. Weinberg, and Sue Kiefer Hammersmith, *Sexual Preference: Its Development in Men and Women* (Bloomington: Indiana University Press, 1981); see also Richard Green's confirming longitudinal study, *The "Sissy Boy Syndrome" and the Development of Homosexuality* (New Haven: Yale University Press, 1987). For a summary of biological findings, see Frederick Whitam and Robin Mathy, *Male Homosexuality in Four Societies* (New York: Praeger, 1986), chapter 7; see also Richard C. Pillard and James D. Weinrich's sibling study, "Evidence of Familial Nature of Male Homosexuality," *Archives of General Psychiatry* (1986) 43:808–12.

people were persecuted, threatened with jail terms, shattered careers, loss of family and housing, exposed to fatal disease and the like for eating, say, rocky road ice cream, no one would ever eat it; everyone would pick another easily available flavor. But gay sex seems not to be like that. If sexual orientation were an easy choice, Kinsey's statistics on the incidence of homosexuality in America, issued as they were when gay sex was everywhere a felony, would not have been shocking—they would simply have been preposterous, utterly unbelievable, virtually self-refuting.

On the other hand, even if establishing a sexual orientation is not like making a relatively trivial choice, perhaps it is like making the central and serious life-choices by which individuals try to establish themselves as being of some type. Again, if one examines gay experience, this seems not to be the case. For one never sees anyone setting out to become a homosexual, in the way one does see people setting out to become doctors, lawyers, and bricklayers. One does not find gays-to-be picking some end—"At some point in the future, I want to become a homosexual"—and then set about planning and acquiring the ways and means to that end, in the way one does see people deciding that they want to become lawyers, and then sees them plan what courses to take and what sort of temperaments, habits, and skills to develop in order to become lawyers.

The gay experience is quite different. Typically, gay persons-to-be simply find themselves having homosexual encounters and yet at least initially resisting quite strongly the identification of being a homosexual. Such a person even very likely resists having such encounters, but ends up having them anyway. Only with time, luck, and great personal effort does the person gradually come, if she does, to accept her orientation, to view it as a given material condition of life, coming as materials do with certain capacities and limitations. The person then begins to act in accordance with her orientation and its capacities, seeing its actualization as a requisite for an integrated personality and as a central component of personal well-being. As a result, the experience of coming out *to oneself* has for gays the basic structure of a discovery, not the structure of a choice. Far from signaling immorality, the coming out process affords one of the few remaining opportunities in ever more bureaucratic, mechanistic, and socialistic societies to manifest courage.

Nevertheless, two groups of self-identified homosexuals hold that sexual orientation *is* a matter of choice and, indeed, is better for being so. One group is lesbians who claim that having same-sex relations is chiefly politically motivated, and that pulling out of heterosexual relations and beginning homosexual ones is the politically correct thing to do, given the horrors of heterosexuality.[33] However, as far as actual sexual behavior goes, this claim simply overlooks the psychobiological truth (seemingly obvious, but in any case proven by Masters and Johnson) that one's sexual arousals are not subject to the blandishments of one's will. Sexual arousal is something that comes over one independently of the will; indeed, willing sexual arousal defeats it.[34] In sexual acts, one does not choose the gender (or genders) which can excite one. One may choose to identify oneself with a sexual orientation, but if one has successful sex acts in accordance with that orientation, it is because one is preconfigured or primed to respond to sexual cues of one sort rather than another.

Other gays who hold that sexual orientation is a matter of choice do so because they believe that the categories of sexuality themselves are not cast up from nature but are products of social construction, in much the way stereotypes are social constructions, so that sexual categories manifest themselves differently in different historical eras.[35] If this belief is true, nature cannot compel one to be, say, a homosexual, for while nature has always been around, homosexuality did not (in this view) exist *as a social category* before the last century. One must therefore choose to fall into one category or another after the categories are socially created. Constructivists accuse biological or social determinists of merely being apologists and excuse-makers trying to fend off moral censure through metaphysics and of actually belittling gays by making

33. For insightful discussion see, Mary Anne Warren, *The Nature of Woman: An Encyclopedia and Guide to the Literature* (Inverness, Cal.: Edge Press, 1980), s.v. lesbianism.

34. See William H. Masters and Virginia E. Johnson, *Human Sexual Inadequacy* (Boston: Little, Brown, 1970), pp. 198–99, 202–203, and *Homosexuality in Perspective* (Boston: Little, Brown, 1979), pp. 267–68, 296–97.

35. The view that society constructs the categories of sexuality was launched by Michel Foucault's *The History of Sexuality, Volume I: An Introduction*, trans. Robert Hurley (1976; New York, Random House, 1980). The thesis has been most carefully defended as applying specifically to homosexuality by John D'Emilio in "Capitalism and Gay Identity" in Ann Snitow, Christine Stansell, Sharon Thompson, eds., *Powers of Desire: The Politics of Sexuality*, pp. 100–13 (New York: Monthly Review Press, 1983) and "Making and Unmaking Minorities: The Tensions between Gay Politics and History," *New York University Review of Law and Social Change* (1986) 14:915–22.

sexual orientation a process as determinate, mechanical, and hapless as the earth circling the sun in 365.25 days or water freezing at 32 degrees.

As a normative theory, constructionism is objectionable in two ways. First, it takes a Stalinistic view of the social and hard sciences in that it calls for drawing their findings into line with a predetermined social ideology. It requires, for instance, dismissing the experience of gay people *discovering* that they are gay as a grand scale self-deception despite the honesty, clarity, and perspicuity with which their stories are told.[36]

Second, to be free does not require that a person be a blank slate capable of creating and then reconstructing every possible component of the self. Rather, to be free is to be able to make something of oneself. One does not hear the social constructivists claiming that blacks cannot be free if it is the case that their race is not chosen. In the social dimensions of sexuality, one acts freely by taking responsibility for it.[37] In taking responsibility for their sexuality—even though it may not be of their choosing—and doing something about it and society's response to it, gays are justifiably proud of themselves and make something of themselves.

That gays do take responsibility for sexuality and come out—virtually always in isolation and even into conditions of pervasive and imminent oppression—is a sign of the indomitability of the *individual* human spirit and a justification for viewing the individual as the proper locus of value in society.

VII. HOW WOULD SOCIETY AT LARGE BE CHANGED IF HOMOSEXUAL ACTS WERE DECRIMINALIZED AND GAYS SOCIALLY TOLERATED OR EVEN ACCEPTED?

Recommendations to change social policy with regard to gays are invariably met with claims that to do so would invite the destruction of civilization itself: after all, isn't that what did Rome in? Actually Rome's decay paralleled not the flourishing of homosexuality but its repression under the later Christianized emperors.[38] Predictions of American civili-

36. For a book full of examples, see Nancy Adair and Casey Adair, *Word Is Out: Stories of Some of Our Lives* (San Francisco: New Glide Productions, 1978).

37. See Joyce Trebilcot's modern classic "Taking Responsibility for Sexuality" in Robert Baker and Frederick Elliston, eds., *Philosophy and Sex,* 2d ed., pp. 421–30 (Buffalo: Prometheus Books, 1984).

38. See Boswell, *Christianity,* chapter 3.

zation's imminent demise have been as premature as they frequent. Civilization has shown itself rather resilient here, i because of the country's traditional commitments to a respect for privacy, to individual liberties, and especially to people minding their own business. These all give society an open texture and the flexibility to try out things to see what works. And because of this, one need not now speculate about what changes reforms of gay social policy might bring to society at large. For many reforms have already been tried out here and there, and nothing weird has resulted from them.

Half the states have decriminalized homosexual acts. Can you guess which of the following states still have sodomy laws: Wisconsin, Minnesota; New Mexico, Arizona; Vermont, New Hampshire; Nebraska, Kansas. One from each pair does and one does not. And yet one would be hard pressed to point out any substantial difference between the members of each pair. (If you're interested: the second of each pair has such laws.) Empirical studies have shown that there is no increase in other crimes in states that have decriminalized gay sex.[39] Decriminalization is not a primrose path to hell.

Neither has the passage of legislation barring discrimination against gays ushered in the end of civilization. Some fifty counties and municipalities, including Los Angeles, Boston, and New York, have passed such statutes and among the states and colonies, Wisconsin and the District of Columbia have model protective codes. Again, no more brimstone has fallen in these places than elsewhere. Staunchly antigay cities like Miami and Houston have not been spared the AIDS crisis.

Berkeley, California, has even passed domestic partner legislation giving gay couples the same rights to city benefits as married couples and yet Berkeley has not become more weird than it already was.[40]

Seemingly hysterical predictions that the American family would collapse if such reforms were passed have proven false, just as the same dire predictions that the availability of divorce would lessen the ideal and

39. See Gilbert Geis, "Reported Consequences of Decriminalization of Consensual Adult Homosexuality in Seven American States," *Journal of Homosexuality* (1976) 1(4):419–26; Ken Sinclair and Michael Ross, "Consequences of Decriminalization of Homosexuality: A Study of Two Australian States," *Journal of Homosexuality* (1985) 12(1):119–27.

40. "Berkeley Council Backs Friendship Benefits," *The New York Times*, December 7, 1984, p. Y12. Subsequently, the American Civil Liberties Union issued a formal policy statement endorsing the elimination of legal barriers to gay marriages. "Rights Group Backs Homosexual Marriages," *The New York Times*, October 28, 1986, p. 20.

desirability of marriage proved completely unfounded. Indeed if current discrimination, which drives gays into hiding and into anonymous relations, was lifted, far from seeing gays raze American families, one would see gays forming them. Virtually all gays express a desire to have a permanent lover. Many would like to raise or foster children—perhaps from among those alarming number of gay kids who have been beaten up and thrown out of their "families" for being gay. A surprising number of gays—especially lesbians—do have children, either from former heterosexual lives or through artificial insemination. Indeed it is not fanciful to suppose that technology will eventually do for the relation between procreation and sexual orientation what it has done for the relation between strength and gender. In general, when afforded the opportunity, gays have shown an amazing tendency to nest.

Society currently makes gay coupling very difficult: a life of hiding is a tense and pressured existence not easily shared with another. And society seems to find gay love even more threatening than gay sex. The latter society might excuse as an aberrant compulsion but the former is surely a matter of choice that shows a commitment and indicates that the homosexual does not view her or his condition as some sort of permanent flaw. In turn, this choice shows that more usual couplings are not a matter of destiny but of personal responsibility. And *that* society finds scary: the so-called basic unit of society—the family—turns out not to be a unique immutable atom, but can adopt different parts, be adapted to different needs, and even improved. Gays might even have a thing or two to teach others about divisions of labor, the relation of sensuality to intimacy, and the stages of development in love relations.

If discrimination ceased, the energies that the typical gay person wastes worrying in the closet would be released for use in personal flourishing. From this release would be generated the many spinoff benefits that accrue to society at large when its individual members thrive—goodwill, charity, and civic spirit.

Finally, and perhaps paradoxically, in extending to gays the rights and benefits it has reserved for its dominant culture and extended selectively to others, America would confirm its deeply held, nearly religious vision of itself as a morally progressing nation, a nation itself advancing and serving as a beacon for others—especially with regard to human rights. The words with which our national pledge ends—"with liberty and justice for all"—are not a description of the present but a call for the future. Ours is a nation given to a prophetic political rhetoric which acknowledges that morality is not arbitrary and that justice is not merely the expression of the current collective will. It is this vision that led, even in the absence of much articulate moral argument, the black civil rights movement to its successes. Those congressmen who opposed that movement and its centerpiece, the 1964 Civil Rights Act, on obscurantist grounds, but who lived long enough and were noble enough, came in time to express their heartfelt regret and shame at what they had done. It is to be hoped and someday to be expected that those who now grasp at anything to oppose the extension of that which is best about America to gays will one day feel the same.

PART TWO

Mr. Justice Douglas at Sodom: Gays and Privacy

2. Why Sodomy Laws Are Bad

The American Civil Liberties Union is occasionally called upon to defend the civil liberties of homosexuals. It is not within the province of the Union to evaluate the social validity of laws aimed at the suppression or elimination of homosexuals.—"Homosexuality and Civil Liberties: Policy statement adopted by the Union's Board of Directors, January 7, 1957," *Civil Liberties: Monthly Publication of the ACLU,* March 1957, no. 150, [p. 3], abutting a sidebar marking the centenary of *Dred Scott.*

I. Introduction
II. The Stakes

I. INTRODUCTION

Some thirty years after this ACLU policy statement, the Supreme Court in *Bowers v. Hardwick* would assert the same of the Constitution's province, holding that gays have no constitutional privacy right to have sex: the Constitution does not "confer[ ] a fundamental right upon homosexuals to engage in sodomy."[1] Perhaps surprisingly—but perhaps not—the Court was able to reach this conclusion without discussing gays, or privacy, or sex. The strategy of the Court was to treat privacy as only a way of denominating a series of cases—"the privacy cases"[2] —yet not as having anything essential to do with why the cases declared various laws unconstitutional. The Court broke the privacy cases into isolated atoms—viewed them as having relevantly in common nothing

1. *Bowers v. Hardwick,* 106 S. Ct. 2841, 2843 (1986). Within two weeks of the *Bowers* decision, the Missouri Supreme Court, citing *Bowers,* upheld Missouri's sodomy law from privacy challenge. *State v. Walsh,* 713 S.W.2d 508, 511 (Mo. Banc 1986). After *Bowers,* the only other sexual privacy challenge to a statute so far to reach a state's highest court, that of Louisiana, also held that homosexual sodomy is not constitutionally protected, again citing *Bowers. State v. Neal,* 500 So.2d 374, 378 (La. 1987) (upheld anti-solicitation statute and, in dicta, a sodomy statute).

2. *Bowers,* 106 S. Ct. at 2844.

more specific than being what are called Substantive Due Process cases. Then for rights to Substantive Due Process the Court applied a test of long-held traditions and consensus that allowed the simple citing of the illegality of gay sex to ground its continued illegality.[3]

The aim of this part is not to criticize, other than incidentally, the Court's opinion in *Bowers*, but to do the work the Court majority—and even in its dissents—chose not to do: to explain why privacy should be viewed as a fundamental, substantive, and quite general constitutional right,[4] why gay sex falls under that right,[5] and in this chapter, why it is important that this should be so recognized by the courts. In the next chapter, I advance a theory based on the ninth amendment and Equal Protection Clause—*not* the Due Process Clause—which explains what rights not explicit in the Constitution are nevertheless fundamental to it. The vehicle for this analysis will be a critical yet sympathetic examination of *Griswold v. Connecticut*,[6] the case in which Justice Douglas for the first time precipitated from constitutional suspension the right to privacy and which remains the Court's only attempt at a systematic explanation of the right's moorings within the Constitution.

Indeed, after some unhelpful remarks in *Roe v. Wade*[7] about the origins of the right, recent invocations of privacy by Supreme Court justices—successful and not—have made no attempt to explain the right's imprimatur. The four-man dissent in *Bowers* does not indicate which Constitutional provisions it would have used to void sodomy laws; it simply cites a successful privacy case announced three weeks earlier which had claimed "[o]ur cases long have recognized that the Constitution embodies a promise that a certain private sphere of individual liberty will be kept largely beyond the reach of government."[8] This privacy case cites in turn the same list of cases that the *Bowers* Court construed only as Due Process cases, but fails to mention any Constitutional provisions or to offer any account of why the Constitution embodies a promise of privacy. The caselaw discussed in the appendix to

3. *Ibid.* at 2844–46.
4. See chapter 3.
5. See chapter 4.
6. 381 U.S. 479 (1965).
7. 410 U.S. 113, 152–53 (1973).
8. *Bowers*, 106 S. Ct. at 2850 (Blackmun, J., dissenting) (quoting *Thornburgh v. American College of Obst. & Gyn.*, 106 S. Ct. 2169, 2184 [1986] [barring abortion regulations under right to privacy]).

this part indeed does point to the conclusion of the four-man dissent in *Bowers,* but such pointing in itself fails to explain why the series of privacy cases should have a first member and so exist at all.

At the level of theory, the analysis in this part answers two important questions: what fundamental rights are implicit in the Constitution, and why is sex a private matter anyway? At a practical level, though, one might well ask whether the game is worth the candle. For sodomy laws are virtually never enforced.[9] And so, before addressing in the next two

9. Sodomy laws are very rarely enforced against consenting adults in clearly private environs. They are sometimes applied when the laws make no distinction between private and public, adults and minors, or consent and coercion. In the nation's capital, for instance, while sodomy is a felony with a maximum penalty of ten years in prison, there are no laws that particularly address the problem of males raping males. The statute defines rapes as involving only female victims. D.C. Code Ann. sect. 22–3502 (1981). Thus sodomy laws are used to fill this breach of the legal imagination. Male victims are left to plead necessity.

Currently, twenty-four states and the District of Columbia have some form of sodomy laws applying to same-sex adult couples. See *Bowers,* 106 S. Ct. at 2845 (citing "Survey on the Constitutional Right to Privacy in the Context of Homosexual Activity," *University of Miami Law Review* [1986] 40:524 n.9). The content of sodomy laws has varied widely from time to time, state to state and country to country. Laws have ranged from banning only anal penetrations of males by males to banning all permutations of contacts between mouth, genitals, and anus except kissing and genital contacts between those married to each other. The arguments of this part apply to all such variations. For one of the most broadly phrased and thus restrictive sodomy laws, see Miss. Code Ann. sect. 97-29-59 (1972) ("Every person who shall be convicted of the detestable and abominable crime against nature, committed with mankind or with beast, shall be punished by imprisonment in the penitentiary for a term of not more than ten years").

Within the last twenty years a number of states, Texas for example, have liberalized their laws to the extent of allowing oral and anal sex among heterosexual couples, but not among gay and lesbian couples. Tex. Penal Code Ann. sect. 21.06 (Vernon 1974). Such a distinction should raise serious questions of the laws' validity under rights to equal protection. See *Commonwealth v. Bonadio,* 490 Pa. 91, 415 A.2d 47 (1980) (Pennsylvania's sodomy law declared unconstitutional on equal protection grounds).

Bestiality is frequently included within the reach of sodomy laws. See, e.g., Miss. Code Ann. section 97-29-59 (1972). Such a facet of a sodomy law may be best upheld on possibly legitimate paternalistic grounds as an animal protection law. I say "possibly legitimate" for Kinsey, who took the time to look, has shown that some nonhuman animals prefer human sex partners over members of their own species: "On the other side of the record, it is to be noted that male dogs who have been masturbated may become considerably attached to the persons who provide the stimulation; and there are records of male dogs who completely forsake the females of their own species in preference for the sexual contacts that may be had with a human partner." Alfred Kinsey, et al., *Sexual Behavior in the Human Male* (Philadelphia: W. B. Saunders, 1948), p. 677.

Most laws banning sex between adults and children may be upheld on legitimate paternalistic grounds. For moral arguments, pro and contra, for pedophilia, see Robert

chapters the source and scope of the constitutional right to privacy, this chapter will argue that quite a lot is at stake in the elimination of even unenforced sodomy laws, but that the stakes have largely been misunderstood. The evil of unenforced sodomy laws is chiefly their assault on dignity and only secondarily their unwarranted causing of unhappiness.

II. THE STAKES

Sodomy laws are so little enforced that it has been difficult for civil libertarians even to bring cases under them into court for constitutional review. Previous unsuccessful challenges to such laws were mounted in Texas and Virginia by claiming that even without the laws' having been enforced, they were unconstitutional on their face.[10] A successful attempt to overturn New York's sodomy law was occasioned by an odd series of events in which a grand jury indictment for the raping of a child was basically reconstructed by the district attorney and judge into a charge of sex between consenting adults.[11] The challenge in *Bowers* started when a policeman came to Mr. Hardwick's home to confront him with an unpaid ticket for public drunkenness. A housemate, not knowing of Mr. Hardwick's whereabouts, admitted the policeman to see if Mr. Hardwick was in his bedroom. He was—entangled with another man's anatomy in ways allegedly violating The Peach State's statute against unnatural acts.[12] His arrest under the statute

---

Ehman, "Adult-Child Sex" and Marilyn Frye, "Critique" both in Robert Baker and Frederick Elliston, eds., 2d ed. *Philosophy and Sex*, pp. 431–46, 447–55 (Buffalo: Prometheus Books, 1984). For an excellent discussion of medical moralizing on pedophilia, bestiality, sadomasochism and other paraphilias, see Frederick Suppe "Classifying Sexual Disorders: The *Diagnostic and Statistical Manual* of the American Psychiatric Association," *Journal of Homosexuality* (1984) 9(4): 9–28.

10. *Baker v. Wade*, 769 F.2d 289 (5th Cir. 1985) (en banc) (upholding Texas's sodomy law against a privacy challenge), cert. denied, 106 S. Ct. 3337 (1986); *Doe v. Commonwealth Attorney for Richmond*, 403 F. Supp. 1199 (E.D. Va. 1975) (upholding Virginia's sodomy law against privacy challenge), aff'd mem., 425 U.S. 901 (1976).

11. *People v. Onofre*, 51 N.Y.2d 476, 415 N.E.2d 936, 434 N.Y.S.2d 947 (1980), cert. denied, 451 U.S. 987 (1981) (New York's sodomy law declared an unconstitutional violation of privacy rights). On the contorted, peculiar, but undisputed facts of the case on appeal, see Brief for the Appellant pp. 2–3, People v. Onofre, 51 N.Y.2d, 415 N.E.2d 936, 434 N.Y.S.2d 947 (1980) (No. 77/405 [Criminal]), cert. denied, 451 U.S. 987 (1981); Brief for Respondent, pp. xiv-xvii, *ibid.*

12. Ga. Code Ann. section 16-6-2 (1984).

was the first in some fifty years for adult private consensual gay sex.[13]

In the absence of anything approaching routine enforcement of sodomy laws, it is not surprising that little attention was paid to them in the early 1970s at the start of the gay rights movement. Rather, civil rights legislation guarding against discrimination in employment, housing, and the like was the paramount issue on gay political agendas. More recently, and especially with the establishment of a number of gay legal defense foundations in the middle and late 1970s, the courts have become the center of serious attention as a possible source of gay justice.

Even so, arguments for bothering with such laws are cast almost entirely in terms of their practical consequences: legal reform is generally called for not because of a perception that the laws are inherently objectionable, but because of real or apparent spinoff effects in areas of public policy that do matter.

Sodomy laws are, so many current activists claim,[14] the bedrock of discrimination against gays. The case for this position is of mixed virtue. Opponents of civil rights legislation for gays do cite the existence of sodomy laws in opposing such legislated rights—how after all can one legitimately force people to hire and rent to unapprehended felons? One suspects, though, that this move is in general a ruse for opposition of foreign origin. For the absence of such laws does not stop people who are otherwise opposed to civil rights for gays from continuing their opposition; at least one never hears of people changing their views on civil rights when the status of a state's sodomy law changes. Rather the existence of sodomy laws simply gives those opposed to civil rights something to say that does not sound patently prejudicial in an area where there may not be a lot to say.

Indeed, most Americans, including gay ones, probably do not even know with any degree of certainty whether the state in which they live has a sodomy law. When Illinois legislators voted in 1961 to repeal the state's sodomy law, making it the first state to legalize gay sex, they did not even know what they were voting on. The repeal was simply one

13. *Bowers,* 106 S. Ct. at 2859 n.11 (Stevens, J., dissenting).

14. For a summary of practical consequences of largely unenforced sodomy statutes, see Arthur S. Leonard, "Keeping the Cops out of Michael Hardwick's Bedroom," *New York Native,* March 24, 1986, p. 24; Nan Feyler, "The Use of the State Constitutional Right to Privacy to Defeat State Sodomy Laws," *New York University Review of Law and Social Change* (1986) 14:976–79.

overlooked and undiscussed technical detail of an omnibus criminal law reform package adopted in entirety from the American Law Institute's Model Penal Code.[15] Two of the toughest gay civil rights laws in the country have been passed in locales where sodomy laws were in force— Wisconsin, the only state to adopt such protections although it decriminalized gay sex only a year later,[16] and The District of Columbia, where sodomy is still a felony.[17]

In general, little weight can be given to claims of some activists that one chief harm of these laws is that they produce severe psychological damage for many gays in states with such laws. The existence of such damage and unhappiness cannot be denied, but it is the result of a general toxic antigay social climate, to which sodomy laws may or may not be a concomitant. At least, sodomy laws are not the substrate or initiating cause of social hostility to gays.

More promising sources of possible indirect practical benefits from the elimination of sodomy laws are found in judicial treatments of sexual solicitation laws, which *are* enforced—almost always through techniques of entrapment.[18] These solicitation laws frequently have devastat-

15. See *Bowers,* 106 S. Ct. at 2845 n.7; John D'Emilio, *Sexual Politics, Sexual Communities: The Making of a Homosexual Minority in the United States, 1940–1970* (Chicago: University of Chicago Press, 1983), p. 146.

16. Wisconsin's bill protecting gays, among other classes, in employment and public accommodations was passed in 1982. Wis. Stat. Ann. section 111.31-.32 (West Supp. 1986). Its sodomy law was revised in 1983 to eliminate consensual adult sex in private as a crime. Wis. State. Ann. section 944.17 (West Supp. 1986) (1983 Act 17, sect. 5, effective May 12, 1983).

17. Washington, D.C. still has a sodomy law with ten years' imprisonment as a maximum penalty. D.C. Code Ann. sect. 22-3502 (1981). It has, however, one of the oldest and strongest gay rights laws in the country, passed in 1977. D.C. Code Ann. sections 1-2501, -2502, -2512, -2515, -2519, -2520 (1981).

18. For a levelheaded treatment of the legal morality of entrapment as a law enforcement technique, see Gerald Dworkin, "The Serpent Beguiled Me and I Did Eat: Entrapment and the Creation of Crime," *Law and Philosophy* (1985) 4:17–39. Dworkin's analysis, however, is not fine grained enough to deal with sexual solicitation and indeed does not address the matter. He shows to be a red herring the Court's current permissive Constitutional standard—that the state in entrapment cases need show only an offender's *predisposition* to commit a crime *(Sorrells v. United States,* 287 U.S. 435 [1932]). He argues that the government should have to show that it has not caused the offender to form the *specific intent* to commit the crime: "if the government, in Learned Hand's phrase, 'solicits, proposes, initiates, broaches or suggests' the offense, then the origin of the intent lodges with the state" (p. 29).

The problem with this formulation is that "broaching" and "suggesting" are bound to be vague when applied to the complex social rituals of the cruising grounds where sexual

ing personal, social, and economic effects for those arrested, even though criminal penalties typically are slight and even if charges are ultimately dropped or a not-guilty verdict reached. Though solicitation is sometimes crabbedly viewed as a species of public nuisance or public indecency, sometimes the relation between solicitation and sodomy is viewed, reasonably enough, as that between an attempt of an act and the offense itself. If the latter is not something that *can* be criminal, neither, so it has been successfully argued in New York, can the former.[19] The California Supreme Court has taken the still stronger position that even when legislative reform rather than constitutional construction has decriminalized consensual private sodomy, laws against solicitation to commit the act violate Due Process rights.[20] Whither sodomy laws go, so too do sexual solicitation laws.

The existence of sodomy laws also significantly affects the way in which judges—who *are* aware of their existence—apply the law in

---

solicitations take place—to the ways, for instance, in which availability for sex is signaled. But in cases—including virtually all sexual solicitation arrests—where arrests require police decoys to know something of the sexual solicitation rituals, the entrapment will clearly violate Hand's criterion. For sexual solicitations for 'public' sex acts, as in washrooms and parks, are conspiratorial rituals in which the one person's predisposition to commit a crime becomes a specific intent to do so here-and-now *only if* the other person also has the same intention. In this context, when one of the actors is the state and where, by playing out the rules and customs of the ritual, willingness has been clarified, it is irrelevant who, as it were, makes the first move—almost always the point at which the arrest is made. For the ritual to work, the state must have the intention to break the law and to invite the breaking of the law, which is both unfair and conceptually incoherent as telling people both to break and not to break the law (see G. Dworkin, pp. 32–34). For detailed description and analysis of sexual rituals in 'public' places, see Laud Humphreys' *Tea Room Trade: Impersonal Sex in Public Places* (Chicago: Aldine, 1970); Jon J. Gallo, et al., "The Consenting Adult Homosexual and the Law: An Empirical Study of Enforcement and Administration in Los Angeles County," *U.C.L.A. Law Review* (1966) 13:643–797. The authors conclude:

> Societal interests are infringed only when a solicitation to engage in a homosexual act creates a reasonable risk of offending public decency. The incidence of such solicitations is statistically insignificant. The majority of homosexual solicitations are made only if the other individual appears responsive and are ordinarily accompanied by quiet conversation and the use of gestures and signals having significance only to other homosexuals (pp. 795–96).

19. *People v. Uplinger*, 58 N.Y.2d 936, 447 N.E.2d 62, 460 N.Y.S.2d 514 (1983) (New York's sexual solicitation law declared unconstitutional as companion legislation to its unconstitutional consensual sodomy law), cert. dismissed, 467 U.S. 246 (1984).

20. *Pryor v. Municipal Court*, 25 Cal. 3d 238, 254, 599 P.2d 636, 645, 158 Cal. Rptr. 330, 339 (1979) (California's sexual solicitation law voided on Due Process grounds); so too, *Commonwealth v. Sefranka*, 382 Mass. 108, 414 N.E.2d 602 (1980) (Massachusetts' sexual solicitation law voided on Due Process grounds).

general. Such influences are apparent when judges make determinations based on what they perceive to be public policy. It would be the rare judge that did not consider the admission of regular violations of the laws as tantamount, at a minimum, to a showing of bad moral character, which by statute or construction is then allegedly a sufficient warrant to deny one the position of school teacher, state licensee, or child's custodian. Such laws have had a concrete impact on many state employment opportunities for gays and lesbians and in custody suits involving lesbian and gay parties. However, as in the realm of legislated rights, the repeal of sodomy laws still might not be sufficient to eliminate blockades to correct judicial decisions in gay employment and related cases. In one of the more noteworthy antigay cases on record, Washington State's highest court, independent of the existence of the state's sodomy law, upheld the firing of a gay school teacher on grounds of immorality, quoting at length the New Catholic Encyclopedia as its rationale.[21]

Further, should sodomy laws be eliminated from the books not by legislation but by a judicial finding that they violate a fundamental constitutional right to privacy, one could reasonably hope that most discriminations against gay people by the state would also be declared unconstitutional. For under Equal Protection analyses, discriminations which impinge or trench on a fundamental right must pass, like laws barring outright actions protected by the right, the highest standard of judicial review: such discrimination must be shown both to have an end that is compelling and to be necessary to that end.[22] Widespread discrimination in government employment both directly in hiring and indirectly

21. *Gaylord v. Tacoma School District No. 10,* 88 Wash. 2d 286, 292, 295, 559 P.2d 1340, 1343, 1345 (Sup. Ct. Wash., 1977) (upholding the firing of a gay teacher for being immoral), cert. denied, 434 U.S. 879 (1977); see also *Rowland v. Mad River Local School District,* 730 F.2d 444 (6th Cir. 1984) (upholding, against first amendment and Equal Protection challenges, the permanent suspension of a school counselor for mentioning her lesbianism at school), cert. denied, 470 U.S. 1009 (1985).

22. The leading case here is *Shapiro v. Thompson,* 394 U.S. 618 (1969), which invalidated year-long residency requirements for welfare recipients as impinging on the fundamental right to interstate travel. However, subsequent to the abortion funding decisions, it is unclear what counts as impinging or trenching on fundamental rights. *Maher v. Roe,* 432 U.S. 464 (1976) (prohibition of abortion funding upheld against Equal Protection challenge); *Harris v. McRae,* 448 U.S. 297 (1980) (abortion funding bar upheld). These cases upheld bans on funding abortions for indigents even when all other medical procedures for them are paid by the state. *Shapiro* suggested that any distinction made with regard to a fundamental right counted as an impingement on that right.

through licensing procedures would likely be eliminated, especially at the state level. Further discrimination against gays in immigration and military policy might be eliminated, though the courts have traditionally given Congress and the executive branch the greatest degree of deference in these two areas.[23] And there is an untried possibility that laws barring gays from marrying would also be struck down on these grounds.[24]

All of these indirect deleterious effects of sodomy laws may, when taken collectively, constitute a strong enough reason for their elimination, even if they are never enforced. But the mere existence of these laws is an evil of a kind different and greater than their damaging consequences. The basic evil of sodomy laws is that they are an affront to dignity. In contrast, their bad indirect effects are mere mischief. An affront to dignity occurs whether the laws are enforced or not, and even whether they are known to exist or not.

Admittedly, dignity is an elusive notion, often appealed to when people have run out of moral reasons and explanations. Nevertheless, the common phrase "adding insult to injury" affords an intuitive grasp of the relevant distinction between two types of evils. An insult is an offense against dignity, while an injury is something that reduces one's happiness or pleasure, or denies one some benefit, wealth, power, useful possession, or generally reduces one's material circumstances in the world. Insults are a graver form of evil, for they are of a class of evils that attacks a person as a person. The most common indignities—invective and name-calling, insults in a narrow sense—attack a person because of some largely irrelevant peculiarity and without regard to anything that he has done. Thus calling someone a "nigger," "faggot," or "cunt" is a star case of insult. Such abuses attack the person as person in two ways. By focusing importance on an irrelevant characteristic, they attack per-

23. See Samuel M. Silvers, "The Exclusion and Expulsion of Homosexual Aliens," *Columbia Human Rights Law Review* (1984) 15:314–22; Peter N. Fowler & Leonard Graff, "Gay Aliens and Immigration," *University of Dayton Law Review* (1985) 10:621–44; John Heilman, "The Constitutionality of Discharging Homosexual Military Personnel," *Columbia Human Rights Law Review* (1980–81) 12:191–204; Rhonda R. Rivera, "Queer Law: Sexual Orientation Law in the Mid-Eighties, Part II," *University of Dayton Law Review* (1986) 11:287–324.

24. When the highest court of New York declared its sodomy law an unconstitutional violation of privacy, the dissenting opinion pointed out this likely consequence as an attempted *reductio ad absurdum* of the court's opinion, *People v. Onofre*, 51 N.Y.2d 476, 504 n.3, 415 N.E.2d 936, 950 n.3, 434 N.Y.S.2d 947, 960 n.3 (1980).

sons as repositories of deserved fair treatment and equal respect. And as holding a person morally accountable without regard for anything he has done, they show disrespect for persons as moral agents.

Now, an offense may be both an insult and an injury or just one or the other. Thus simple theft without aggravating circumstances, particularly theft of a luxury item, is chiefly an injury without being an affront to dignity, unless of course one views a person essentially as a consumer and possessor of luxuries. Cutting someone is likely to be both an injury and an insult, since it will both cause pain and affront dignity by violating bodily integrity, a precondition for a person being in the world at all.[25]

Some acts can be insults and yet provide no injury. Lying, or more particularly lying that actually benefits its hearer, provides many examples. Lying attacks persons in pretty much any conception of what a person is. On a Kantian notion of a person as a creature who has ends of his own, who can recognize others as having ends of their own, and so who is capable of respecting others, lying to a person shows a lack of respect for her by treating her merely as a means to one's own ends. The chief problem in this conception is not that the person will come to have a false belief or even act upon a false belief to her detriment, but that in lying one treats another like a found object, treating that person entirely as an instrument for one's own ends. Alternatively, if one views a person quasi-Platonically as essentially a thinker, knower, seer, poet, or contemplator, then causing a person to have false beliefs is sufficient to assault persons in that conception simply as casting the contemplated world in a false light.

Invasions of privacy typically entail disrespect and not mere harm. Admittedly some invasions of privacy produce injuries, sometimes grave ones. When police place hidden movie cameras in washroom stalls, men lose jobs, families are destroyed, men kill themselves. But invasions of privacy usually are also assaults on dignity. They are particularly grave failures to respect persons if the notion of person as thinker is fused with that of person as a creature with her own ends, into a unified view of person as chooser—a subject conscious of herself as an agent with plans, projects, and a view of her own achievements.[26] In this conception, one

25. See chapter 4, section V.
26. This definition and paragraph adapt views from Stanley I. Benn's "Privacy, Freedom, and Respect for Persons" in Ferdinand D. Schoeman, ed., *Philosophical Dimensions of Privacy: An Anthology*, pp. 228–31 (Cambridge: Cambridge University Press, 1984).

respects a person not by treating her essentially as one who is happy or sad—that would be a ground for sympathetic joy or pity but not respect. Rather one shows respect by not manipulating the conditions in which a person makes choices.

On this account, observed uninvited scrutiny effects such disrespectful manipulation by forcing the agent to become self-reflective, to become continuously aware of what he is doing, thus forcing an alteration of an agent's perception of himself. But even covert observation—spying—is objectionable. For it, like lying, "deceives a person about his world for reasons that *cannot* be his own reasons."[27]

Thus a person need not be aware of the act that insults her in order to be insulted nonetheless. When the state, through sodomy laws, reserves for itself the power to snoop on activity that is both traditionally and inherently private,[28] it insults gays even if gays are not harmed by the laws and even if they are unaware of the laws' existence.

Sodomy laws assault dignity in another way as well. As mentioned, the largest class of insults and assaults to dignity arise when a person is held in low esteem for widely irrelevant features and without regard to anything he himself has done. These violate a person's essential desert for equal respect and respect as a moral agent. Equal respect is violated because a person's desires, plans, aspirations, and sense of the sacred are not considered worthy of social care and concern on a par with those of others. And respect for moral agency is violated because a person is being judged without regard to her individual merits or accomplishments. Unenforced sodomy laws are invective by government.

When a state has unenforced sodomy laws on its books—not by oversight but even after the failure of law reform has drawn attention to their existence, and yet no attempt is made to enforce them though their frequent violation is a secret to no one—then insult is their main purpose. If the law is virtually never enforced, the law exists not out of a concern with the *actions* of gay people, but with their *status*. At oral argument in *Bowers,* Georgia claimed the purpose of its sodomy law was "symbolic."[29] And that claim unwittingly is true. For sodomy laws

27. *Ibid.,* p. 230.
28. See chapter 4, sections II and III.
29. See *Bowers,* 106 S. Ct. at 2859 n.12 (Stevens, J., dissenting); see generally Brief for Petitioner, at section II D, *Bowers v. Hardwick,* 106 S. Ct. 2841 (1986) (No. 85–140). Once Georgia admitted it had not prosecuted anyone under its sodomy statute in fifty

afford an opportunity for the citizenry to express its raw hatred of gays *systematically* and *officially* without even having publicly to discuss and so justify that hatred. There are, of course, nonsystematic means to this end, queerbashing, for instance. Still, unenforced sodomy laws are the chief systematic way that society as a whole tells gays they are scum.[30]

Slandering someone behind his back is an insult, even if he never learns of the slander. So again gays, even if unaware of sodomy laws, are insulted behind their backs by them. Even if some gays are unaffected by them in the sense that their happiness or fortunes do not depend upon the laws' removal, nevertheless their dignity is diminished by the laws' very existence.

The natural human responses to harms are pain and an analogue to pain—the form of anger that is being riled-up. Proper remedies are compensation and perhaps retribution. The response to insult is not pain and its analogue, but resentment and indignation—an anger that does not lash out in retaliation, but a pure, cool anger. The remedy sought cannot be compensation—another cannot make one a person. The proper action of the offended party is one that directly reasserts the dignity that was denied, in order to secure that dignity in a way that cannot be denied again, even if the person who thus asserts her dignity places herself at risk for harms by doing so. At an individual level, *expressing* indignation to the offender is the means to this end, even if one is under the power of the offender, such as an employer or even a friend. At the level of individual interactions, the goal of such assertion is heartfelt apology from the offender.

The social form of asserting dignity in the face of its social denial is nonviolent yet assertive civil disobedience. The end reasonably sought is the recognition of rights and the withdrawal of the sling of insult from the society's arsenal. Gays have not even entertained the possibility of nonviolent civil disobedience as part of what gay social justice might look like and might require. There has been no gay counterpart to Rosa

---

years, and after having failed to prosecute Mr. Hardwick in a case where conviction, as Justice Stevens noted, appeared to have been "served up on a platter," Georgia could hardly offer any justification for the law *other than* symbolism. For any justification that presumes certain effects on behavior flowing from the coercive threat of punishment, any rationale appealing to a need to deter behavior, is gutted by Georgia's admissions at trial. On Justice Stevens' remark, see "Supreme Court Hears Sodomy Challenge in Restrained Mood," *Lesbian/Gay Law Notes* [New York], April 1986, p. 21.

30. See further, chapter 4, section IV.

Parks.[31] No one has even thought to be her. That requires courage, openness, a willingness to put one's happiness at risk, and a solid sense of self. As a result gays have resorted chiefly to the low-key lobbying efforts of business-as-usual politics and have had little success.[32] Perhaps the target was mistaken.

In extreme circumstances, gays have occasionally resorted to unorganized mass violence in response to specific failures of the criminal justice system. The gay rights movement was launched in late June of 1969 in the aftermath of three days of street violence and demonstrations which have come to be called the Stonewall Riots. The disruptions were sparked by drag-queens violently resisting arrest in a routine harassing police raid of a Greenwich Village gay bar, the Stonewall Inn.[33] Or again, when a wholly heterosexual San Francisco jury found the assassin of city supervisor and gay hero Harvey Milk guilty of only a relatively piddling charge, gays in a dramatic mass uprising trashed the front of the city hall and torched a dozen squad cars in what have come to be called, after the assassin, the White Night Riots.[34]

Born of understandable frustration, such mass violence nevertheless requires not courage but temerity, not a sense of self but lack of it, not openness but anonymity, and not a sense of dignity but retribution. Such measures are justified—if at all—only when all others have failed, and yet some routes toward justice have hardly been explored. In chapter 3, I discuss the courts as one route. In chapter 14, I discuss civil disobedience as the alternative route to be tried when the courts fail in their mission.

In America there is a forum for the redress of those assaults to dignity that are perpetrated by government: the courts as expounders of Constitutional immunities against the state's monopoly of legitimate coercive

31. In 1955, Rosa Parks was arrested for refusing to leave the whites-only section of a city bus in Montgomery, Alabama. Her civil disobedience catalyzed the black civil rights movement. See Juan Williams, *Eyes on the Prize: America's Civil Rights Years, 1954–65* (New York: Viking, 1987), pp. 63–70. For discussion and justification of gay civil disobedience, see below chapter 14.

32. See, for example, Stephen Kulieke, "The Houston Defeat: Why?" *The Advocate* [Los Angeles], March 19, 1985, no. 416, pp. 10–11.

33. See D'Emilio, *Sexual Politics*, pp. 231–33.

34. On the White Night Riots, see Randy Shilts, *The Mayor of Castro Street: The Life and Times of Harvey Milk* (New York: St. Martin's, 1982), pp. 325–39. The day after the *Bowers* decision was announced, gays in New York City blocked Sixth Avenue for three hours. It is not clear whether this reactionary move should be counted as civil disobedience or mass violence. The gay press, even the conservative gay press, viewed the blockade as similar to the Stonewall Riots. See *The Advocate*, August 5, 1986, no. 452, pp. 12–13.

powers. To the extent that sodomy laws are an assault on dignity and to the extent that dignity is not, as it is not, something which ought morally to depend on the whims of majorities, then the courts are not just an available forum to overturn sodomy laws, but are also the proper forum.[35] There is, I think, no effective social equivalent to an individual's heartfelt apology. There is only the assertion of rights.

35. See generally, Ronald Dworkin, *A Matter of Principle* (Cambridge: Harvard University Press, 1985), chapter 2.

3. Mr. Douglas' Emanations: Whence and Whither Fundamental Rights

I. INTRODUCTION

Using Douglas' opinion in *Griswold v. Connecticut*[1] as a point of departure, this chapter offers an understanding of the Constitution which justifies a general and substantive constitutional right to privacy, but avoids standard objections to theories of constitutional interpretation which construe rights broadly. The result is a theory of interpretation that is neither narrow and mean-spirited nor unwieldy and amorphous, but is comprehensive yet clearly defined—a theory of equality-based coherence.

Douglas argues in a short, intense, rhetorically charged, metaphor-packed opinion that though the term "privacy" does not occur in the Constitution, there is nevertheless a constitutional right to privacy as fundamental as other substantive rights in the Bill of Rights. This right is so powerful that no analysis is even offered of Connecticut's alleged interests in the marital contraceptive law which the case voids.[2]

---

1. 381 U.S. 479 (1965).
2. *Ibid.* at 480–86. Perhaps Douglas intentionally left this task to Justice White, who concurred on the ground that the aims of the law were patently irrational. *Ibid.* at 502–7 (White, J., concurring).

The case pursues, often simultaneously, three diverse lines of argument, lines which are tangled, uneven, and unclear. One strand of argument is delivered stillborn[3] and the other two stand unwittingly at odds with each other.[4] One of the latter two, however, succeeds in establishing a general substantive right to privacy.[5]

II. PRIVACY AS ASSOCIATION: STRIKE ONE

One prominent but unsuccessful line of argument in *Griswold* holds that the right to privacy is pendant from a right to association. The steps of this argument seem to run as follows: (1) there is a right to association which is a first amendment right;[6] (2) the scope of the right to association is not limited to political activities but includes other relations and activities as well;[7] (3) the benefits of the right are not merely political benefits but include social and material benefits;[8] and (4) marriage is an association—an important one—of which, by virtue of the right to association, access to contraception is a protected material and social benefit.[9]

The first of these four premises is strong but the second very weak. In support of it Douglas cites only *NAACP v. Button*,[10] but he seems, at best, to have in mind that case's passing suggestion that the "personal satisfaction" received from[11] and a small fee attendant to a lawyer's political advocacy work using his skills[12] does not automatically make that work subject to the powers of the state to regulate the professions.[13] The benefits of the right may extend beyond political ones, but the association protected in *Button* is purely a political one, not a social one. Douglas thinks he has established the second premise when at most he

3. See sections II and III below.
4. See sections IV and V below.
5. See section V below.
6. *Griswold*, 381 U.S. at 482.
7. *Ibid.* at 483.
8. *Ibid.*
9. *Ibid.* at 486.
10. 371 U.S. 415, 430–31 (1963) (under the right of association, lawyers acting for political organizations are not subject to the same professional restrictions as other lawyers).
11. *Ibid.* at 444.
12. *Ibid.* at 443.
13. *Ibid.* at 442.

supports the third. To reach the requisite second premise and to include marriage under it, there must be at least one additional suppressed premise—a dubious one. Either marriage itself is being viewed as a first amendment right or all (important) associations and relations are protected by the right to association. The first alternative is absurd. The second is vague and dangerous: it would void a great deal of law. It would void, for example, the 1964 Civil Rights Act if business relations are viewed as important. Indeed the courts have been hesitant to expand the right to association beyond associations clearly political.[14]

This restriction of associational rights to politics has indeed worked to the advantage of gays. On the one hand, the only area of constitutional rights in which gays have had consistent success in federal courts is the establishment of gay political groups on state university campuses. They have won cases under the right to association in each of the many federal circuits where the issue has come up.[15] On the other hand, attempts to void gay provisions of local human rights ordinances by appeal to associational rights have generally failed. The best known case here is The Boy Scouts of America's constitutional failure to trim the wings of a gay Eagle Scout. The California Supreme Court ruled that the Boy Scouts are a public accommodation under a state public accommodations statute which bars discrimination against "all persons" and then ruled that associational rights of the Scouts did not void the act as it applied to gays.[16]

14. It is true that in *Roberts v. United States Jaycees*, 468 U.S. 609, 618–19 (1984), which upheld civil rights laws against associational challenge, Justice Brennan speaks of a right to intimate association, but it is clear from the cases he cites, including importantly *Stanley v. Georgia*, 394 U.S. 557 (1969), which protected the relation between a man and his pornography collection, that Brennan is really speaking of privacy in general here and not a separate right which deals only with relations between persons.

15. In the First, Fourth, Fifth, Eighth, and Eleventh Circuits; for example, *Gay Lib v. University of Missouri*, 558 F.2d 848 (8th Cir. 1977), cert. denied, 434 U.S. 1080, reh'g denied, 435 U.S. 981 (1978); *Gay Alliance of Students v. Matthews*, 544 F.2d 162 (4th Cir. 1976); *Gay Student Org., University of New Hampshire v. Bonner*, 509 F.2d 652 (1st Cir. 1974). All these cases voided prohibitions barring gay student groups on state university campuses under the right to association. See National Lawyers Guild Anti-Sexism Committee of San Francisco Bay Area Chapter, Roberta Achtenberg, ed., *Sexual Orientation and the Law* (New York: Clark Boardman, 1985), chapter 9.02 [1–2].

16. *Curran v. Mount Diablo Council of Boy Scouts of America*, 147 Cal. App. 3d 712, 195 Cal. Rptr. 325 (1983) (upholding public accommodation protections against associational rights).

III. INTIMATE ASSOCIATION?

[Marriage] is an association that promotes a way of life, not causes; a harmony in living, not political faiths; a bilateral loyalty, not commercial or social projects. Yet it is an association for as noble a purpose as any involved in our prior decisions.[17]

On the basis of these thundering last two sentences of *Griswold*, the liberal constitutional theorist Kenneth Karst has tried to rehabilitate associational rights as part of a general attempted revival of Substantive Due Process.[18] Douglas specifically denies that he is reviving Substantive Due Process in *Griswold*[19]—a point conveniently overlooked by both Karst and the *Bowers* Court. And Douglas had a finely tuned detector for Substantive Due Process.[20] Under the interpretation proposed here, Douglas is indeed right in not seeing *Griswold* as a revival of Substantive Due Process.

Karst claims that *Griswold*, as the generator of broad constitutional interpretation, launched not a right to privacy but a right to *intimate* association. Karst does not define intimacy by giving its marks but only by cataloguing quite heterogeneous examples of intimate relations: marriage, marriage-like relations, other familial relations, and close friendships.[21] Nonetheless, he supposes this amorphous right is the driving force behind and affords the best overall understanding of the later "privacy" cases[22] and most of the other "fundamental rights" cases of the last twenty years,[23] and points to many other rights, including even a right to gay marriage.[24]

17. *Griswold v. Connecticut,* 381 U.S. 479, 486 (1965).

18. Kenneth L. Karst, "The Freedom of Intimate Association," *The Yale Law Journal* (1980) 89:624–92. This article seems to provide the intellectual backdrop of the four-man dissent in *Bowers v. Hardwick,* 106 S. Ct. 2841, 2851, 2854 (1986) (Blackmun, J., dissenting).

19. *Griswold,* 381 U.S. at 482–83.

20. See, for example, Douglas' concurrence in *Boddie v. Connecticut,* 401 U.S. 371, 384–85 (1971) (Douglas, J., concurring) (under Due Process, the case voided requirements of filing fees from indigents in divorce petitions; Douglas would have voided the fee under an Equal Protection analysis holding indigents to be a suspect class rather than under the Due Process Clause).

21. Karst, "Intimate Association," p. 629.

22. *Ibid.,* pp. 641–42, 655, 689.

23. *Ibid.,* pp. 652–53, 663–64, 667, 671, 676–82; for example, the right to marry and even enhanced Equal Protection rights of illegitimate children.

24. *Ibid.,* p. 684.

However, Karst cannot give an adequate account of the privacy decisions nor adequately ground rights to sexual activity. Karst is unable even to explain adequately the Court's second privacy case, *Stanley v. Georgia*,[25] which established the specific privacy right to possess and use materials that are constitutionally obscene—ones which appeal to prurient interest and which a person has the right neither to produce nor even to purchase. Reading and solo masturbation are private acts if any are, yet neither is an act of intimacy. Further, according to Karst, a state's barring abortion is not an intrusion into a private affair of a pregnant woman, but (oddly enough) is a sort of shotgun marriage between fetus and mother, a coerced intimacy.[26] In general, private acts need not be intimate, because they need not engage relations with other persons at all. A correct account sees intimacy as a protected dimension of privacy rather than privacy as a dimension of intimacy.

Karst claims that casual gay sex acts are constitutionally protected under a right to association not because they are private but because they "may" lead to a relation that is intimate or marriage-like.[27] But this strategy implicitly sets out a hopelessly open-ended constitutional test. For if every instance of something that "*may* lead to *x*" is protected to "the right to *x*," there will not be anything that is not constitutionally protected, since every act *may* lead to intimacy. If Karst were to alter the protection-invoking formulation to "likely or probably leads to *x*," he might save the test, but would lose gay sex as meeting it, since traditionally the majority of male homosexual encounters have been impersonal.[28] Nor could Karst have sex be relevantly covered by "the right to *x*, such as, intimacy" because "necessary for *x*, such as, intimacy." For then he would lose most familial relations and friendships as intimate relations, since by tradition, taboo, common sense, and good taste, most familial relations and friendships do not entail sex between their mem-

25. 394 U.S. 447 (1969) (right to possess obscene materials in one's own home).

26. Karst, "Intimate Association," p. 641. However, it is unclear why, if this is the problem, the remedy is one to which the mother, but not the fetus, has access—killing the "spousal" counterpart.

27. *Ibid.*, p. 633.

28. See Alan P. Bell and Martin S. Weinberg, *Homosexualities: A Study of Diversity Among Men and Women* [An official Kinsey Institute study] (New York: Simon and Schuster, 1978), pp. 73–78; James Spada, *The Spada Report* (New York: Signet, 1979), pp. 63–76, 326–27; Karla Jay and Allen Young, *The Gay Report* (New York: Summit Books, 1979), pp. 161, 248–49, 251–52.

bers. The right to intimate association, at least as construed by Karst, will not protect gay sex as Karst thinks it will.

IV. PRIVACY AS A "PERIPHERAL" RIGHT: STRIKE TWO

A second line of argument in *Griswold* advances the theory that zones of privacy are adjuncts to specific explicit constitutional guarantees, which are said to "create" the zones.[29] In this view there are various specific rights to privacy, not one single overarching right to it. Each protected privacy is derived from one or more specific guarantees of the Bill of Rights. The explicit guarantees, on this account, severally determine the content and gravity of implicit privacy rights.

"Peripheral" is Douglas' favored metaphor for describing and justifying these protected privacies which are not themselves explicit guarantees: the explicit guarantees have peripheries that protect activities which do not in any direct, obvious way fall under the specific guarantees proper.[30] Thus, Douglas' first theoretical step in the case is to say that the right to association, though not mentioned in the Constitution, is "necessary" to the political rights of the first amendment if they are to be "fully meaningful" and that a right to privacy covering party membership lists is, in turn, similarly necessary to this right.[31] This line of thought, however, fails both as a general method of constitutional interpretation and as a specific method for locating the privacy actually protected in the case—marital contraception. The view that peripheral rights are what constitute the implicit fundamental rights of the Constitution lets in both too many rights and too few.

First, if a sufficient condition for the existence of a constitutional right is that it is simply *necessary* to the meaningful possession or expression of some specific provision of the Bill of Rights, then the Constitution becomes a net so broad as to be completely unmanageable. If one has a right to association in political activity simply because it is necessary to

29. *Griswold*, 381 U.S. at 484.
30. For example, *ibid.* at 483.
31. *Ibid.* at 483. The reasoning given here by Justice Douglas continues to be the Court's rationale for rights to political association. See *Roberts v. United States Jaycees*, 468 U.S. 609, 618 (1984): "In another set of decisions, the Court has recognized a right to associate for the purpose of engaging in those activities protected by the First Amendment. . . . The Constitution guarantees freedom of association of this kind as an indispensable means of preserving other individual liberties."

political speech, then it would seem that one must have, to an even greater degree, a constitutional right to breakfast and kidney machines. To claim this, though, one would have stepped upon a very steep and slippery slope into constitutionally mandated welfare rights. The courts would then be managing the economy in the most severe of ways. The courts would not simply be determining the shape of economic policy by setting limits to government's intervention into economic matters, as the Supreme Court did some 200 times in the now generally bemoaned *"Lochner* era" (1905–1936) by barring, under the banner of Substantive Due Process, state-mandated commercial and labor regulations.[32] Far worse, the courts would have to assume for themselves final authority and control over the creation and enforcement of social and economic regulations to guarantee that every need for food, shelter, clothing, medicine, and probably education is met for all those who might speak, print, assemble, or petition—to wit—everyone.

Practical necessity dictates that the courts ought not assume such a massive role in social policy, and moreover, such a role for the courts is clearly out of keeping with the general tenor of the rights of the Bill of Rights. All of its provisions, save one, are *immunities* from government coercion. They say what the government cannot do—how the government may not deploy its power, its legitimate monopoly of coercion. Only the sixth amendment right to compulsory process for obtaining witnesses in one's favor is an exception to the rule that rights are immunities. Only that amendment requires the government to do or to provide something. Only it gives the citizen a demand claim upon the government. But even here the right is not a free-standing positive right existing independently of state actions. Rather it is triggered or engaged only because the government has already deployed its power—by arresting the right-bearer. Therefore, if the government did not exist at all, did nothing at all, everyone would have all the rights of the Bill of Rights. But obviously welfare rights in general, positive rights that the govern-

---

32. The case from which the era takes its name declared unconstitutional a state law setting a 60-hour maximum work-week for bakers, *Lochner v. New York,* 198 U.S. 45 (1905). See also, *Adkins v. Children's Hospital,* 261 U.S. 525 (1923), in which the Court voided statutes establishing minimum wages for women and children. On the *"Lochner* era" and the triumph of Substantive Due Process in the economic arena, see Benjamin Wright, *The Growth of American Constitutional Law* (1942; Chicago: University of Chicago Press, 1967), pp. 153–79. For statistics on numbers and kinds of laws struck down, see page 154.

ment provide goods and services, are not even rights of the sort that are triggered (like rights to witnesses on one's behalf) by some deployment of government coercion, let alone immunity rights of the sort found in the rest of the Bill of Rights. A general constitutional principle cannot then be asserted in the claim that one has the right to whatever is necessary for meaningful possession of specific provisions of the Bill of Rights.

Second, Douglas' "peripheral rights" analysis will not generate a right to privacy that either is on all fours with explicit guarantees of the Constitution or is by itself a general right—*the* right to privacy. The analysis fails to explain why the right is fundamental in force. Rights have cores and edges with correspondingly varying strength as to what they protect or do not protect. Thus regulations of speech that distinguish *what* various speakers say—the content of speech—engage the core of first amendment freedoms of speech and, in order to be upheld against challenges, have to pass the most stringent constitutional standards—namely, they must be necessary means to compelling ends.[33] By contrast, regulations that are neutral with regard to the content of speech and regulate rather, say, the time, place, and manner of speech are at the edges of first amendment protection and must meet only a weaker constitutional standard in which the weight of the regulation's impact on the speaker is balanced against the weight of the state's interest in the regulation.[34] In treating privacy as a "peripheral" right tied to specific guarantees, Douglas places privacy (to continue his spatial metaphor) beyond the pale. In view of its conceptual dependence on specific explicit provisions, privacy ought to have less force than the specific guarantees have. If, as Douglas claims, privacy is peripheral to the first amendment, then it ought to generate a protection even weaker in force than the scrutiny given to content-neutral regulations. But it does not. Douglas claims, and ensuing privacy cases have maintained, the same constitutional standard holds for privacy as for content-based regulations of speech, and this is also what is really needed if the right is

33. See *Consolidated Edison Co. of New York v. Public Service Comm'n,* 447 U.S. 530, 540 (1980) (held unconstitutional an administrative order barring a utility company from discussing controversial issues in its billing statements, as failing to be necessary to a compelling state interest).

34. See *United States v. O'Brien,* 391 U.S. 367, 377 (1968) (burning a draft card as symbolic speech fails a complex balancing test for regulations of the manner of speech).

to have any impact.[35] Douglas' peripheral rights analysis should be seen as failing to establish privacy rights sufficiently powerful enough to override any legitimate state interests.

Further, as conservative constitutional theorist, former Federal Appellate Judge, and rejected Supreme Court nominee Robert Bork has correctly noted, Douglas' peripheral rights analysis does not generate a *general* right to privacy.[36] At best it generates diverse privacy satellites variously tethered to various specific guarantees. Thus one gets *a* right to privacy in political party membership lists, but not *the* right to privacy: the peripheral "right has no life of its own as a right independent of its relationship to a first amendment freedom. Where that relationship does not exist, the [peripheral] right evaporates."[37] Douglas' reasoning establishes a "zone of privacy," not a right to privacy in general. Yet it is *the* right to privacy that is needed if marital contraception is to be constitutionally protected. Despite his analysis, Douglas correctly does not attempt to find the use of contraceptives in the peripheries of some one or more specific explicit provisions of the Constitution. Douglas' talk of peripheries simply fails to give the requisite generality to privacy.

V. SPECIFIC PRIVACIES AS PENUMBRAL RIGHTS: A TWO BAGGER

A more promising approach for developing a general right to privacy through *Griswold* comes from a converse, competing line of thought at which the case only hints. This conception of implicit rights does not credit the Constitution's explicit guarantees severally as the substantive source for specific implicit rights but rather finds, in the specific explicit guarantees, indicia of broad structure and coherence, which in turn suggest specific implicit guarantees. In this view, explicit guarantees do not explain the source and content of specific parts of the right to privacy (like marital contraception),[38] but rather the explicit guarantees and the

35. *Griswold v. Connecticut,* 381 U.S. at 485, *Roe v. Wade,* 410 U.S. 113, 155–56 (1973) (voiding most bars to abortions on privacy grounds).

36. *Dronenberg v. Zech,* 741 F.2d 1388, 1392 (D.C. Cir. 1984), an otherwise rebarbative opinion denying privacy rights to gays; for a critique, see Ronald Dworkin's "Reagan's Justice," *The New York Review of Books,* November 8, 1984, pp. 27–31.

37. *Dronenburg,* 741, F.2d at 1392 (Bork, J.).

38. See *Griswold v. Connecticut,* 381 U.S. 479 (1965). For subsequent Supreme Court

implicit guarantees have the same origin. The various parts of the right to privacy not articulated in the Constitution have the same source as the specific explicit provisions. The right to privacy is a general right that informs and gives substance to both explicit and implicit provisions of the Constitution.

After citing some dozen cases that construe constitutional rights broadly, Douglas claims:

> The foregoing cases suggest that specific guarantees in the Bill of Rights have penumbras, formed by emanations from those guarantees that help give them life and substance.[39]

If one parses the sentence and assumes that the last clause is, as the punctuation and wording require, a restrictive subordinate one, then the sentence must be understood as follows:

> Specific guarantees have penumbras that are formed by emanations from those *general* guarantees that help give the specific guarantees life and substance.

Douglas' widely misunderstood "penumbra" metaphor also suggests this interpretation. Penumbras—areas of half light and half shadow—are not caused by the areas of full light which they abut. Rather the light of penumbras and the light of areas of full illumination have *the same source*. The "penumbra" metaphor can be spelled out as follows: The specific explicit guarantees of the Constitution are areas of full illumination. Rights to marital contraception and the like are areas of half light and half shadow. And what the state may bar or require is an area of total shadow. Privacy understood as a general right is the source of light producing *both* explicit *and* implicit provisions of the Constitution. Those critics of Douglas who cynically claim that he found the right to privacy "lurking in the shadows" of the Constitution have simply misconstrued his careful metaphor.[40]

---

decisions affirming aspects of the right to privacy, see *Stanley v. Georgia*, 394 U.S. 557 (1969) (possession of obscene materials); *Eisenstadt v. Baird*, 405 U.S. 438 (1972) (single adult nonmarital contraception); *Roe v. Wade*, 410 U.S. 113 (1973) (abortion); and *Carey v. Population Services Int'l*, 431 U.S. 678 (1977) (plurality opinion) (minors' contraception).

39. *Griswold*, 381 U.S. at 484.

40. See, for example, *Whalen v. Roe*, 429 U.S. 589, 598 n.23 (1977) ("As the basis for the constitutional claim they rely on the shadows cast by a variety of provisions in the Bill of Rights.") and Walter Berns, "Taking Rights Frivolously," in Douglas MacLean and

This interpretation is further supported by the tack Douglas takes following his initial statement of the penumbra metaphor. He begins to enumerate specific provisions of the Bill of Rights which are each a "facet" of the right to privacy.[41] Since he does not suppose that any one of these specific "facets" covers marital contraception, the procedure would be wholly gratuitous if he did not suppose that the enumeration was building the case that there are some general principles, including privacy, which inform large stretches of the Constitution and provide a warrant for specific guarantees not explicit in it.

Douglas again mentions the zone of privacy in the first-amendment-derived right of association.[42] Usually, first amendment rights are understood essentially as ones which protect *public* expression, like uttering, printing and distributing, not *private* acts. And this understanding will be all the more strong to the extent that freedom of speech and press are chiefly construed as political rights. However, to the extent that freedoms of speech and press include freedom of conscience[43] and the right to read and receive information,[44] privacy is directly entailed by the first amendment and is not dependent at all on derivative associational rights. Douglas might also have strengthened his case by mentioning that freedom of religion is at heart a right to privacy. For as one of the century's leading Baptist ministers—in clarifying "the purposes underlying the Establishment Clause"—had recently claimed: "the Establishment Clause stands as an expression of the principle on the part of the Founders of our Constitution that religion is *too personal*, . . . to permit its 'unhallowed perversion' by a civil magistrate."[45]

Douglas also makes prominent use of the third amendment's prohibition against nonconsensual peacetime billeting of soldiers in any house.

Claudia Mills, eds., *Liberalism Reconsidered*, p. 63 (Totowa, N.J.: Rowman and Allanheld, 1983). Berns refers to *Griswold* as a case "where Justice Douglas found [the constitutional right to privacy] lurking in shadows cast by a potpourri of constitutional provisions."

41. *Griswold*, 381 U.S. at 484.

42. *Ibid.*

43. For example, *West Virginia Board of Education v. Barnette*, 319 U.S. 624 (1943) (under first amendment students cannot be required to salute the flag or else face expulsion).

44. *Griswold*, 381 U.S. at 482; *Stanley v. Georgia*, 394 U.S. 557, 564–64.

45. Justice Black in *Engel v. Vitale*, 370 U.S. 421, 431, 432 (1962) (majority opinion) (emphasis added) (voluntary school prayer is an unconstitutional establishment of religion) (citing "Memorial and Remonstrance against Religious Assessment," in *Writings of Madison*, 2:187).

This appeal is extraordinary in two ways. First, the Court has never heard a case under the third amendment.[46] In retrospect, the amendment is a historical anomaly. It was born of peculiar circumstances which passed with the passing of the Revolutionary War. And yet there it is on the same textual footing as the grandeurs of the first amendment. Second, privacy seems to exhaust the content of this right. Unlike the first amendment, the third amendment protects privacy and almost nothing else. By incorporating this amendment in his interpretation, Douglas is implicitly saying that the Bill of Rights is not to be construed as a laundry list or a mishmash of unrelated, historically arbitrary provisos. The document becomes coherent both as a document and as a constitution—a *framework* for national governance—if the third amendment owes its status not to historical quirk but to its function as a facet of a privacy which informs and unifies large stretches of the document.

In this vein, Douglas quotes at length from *Boyd v. United States*,[47] a case which he elsewhere calls the "fountainhead" of the right to privacy.[48] *Boyd* is a century old case which held the fourth amendment's protections against unreasonable searches and seizures and the fifth amendment's protections against self-incrimination in "essence" jointly "apply to all invasions ... of the sanctities of a man's home and the privacies of life" and of "his indefeasible right of personal security [and] personal liberty" and do not merely protect against "the breaking of his doors and the rummaging of his drawers."[49]

Its understanding of the scope of the amendments aside, the *Boyd* Court correctly saw the values at stake in the amendments. Invasions into the privacies of life attack a "sacred right."[50] By "sacred right" the Court does not mean values of divine origin, but rather those that are like religious values in an individual's system of values in that they override considerations of prudence and utility. Such sacred values are different in kind from and trump others. In a social context, they are

46. Ronald Rotunda, *Modern Constitutional Law* (St. Paul: West, 1981), p. 382.

47. 116 U.S. 616 (1886) (coerced production of personal papers by a defendant at trial violates both fourth and fifth amendment protections against searches, seizures and self-incrimination).

48. *Doe v. Bolton*, 410 U.S. 179, 209 n.2 (1973) (Douglas, J., concurring) (barring abortion regulations on privacy grounds).

49. *Boyd*, 116 U.S. at 630.

50. *Ibid.*

rights and values which are not for sale to the government for its uses in promoting social utility and ones against which government interests or public goods cannot be weighed.[51] The breaking of doors and rummaging of drawers, by contrast, are mere mischief, "circumstances of aggravation," and sources of unhappiness.[52]

The *Boyd* Court's thinking in establishing a broad scope for the amendments, however, is less clear and compelling than its understanding of the stakes. In its specific holding, the *Boyd* Court refused to allow the state to coerce a defendant into producing papers from his home as evidence in his criminal trial. Claiming that "[in] this regard the Fourth and Fifth Amendments run almost into each other,"[53] the Court ruled the state's trial procedure violated both the fourth and the fifth amendments.[54] But the fact that the two amendments run together is not the result of what each is separately, but the result of the "essence" in which they jointly share. The concurrence in *Boyd* correctly notes that the state's procedure cannot in any ordinary sense be construed nonarbitrarily as a "search."[55] The Court's opinion retorts that anything that has the exact same purpose as a search is a search.[56] But this is simply false: it would be as good to say that all strategies that have exactly the same purpose are the same (type of) strategy. The concurrence supposed that the state's procedure of forced production of papers violated just the fifth amendment and its provision that no "person . . . shall be compelled in any criminal case to be a witness against himself."[57] But this is not quite right either. For a person and his papers are quite different things. One can, for instance, sell one's papers but one cannot permanently sell oneself. The only proper way for the *Boyd* Court to reach the result it does is to acknowledge, as Douglas does in *Griswold,* that the state provision is not unconstitutional under any specific explicit guarantee in the Bill of Rights but violates principles that the specific guar-

---

51. On sacred values in public policy, see Douglas MacLean, "Social Values and the Distribution of Risk," in Douglas MacLean, ed., *Values at Risk,* pp. 85–93 (Totowa, N.J.: Rowman and Allanheld, 1986).

52. *Boyd,* 116 U.S. at 630.

53. *Ibid.*

54. *Ibid.* at 633, 635.

55. *Ibid.* at 641 (Miller, J., concurring).

56. *Ibid.* at 622.

57. *Ibid.* at 649 (Miller, J., concurring).

antees share—in the words of *Boyd*—"the privacies of life" and "personal liberty." The fourth and fifth amendments run together because in significant measure they express the same general right.

VI. THE SOURCE OF PRIVACY'S GENERALITY

What would warrant the interpretative strategy of claiming that common values in the Bill of Rights generate nonexplicit substantive constitutional guarantees? The answer, at which Douglas only vaguely hints, is the ninth amendment taken in conjunction with the Equal Protection Clause, *not* the Due Process Clause, of the fourteenth amendment.[58] The ninth amendment guarantees that there are personal rights over and above those that are specifically enumerated in the first eight amendments. It reads: "The enumeration in the Constitution, of certain rights, shall not be construed to deny or disparage others retained by the people." That individuals retain certain unmentioned rights is reinforced by the tripartite distinction in the tenth amendment between federal power, states' "rights," and the rights of "the people"—that is, individuals severally in contrast to their aggregates, the states. The amendment reads: "The powers not delegated to the United States by the Constitution, nor prohibited by it to the States, are reserved to the States respectively, or to the people."

The ninth amendment, however, fails to provide any guidance about where the additional implicit individual rights are to be found; and for this reason some interpreters suggest that there are none and that it is ridiculous to cite the amendment as the source for any right.[59]

A. Tradition and Consensus Considered: Strike One

For others the criterion for reserved rights is a vague appeal to long-held tradition and broad consensus. The rights are those "so rooted in the traditions and conscience of our people as to be ranked as fundamental"[60]

58. *Griswold,* 381 U.S. at 484.
59. See *Griswold,* 381 U.S. at 511, 519–20 (1965) (Black, J., dissenting); *ibid.* at 529–31 (Stewart, J., dissenting).
60. *Ibid.* at 487, 493 (Goldberg, J., concurring) (citing *Snyder v. Massachusetts,* 291 U.S. 97, 105 [1934]).

or those "which the State . . . always and in every age . . . has fostered and protected."[61] And this was the test used in *Bowers*.[62]

The usual and a correct retort to the use of this criterion is that there is no good way to detect what falls under it. Tradition and collective conscience will appear to be whatever justices see them to be.[63] In *Bowers* the Court considered appeal to tradition a protection against "the imposition of the Justices' own choice of values on the States and the Federal Government."[64] But this is simply not so. For just consider marriage—the institution trumpeted as eternal and universal in the closing lines of Douglas' opinion in *Griswold* and the institution Justice Harlan had in mind when enunciating the "tradition and consensus" standard. Recent scholarship has shown that far from being a universal institution through all of Western history, marriage as a widespread institutional arrangement is a rather recent phenomenon in any but the wealthiest classes. Even for the wealthy, it was not a sacred bond, but chiefly a commercial relation developed and structured to deal with the problem of the transfer of wealth and property.[65] Douglas and Harlan were simply manifesting the tendency of many humans to project their particular circumstances into eternal verities in an attempt to view them as necessary and good. The same turn of mind names the constellations after heroes and other utensils in an attempt to find purpose and comfort in the cosmos. If marriage fails the "traditions and consensus" test, it is not clear whether anything will pass it, though perhaps slavery, an institution of longer and broader standing than civic marriage, might.[66]

61. Justice Harlan's widely cited standard in his dissent in *Poe v. Ullman*, 367 U.S. 497, 553 (1961), also quoted in *Griswold*, 381 U.S. at 499 (Goldberg, J., concurring). For a recent case using this standard for what is fundamental, see *Moore v. City of East Cleveland, Ohio*, 431 U.S. 494 (1977) (plurality opinion) (zoning ordinance barring grandchildren from living with their grandparents violates Due Process).

62. *Bowers*, 106 S. Ct. at 2844.

63. *Griswold*, 381 U.S. at 519 (Black, J., dissenting).

64. *Bowers*, 106 S. Ct. at 2844.

65. For a review of the literature on the vagaries of marriage as an institution, see Lawrence Stone, "Sex in the West: The Strange History of Human Sexuality," *The New Republic*, July 8, 1985, pp. 25–37.

66. See Orlando Patterson, *Slavery and Social Death: A Comparative Study* (Cambridge: Harvard University Press, 1982), p. vii:

There is nothing notably peculiar about the institution of slavery. It has existed from the dawn of human history right down to the twentieth century, in the most primitive of human societies and in the most civilized. There is no region on earth that has not at some time harbored the institution. Probably there is no group of people whose ancestors were not at one time slaves or slaveholders.

It is to be hoped that few would want to claim that, but for the thirteenth amendment, the fourteenth would prevent the state from barring slavery, the long Western tradition of which establishes slave owning as a fundamental right.

Judges have no special insight to *Geschichte;* their job neither allows them time nor invokes the talents required for honing historical skills to a level that might permit impartial findings; not even professional historians usually achieve that. Even for experts, *Historie* is controversial and as ideologically laden as any of the humanities and social sciences. Judges are as likely as any amateurs to pick and choose its variety in ways that fit their preconceived ends. Justice Burger's concurrence in *Bowers* provides a particularly clear instance of this vice. He claims that "homosexual conduct [has] been subject to state intervention throughout the history of Western Civilization" and that to protect homosexual acts "would be to cast aside millennia of moral teaching."[67] He cites but one historian[68] and makes no mention of John Boswell's magisterial *Christianity, Social Tolerance, and Homosexuality: Gay People in Western Europe from the Beginning of the Christian Era to the Fourteenth Century* which thoroughly criticizes Burger's one source and shows that far from a uniform condemnation of gay sex "throughout the history of Western Civilization," over the largest stretch of that civilization—the sixth century B.C. to the twelfth century A.D.—there was a large variety and considerable flux in the moral, social, legal and religious evaluation of gays and gay acts.[69]

In any case, it is clear that many of the cases cited by the *Bowers* Court as Substantive Due Process cases could not possibly have passed its "tradition and consensus" test. This is particularly true of the cases which declared anti-miscegenation laws and bars on abortion unconstitutional.[70] It therefore is particularly unfair for the Court to have selectively invoked the test against gays.

67. *Bowers,* 106 S. Ct. at 2847 (Burger, C. J., concurring).

68. *Ibid.* (citing Derrick Sherwin Bailey, *Homosexuality in the Western Christian Tradition* [1955; Hamden, Conn: Archon Books, 1975], pp. 70–81).

69. John Boswell, *Christianity, Social Tolerance and Homosexuality* (Chicago: University of Chicago Press, 1980). Of Chief Justice Burger's one source, Boswell writes: "[Bailey's] work suffers from an emphasis on negative sanctions which gives a wholly misleading picture of medieval practice, ignores almost all positive evidence on the subject, is limited primarily to data regarding France and Britain, and has been superseded even in its major focus, biblical analysis" (p. 4, n.3).

70. See *Bowers,* 106 S. Ct. at 2848 n.5 (Blackmun, J., dissenting). *Loving v. Virginia,*

Problems of impartiality and equitable application aside, other problems beset the test. If fundamental rights are as broadly based and widely believed in as those who advance the consensus-based criterion claim, then any violation of such rights is self-correcting. A person who thinks such a right has been violated simply needs to point out the violation to the people for legislative remedy and can do so, thanks to the explicit political freedoms she has under the first amendment. The courts need not intercede at all, if rights are just overarching customs. And in any case, the people acting through the ballot box are a much better gauge of what their own widely held customs are than are nonelected judges.

Another path to this same end is to notice that all constitutional rights are rights of minorities; in a working democracy the majority, particularly a wide one, has no need to resort to courts as the guarantors of what it wants. Only minority members will have occasion to appeal to rights; it would then be bizarre and grossly unfair if the majority can deploy the power of the state as well as determine what immunity rights are prescribed against that power. The consensus-based view of rights renders rights wholly vacuous.[71]

One must suppose that the guiding rationale behind the "tradition and consensus" standard is a belief that tradition and consensus represent the wisdom of the ages. However, if an activity has persistently been illegal, one is unable to determine from an examination of the activity itself what its value is. This inability will more or less be automatic in the case of utilitarian evaluations for actions of disputable worth. For one will not be able to see what an activity's value is from its

---

388 U.S. 1, 12 (1967) (anti-miscegenation laws voided) and *Roe v. Wade*, 410 U.S. 113 (1973) (most bars to abortion voided). It is not even clear that the plurality opinion in *Moore v. East Cleveland*, 431 U.S. 494 (1977), which provides the specific formulation of the test used in *Bowers*—liberties "deeply rooted in this Nation's history and tradition," *Bowers*, 106 S. Ct. at 2844—itself really passes its own test, although an attempt is made. *Moore*, 431 U.S. at 504–5.

71. Still other problems highlight the test's vagueness: Is the test positive acceptance over the long haul or is mere tolerance sufficient?—after all, constitutional rights simply dictate state tolerance. Further, how long is long? Must a protected behavior be approved of (or tolerated) for one century, two centuries, five, fifteen, twenty-five? Will three weeks in a society needing to forget its past be sufficient? And why limit the test to Western traditions? What if there are multiple and conflicting traditions within one culture? Which then will serve as the standard for fundamentalness? None? For other criticisms of the "tradition and consensus" standard for fundamental rights, see Michael Perry, *The Constitution, the Courts, and Human Rights* (New Haven: Yale University Press, 1982), pp. 93–96.

consequences since the activity has not been allowed to have them. But utility aside, the mere existence of law has an influence on the intellectual and social climate surrounding an activity and generates a prima facie presumption in the typical person's mind that there is something wrong with the activity. This creation and fixing of such a presumption is one chief reason why law ought not to be justified as an instrument of moral education. The use of coercion simply freezes moral progress, turns claims of immorality into self-fulfilling prophecies, and eliminates those processes of examination and of trial and error which instill social institutions with value.[72] So even if one could overcome problems of vagueness for the "tradition and consensus" test, in cases where the examined activity has been traditionally illegal, or stigmatized to such a degree that it is not subject to continuous reevaluation, as gay sex has been for the last seven centuries, then the test simply is inapplicable. For when confronted with a history of coerced behavior, the test affords no way of distinguishing between the wisdom of the ages and their prejudices.

The proper stance to take then toward the test as applied to homosexuality is one of necessarily suspended judgment, as though one were asked to use a ruler to judge the length and breadth of the number six. Homosexuality, given its social treatment, is not the sort of object that can properly be said to be measurable by the "tradition and consensus" standard. However, if the test were applied, anyway, to homosexual acts, it would presumably rule out fundamental rights covering them.[73]

Nevertheless, the liberal constitutional theorist Laurence Tribe, who argued the gay side before the *Bowers* Court, has claimed that a "collective consensus" or "traditional values" approach to fundamental liberties will generate a right to sexual privacy covering gay sex, *despite* widespread traditional and contemporary objection to gay sex acts—if only one pays attention to "what level of generality one employs to test the pedigree of the asserted liberty claim. . . . It is crucial, in asking whether an alleged right forms part of a traditional liberty, to define the

---

72. See H. L. A. Hart, *Law, Liberty and Morality* (Stanford: Stanford University Press, 1963), pp. 69–77, especially pp. 74–75.

73. *Poe v. Ullman*, 367 U.S. 497, 547, 552 (1961) (Harlan, J., dissenting). So too, *Bowers*, 106 S. Ct. at 2846: "[T]o claim that a right to engage in such conduct [i.e., gay sex] is 'deeply rooted in the Nation's history and tradition' . . . is, at best, facetious."

liberty at a high enough level of generality to permit unconventional variants to claim protection along with the mainstream versions of protected conduct."[74] Even if this strategy is neither simple question begging nor an Equal Protection analysis in disguise, it will not work. If tradition or broad consensus is the feature that generates a right as the right it is, then if one changes the conditions of the question asked of the tradition or members of the consensus, what the consensus is and what the tradition asserts may very well change, and in turn the scope of the derivative right may change. If one asks a group whether they believe in sexual privacy rights, perhaps the vast majority would say "yes"; but if one asks the same group "well, do you believe in general rights to sexual privacy *if* that ends up protecting homosexual acts," the answer may well be "no." If so, what the consensus has been will change and so will the consensus-generated right. If it is simply consensus that generates the right, without more there is no requirement that the right be coherent or general in scope.

B. The Good: Strike Two

Still others suppose that political philosophy should largely determine what rights there are. In this view, judges should hold as constitutional rights, vaguely on fourteenth amendment grounds, those rights asserted by the best political theory of the times limited only by a requirement that the rights be *consistent* with past judicial precedents and with explicit language of the Constitution.[75] Yet still others, without resorting

74. Laurence Tribe, *American Constitutional Law* (Mineola, N.Y.: Foundation Press, 1978), pp. 944, 946.

75. Ronald Dworkin, *A Matter of Principle* (Cambridge: Harvard University Press, 1985), pp. 125, 149, 153, 159, 161–63, 165–66; similarly but with even fewer restraints, David A.J. Richards, *Sex, Drugs, Death and the Law* (Totowa, N.J.: Rowman and Littlefield, 1982), pp. 7–20, and especially pp. 30–33.

Dworkin thinks that constitutional interpretation is essentially like literary interpretation. Constitutional interpretation, he claims, should give a reading of the text that makes the text the best story it can be. In this analogy, political theory's role in constitutional and legal interpretation is rather like a (mere) principle of charity in interpreting a literary author. At first blush, this interpretative stratagem seems innocuous enough. However, the Constitution and, say, a novel have divergent densities of texture. A detail-laden and event-packed 500-page novel places lots of restraints on what its best story can be; the principle of charity simply fills in small gaps. But the Constitution is a rather thin tome: the first

to a general skepticism about fundamental rights, hold that though there is no criterion to be found within the Constitution for what counts as a fundamental right, judges are those persons best situated through their functional roles both in society as a whole and in the government's separation of powers to have a vision of what rights there are. And because America has a quasi-religious view of itself fundamentally as a morally progressing nation, judges should assert as constitutional rights those that appear in their visions—quite independently of any constitutional provisions and limited only by political and social forces in which judges necessarily find themselves enmeshed: "judicial review represents the institutionalization of prophecy."[76]

C. Equality-Based Coherence: RBI

My own suggestion is less venturesome and heady than these interpretative theories which have The Good as the wind in their sails. The guide needed and warranted to determine what rights there are implicit in the Constitution is to be found in a reflexive application of the fourteenth amendment's guarantee of equal protection of the laws to the Constitu-

---

amendment is but forty-five words, the Equal Protection Clause fourteen—nearly all generalities. Here literary economy leaves political theory determining virtually the whole content of constitutional rights and so this position leads back to the view, as on the "tradition and consensus" model, that rights are whatever five justices think they are.

Precedent, admittedly would fill in a great deal of "literary" detail, but Dworkin is unable to clarify why precedent should be given any special weight within his scheme, especially when precedents are generated out of theories of constitutional interpretation different than his own. Precedent is a poor guide exactly because there has been a general flux of doctrine on major constitutional issues in large part as a result of the changing fortunes of the very sort of interpretation that Dworkin advocates. Should only the precedents that accord with the general broad interpretative theory be taken as valid?

Richards quite radically claims that the explicit provisions of the Constitution are without "any meaning at all" unless they are embedded in a general theory of human rights "that the Constitution assumes as its communicative context" (p. 32). Now while it is true that sentences are unintelligible unless they are part of some language and conform to the linguistic conventions of the community of speakers, it is not true that this required embedding determines the positive content of any particular sentence: "John Henry is 6'2" " and "John Henry is 5'10" " will both be embedded in the same way in the same context and yet cannot mean the same thing. Richards tries to import a general principle of autonomy or independence into the Constitution by claiming this value to be the communicative context in which the Constitution's provisions are embedded and so must be what they mean. But this analogical strategy mistakes, as indicated, the nature of language and its relation to social contexts.

76. Perry, *The Constitution*, pp. 97–145, quote from p. 98.

tion itself taken as the primary part of "the supreme law of the Land."[77] As part of the supreme law of the land, the Constitution is subject to the restriction that the Equal Protection Clause imposes upon all law. It is sufficient for the interpretation of reflexive application that the Clause impose on specific constitutional provisions only a weak notion of equality—that is, the treating of relevantly similar cases similarly: or fairness, as that term is ordinarily understood. The Equal Protection Clause applied to the Constitution itself calls for a normative consistency among specific rights. At the level of constitutional precept, it holds that the values that inform specific guarantees also apply to unmentioned guarantees which express similar values. The Clause commits the Constitution to a rule of consistent application of principles at the level of constitutional guarantees, though not to any principle that just happens to be a good one or is even the best one.

The claim of Equal Protection as applied to the Constitution itself is simply that the protections of the Bill of Rights shall not be allowed to be underinclusive. The principles to which the Equal Protection Clause gives life are those that inform and give substance to the specific explicit guarantees. One looks, then, not to natural law, or cultural consensus, or wide majorities or The Good to determine the scope of fundamental rights in the Constitution's broad clauses, but rather to the specific explicit guarantees, which determine the content of the fundamental rights in that they are highly illustrative instances of the principles that inform the document. Fundamental rights are not the ones that are good ones and *merely consistent* with the specific explicit guarantees of the Constitution[78] but rather ones that are *positively suggested* as principles by the specific explicit provisions. One's guide then is not disputable political theory but the specific provisions of the Bill of Rights.

The method of broad constitutional interpretation suggested here proceeds in a manner similar to the artist in the following analogy: A police artist is taken to a gallery of portraits of Hapsburgs and is asked to draw a composite sketch of the Hapsburg look, which then can be used to identify still other paintings as being paintings of Hapsburgs. The interpretative artist's sketch does not come out of thin air, nor does it represent the best looking person that might by some stretch of the imagination be taken as a Hapsburg; rather its contours are positively

77. U.S. Constitution, article VI, clause 2.
78. Ronald Dworkin's position, on which see section VI B above.

suggested by the various paintings which the artist observes. If the artist is clever her sketch need not be simply an abstraction presenting only the most basic common denominator of all the paintings—there may not be one—but rather might display salient features found in some of the paintings. If the artist is a cubist she could possibly incorporate into the painting that is to serve as a model a very high degree of complexity and variation drawn from nothing other than the specific paintings.[79]

Analogously in the version of constitutional interpretation espoused here, specific explicit constitutional provisions "generate" or "create" other guarantees only epistemologically, not causally or substantively; they are the source from which one perceives more general, but not necessarily more abstract, precepts. These precepts are warranted in their generality through the Equal Protection Clause. The clause directs the investigator to look for the values that underlie the specific explicit provisions; the ninth amendment in turn lends substance to those general values. Fundamental constitutional rights, then, get their scope and content from an examination of the specific explicit provisions, but they do not get their substance and force from the specific explicit guarantees, as they do on the rejected peripheral rights model. Instead the ninth amendment tells judges that they are warranted in finding additional implicit rights in the Constitution. It tells them *that* they should look and that they should construe what they find as substantive rights; the Equal Protection Clause tells them *where* and *how* they should look.

Admittedly, equal protection construed as mere consistency is not the weakest possible sense of equality; one might claim that equality means only equal *access* to whatever rights one has. Analogously, one might claim that liberty is merely the right to do whatever is not prohibited. Neither of these understandings places any restrictions on the scope, substance or content of laws. In both cases only weak procedures in the application of law are invoked. For instance, in the case of liberty construed as whatever is not prohibited, laws may not be applied *retroactively,* for, if they were, one and the same individual act could be both allowed and forbidden, and this possibility is incoherent. In the case of equality taken as equal access to whatever rights there are, plaints can be lodged only against the selective *enforcement* of laws, not against

79. See generally, Richard Mohr, "Family Resemblance, Platonism, Universals," *Canadian Journal of Philosophy* (1977) 7:593–600.

their *content*. Yet, no court has ever construed the Equal Protection Clause that weakly. Even on its weakest interpretation it requires that laws show some rational relation to a legitimate state interest and not be wholly arbitrary and capricious *in their content*.[80]

On the other hand, the Court's weak interpretation of Equal Protection has uniformly allowed for overinclusion and underinclusion of means to legitimate legislative ends. Under the interpretation advanced here, underinclusions in applying the Equal Protection Clause to the Constitution itself must be ruled out. The interpretation does not permit, for instance, that some substantive privacies be protected, for example, third amendment protections of the home, but not others, such as marital contraception.

The standard arguments, though, for allowing deviations from a prima facie constitutional presumption of consistency in the legislative realm are pragmatic ones peculiar to that realm. The Court regularly points out the need for flexibility in legislative functioning and the benefits of learning from legislative experimentation: "It is by such practical considerations based on experience rather than by theoretical inconsistencies that the question of equal protection is to be answered. ... It is no requirement of equal protection that all evils of the same genus be eradicated or none at all."[81] However, neither the need for legislative flexibility nor for social experimentation in admitting over- and underinclusions holds of the Court itself. In the judge's chambers, political compromises are both unneeded and inappropriate and social experimentation is wholly out of place, for whether one construes constitutional rights as trumps over social utility or only as counterweights to it, judges, as preservers of rights, cannot have as their function the maximization of social utility.

Moreover, while consistency and coherency may be too much to hope for from politicians, especially acting in groups, these procedures are the main tools of the judge's craft. Consistency and coherence, for instance,

80. For cases that construe the Equal Protection Clause weakly, yet not as a mere procedural right, see, for example, *Lindsley v. Natural Carbonic Gas Co.*, 220 U.S. 61, 78–79 (1911); *Railway Express Agency, Inc. v. New York*, 336 U.S. 106, 110 (1949); *McGowan v. Maryland*, 366 U.S. 420, 426 (1961): "A statutory discrimination will not be set aside if any state of facts reasonably may be conceived to justify it."

81. *Railway Express Agency, Inc. v. New York*, 336 U.S. at 110 (1949) (upholding a business regulation against Equal Protection challenge).

are central to the rule of precedent. When judges apply past cases to new ones, distinguish new ones from old ones, recognize areas of discretion and even explicitly overturn past rulings, consistency and coherence are their methods. Judges *must* presume themselves capable of operating closely under a principle of consistency, even if they cannot presume the same of legislators. Precise consistency—no over- or under- inclusions —can be a guiding principle in the determination of *what rights there are* and should be if Equal Protection is not to be rendered vacuous or merely procedural.

Admittedly, the process of discovering implicit rights advances piecemeal. Implicit rights are likely to be discovered and successfully asserted first in cases that in fact promote the interests of the dominant culture. It is slight inconsistencies or glitches in dominant cultural forces and social structures that will first point up the need for a right, and spark, call forth, and successfully reveal the right. The benefits drawn from the right by the dominant culture also figure significantly in the establishment and stabilizing of the right in the social fabric. The Magna Carta applied not to Average Joes but to the ascendant nobility. Its rights extended to the lower classes only much later.[82]

It should be no surprise that when the violation of privacy became established in England as a common law ground for suing the violator, the plaintiffs were The Queen and her consort.[83] It is no accident that the U.S. Supreme Court should first advance the notion that there are protected "privacies of life" in a case that protected captains of commerce.[84] And it is not surprising that privacy should first be precipitated as an independent right in a case strengthening the power of people in marriage—a dominant institution of the dominant culture—and not,

82. Though Chapter 29 of the Magna Carta is the forerunner in both wording and substance of the U.S. Constitution's fifth amendment, the vast majority of the Magna Carta's 63 chapters deal with the rights and powers of only some 30 barons. See William Sharp McKechne, *Magna Carta: A Commentary on the Great Charter of King John* (Glasgow: J. Maclehose and Sons, 1914), pp. 109–20; Faith Thompson, *Magna Carta: Its Role in the Making of the English Constitution, 1300–1629* (1948; New York: Octagon Books, 1972), pp. 68–99; Lord Hubert Lister Parker of Waddington, *Magna Carta and the Rule of Law* (Richmond: Magna Carta Commission, 1965).

83. See Samuel D. Warren and Louis D. Brandeis, "The Right to Privacy," *Harvard Law Review* (1904) 4:199 n.5, discussing *Prince Albert v. Strange*, 2 DeGex & Sm. 652, 659 (1849) (injunction against press issued to protect royal privacy).

84. *Boyd v. United States*, 116 U.S. 616 (1886) (declared a customs revenue law unconstitutional as applied against an importer).

say, pornographers[85] or abortionists.[86] It is not merely the blandness of the specific holding in *Griswold*[87]—the protection of marital contraception—that let the implicit right to privacy be established without ruffling feathers, but also the group to whom the right was addressed—middle and upper class heterosexuals. However, one would be mistaken to say that these social and political realities, though they *explain* the discovery and establishment of rights, *justify* the rights' existence or set the limits of the rights' legitimate scope. Once a right is established, it is particularly important that considerations of fairness extend the right to relevantly similar cases. For only then, as rights extend beyond the dominant culture, do the rights have their proper purpose—the protection of minorities from legislative majorities.

It will be useful to an understanding of the method of broad constitutional interpretation advanced here—equality-based coherence—to examine some rights that it will and will not ground.

The mode of interpretation offered here grounds the right to political association better than does the justification afforded by the *Griswold* Court. The right to association is not to be justified as being "necessary" to the "full meaning" of the political rights of the first amendment.[88] Rather it is to be seen as *part* of a general right to political participation which the fourteenth amendment's Equal Protection Clause generates out of freedoms of speech, press, assembly, and petition, by viewing them collectively and consistently as rights of political participation. The Clause applies as well to other forms of political participation, including membership in political associations. Construing these first amendment rights as political rights does not exhaust their content, but their political dimension is undeniable, gives them a coherency, and positively points toward a general right of political participation of which they are parts. Political participation is a right that gives life and substance to the specific political rights of the first amendment. Consistency then requires the general right also to encompass a specific right to political association.

However, the same principle of equality-based coherence does not generate a right to a wider range of associations. For there are no other

85. *Stanley v. Georgia*, 394 U.S. 557 (1969) (right to private possession of obscene materials).

86. *Roe v. Wade*, 410 U.S. 113 (1973) (privacy right to abortion).

87. *Griswold v. Connecticut*, 381 U.S. 479 (1965).

88. For the reasons given in the discussion of privacy in membership lists discussed above, section IV.

specific guarantees in the Bill of Rights, save possibly the Free Exercise of Religion Clause, that would suggest that association, in general or intimate association in particular, is a right with which the Bill of Rights is chiefly concerned in prescinding from legislative control. No intimate relations, for example, of family, marriage, or friendship are mentioned in the Bill of Rights. If intimate relations are protected in the Constitution, it is because they are private relations and privacy in general is protected.

Equality-based coherence also explains why it is correct that the Court has for over a hundred years held voting to be a fundamental right.[89] Voting is part and parcel of the political activities protected by the first amendment and other provisions of the Constitution. It is fundamental because it is part of a general right of political participation, not because it independently is some natural right or because it is preservative of all other rights—a reason the Court has sometimes mistakenly advanced for viewing voting as fundamental.[90]

The right to privacy has an even wider base than the right to political participation. Privacy rights permeate virtually the whole of the Bill of Rights. It is important to note that specific privacies explicitly protected are not limited to informational privacy—the claim, entitlement, or right of an individual to determine what information about himself may be communicated to others. The specific, explicit privacies also protect substantive privacy—the status or condition of limited access to a person.[91] The Constitution protects not only private information but also private matters. Religious rights, as privacy rights, are primarily substantive rights and not simply procedural rights regulating how or what information may be gathered about one.[92] Similarly, the right against billeting soldiers in peacetime is such a substantive privacy right.

Although informational privacy seems to be the paramount concern

89. *Yick Wo v. Hopkins,* 118 U.S. 356, 370 (1886) (administrative practice with disparate impact against a racial group violates Equal Protection); *Reynolds v. Sims,* 377 U.S. 533, 562 (1964) (right to suffrage requires equally proportioned electoral districts); *Harper v. Virginia Board of Elections,* 383 U.S. 663, 668 (1966) (poll tax violates right to vote).

90. *Yick Wo,* 118 U.S. at 370. For discussion and criticism, see chapter 6, section IV.

91. These definitions are adapted from Ferdinand Schoeman, "Privacy: Philosophical Dimensions of the Literature," in Ferdinand Schoeman, ed., *Philosophical Dimensions of Privacy: An Anthology,* pp. 2–3 (Cambridge: Cambridge University Press, 1984).

92. See *Engel v. Vitale,* 370 U.S. 421, 431, 432 (1962) (voluntary school prayer is an unconstitutional intrusion into personal choices and actions).

of the fourth and fifth amendments,[93] it would be gratuitously conservative to see them as limited to informational privacy. What makes a search reasonable is not merely the procedures that are used in its execution but also the object sought.[94] A search for ghosts in violation of a law barring the harboring, aiding, and abetting of ghosts would be unconstitutional even if the search was carried out with warrants supported by oaths and affirmations and particularly describing the place to be searched and the things to be seized. It would be unreasonable not because of the means used but because it is irrational to look for ghosts.

The sixth amendment right of a person to defend himself at trial without counsel is still another substantive privacy right rather than a mere procedural right.[95] Indeed, the Court, in rejecting, as controlling, paternalistic arguments requiring counsel, frankly admits that as a procedure the right to defend oneself, in all but the rare case, will interfere with the achievement of justice in the courtroom and will have results unfavorable to the defendant.[96] Instead of a procedural justification, the Court correctly claims "[T]he right to defend is personal"[97] and that "the right to appear pro se exists to affirm the accused's individual dignity and autonomy."[98]

93. It is arguable, however, that the Court sees even the fourth amendment's protection of informational privacy chiefly as a useful means of protecting substantive privacy. See *Mapp v. Ohio*, 367 U.S. 643, 656 (1961) ("The right to privacy" is "no less important than any other right carefully and particularly reserved to the people"); *Katz v. United States*, 389 U.S. 347, 353 (1967) (fourth amendment protects conversations placed from *public* telephone booths, because it "protects people—and not simply 'areas' ").

94. For a recent case that holds the protection against unreasonable searches to be a substantive rather than merely a procedural right, see *Winston v. Lee*, 470 U.S. 753 (1985) (bodily search for a deeply buried bullet held unreasonable even when likely to produce incriminating trial evidence). See also *Rochin v. California*, 342 U.S. 165, 172 (1952) (stomach pumping violates Substantive Due Process, because it "illegally break[s] into the privacy of petitioner").

95. See *Faretta v. California*, 422 U.S. 806 (1975) (right to defend oneself at criminal trial without counsel established as a free-standing sixth amendment right); *McKaskle v. Wiggins*, 465 U.S. 168 (1984) (setting boundaries for *Faretta*). In *Faretta*, the implicit right to appear pro se is derived in a manner strikingly similar to Douglas' argument for a general right to privacy in *Griswold*. After pointing out that the explicit guarantees of the sixth amendment have the individual accused, not his counsel, as their focus, the Court concludes: "Although not stated in the Amendment in so many words, the right to self-representation—to make one's defense personally—is thus necessarily implied by the structure of the Amendment." *Faretta*, 422 U.S. at 819.

96. *Faretta*, 422 U.S. at 832–33.

97. *Ibid.* at 834.

98. *McKaskle*, 465 U.S. at 178.

Finally, most of what are cruel and unusual punishments,[99] such as dismemberment and the intentional infliction of pain are at heart violations of privacy. Thus privacy rights inform and give substance to even the eighth amendment and they are there too chiefly substantive, not procedural.

It should not be surprising that privacy as a substantive principle permeates the Bill of Rights. For privacy is closely allied to what a right essentially is. A right is, at heart, an individual's immunity against others who would, in its absence, use the individual for their own purposes. Private acts do not fulfill some social function but rather are peculiar to the participants involved or acquire value simply because they are the individuals' actions. Thus, private relations, unlike, say, commercial transactions or relations with government agents, are intimate or personal rather than functional and impersonal. An appeal to the value of privacy insulates the private act from possible uses in the projects of others.[100] A constitution that protects rights, then, does not accidentally find itself protecting privacy.

The method of broad interpretation advanced here would find another important but as yet unarticulated general right in the Bill of Rights, one even broader than the right of privacy. It is suggested by virtually all of the specific explicit guarantees and approaches exhausting their content. This is the right not to be picked on. Justice Brandeis may have been looking for a similar concept in his famous formulation that there is a "right to be let alone—the most comprehensive of rights and the right most valued by civilized man."[101] The right not to be picked on springs from and encompasses privacy rights, political and religious rights, rights to the fair administration of justice and fourteenth amendment rights of "discrete and insular minorities."[102] Yet it has an important reach that

99. See *In re Kemmler*, 136 U.S. 436, 446–47 (1890) (dicta) (crucifixion and breaking on the wheel are cruel and unusual punishments); *Chambers v. Florida*, 309 U.S. 227, 237 (1940) (dicta) (quartering and rack are cruel and unusual under Due Process); *Weems v. United States*, 217 U.S. 349 (1910) (intentional nonincidental infliction of pain is cruel and unusual punishment). But see *Hudson v. Palmer*, 468 U.S. 517, 530 (1984) ("[W]e conclude that prisoners have no legitimate expectation of privacy").

100. See generally, Ferdinand Schoeman, "Privacy and Intimate Information" in Schoeman, ed., *Philosophical Dimensions of Privacy*, pp. 413–16.

101. *Olmstead v. United States*, 277 U.S. 438, 478 (1928) (Brandeis, J., dissenting). Brandeis' dissent on this point was eventually vindicated in *Stanley v. Georgia*, 394 U.S. 557, 564 (1969), where it is absorbed into the majority opinion.

102. *United States v. Carolene Products Co.*, 304 U.S. 144, 152–53 n.4 (1938). Under

they do not have: it protects, for instance, against some forms of government speech. There is no speech counterpart to the Establishment Clause: the first amendment prohibits the state from interference with the free exercise of religion and the freedom of speech, but bars the state establishment only of religion. In general there should probably not be a speech counterpart to the Establishment Clause; if there were, it would likely, for example, void the government's operation of public schools.[103] Yet, constitutionally, government speech ought not to be wholly unbridled.

Consider the ugly case of Edward Charles Davis III.[104] A Louisville Police Chief had published and publicly circulated flyers that featured Davis' picture as part of an anti-shoplifting campaign. Davis had never been found guilty of shoplifting but was nevertheless described on the posters as an "active shoplifter."[105] The Court found that no constitutional right of Davis' had been violated and so he could not sue the police chief under federal civil rights law.[106] Justice Brennan in heated dissent had to reach clear back to a *Lochner* era Substantive Due Process case, *Meyer v. Nebraska*,[107] to find a "liberty right" broad enough to cover the sheriff's actions as violations of the right.[108] But the core of *Meyer* is a laundry list of "liberty rights" with no guiding principle and enunciated in a catalogue of cases many of which were subsequently overturned.[109] Now, the police chief's actions in *Davis* were clearly an outrage and what they violated was the right not to be picked on.

---

this case, politically dispossessed groups—to date, racial groups, legal aliens, women, and illegitimate children—have been afforded enhanced Equal Protection rights, which require that laws affecting these groups be judicially found not simply to be rationally related to a legitimate state interest (as all laws must be found) in order to pass Equal Protection muster, but also to be substantially related to an important state interest (for classifications by gender and legitimacy) or even necessary to a compelling state interest (for classifications by race and alienage).

103. If compulsory school prayer, the advocacy of religion in schools, and the provision of religious textbooks are establishments of religion, then all recitation, advocacy, and reading in schools would appear to be establishments of speech. Perhaps a right against establishment of speech would permit moments of silent thinking.

104. *Paul v. Davis,* 424 U.S. 693 (1976) (held no privacy or Due Process rights are violated by the police publicly posting an innocent person's picture with the caption "known shoplifter").

105. *Ibid.* at 697.

106. *Ibid.* at 699–713.

107. 262 U.S. 390 (1923) (Due Process encompasses a parents' right to have their children taught German).

108. *Davis,* 424 U.S. at 722.

109. *Meyer,* 262 U.S. at 399.

It should not be surprising that this right, foreshadowed in the Constitution's provisions against both federal and state bills of attainder,[110] should be the broadest of rights in the Bill of Rights. For the specific rights of the Constitution jointly direct their immunities against governments—against monopolies of coercion over citizens. Among equals there is no need for a right not to be picked on, but where power is as asymmetrically divided as it is between an individual and the state, the need is paramount.

The rights generated by equality-based coherence are broad and specifically protect substantive privacy. However, the rights of the Constitution and specifically the right to privacy are not so broad as to be equivalent to a general principle of independence. By independence I mean the ability to guide one's life by one's own lights to an extent compatible with others' ability to do the same. A right to independence, as a constitutional precept rather than simply a general social ideal, would bar all government regulation of voluntary associations, since mutual consent guarantees that the "compatible extent" proviso in the definition of independence is fulfilled; and thus would be generated the "right to contract"—the judicial chimera of the *Lochner* era. But if one goes looking for specific guarantees of the Constitution that would suggest independence as a general right informing and giving substance to specific guarantees, one will not find any that are not covered and accounted for more economically and concisely by the narrower principle of privacy. Specifically, the Liberty Clause of the fourteenth amendment will not help in this search. The content of the right to liberty in the fourteenth amendment lies entirely in its exemption clause—liberty shall not be denied *except* through due process of law. Since this protection itself draws a distinction between the substance of liberty and the process of its denial, the Due Process exception itself can hardly be considered a source of substantial liberty. Nevertheless, even after the *Lochner* era, the Court has occasionally used Due Process to that end when faced by a law it just cannot stand.[111]

Justice White ends the body of his opinion for the Court in *Bowers* by

110. U.S. Constitution article I, section 9, clause 3 and section 10, clause 1.
111. For good examples, see *Boddie v. Connecticut*, 401 U.S. 371 (1971) (held indigents not required to pay divorce filing fees) and *Moore v. City of East Cleveland, Ohio*, 431 U.S. 494 (1977) (invalidated a prohibition on grandchildren living with their grandpar-

suggesting that a constitutional recognition of rights of gays would likely lead the Court back to the unrestrained judicial interference in government demonstrated in—horror of horrors—the *Lochner* era.[112] On the one hand, this concern is highly implausible both in general[113] and in the context of the rights discussed above. On the other hand, if the Court, with a slightly different membership, thought laissez-faire markets traditional in and fundamental to America's heritage, it might very well take White's test for Substantive Due Process in *Bowers* and work with it the same deeds done by the *Lochner* Court's "natural" right to contract.[114] There are rights still to be articulated within the interpretive method of equality-based coherence, but there should be no fear that it will lead back to the era of freewheeling Substantive Due Process and the overthrow of economic regulations.

Having established in this chapter that there is a general right to substantive privacy, the discussion turns in the next chapter to a multi-dimensional analysis of why gay sex acts should be seen as falling under this right.

---

ents). The author of the Court's plurality opinion in *Moore,* Justice Powell, upon his retirement from the Court told *The New York Times*

> that he had no hesitation about invoking substantive due process when necessary to correct what he regarded as a manifest injustice. He recalled his 1977 opinion for the Court that a woman had a Constitutional right to share a household with her two grandsons, contrary to local zoning law. "I thought it would be outrageous to separate that family," he said.

"Powell on His Approach," *The New York Times,* July 12, 1987, p. Y9, col. 4. Here Justice Powell reveals that the judicial "thinking" that went into deciding *Moore* had nothing whatsoever to do with the reasons for the case's result *as stated in his opinion* in the case, which set forth (and then applied on the shakiest of historical grounds) a "tradition and consensus" standard for Mrs. Moore's aval right. Though this standard had nothing to do with the judicial decision making that determined the outcome in the case in which the standard was announced, the standard was the one used in *Bowers* as though it were abiding, clear, official doctrine. *Moore* at 504–5; *Bowers,* 106 S. Ct. at 2844. Despite his confessed "thinking" in *Moore* and his opinion in the case, which together both falsely and hypocritically turned a personal animadversion into an eternal verity, Powell explained his changing his vote in, and so the result of, the 5–4 *Bowers* decision by claiming that judges should not "substitute their social and economic beliefs for the judgment of legislative bodies, who are elected to pass laws." *The New York Times,* July 12, 1987, p. Y9, col. 4. Powell was not a principled justice; he was a loose cannon on the deck of Constitutional law.

112. *Bowers,* 106 S. Ct. at 2846.

113. The *Bowers* Court fails to explain why a right to gay sex would lead back to *Lochner* when abortion and contraception rights have not had this effect.

114. See above note 32.

4. Why Sex Is Private

I. INTRODUCTION

When Canada went through the national trauma of decriminalizing gay male sex in 1969, Prime Minister Trudeau's slogan for reform was that "the state does not belong in the bedrooms of the nation." His Conservative opponents pointed out that if murder was going on in the nation's bedrooms, the state had surely better be there. And they of course were right. That an act occurs behind four walls does not give it even a prima facie presumption of substantive immunity from the state. Consensual domestic bomb production and boudoir homicide do not invoke any substantive rights that would protect the activities if the state used just procedures to find them out. Is sex private in a way that invokes a substantive right from state prosecution?

This chapter gives four arguments, each sufficient to answer the question affirmatively. It does not offer a "theory" of the state, and then show how privacy rights covering sex fall out deductively from the theory. Nor does it offer an analysis of what privacy is and only then discuss its concomitants affecting the state. That would be a hopeless and needlessly Platonic task. Privacy has proven recalcitrant to conceptual analysis and to attempts to reduce it to a univocal or even focal sense.[1] Privacy is a star case of a cluster term or a family-resemblance

---

1. Contrast, for example, the conflicting reviews of the literature offered by Ferdinand Schoeman, "Privacy: Philosophical Dimensions of the Literature," in Fredinand Schoeman, ed., *Philosophical Dimensions of Privacy: An Anthology*, pp. 1–33 (Cambridge: Cambridge University Press, 1984) and William A. Parent, "Recent Work on the Concept of Privacy," *American Philosophical Quarterly* (1983) 20:341–56.

term. Its various senses crisscross and overlap. Yet its various senses have in common that they are both norm-dependent and norm-invoking: they rely for their sense on normative notions and in turn have normative consequences. This chapter shows that sexual activity engages various dimensions of privacy—sufficiently fulfills norms upon which some of its senses depend—and shows that these senses in turn each invoke norms which make it reasonable that state interference in sex acts should be presumptively barred and so that sex acts ought to engage any general, substantive constitutional right to privacy.

II. SEX AND CULTURAL PRIVACY

The contours of privacy, in some of its forms, are culturally defined. In all societies there are obligations flowing from customs and mores to keep some activities, possessions, thoughts and things out of the public eye. These obligations vary widely from culture to culture. In some Muslim countries women have an obligation to veil their faces in public, yet among the North African Tuareg Muslims only men have such an obligation.[2] In some Inuit tribes, one's name, like the third name of Eliot's cats, is private.[3] Now, some of these diverse privacy customs strike Americans as quaint, silly, or impractical. Others produce horror. That Vietnamese villagers defecate virtually anywhere led many American servicemen to rationalize that the Vietnamese are subhuman.[4]

Some privacy obligations vary widely over time within a culture. Customs, for instance, restricting eating in public have radically liberalized within one generation of Americans, while illness, deaths, and perhaps births are becoming increasingly private matters here.[5] And while colleagues would never dare read what one was composing at a typewriter, they consider what appears on one's wordprocessor screen as public as advertisements on billboards.[6]

2. See Robert Murphy, "Social Distance and the Veil," in Schoeman, ed., *Philosophical Dimensions of Privacy*, pp. 34–55.

3. See Alan Westin, "The Origins of Modern Claims to Privacy," in Schoeman, ed., *Philosophical Dimensions of Privacy*, p. 73 n.57.

4. See Charles Nelson, *The Boy Who Picked the Bullets Up* (New York: Morrow, 1981); cf. Westin, *ibid.*, p. 62.

5. Westin, *ibid.*

6. For eye-opening examples of cultural variation in privacy customs, see, for example, Alan Westin, *ibid.*, pp. 56-74.

Some privacy obligations, however, are nearly universal. Sexual privacy falls into this category, though in many societies this privacy is sought out *not* in the home but in the wild: "[T]he sexual act is usually performed outside, so that privacy can be obtained, in bush, field, forest, or [on a] beach."[7] Mandatory privacy holds true of homosexual as well as heterosexual behavior. Among the "Sambia" of Papua New Guinea, compulsory homosexual behavior is integral to the rites of male maturity and is embedded in a corresponding sexual theology and ideological biology. Yet the mandated homosexual acts are carried out strictly in private—indeed in secret from women.[8] It is not surprising that those states of the United States which have decriminalized and socially tolerate homosexual acts nevertheless do not allow them to scare the horses.

Now, across the range of actions for which there is an *obligation* to privacy, that very obligation generates, in turn, a *right* to privacy. For society cannot consistently claim that these activities must be carried out in private (despite their sometimes manifest public consequences, like population growth) and yet retain a claim to investigate such activity and so, to that extent, make it public behavior. Where there is an unconditional requirement to keep some activity out of the public eye, the activity sufficiently fulfills the requirements of privacy when privacy means that nobody may rightfully spy on an activity.[9]

This right not to be spied on holds all the more strongly where the would-be investigator is the police—acting as a representative of the moral will of society as a whole. The investigation of the act by the police violates any obligation to privacy completely, for it exposes the act to the public as a whole, not only through the publicity of arrest and trial but also simply through the police's role as moral representative

7. *Ibid.,* p. 63.

8. Gilbert Herdt, *Guardians of the Flutes: Idioms of Masculinity* (New York: McGraw-Hill, 1981), pp. 232-39, 284-88. See generally, Gilbert Herdt, ed., *Ritualized Homosexuality in Melanesia* (Berkeley: University of California Press, 1984) and Walter Williams, *The Spirit and the Flesh: Sexual Diversity in American Indian Culture* (Boston: Beacon, 1986), pp. 252-75. Williams provides an eye-opening international survey of historical and anthropological findings of socially endorsed, institutionalized forms of homosexuality.

9. If the obligation to privacy is conditioned by an additional requirement of full disclosure through reports (say, in the form of records, affidavits, or videos), then the obligation does not automatically trigger the right. For, in that case, if one fails to provide the reports, then one may be investigated. But the obligation to keep sexual activity private, especially gay sex, is not so qualified. People don't want to see it and especially don't want to hear about it.

of society. To cast the point in constitutional terms, the searching out of socially mandated private behavior causes the search to be unreasonable. The search is irrational because it entails a contradiction: that its object be both hidden and public—made hidden by social demand and public by society's agents.

It makes no difference here whether the behavior itself is socially approved or not. The obligation to privacy cuts across both what is socially condemned—most of the seven deadly sins—and what has society's highest commendation—heterosexual intercourse with benefit of clergy for procreation. To say that something ought not to occur at all is not to say that it ought not to be carried out in private when it does occur. In society's judgement, homosexuality is an evil of this sort. Now not all evils ought to be practiced in private if practiced at all. Murders, rapes, and child abuse, if they must occur, would be better to take place in public—to facilitate arrest. But the plaint from conservative quarters that gays objectionably "flaunt" themselves would have no force if this were the sort of evil involved. So, in general, the argument here does not presuppose tolerance, let alone acceptance of gays, nor does it beg the question by presuming that gay sex acts are already legal. Disgust will do. So when gay sex does occur in private, it cannot be rightfully spied on—especially by the police.[10]

10. Does this analysis of obligation-engendered privacy rights void income taxes, as at first blush it might appear to do? *Knowledge* of personal wealth and income in contemporary American society is considered a private matter in *certain* dimensions. There is a social obligation not *to ask* another person about his wealth and income, but there is no obligation on him to keep such knowledge private, at least not a very strong one. A person is permitted to say what her income is. The search for knowledge about wealth and income for tax purposes, then, is not irrational and contradictory. Society is not saying, "You may not tell us your income and yet must tell us your income." The case would be different if there were a social obligation to keep one's wealth itself private—as is the case, for instance, among the timocrats of Plato's *Republic*, for whom conspicuous wealth is a source of shame, not honor. But for here and now, one need, for tax purposes, only overcome the social presumption against *asking* after wealth and income. In this case, state and society will be relevantly different. Here the state is not functioning as the representative of the populace. Rather, it is fulfilling a role which is specific to the state as state and which is not appropriate for individuals to fulfill, just as criminal arrest procedures are not "representative" of vigilantism, but serve a different function—the administration of justice. The state is not simply efficiently pinch-hitting for the populace as a whole; it is fulfilling a uniquely governmental function, as when at trials the state compels testimony—even that touching on (some) private matters. Nevertheless, society has gone out of its way to protect the private knowledge of income, by narrowly drafting tax procedures and indeed largely relying on voluntary compliance. How much greater then ought the pre-

Some gay activists have opposed appeals to privacy as the mainstay of gay rights strategies: privacy, especially enforced privacy, is the closet. They claim that what is needed is not gay privacy but gay publicity—to break through the silence and taboos surrounding gay issues and to confront people's unsubstantiated fears of gays.[11]

Now admittedly access to the public is necessary if gays are to make any progress toward social acceptance and in the rough-and-tumble of electoral politics.[12] But here is a case where the activist can have her cake and eat it too. Both gay privacy and gay publicity ought to be and can be protected. The two are not mutually exclusive *even* on an analysis that derives privacy rights in part from privacy obligations—for two reasons.

First, even a rough distinction drawn between privacy and secrecy will allow for publicity, since not all that needs to be private needs to be secret. Second, society can be held accountable to act consistently in its requirements for both privacy and secrecy.

At least in the realm of the sexual, the privacy that society can consistently require applies to specific acts and not to patterns of behavior or to the telltale signs of specific acts. Required privacy applies consistently to tokens of action rather than types. It is specific sexual performances that are to be kept from the public eye—no scaring the horses. But no one supposes that a conspicuously pregnant woman out in public has somehow violated the requirement of sexual privacy that society places over sexual performances, though everyone can make the simple inference that she has had sex. One can infer that (rape and artificial insemination aside) she's that type of person who engages in heterosexual behavior. Similarly, no one supposes that heterosexual couples who wear wedding rings or who take their offspring for walks in parks have violated the obligation to privacy surrounding sex acts, even though the

sumption of protections for privacy be in cases where there is an actual obligation to it—as in sexual behavior?

11. See, for example, Marilyn Frye, *The Politics of Reality: Essays in Feminist Theory* (Trumansburg, N.Y.: The Crossing Press, 1983), pp. 152–74; Lisa Bloom, "We are all Part of One Another: Sodomy Laws and Morality on Both Sides of the Atlantic," *New York University Review of Law and Social Change* (1986) 14:1011–16. Bloom calls for the abandonment of a "rights-based legal model" which focuses on individuals' privacy in favor of "the feminist morality model of mutual concern and social cohesion." (p. 1015).

12. See chapter 6, section III.

rings publicly commit them to having had sex—the consummation of marriage—as do usually the children, and so all collectively suggest a pattern of heterosexual behavior. It's no secret what type of people we have here. Correspondingly, gays should resist any requirement that makes a secret of what type of people they are.

It is completely coherent to be nonsecretive about what is obliged to be private. It is indiscreet among acquaintances who have not developed some level of trust to ask after the other's religion, though either may offer that information in appropriate contexts. Similarly, while it is indiscreet for someone to ask another whether he had sex last night, the latter may proffer this information if it is apposite to the conversation. Secrets are essentially reports rather than sensations.

Thus generally, an obligation to *privacy,* an obligation to shield specific acts from the vision and hearing of nonparticipants, does not entail a requirement of *secrecy* about the acts—and vice versa. For there can be secrets about things that are perfectly public, like the king's new clothes. Keeping a secret means only living by an obligation not to report some information, but does not entail that one is prevented from having the sensation or experience which might be reported or even that the sensation or experience be kept out of sight.

Now, there is in current society a general requirement of secrecy covering gay behavior patterns and sexual types. (That is why there are no gay characters in comic strips and television advertisements and the like.) But once one passes into the realm of information, reportage, and opinion, one is in the realm of protected free speech rights. Both the general utility of the free flow of information in society and the right of people to speak their minds outstrip quickly any merely conventional obligation to secrecy.[13]

In any case, the enforced secrecy and mandated discreetness surrounding many sex-related matters are often themselves perfectly objectionable, when, for instance, they serve as sources of stigma against whole classes of people. Such current taboos surrounding menstruation, for example, bring home to women that, in society's view, what makes them different from men makes them—in the long shadow of Leviticus—

13. *Carey v. Population Sevices Int'l,* 431 U.S. 678, 700–2 (1977) (offense and embarrassment held illegitimate grounds for banning display and advertisement of contraceptives).

dirty, unwholesome, and inferior.[14] For gays, the taboos mark them as unspeakably gross and disgusting—like shit.

Further, the obligation to secrecy is radically inequitable in its application against gays. Sometimes the inequity is blatant, as when only signs of heterosexual behavior are socially or legally allowed, like public kissing. Sometimes it is more subtle, as when seemingly neutral pressures not to talk of *any* sexual matters have a radically disparate impact against gays. Since social institutions are already tooled to promote heterosexuality, any general bar to discussing sexual matters simply further entrenches the dominant culture. Pseudo-liberal school boards that claim they do not want any teachers' sexual orientation—gay or not—to be known to students and so fire openly gay teachers for allegedly flaunting themselves are simply being disingenuous in theory—and inconsistent in practice. At least, history has yet to record a case of wedding rings causing teachers to be fired by such school boards for flaunting heterosexuality. The gay activist then might well adopt as a slogan: "privacy yes, secrecy no."

III. THE INHERENT PRIVACY OF SEX

Even if there were no social customs that generate a right to privacy from an obligation to privacy, sex acts would still be covered by any general, substantive right to privacy. For the privacy of sex acts is not only culturally based but also inherent to them. Sex acts are what I shall call "world excluding." Custom and taboo aside, sexual arousal and activity, like the activities of reading a poem or praying alone, are such as to propel away the ordinary world, the everyday workaday world of public places, public function, and public observation.[15]

14. Leviticus 15:19–27.

15. This section in part draws on some ideas and metaphors in Part One of Murray S. Davis' *Smut: Erotic Reality/Obscene Ideology* (Chicago: University of Chicago Press, 1983), which provides an excellent descriptive phenomenology of sex acts. Davis, in turn, owes a great deal to Jean-Paul Sartre's discussions of sex in *Being and Nothingness,* trans. Hazel Barnes (New York: Philosophical Library, 1956), pp. 382–407 and to Thomas Nagel's classic article "Sexual Perversion," *Journal of Philosophy* (1969) 66:5–17. All three of these authors are confessed heterosexuals. Specific sexual behavior is diverse in kind and implications, but the account of sex acts in this section is intended to be pitched at a level of generality such that—for the issues it addresses—it covers both heterosexual acts and homosexual acts, both gay male and lesbian. For three diverse accounts by lesbians of the nature and implications of lesbian sex, see Audre Lorde, "Uses of the Erotic:

There are several ways in which sex acts are world-excluding. First, sexually aroused people experience the world in an altered way. Sexual arousal alters perception of reality in some of the same ways powerful drugs do.

Space recedes. Arousal is an immersion into a different medium, as into sleep fraught with scary possibilities, or as into a liquid, where one either is contiguous with another or has no contact at all. One could not have a public, shared space in syrup. In continued arousal, perception becomes more and more focused and narrow. One attends only to what is near. One's gaze no longer roams or scans at large, but increasingly becomes a form of attention. The focusing process calls for and is enhanced by nightfall. Only what is near, if anything at all, is seen. Gradually, perception is channeled away from vision—the supreme sense of the everyday public world, a sense that requires a gulf of open space. Perception shifts from vision to touch, the sense which requires the absence of open space. At peak arousal, as in a liquid or in a blizzard, the horizon is but the extent of one's flesh. One is hermetic save for the continuation of one's flesh with and in the flesh of another.

No less, sex withdraws one from the world of waking and talking, from reason, persuasion, and thought. Sex is essentially a world of silence; words, such as they are, are not reports, descriptions, or arguments, but murmurs and invocations which emphasize silence and its awe.

Time, like space, recedes with arousal. Suspended is the time by which one gauges the regularity and phases of the workaday world. Time is interrupted and becomes inconsequential, as in the spontaneity and attention-absorbing fascination of games.

Second, social relations alter importantly during the shift into erotic reality; people who were important in everyday reality recede from importance. People with whom one has functional, public roles fade away entirely or at least as persons strictly identified with those roles. Colleagues and service personnel fade from consciousness. One becomes focused only upon those who potentially jibe with one's tastes, the particularities of one's erotic choices or desires. Anyone could have sold

The Erotic as Power," in Laura Lederer, ed., *Take Back the Night: Women on Pornography*, pp. 285–300 (Toronto: Bantam, 1982); Jeffner Allen, *Lesbian Philosophy: Explorations* (Palo Alto, Cal.: Institute for Lesbian Studies, 1986), pp. 89–106; Pat Califia, *Sapphistry: The Book of Lesbian Sexuality* (Tallahassee, Fla.: Naiad Press, 1980).

you a train ticket through a wicket; even a computer could. But only someone particular in appearance, mien, pose and act could arouse you. Even the most 'impersonal' or 'anonymous' sexual encounters are intimate in this way—rarely does a name arouse—and, communist ideology aside, such encounters are not marked by mere functioning in accord with social or economic roles. Even in sexual environments where there are ample numbers of ready, willing, able, and intentionally sexual bodies, as in bathhouses, parks, and backroom bars, still virtually everyone is picky about their partners, even to the point of completely frustrated desire.[16]

Third, in the process of sexual arousal, one becomes increasingly incarnate, submerged in the flesh. When this process is mutual and paired with the shift in perception to touch, it achieves an unparalleled intimacy. Social and psychological characteristics, one's own and those of the object of erotic desire, pale in this focusing on and submerging into flesh. In sexual disengagement from spatial, social, and psychological circumstances, the body ceases to be merely a coathanger for personality, but assumes an independent life of its own.

One perceives the other as flesh and desires the other to be flesh. Usually one becomes, in turn, flesh for another, in part because one's own submersion into the flesh sparks or enhances desire in the other. The recognition of this effect on the other, in turn again, facilitates one's own further submersion. This process of mutual reciprocal incarnations may be iterated at many levels, though eventually the body submerges even the mind's ability to carry out the requisite recognitions and one becomes just the body sensing.

This sexually aroused body, in turn, works as an alembic on sensations typical of the everyday world. A touch—say, a light brushing of the flesh that would go largely unnoticed in the everyday world, save possibly for its social significance—here becomes an intense yet diffuse pleasure and, as the nontimid masochist knows, what was pain in the ordinary world, say, having one's tits twisted, here transmutes into a coursing yet careening pleasure.

The recognitions constitutive of mutual incarnations, the very slide into the purely sensing body, and the immediacy and simultaneity of touching and being touched produce a transparency in the flow of

16. On the dynamics of the impersonal sex scene, see John Rechy, *The Sexual Outlaw* (1977; New York: Grove Press, 1984).

information and sensation between partners. The vagueness and ambiguity typical of everyday interactions and the obscurity of connections between intent and response are here distilled into a clarity of cause and effect unmatched in human experience. One is as intimate as one could be.

Fourth, the everyday world of will and deeds fades away with sexual arousal. The will is not a chief causal factor in the fulfillment of sexual desire and indeed impedes sexual arousal. One can effectively use one's will to raise one's arm but cannot use one's will to raise, well, to effect the transition from sexual desire—horniness—to sexual arousal—the engorging and sexual sensitizing of the genitals. Indeed, quite the opposite is true: the willing of sexual arousal guarantees it will not occur. Sexual arousal must happen *to* one; it is a passion, not an action, project, or deed. It can occur only in situations in which one is not observing one's progress and judging how one is doing. As Masters and Johnson have shown, self-observation, self-judging, and the willing of arousal are the chief causes of—and virtually guarantee—impotence.[17] One has to be lost in the sex for it to work upon one.[18]

For all these reasons, the sexual realm is inherently private. The sex act creates its own sanctuary which in turn is necessary for its success. The whole process and nature of sex is interrupted and destroyed if penetrated by the glance of an intruder—unless that glance itself becomes incorporated in the process just described. The gazes of nonparticipants in sex are not the harmless matrix of intersecting looks of the marketplace or town meeting, which, by virtue of their very complexity, cancel each other out like randomly intersecting waves. Rather, being viewed by an uninvited other is as intrusive in sex as the telephone ringing. For, like the unwelcome ringing, such observation brings crashing in its train the everyday world of duration and distance, function and duty, will and action. Further, the gaze of others injects into sex the

17. See William H. Masters and Virginia E. Johnson's *Human Sexual Inadequacy* (Boston: Little, Brown, 1970), pp. 198–99, 202–3 and their *Homosexuality in Perspective* (Boston: Little, Brown, 1979), pp. 267–68, 296–97.

18. Don't be mistaken: sadism is no exception. One can be aroused by one's dominating or successfully manipulating another. But in this case, power effectively deployed has become the object of one's arousal; the body of the other not as body simpliciter but as body disposed in a certain way is what arouses one. Still, however, it is not one's will to be aroused that is causing one to be aroused, though it may be one's will that effectively dominates the other.

waking world of vision, not the submerged and submerging world of flesh. Most importantly, it judges—even if sympathetically—causing self-reflection. Even if such reflection may only take the form of felt uncertainty, it virtually always causes a great deal more disruption. For, where a socially imposed obligation to maintain an act as private mounts to the level of taboo (as is the case with sex and excretion in America), *any* observation, even a seemingly disinterested one, is bound to be construed by the observed as a harsh intrusive judgment. There is no such thing as casual observation of people fucking.

Each component of the world-excluding nature of sexual encounters is destroyed by an intruding observer. To observe sex but not participate in it is to violate the sexual act. Sex is possible only in the realm of *presumed* privacy, and so is violated even by an unobserved observer. Sex is inherently private. Any moral theory that protects privacy as sanctuary and as repose from the world must presumptively protect sexual activity.

The inherently private nature of sex has an important legal consequence: consent is the mark of the private in the realm of the sexual. Those present at a sexual encounter are either part of it or an intrusion into it; there can be no neutral observers, a public at large, here. If all the members present at an encounter are there by mutual consent, it is the rest of the world that is thereby excluded by the nature of the sexual encounter. Therefore, nothing about the nature of sexual encounters requires that the number of persons engaging in private sexual acts be limited. The traditional and sometimes legally enforced belief that two participants at most constitute a private sexual encounter—that three or more people automatically make sex a public act—is a displaced vestige of the view that sex is only for reproduction: since humans have litters of but one, only two can effect procreation.[19]

As usual in matters sexual, Canada gets the prize for legal zaniness when it comes to numbers and privacy. Even in the face of national consenting adult laws, provincial bawdyhouse statutes have been applied to private dwellings where the allegedly publicity-producing magic number three is achieved only by counting two different pairings on two

19. For an improperly decided case, see *Lovisi v. Slaton,* 539 F.2d 349 (4th Cir. 1976) (en banc) (held that a husband and wife automatically waive privacy rights by inviting a sailor to engage in sex with them).

different nights.[20] While most people would find this absurd, many may find orgy rooms at bathhouses and backrooms in bars not to be private.[21] This view is wrong, for if the participants are all consenting to be there with each other for the possibility of sex polymorphic, then they fulfill the proper criterion of the private in the realm of the sexual. If, as is the case, gay cruising zones of parks at night have as their habitues only gay cruisers, police cruisers, and queerbashers, then they too are private in the requisite sense; and, in the absence of complaints against specific individuals, arrests should not occur there for public lewdness.

Now, consent is not the mark of the private *überhaupt*. Not everything that is consensual is private. Except for commercial interactions which are illicit or in which the product exchanged itself invokes certain privacy conventions (say, the formerly discreet purchasing of condoms), acts of buying and selling are perfectly public. They entail none of the world-excluding features of sexual encounters and are paradigmatically public in being largely functional encounters. In such a commercial encounter, the peculiarities of the individuals involved and the uniqueness of the encounter as developed by its participants are irrelevant to its significance and success. Except for xylophiles, buying lumber is not an intimate act.[22]

That consent is the mark of the private in the realm of the sexual should allay some fears that feminists have expressed against advancing privacy as an engine for social reform. They see the valuing of privacy as legitimizing marital rape, incest, and child abuse, and so as a chief tool and manifestation of patriarchy. But marital rape is not consensual and so is no more privacy-invoking than a bedroom murder. Again: it is not

---

20. See Gerald Hannon, "Bedroom, Not Bawdyhouse," *The Body Politic* [Toronto], November 1981, p. 9: The acquitted defendant's case "represented the first time that bawdyhouse charges had been brought against a man for having sex with other men on a repeated basis in his own home."

21. On state regulation of gay bathhouses on medical and paternalistic grounds, see chapter 8.

22. Prostitution is a difficult case. Is it private or not by this standard? Like traditional marriage, prostitution undeniably has structural components that are fixed by economic relations and social roles. So if traditional marriage is considered covered by privacy then probably fairness requires that prostitution be so too. The state, however, may regulate the commercial and socially determined components of prostitution, as it ought also to be able to do with corresponding parts of marital relations. Gay marriages, invoking, as they do, no social roles, are more private than garden variety ones.

four walls that define an act as private. Rather, they are conditions by which inherently private acts may be maintained as private. Feminists' legitimate complaints are against interpretations of civic marriage that have traditionally and legally voided the application of rape laws to husbands and against inequitable police procedures in addressing public acts that occur behind four walls.[23]

IV. SEX AS A CENTRAL PERSONALLY-AFFECTING VALUE

The Supreme Court's analyses of privacy in the contraception and abortion cases suggest that a sufficient mark for acts being *constitutionally* protected by privacy is that they embody central personally affecting values.[24] Now, this analysis is not meant (and should not be meant) as a mark of privacy *per se* nor as the gauge of the strength of the constitutional right to privacy, but rather means that only *important* self-affecting values rise to the level of constitutional protection. Not every little thing that might reasonably be considered private invokes the strict scrutiny analyses of cases like *Griswold v. Connecticut* and *Roe v. Wade*.[25] The importance of the self-affecting interest triggers the constitutional right—at whatever strength it has.

There are good practical reasons for the Court to place importance on importance here. Friendship is typically and analytically private because it is intimate. It is based on the participants' uniqueness and has value chiefly because it is they who value it and not chiefly because they fulfill some social function in the relation. But the law must draw the line somewhere between constitutionally protected relations and relations among people who *in the eyes of the law* are strangers. It has never occurred to anyone to suggest, for instance, that friends ought to have

23. On substantive and procedural abuses in traditional marriage "contracts," see generally Sara Ann Ketchum's excellent "Liberalism and Marriage Law," in Mary Vetterling-Braggin, et al., eds., *Feminism and Philosophy*, pp. 279–89 (Totowa, N.J.: Littlefield Adams, 1977).

24. *Eisenstadt v. Baird*, 405 U.S. 438, 453 (1972) (right to contraception extended to the unmarried); *Roe v. Wade*, 410 U.S. 113, 152–53 (1973) (right to abortion contained within the right to privacy).

25. *Griswold v. Connecticut*, 381 U.S. 479 (1965), was the Court's first case establishing privacy as a free-standing, substantive, constitutional right. For an analysis of this case, see chapter 3.

the same legal immunities of privacy against the state forcing them to testify against each other as is possessed by husbands and wives, penitents and priests, doctors and patients, and clients and lawyers. Our general cultural intuitions have been to draw the line of protected privacy near the boundary of the family unit, or more precisely near the means by which individuals jointly fulfill the necessities of life, and so to exclude friends, especially of the bridge partner and old crony varieties, from the reach of protected privacy. Perhaps this exclusion is wrong, but, given our cultural intuitions, someone would have to argue it is wrong.

Is one's interest in having a sex life as important as a number of other personally affecting acts that the Court has protected under the right to privacy? The answer is an obvious yes. The Court in *Carey,* in addition to extending contraceptive rights to minors, barred on privacy grounds a restriction allowing only licensed pharmacists to sell contraceptives: the mere inconvenience of having to find a drugstore in order to buy condoms and their increased cost in a market thus restricted were enough to trigger the right to privacy and strict scrutiny.[26] In *Roe v. Wade,* the interests mentioned as sufficient to trigger strict scrutiny are more substantial though still modest. They are two. First, there is an interest against medically "specific and direct harm" resulting from the prohibition of abortion.[27] However, since the case does not limit the right to abortion to medically indicated ones, this interest is highly suspect in triggering a *general* right to abortion. Second, an interest exists in avoiding the "distress" produced by legal bars to abortion—possible stigma and the strain of caring for an unwanted child.[28] Only the latter interest would be universally applicable to all barred abortions, and indeed fades as an interest to the degree that adoption becomes a reasonable option.[29]

If these interests are the sort sufficient to convert a personal interest into a privacy right, then one's interest in having a sex life at all will surely pass the test. First, casting gay acts as felonies certainly contributes to the general stigmatizing of gays in society. Although all criminal law will bring some stigma against all violators, admitting to breaking

26. *Carey,* 431 U.S. at 689.

27. *Roe v. Wade,* 410 U.S. 113, 153 (1973).

28. *Ibid.*

29. *Roe v. Wade* simply fails to mention the intrusiveness of actually carrying a fetus to term—inevitable and all-consuming in all full-term pregnancies. This would have been a surer interest to have cited as triggering privacy protections.

sodomy laws has an added dimension of stigma. For such an admission of law breaking, like bearing a child out of wedlock or publicly espousing communist beliefs, casts one into a class that is stigmatized *quite independently* of legal sanctions. Legal sanctions and the charge of being "an unapprehended felon" are not the origin of stigma against gays, but they help maintain and enhance that stigma against one as a member of a class on which derision is cast regardless of the acts that place one in that class. Indeed, when no attempt is made to enforce sodomy laws, the dubious "educational function" of stigmatizing gays as a class seems to be their main purpose.

It can not be claimed that sodomy laws, like Georgia's, which fail to distinguish between heterosexual and homosexual sodomy, do not stigmatize gays any more than they stigmatize nongays. In his curious hairsplicing dissent in *Bowers v. Hardwick*,[30] Justice Stevens errs along this line. He accepts Georgia's position at oral argument that it is legitimate for laws to have a "merely symbolic" function, "a purely symbolic role," but seems to claim that Georgia's law obviously fails to be rationally related to this legitimate state function because it does not distinguish between homosexual and heterosexual acts.[31] This view fails to understand symbols. The meaning and force of a *mere* symbol cannot be derived independently of the social behavior in which it is embedded. Whether black cats are taken as symbols of life or death has nothing to do with the nature of cats. Whether a raised middle finger is an obscene gesture or a prayer has nothing to do with the nature of digits. The meaning of such symbols depends entirely on social custom. Symbols that stigmatize are no different. Whether segregated washrooms stigmatize certain segregated groups depends entirely on social custom. White-only washrooms stigmatize blacks as allegedly being dirty—they appeal to and enhance an already existing socially concocted stereotype. But while there may be competing social theories to explain gender-segregated washrooms, few people would think that the social function of men-only washrooms is to stigmatize women. Therefore if law is being treated as *mere* symbol, it is not enough simply to point to its wording or structure to determine its symbolic significance. One must look to the social behavior in which it is embedded and whence it is plain that even

30. *Bowers v. Hardwick*, 106 S. Ct. 2841 (1986) (held homosexual sodomy is not protected by the constitutional right to privacy).
31. *Ibid.* at 2858–59 n.12 (Stevens, J., dissenting).

generic sodomy laws stigmatize gays as a group but are never used to stigmatize heterosexuals as a group. While this should be obvious, one example will clear any doubt: People who call for the retention of immigration discrimination against gays use as their main rationale that gays have to be kept out of the country lest they break state sodomy laws. Would anyone ever think of mounting the same argument for keeping heterosexuals out of the country? So sodomy laws stigmatize gays even if they do not specifically draw attention to the similarity in gender of the offending parties.

Putting aside the importance of avoiding stigma, an impartial examination of sex's role in an individual's life would show first that, far from having any imaginable value or at most a nugatory one, sex is in general a central personal concern, and second that for those people with a sex drive, addressing sex as central and appropriating it to oneself in some way or another is probably necessary to fulfilled life.[32] Or at least the lives of those like priests and nuns who renounce sex altogether would support a belief that one's sexual choices are as central as any aspect of

32. For a quite different account of the importance of sex in life, see David A. J. Richards, *Sex, Drugs, Death and the Law* (Totowa, N.J.: Rowman and Littlefield, 1982), pp. 51–54. For Richards, sex is largely a matter of thought rather than sensation. He thinks human sexuality is "extraordinarily plastic and malleable" (p. 51) and that the chief role of sex is as a sort of psychotherapy which works over malleable sexuality by producing and critically examining an individual's fantasies, so that he may decide what sort of person he wants to be, and then become that person (p. 52). Thus, for Richards, sex is not simply some specific end that an independent or autonomous person might choose as one of her ends but rather part and parcel of what it means to be autonomous: to have the capacity to revise one's ends. This position, however, stands at odds with Richards' claim that sexual orientation itself is permanently fixed at least by early childhood (p. 42). If the latter is true, having a sexual orientation is not *part* of what autonomy is or even an *instance* of a person acting autonomously; all that is up for grabs in that case is whether one will *act* on one's orientation.

The four-man dissent in *Bowers* manifests the same stresses as are found in Richards' account. On the one hand, the dissent claims that "neither is [sexual orientation] simply a matter of deliberate personal election," *Bowers* 106 S. Ct. at 2850 n.2 (Blackmun, J., dissenting), and yet on the other hand sees the protection of sexual orientation as based on a right to make "certain *decisions* that are properly for the individual to make"—ones that "dramatically [alter] an individual's self-definition" and entail an "ability independently to define one's identity." *Ibid.* at 2850–51 (Blackmun, J., dissenting) (emphasis in original).

For Richards sex is also supremely important as part of something he calls "sexual love" (p. 53), the mechanics of which, however, seem to have little or nothing to do with sexual behavior, and indeed sex finally drops out of the picture altogether as Richards asserts *"the principle of love as a civil liberty"* (p. 54, emphasis in original).

one's life. For vows of chastity are as central to their religious life—their most meaningful life—as any vows they take.[33]

The centrality of sex as a value is indicated by the very vocabulary, or *lack* of it, that surrounds sex. Sex used to seem so central, and yet seemingly frightening, that for centuries, only theologians and pornographers could discuss it: "Sex must have at least the potential of being one of life's boundary experiences if it could be treated by only the highest and lowest literary genres."[34]

Only the power of entrenched and complex institutions, a power so pervasive as to appear invisible, was strong enough to preserve this gap in discourse and thought. Thus when one looks at a newspaper's cavalcade of engagement and wedding photos, it never even crosses one's mind to think "gosh, what a slew of heterosexuals." When discourse about sex simply could not be avoided, some institutions were strong enough to fill the void with euphemisms so automatic and arcane as not to suggest a present presence—the language of "to have and to hold," "blessed events," and "the facts of life." Even so, some "things" were so powerful and frightening that they had to remain unnamed and unmentionable, to be dealt with not by appeal to and through institutional arrangements but only by extraordinary, direct appeal to some allegedly preinstitutional fundament.

When now sex is discussed somewhat more forthrightly, the terms are not merely those of desire but also those of need, and correctly so for two reasons. First, though sexual activity is not necessary to the continued biological existence of an individual as are some things that are called natural needs, it is a desire (unlike addictions) that recurs independently of its satisfaction—a natural object, not a product. It is a desire that, if one has it at all, constantly presses itself upon life no matter what one does. For the state to bar one from having sex *at all* is to cast one automatically into a perpetual despair analogous to that of those whose plans are frustrated daily by ghetto, prison, or disease. But worse still, at least in prison, ghetto, or illness, one can achieve the consolation of the resigned, the comparative happiness of those who have reduced their expectations to match their prospects, or even the finality of giving up. The recurrent nature of sexual desire trips up even these joys.

33. John L. McKenzie, *The Roman Catholic Church* (New York: Holt, Rinehart and Winston, 1969), pp. 74–80.
34. Davis, *Smut*, p. xx.

Second (like addictions and the desires for the prerequisites of continued biological existence) sex's frustration tends to sponsor aggression. This may take blatant forms as when a young man enters gay life first by being a queerbasher, then a "rough trade" hustler who assaults his johns, and only finally scrapes together enough something to allow himself a pleasure not vouchsafed by violence.[35] Such violence born of sexual frustration is the order of the day in medium and maximum security prisons where violence and domination themselves, not their male sufferers, become the chief objects of sexual arousal.[36]

Alternatively, aggression born of sexual frustration may take more subtle and insidious forms. It can chiefly be directed not against specific others, but against the world as a whole or even against oneself. One could wade through Freud for the same point but a novelist has made it better. Consider the following remarkable passage from the 1929 récit *Alexis* in which the twenty-four year old Marguerite Yourcenar has her homosexual title character describe the effects of a year of abstinence at about the same age:

> Our body forgets like our soul; that is possibly what explains why some of us experience renewals of innocence. I attempted to forget; I almost did. Then, that sort of amnesia appalled me. My memories, which always seemed to me incomplete, tortured me even more. I embraced them in order to bring them to life again. I grew desperate when they paled. I had nothing but them to compensate me for the present, and for the future I had renounced. . . .
>
> Sometimes one controls one's acts; one controls less often one's thoughts; one never controls one's dreams. I had dreams. I came to know the danger of stagnant waters. It seems that acting absolves us. There is something pure, even in a culpable act, compared to the thoughts we form about it. Or, if you wish, you could say that acts are less impure because of the element of mediocrity reality always possesses. The year in which I did, I assure you, nothing reprehensible was troubled with more obsessions than any other, and with viler ones. One would have said this wound, closed too quickly, had reopened in the soul and ended up by poisoning it. . . . And so, I loved life. It was in the name of life, that is to say, my future, that I forced

35. See Bruce Fischer and Toby Marotta, *Adolescent Prostitution: A Study of Sexual Exploitation, Etiological Factors, and Runaway Behavior with a Focus on Adolescent Male Prostitutes: Executive Summary* (San Francisco: Urban and Rural Systems Associates, 1982).

36. See Wayne Wooden and Jay Parker, *Men Behind Bars: Sexual Exploitation in Prison* (New York: Plenum, 1982).

myself to triumph over myself. Yet one hates life when one suffers. I had suicidal obsession; I had others even more abominable. I saw in the humblest objects of daily life nothing more than the instruments of potential destruction . . . .

I became hard. Up to that point I had refrained from judging others; I would have ended up, if I had had the strength, by being as pitiless to them as I was to myself. I did not pardon the next man his smallest transgressions; I feared that any indulgence toward someone else would lead me, confronted with my conscience, to excuse my own faults. I was suspicious of the softness provided by sweet sensations; I came to hate nature because of the tenderness of spring. I avoided as much as possible the music that moved me: my hands, placed before me on the keys, troubled me with the memory of caresses. I feared the unforeseen in social encounters, the danger in human faces. I was alone. Then my solitude made me afraid. One is never completely alone: unhappily one is always with oneself.[37]

Sexual interests are not then pleasures one can merely forgo like the quest for sugar, or even for gains normally ill-gotten:

For both the difficulties involved in the repression of sexual impulses and the consequences of repression are quite different from those involved in the abstention from "ordinary" crime. Unlike sexual impulses, the impulse to steal or to wound or even kill is not, except in a minority of mentally abnormal cases, a recurrent and insistent part of daily life. Resistance to the temptation to commit these crimes is not often, as the suppression of sexual impulses generally is, something which affects the development or balance of the individual's emotional life, happiness, and personality.[38]

37. Marguerite Yourcenar, *Alexis,* trans. Walter Kaiser (1929; New York: Farrar Straus Giroux, 1985), pp. 60, 61, 62.
For Freud, though, for example:

The position agreeable to all the authorities, that sexual abstinence is not harmful and not difficult to maintain, has also been widely supported by the medical profession. It may be asserted, however, that the task of mastering such a powerful impulse as that of the sexual instinct by any other means than satisfying it is one which can call for the whole of a man's forces. Mastering it by sublimation, by deflecting the sexual instinctual forces away from their sexual aim to higher cultural aims, can be achieved by a minority and then only intermittently, and least easily during the period of ardent and vigorous youth. Most of the rest become neurotic or are harmed in one way or another. Experience shows that the majority of the people who make up our society are constitutionally unfit to face the task of abstinence.

Sigmund Freud, " 'Civilized' Sexual Morality and Modern Nervous Illness" (1908), in James Strachey, ed. and trans., *The Standard Edition of the Complete Psychological Works of Sigmund Freud,* 9:193 (London: The Hogarth Press, 1959).
38. H. L. A. Hart, *Law, Liberty and Morality* (Stanford: Stanford University Press, 1963), p. 22.

The intrusiveness and perpetual return of sexual desire means that for a healthy personality, the total forgoing of a sex life would itself have to be a major life commitment, possible only if the resignation were itself voluntary. Mere external restraint could never produce "virtue" here.

Yet, it is not merely as a need that sexual pleasure is central to human life; in intensity and in kind it is unique among human pleasures; it has no passable substitute from other realms of life. For ordinary persons— not mystics or adolescent poets—orgasmic sex is the only access they have to ecstasy. This may take a number of forms: self-transcendence, a standing outside of self *(ex + histanai);* deliquescence and fusion; engulfing embrace; quiet peace; and self-negation *(la petite mort)*, all of which have clear counterparts only in religious visions of the end of life and the ends of life. It is no accident therefore that religions have provided a fairly constant opposition to sex. The stiff and immediate competition that sex gives to religion as an end of life, paired with the fact that sexual arousal is not chiefly an act of will but something that comes over one, is too much for most religions to address adequately, especially many Western ones that hold good will and good acts as the paths to salvation and its ecstatic achievement.[39] If pleasure is its own bottom— and only fanatics could deny that—then sex as the most intense of pleasures is one of the central free-standing components of the good life. Not only must sex be central as a need, it ought to stand centrally as what for most persons causes them to feel most alive.

Further, if matrimonial love is central to the good life, sex will be central for this reason as well. Those who do not see sex as having its own bottom but who cannot deny its daunting force generally try to incorporate sex safely and tamely into other relationships by giving it a use in their upkeep. Sex on this high romantic model is viewed as a

39. See, for example, "Doctrinal Congregation's Letter to Bishops: The Pastoral Care of Homosexual Persons" (Rome, October 1, 1986). The Vatican's English translation is published in full in *Origins: NC Documentary Service* (November 13, 1986) 16:377–82. After twenty years of considering a homosexual *status* morally neutral as long as one did not *act* on one's orientation, the Roman Catholic Church now considers even a congenitally constitutional homosexual orientation an "objective disorder" (at No. 3). The Church fails to give any account of what one is to do about the existence of one's congenital homosexual desires—one's permanent objectively disordered status (at No. 12). No such account, of course, could be given—once permanence and disorder are linked. Far from offering moral guidance, the Catholic Church has invented a class of innately inferior persons. The Church's position, in holding that one's moral worth is dependent in part upon one's genes, is conceptually indistinguishable from racism.

symbol or a channel of communication.[40] In this model, sex becomes morally tolerable if it is viewed as a token, expression, or physical embodiment of love: sex stands to love as wedding rings stand to marriage. One problem here is that many other things would serve much better than sex for this purpose. If mere symbolism and communication are the purposes of sex, one would do better to work up one's prose style than one's bedtop manner. Further, of the various modes of orgasmic sex only deliquescence and fusion is even possibly analogous to love relationships. It is the only one, for instance, that is a symmetrical relation between partners, as one assumes matrimonial love is supposed to be. Yet the model of sex as a fusion of partners has been a source of extreme consternation to traditional views of sex, for it suggests the destruction of sacred boundaries and traditional divisions between, for instance, genders.[41] If there is no analogy, the symbol becomes arbitrary and is, in any case, a dispensable one.

Rather, to use a different cluster of metaphors, the relation of sex to love is like the relation of a figured bass to a piece of music with a figured bass or, more so, the repeating bass line of a passacaglia to the passacaglia as a whole. The bass line does not fix the form of the piece, as does the opening series in change ringing, nor is it even so determinate in its relation to the whole as to be like the relation of a theme to a fugue or even of a theme to its variations. Yet it is a necessary and positive contribution, which provides thematic material and supports and shapes the whole as a foundation does a house. And this is why friendships for whatever their emotional and spiritual intensity lack the warmth and depth of love relationships. Even if only as possible or recollected, sex acts are the pedal points and diapason of love relationships. This recognition is the kernel of truth left in the religious dogma that a marriage unconsummated is not a marriage at all.[42] In blocking gays from having sex, the state would also deny them love.

40. For the view that good sex is talk, see Robert Solomon "Sexual Perversion," in Robert Baker and Frederick Elliston, eds., 1st ed. *Philosophy and Sex*, pp. 279–82 (Buffalo: Prometheus Books, 1975): "Sexuality is primarily a means of communicating with other people, a way of talking to them, of expressing our feelings about ourselves and them. It is essentially a language. . . ." (p. 279).

41. See Davis, *Smut*, Parts Two and Three.

42. See McKenzie, *The Roman Catholic Church*, p. 176: "[T]wo people are not really married until they have known each other carnally—after the marriage ceremony, one might add."

V. PRIVACY AND THE BODY

Intermittently, the Court has correctly recognized the special status of a person's body in grounding an important dimension of privacy. In 1891, the Court held that in a civil suit a judge could not order a plaintiff, at the defense's request, to strip before a third party doctor in order to verify or refute her claim of injury. The Court held:

> No right is held more sacred or more carefully guarded, by the common law, than the right of every individual to the possession and control of his own person, free from all restraint or interference of others, unless by clear and unquestionable authority of law. . . . "The right to one's person may be said to be a right of complete immunity: to be let alone." . . . The inviolability of the person is as much invaded by a compulsory stripping and exposure as by a blow. To compel any one, . . . to lay bare the body, or to submit it to the touch of a stranger, . . . is an indignity, an assault and a trespass.[43]

The inviolability of the body is here upheld even over the efficient administration of justice.[44] Now, this "complete immunity" does not cover just the body but also importantly devolves upon one's control of the body, such as, one's choice of clothing. The Court claimed that under this right a court could not order the taking of what one is wearing—even a pocketwatch or jewelry—to settle one's debt come due.[45] Therefore culturally based privacy or mere modesty cannot be the source of this right; rather the right is grounded in bodily based privacy. What one does to one's own body has a special status that is derived from the importance of the body itself.

In elevating privacy from a common law to a constitutional principle, though, the Court has been skittish in seeing the status of the body as a guiding concept.[46] In *Roe v. Wade,* the Court commented in its only theoretical claim about privacy since *Griswold:*

43. *Union Pacific Railway Co. v. Botsford,* 141 U.S. 250, 251 (1891) (quoting Cooley on Torts 29) (asserting a common law right against judicially ordered body inspections).
44. *Ibid.* at 258. Similarly, in another early privacy case, the Court ruled that Congress did not have within its enumerated powers the legitimate capacity to conduct a coercive "investigation into the private affairs of individuals." *Kilbourn v. Thompson,* 103 U.S. 168, 195 (1880) (establishing a civil cause of action for false imprisonment for refusing to reply to questions concerning a real estate partnership).
45. *Botsford,* 141 U.S. at 251.
46. Compare the two cases *Rochin v. California,* 342 U.S. 165 (1952) (coercive extraction of stomach's contents offends a sense of justice and so violates Substantive Due Process) and *Winston v. Lee,* 470 U.S. 753 (1985) (held as an unreasonable search court-

It is not clear that the claim that one has an unlimited right to do with one's body as one pleases bears a close relationship to the right to privacy previously articulated in the Court's decisions. The Court has refused to recognize an unlimited right of this kind in the past.[47]

Here Justice Blackmun's formulation of one's bodily right is simply tendentious.[48] No one would claim that a person has even a prima facie

ordered surgery on a defendant for purpose of removing a bullet which is expected to prove that the defendant is the robber hit by the victim's gunfire) with *Breithaupt v. Abram*, 352 U.S. 432 (1957) (coercive extraction of blood upheld against Due Process challenge).

47. *Roe v. Wade*, 410 U.S. 113, 154 (1973) (citing *Jacobson v. Massachusetts*, 197 U.S. 11 [1905] [upholding compulsory vaccination law] and *Buck v. Bell*, 274 U.S. 200 [1927] [upholding compulsory sterilization order]).

In fine contrast, the Canadian Supreme Court in the lead opinion of its lopsided but fragmented 1988 decision declaring Canada's restrictive abortion law unconstitutional found the status of the body controlling in determining that a right to abortion both falls within the reach of the 1982 Canadian Constitution's broad clauses—Section 7, the rough equivalent of the U.S. Constitution's Due Process Clause—and overcomes the wide deference which the Canadian Constitution gives to all "reasonable" laws—Section 1. The opinion held:

> State interference with bodily integrity, . . . at least in the criminal law context, constitutes a breach of security of the person. [The federal anti-abortion law] clearly interferes with a woman's physical and bodily integrity. Forcing a woman, by threat of criminal sanction, to carry a fetus to term unless she meets certain criteria unrelated to her own priorities and aspirations, is a profound interference with a woman's body and thus an infringement of security of the person.

R. v. Morgentaler, 82 National Reporter [Canada] 1, 23, 24 (1988).

48. Both of the cases Blackmun cites—*Buck v. Bell*, 274 U.S. 200 (1927) and *Jacobson v. Massachusetts*, 197 U.S. 11 (1905)—are judicial embarrassments. *Buck*, based on stereotypes, unsubstantiated fears, and thinly disguised prejudices, approved in venom-tipped prose the court-ordered sterilizations of the mentally challenged. The case was greatly restricted by *Skinner v. Oklahoma*, 316 U.S. 535, 542 (1942), which asserted procreation as a fundamental right requiring strict scrutiny. *Ibid.* at 536, 541. For a detailed, critical examination of *Buck*, see Robert Cynkar, "*Buck v. Bell*: 'Felt Necessities' v. Fundamental Values?" *Columbia Law Review* (1981) 81:1418–61.

Jacobson, still after 80 plus years the Court's leading medical case, upheld a law setting a five dollar fine for refusing to take a free vaccine. Because the case leaves the notion "public health" wholly unanalyzed, it contradicts its own declaration that independence is to be overridden only by public goods on a par with national defense (at 29), i.e., ones which protect against indiscriminate harms to "the people at large" (at 28). The law's resort to criminal penalties rather than direct coercion of the vaccine shows that the law is incoherent as a measure to protect the public against indiscriminate harms. Anyone with five dollars can avoid the vaccine altogether and so potentially contribute to the pool of disease-exposed and contagious persons, while those who want protection from the disease can get it simply by themselves taking the vaccine for free. The merits of the decision aside, the Court was not asked to declare upon a measure that, as in the case of sterilization,

right, let alone an absolute right, to do *with* his body as he pleases or that such use of the body grounds a right to privacy or any other. One does not have even a prima facie right to smash one's fist unprovokedly into another's face however much one might enjoy doing so. Blackmun's formulation implicitly construes bodily privacy as a branch of license— acting as one pleases—an understanding of liberty that is incoherent as a social principle. For, aside from chaos ensuing upon its adoption, one cannot consistently will everyone to have this right: one cannot consistently claim a right to do whatever one pleases and at the same time suppose that another has a right to stop one, derived from the other person's same right to do as she or he pleases. The relevant question— one not even entertained by the Court—is whether one has a right to do *to* one's body as one pleases. Such a right would be wholly different from license and it would be more restricted in the scope of intrusions into the world it protects than even a general right to independence— the ability to do as one pleases *to the extent* that others have the same ability.

Had the Court raised the relevant question, it might have had a chance to acknowledge that the body is the primitive precondition and foundation for a person's being in the world at all, for his projection of himself into the world through actions and for his instilling value in things. The body is not merely necessary for existence and action—as food, shelter and a kidney machine might be—but also is part of that in virtue of which a person is and acts. To use Aristotelian vocabulary, the body is not merely a material condition of a person as a being and as an actor. It is *a* formal cause as well. It is the full actuality of a person's existence —one's body completely colors one's existence.[49] In addition, an individual's body stands to his actions as flesh stands to (vertebrate) animality. The body's degree of actuality is entailed by the full actuality of

provided for the invasion of a person's body, such as compelled vaccination by strapping a person down and injecting the vaccine. In dicta, the Court commented that it would probably not uphold a law that required the vaccine if an individual could show that it was likely to cause him severe harm (at 38–39). Thus the case does not raise questions of bodily integrity and so is not even clearly apposite to Blackmun's purpose in citing it. At most, the relevant analogue in a sex law would be the placing of a five dollar tax on sexual performances as a measure against the spread of sexually transmitted disease. For a conceptual and moral analysis of "public health," see chapter 8, section VII.

49. See Aristotle, *De Anima* 412a10–413a10 (on grades of actuality) and *Physica* 193b31–194b15 (on the relative attachment of bodies to their full actualities).

one's acts. So one's body not only colors one's existence, it colors one's acts as well.

If a person is to be free in any of her actions, she must have control of her own body—not in the sense of doing with it as she will, but doing to it as she will—so that it is hers. For if one's existence and actions are to be one's own other than accidentally, one must be able to do *to* one's body as one pleases. In order that an action is one's own, it is not enough that the action have one's intentions as its efficient cause. For one's intentions are presented not merely by and through but inextricably *with* one's body. Therefore, if one's acts are to be one's own, one's body as well as one's intentions must be one's own—and not accidentally so.

Now, no one could assert that one's thoughts were really one's own —formed the basis of a free action—if they were the thoughts one just happened to have—if, for instance, they were simply installed there in one's mind by brainwashing, electrodes, or God. And they would not even be one's own if one fell into them by chance—if they just happened to be "in the air" and one passively absorbed them. The ideas would be one's own in a significant sense only if one had considered them, worked them over, appropriated them, and especially if one produced them new. Without the last at least as a possibility, one's thoughts are not truly one's own.

Similarly, if one's existence is to be one's own other than by accident and if one's actions are to be free, one's body must not belong to one merely by accident. One must not be forced merely to accept what is given by nature or by others' volitions. One must be permitted the opportunity to mold it, shape it, alter it, and even to make it as boldly new as it is capable, not as others allow—assuming, of course, all the usual restraints on what one may do *to* others *with* it. One cannot reshape one's fist by cutting it with another's bones as one puts it through the other's skull. One may not be able to cut one's hand at all if that would cause one preemptively to fail of some positive duty justifiably incumbent upon one—say, military service in defensive war. But such relatively clear positive and negative duties aside, one must be free to do to one's body as one sees fit, if one is to be free at all.

If, as is the case, the Constitution contains at least *some* substantive rights, it must also protect the root of those rights. Control of one's body in the requisite sense is not merely a necessary condition for possessing (meaningfully) some right, as obtaining at least subsistent nutrition would be. Instead, control of the body is also part and parcel of what any right is as a right, simply because a right is at least an opportunity to act. A conception of the private in the sense of the personal cannot exist without including a right to do to one's body as one will.

Another route to the same conclusion is to notice that the body is not just one more damn thing in the world that one might have or own, but rather has a special value and standing, as that in virtue of which one possesses other things and as the chief means by which other things come to have value. "My body" has a wholly different status than even "my house." A house belongs to its owner because he built it with his body, or bought it with fruits of the labor his body provided him. In the classical labor theory of property, an unappropriated object in the world becomes one's own as one mixes one's labor with it, for it would then be unjust for anyone else to take it. No one else in this circumstance deserves it.[50]

One's property rights then devolve from a special status that one has as a body. If there is some of the world that is one's own, it is so because of one's body. The body is not merely a necessary condition for one's appropriating what is one's own, it is also the chief causal condition for appropriation. If, then, one speaks of one's body as "mine," it is nevertheless not subject to the same restraints and controls as other things that one owns, for it is morally and causally prior to their being one's own.

The body of a person is therefore not available to the state for its legitimate projects in the way her (other) property is. Even the taking of one's (nonbodily) property requires due compensation. All would agree that the coerced taking of one's body or its parts by the state must pass a much higher standard and is probably to be barred altogether as a legitimate thing the state might do, even if, for example, by medical dismemberment, one's fifteen major organs could be used to maintain one each the lives of fifteen other people who otherwise would die.

50. For a careful defense of this version of the labor theory, see Lawrence C. Becker, *Property Rights: Philosophical Foundations* (London: Routledge & Kegan Paul, 1977), chapter 4. My analysis in this section also draws on Sara Ann Ketchum's excellent article "The Moral Status of the Bodies of Persons," *Social Theory and Practice* (1984) 10: 25–38.

Correspondingly, if one's labor and negotiations with others over money and property, the projects in the world by which one acquires property, are subject to state regulation only so long as the regulation is rationally related to some legitimate state goal, then state regulations of the projects, labor, and actions that one directs not for profit or property but rather to one's normatively prior body must pass a considerably higher standard and be justified only by the most compelling ends. While the state, with adequate justification, can take away the value an individual has instilled in other things and even temporarily control his means of instilling these values, it cannot prevent the individual from valuing himself and possessing himself and yet still suppose that—at least in some areas such as those protected by substantive rights—he is not merely a tool of and for the state but has his own projects and values that take precedence. If there are any substantive liberties, one has a right to instill value in oneself and possess oneself.

A very powerful right to privacy then is generated by and over the body because of its special status in one's projects, one's values, and one's very presence in the world. As the means by which one both projects oneself into the world and appropriates what is one's own to oneself, the body engenders special protections for one's actions that chiefly affect it, even if the features of the world which it affects, produces, or appropriates are not covered by the same right and thus remain generally subject to state control.[51]

The general right to control one's body has at its core a cluster of

51. The argumentation in this section has a surface similarity to arguments in the early works of Charles Fried, arguments which view the body as the root of fundamental rights. Thus in his important treatise on medical ethics, Fried writes:

In the most general terms, the goal of health care as it pertains to such fundamental human values relates to the maintenance of the integrity, of the coherence of the human person, with specific reference to the physical substrate of that integrity. The human person identifies himself with his body; he knows that he *is* his body, that his knowledge of and relation to the whole of the outside world depends on his body and its capacities, and that his ability to formulate and carry out his life plan depends also on this body and its capacities. . . . The person comes logically and morally before the various ends he pursues. . . .

The doctor stands in a special relation to his patient because he ministers to the basic unit which is the person, rather than to the attributes and creations which that person gathers around him in pursuit of his purposes. For the person is his body.

Charles Fried, *Medical Experimentation: Personal Integrity and Social Policy* (Amsterdam: North-Holland Publishing Co., 1974), pp. 95–96, emphasis in original. Or again:

The connection between the concept of personality and the special moral quality of directly caused specific bodily based liberties: one has a strong presumptive right to feed one's body, to manipulate it, to exercise it, to dress it as one sees fit, to seek medical treatment, to inject foreign bodies into it, to permit others to do so, to touch it, to have others touch it, to allow others to present their bodies to it, and to be the chief governor and guarantor of one's own feelings, emotions and sensations [52] — compatible with a like ability

harm is based on the (metaphysical) fact that persons, the ultimate object of moral judgments, are particular entities, and more precisely particular *bodies*.

Charles Fried, *Right and Wrong* (Cambridge: Harvard University Press, 1978), p. 33, emphasis in original.

Fried, however, implicitly presupposes that the body is a fixed uniform given from individual to individual, capable of degeneration and decay but not of improvement or even individual distinctive variation. He pays no attention to a person's possible reflexive actions directed at his body — to make it his own other than accidentally and to instill it with value. Fried therefore draws many quasi-paternalistic conclusions, morally condemning and sometimes calling for outright legal bars to activities like selling one's bodily parts and prostitution. For he views these acts as ceding away the substrate of personality (*Medical Experimentation*, pp. 166–67; *Right and Wrong*, p. 142).

The position advanced in this section, by paying attention to the importance of reflexive actions upon the body, argues, to the contrary, that one's body is finally one's own *only if* one can significantly alter it, even partially dismember or temporarily sell it, subject to the limit that it remains as a vehicle for one's actions and projects in the world. One's ear is only really one's own if one can cut it off and send it as a gift to one's friend.

It further follows, for instance, that the ability to enter into binding contracts as a surrogate parent ought to be protected by the constitutional right to privacy. So correctly, *In re Baby M*, 13 *Family Law Reporter* (BNA) 2001, 2022–23 (N.J. Super. Ct. Ch. Div. March 31, 1987). Respecting people's ability to enter into enforceable contracts is one of the chief means by which people are respected as free, moral agents. For in a binding contract an agent limits his own freedom, through commitment, in anticipation of getting what he wants. All the more illegitimate then is any state attempt to bar a woman from entering into binding contracts over that which is most a woman's to control — her body. A bar to binding contracts here cannot be thought of as promoting independence or autonomy, as bars to contracting into slavery or enforced ignorance might be, but only as paternalistic control over women for what others think is women's own good.

In February of 1988, the New Jersey Supreme Court unanimously reversed the ruling of the bench trial in the Baby M case. The Supreme Court's opinion, dripping with liberal condescension and hedged around with appeals to the "natural" and the "normal," held surrogacy contracts void as against public policy, basically on the ground that women — though not men — are too dumb and too emotional to enter into binding contracts. The court held in effect that women are children when it comes to their own bodies. *In re Baby M*, 14 *Family Law Reporter* (BNA) 2007, 2016–18 (Sup. Ct. N.J., February 3, 1988).

52. The Court has stated:

For also fundamental is the right to be free, except in very limited circumstances, from unwanted governmental intrusions into one's privacy.

The makers of our Constitution . . . sought to protect Americans in their beliefs, their thoughts,

on the part of others and with other requirements for civil society. Consensual sex engages and nearly exhausts the core protections of the general right to bodily based privacy. Indeed it comes close to being a perfect or complete exemplification of its provisions.

The right to bodily based privacy rests at the very heart of the conception of personal security.[53] To inhibit the actions by which one makes one's body what it is is more a violation of personal security than even causing it reparable damage. Reparable damage can be rectified and compensated. But barring one from acting upon oneself annihilates one as a free agent in all of one's projects. Therefore, if the state cannot damage one's body—inflicting wounds to advance its projects (even as punishment)[54]—*a fortiori* it cannot bar one from acting upon oneself in consensual sex.

Individuals cannot be assumed to have waived the personal security of bodily based privacy as a condition for receiving the benefits of entry into civil society. For, as the root of all free acts, it is a generative condition of a person's being in a position to make social contracts at all. Such privacy is therefore inalienable and indefeasible. It is so even without appeals to a right to privacy derived from natural law, as it was thought to be by Justice Cobb who "recognized" it "intuitively" as such.[55] Even without resort to intuitions and natural law, bodily based privacy is "implicit in the concept of ordered liberty" and so passes the

---

their emotions and their sensations. They conferred, as against the Government, the right to be let alone. . . .

These are the rights the appellant is asserting in the case before us. . . . [T]he right to satisfy his intellectual and emotional needs in the privacy of his own home.

Stanley v. Georgia, 394 U.S. 557, 564–65 (1969) (quoting *Olmstead v. United States,* 227 U.S. 438, 478 [1928] [Brandeis, J., dissenting]).

53. Bodily based privacy is the chief conceptual ground for rights against cruel and unusual punishment. It gives one, even in punishment, a right not to be bodily invaded: not to be raped, mutilated, or unnecessarily pained, and a right not to have one's body neutralized as a body or turned against itself: not to be shackled into immobilty, crucified, hanged, or left to starve. A *fortiori,* one has a right against these in other government projects—for example, in torture for either information gathering or terror. For a competing account of the error of torture, see Henry Shue, "Torture," *Philosophy and Public Affairs* (1978) 7:124–43.

54. *Weems v. United States,* 217 U.S. 349 (1910) (intentional infliction of pain held cruel and unusual punishment).

55. In his seminal privacy opinion in *Pavesich v. New England Life Ins. Co.,* 122 Ga. 190, 194, 50 S.E. 68, 69 (1905) (establishing common law cause of action for violations of "false light" privacy).

Court's strictest criterion for protection as a fundamental right: since bodily based privacy is a root of all free actions "neither liberty nor justice would exist if [it] were sacrificed."[56]

VI. CONCLUSION

Two years after the Supreme Court in *Griswold* asserted a constitutional right to privacy covering at least some sexual matters, the American Civil Liberties Union reversed its official position on homosexual sodomy. But even then, it did so not by claiming that gay sex should be protected under the *Griswold* right to privacy, but by claiming that government had no legitimate interests in barring gay sex.[57] To this day, Amnesty International has declined to consider even life sentences for homosexual status a human rights violation.[58] But sodomy laws, even when unenforced, are grave injustices.

Sodomy laws not only cause unwarranted harms through indirect spinoff effects but more importantly are assaults on dignity. Unenforced sodomy laws are invective by government. They violate a person's essential desert for equal respect because they represent a failure of the members of the majority to hold the desires, plans, and aspirations of

56. *Palko v. Connecticut*, 302 U.S. 319, 325 (1937) (prohibition against double jeopardy ruled not a fundamental right under the fourteenth amendment). This is Cardozo's very high standard for nonexplicit fundamental constitutional rights. It is the "objective" constitutional test that has vied over recent decades with the more "subjective" long-held-traditions standard for what are to count as fundamental rights. The *Bowers* Court treated the two tests as though they were the same test—*Bowers*, 106 S. Ct. at 2844—implicitly assuming that ultimately justice is merely a matter of convention.

57. "Deportation for Homosexuality Violates Due Process," *Civil Liberties: Monthly Publication of the American Civil Liberties Union* (April 1967), no. 245, p. 6. See generally, John D'Emilio, *Sexual Politics, Sexual Communities: The Making of a Homosexual Minority in the United States, 1940–1970* (Chicago: University of Chicago Press, 1983), pp. 212–13; Vern Bullough, "Lesbianism, Homosexuality and the American Civil Liberties Union," *Journal of Homosexuality* (1986) 13 (1):23–33.

58. "Amnesty Expands Commitment to Gays at Italian Council," *The Advocate* [Los Angeles], November 11, 1982, no. 355, p. 10; "Amnesty Withholds Recognition Again," *The Body Politic*, November 1983, no. 98, p. 22; International Association of Lesbians, Gay Women and Gay Men, *IGA Pink Book: A Global View of Lesbian and Gay Oppression and Liberation* (Amsterdam: COC-magazijn, 1985), p. 11: "Even the world-wide human rights organization Amnesty International has not helped to document cases where lesbians and gays have been imprisoned because of their sexual orientation." In December 1987, Amnesty International voted yet again against holding gays to be covered by its conception of human rights. *The Advocate*, February 16, 1988, no. 492, p. 30.

gay people on a par with their own. Further, as aspersions, like racial, religious, or gender slurs, appealing to widely irrelevant characteristics, unenforced sodomy laws fail to respect gays as moral agents, for they judge gays without regard to their individual merits or accomplishments. To the extent that the assertion of rights is the proper remedy for assaults on dignity, the courts rather than legislatures are the proper forum for the elimination of sodomy laws.

The Constitution, through the right to privacy, can provide a remedy for legislative assaults on the dignity of gays. A proper understanding of the Constitution does not assert that privacy is a substantive right wrested mysteriously from rights to fair procedures. The right is not generated from the Due Process Clause but from the ninth amendment and the Equal Protection Clause. The ninth amendment warrants the discovery and assertion of rights implicit in the Constitution. The equal protection of the *laws,* as applied reflexively to the Constitution as itself the supreme *law* of the land, provides the tool of discovery. When taken together with the ninth amendment, the Equal Protection Clause holds that whatever general principles give life and substance to the particular, explicit guarantees of the Constitution must be extended to other relevantly similar specific guarantees. A right to political participation and a right not to be picked on are two such general principles. A third is a right to substantive privacy—a right to bar access to oneself and not merely a right to control what is known about oneself.

The argument of this part has made no attempt, however, to give necessary and sufficient conditions for what constitutes a private act. Privacy is a notion that has successfully eluded precise conceptual analysis. Some concepts (like unity, good, and red) resist analysis because they are simple; other concepts (like game, tool, and language) resist because they are complex. Privacy is of the latter sort. However, merely because a notion is complex and multidimensional, having senses that crisscross and overlap, does not mean that no clear recognition and identification of its kinds and instances is possible. No one doubts that a hammer is a tool, solitaire a game, or English a language, even if everyone would be hard pressed to give crisp necessary and sufficient conditions for what a tool is, what a game is, and what language is. For such notions, and for privacy, the search for uniformity of definition is misplaced and unnecessary.

Further, that a notion admits of instantiation by degrees is no bar to recognizing and identifying clear cases and kinds of it. One may be uncertain whether a rust patch is more nearly an instance of orange, red, or brown. And yet, no one doubts that oranges are orange. Not everything that admits of continuous variation has a slippery slope of applications. Privacy is a concept that admits not only of definitional complexity but also of degrees of instantiation. But that it applies in degrees also does not entail that all or even most of its applications are uncertain and disputable.

In accordance with these methodological tenets, this chapter has offered four independently sufficient reasons why consensual sex acts conducted out of sensory range of nonparticipants ought clearly to invoke substantive immunities from government intrusions, and so fall squarely under the constitutional right to privacy understood as a general right to substantive privacy.

First, across the range of social phenomena for which there is an obligation to keep behavior out of the sensory range of others, that very obligation generates a corresponding right not to have such behavior investigated by society. The searching out of such behavior by the police as society's moral representatives contradicts society's requirement that such behavior is to be conducted out of the public eye. The search becomes unreasonable because contradictory.

Second, sex acts are inherently private. They work to exclude the world from their participants' perceptions and conversely, in order to work, require such exclusion. They create sanctuary and require sanctuary. Any right to substantive privacy that protects repose and sanctuary will protect the inherent privacy of sex.

Third, even if the perimeter of what counts as a self-affecting action is fuzzy, the role of sexual behavior in a person's life clearly gives sex *a* central place among self-affecting activities. As the fulfillment of need, as an access to ecstasy and as a necessary substrate for matrimonial love, sexual pleasure is set apart from casual pleasures and assumes a role more central in the configuration of human emotions than even friendships have. Any right that protects central self-affecting values, then, will also protect the right to consensual sex.

Finally, because a person's body is a necessary source for all free actions and for any action that instills value in his world, if there are any areas of life in which an individual's plans and projects take precedence over those of society, then the individual must be able to act reflexively on his own body to make it as he wills it and to instill value in it. Moreover, because of the moral priority of the body to an agent's actions in the world, the state's blocking a person's reflexive actions on his own body is an offense on a moral par with a direct violation of a person's body by the state. To be raped by a policeman and to be prevented by the police from having consensual sex are moral equivalents. Therefore, in general, if there are any substantive rights to act in the world, the right to do *to* one's body as one will is necessarily protected. Only when one's control of one's body is protected does one have a right to bodily integrity, and only when one has bodily integrity is one a person at all. Any moral systems, then, in which persons are a locus of value—systems of humans, not systems merely of angels and animals—will be obliged to protect from government those persons' acts of consensual sex.

Appendix to Part Two:
The Privacy Caselaw

It is here argued that the rule of precedent alone should have compelled a different conclusion than the Supreme Court reached in *Bowers v. Hardwick*, where it denied that homosexual acts are protected by rights to privacy.[1] Previous privacy cases simply cannot be squared with the *Bowers* holding.

Privacy cases from *Griswold* up to *Bowers* had gradually expanded rights of sexual privacy. *Griswold*'s holding was limited to the use of contraceptives in the marital bedroom.[2] Four years later, in *Stanley*, the Court protected the right to read and use obscene materials in one's home, but made no reference at all to marriage.[3] In 1972, *Eisenstadt* expanded *Griswold*, on Equal Protection grounds, to cover contraception among the unmarried.[4] The next year, in *Roe v. Wade*, the Court reconstructed *Eisenstadt* as a privacy case proper and held that privacy rights cover abortion whether the woman affected is married or not.[5]

1. *Bowers v. Hardwick*, 106 S. Ct. 2841 (1986).
2. *Griswold v. Connecticut*, 381 U.S. 479 (1965).
3. *Stanley v. Georgia*, 394 U.S. 557 (1969).
4. *Eisenstadt v. Baird*, 405 U.S. 438 (1972).
5. *Roe v. Wade*, 410 U.S. 113, 152 (1973). The post-*Griswold* cases, *Eisenstadt*, 405 U.S. at 453–54, *Roe*, 410 U.S. at 152–53, *Whalen v. Roe*, 429 U.S. 589, 600 n.26 (1977) (upholding a drug registration program against privacy challenge), *Carey v. Population Services Int'l*, 431 U.S. 678, 685 (1977) (barring bans on sale of contraceptives to minors) and *Zablocki v. Redhail*, 434 U.S. 374, 384–85 (1978) (financial circumstances cannot be a bar to marriage), have also reconstructed a number of earlier cases going back to *Boyd v. United States*, 116 U.S. 616 (1886), explicitly as privacy cases rather than Due Process cases or Equal Protection cases, and in doing so made them much more coherent than they stood on their own. These retrospectively reconstructed privacy cases include: *Meyer v. Nebraska*, 262 U.S. 390 (1923) and *Pierce v. Society of Sisters*, 268 U.S. 510 (1925) (both cases establish rights to parents' control over their children's education); *Skinner v. Oklahoma*, 316 U.S. 535 (1942) (barring sterilization as a punishment for some crimes when it is not used for other similar crimes); *Loving v. Virginia*, 388 U.S. 1, 12 (1967) (right to marriage invoked as a free-standing right barring anti-miscegenation laws).

Two other cases have also been treated as establishing the right to privacy, even though both cases upheld challenged laws. They are *Jacobson v. Massachusetts*, 197 U.S. 11

Four years after *Roe v. Wade,* a plurality opinion in *Carey* extended contraceptive privacy to minors.[6]

The principle that holds these cases together is that privacy affords one the right to guide one's sex life by one's own lights. It follows by the force of precedent alone that sex between partners of the same gender ought to be constitutionally protected. The *Bowers* Court dealt with these past privacy cases in only the most summary fashion, indeed in one sentence, by simply asserting without more: "No connection between family, marriage, or procreation on the one hand and homosexual activity on the other has been demonstrated."[7] The Court did not even make a good faith effort to see whether the holdings of past privacy cases have had anything in common or to clarify how the protection of gay sex is to be distinguished from those cases.

Gay sex cannot be distinguished from the line of privacy cases by a claim that the implicit constitutional right to privacy is inherent only in the marital relation.[8] *Stanley, Eisenstadt, Roe v. Wade,* and *Carey* all contradict this claim.

There are solid conceptual reasons as well why the claim is wrong. First, constitutional rights apply to individuals as individuals and not to groups. If applied to groups, the application derives from their application to individuals. The right to association does not apply only to those individuals who happen to be in associations; other individuals also enjoy this right. It does not apply directly to already existing organizations and apply only indirectly to their individual members as members of the organizations. Rather, the right to association, like any other constitutional right, is a right that *each and every* individual possesses. It is the right to establish organizations and associations which then are

---

(1905) (upholding a vaccination requirement) and *Prince v. Massachusetts,* 321 U.S. 535 (1944) (upholding child labor regulations against parental and religious rights).

It is telling that the *Bowers* Court treats *Prince* as a "privacy case," *Bowers,* 106 S. Ct. at 2843, 2844, on a par with *Griswold,* but fails to mention *Jacobson* as one. This oversight tips the Court's hand. For if it had been consistent and used *Jacobson* as it did *Prince,* it could not possibly have construed the "privacy cases" as only "dealing with," *Bowers,* 106 S. Ct. at 2843, family, marriage, and procreation. For the relevant privacy right in *Jacobson* is a right to control one's body. *Jacobson,* 197 U.S. at 29.

6. 431 U.S. 678 (1977) (held unconstitutional a law barring the advertising and display of contraceptives and the sale of contraceptives to minors).

7. *Bowers,* 106 S. Ct. at 2844.

8. As Justice Harlan had claimed in his famous dissent in *Poe v. Ullman,* 367 U.S. 497, 547–48, 552 (1961) (Harlan, J., dissenting).

derivatively protected because the individuals in them are protected. People both in and out of associations have the same rights. Justice Brennan is on the track of this point in *Eisenstadt:*

> It is true that in *Griswold* the right to privacy in question inhered in the marital relationship. Yet the marital couple is not an independent entity with a mind and heart of its own, but an association of two individuals each with a separate intellectual and emotional makeup. If the right of privacy means anything, it is the right of the *individual,* married or single, to be free from unwarranted governmental intrusion into matters so fundamentally affecting a person as the decision to bear or beget a child.[9]

The right to privacy cannot be contingent upon individuals already being in some sort of relation, like marriage or family, just as the right to association is not contingent upon individuals already being in an association.

Second, in all these cases the right to privacy is a *substantive* right, not merely a procedural right. As a constitutional principle, privacy is like a first amendment right, not a Due Process right. One has occasion to perform the actions protected by first amendment rights (e.g., speaking, printing, going to church) if the state *does nothing,* and even if it does not exist. In contrast, an individual has no occasion to use the procedural rights of, say, the fifth, sixth, or seventh amendments until the state has done something to him, like arresting him.

Now, if privacy inheres only in marriage or legally engendered families, problems instantly arise for this schema. If marriage is viewed as a religious institution, then churches rather than courts properly determine the scope of privacy rights. This determination is unquestionably objectionable.[10] Alternatively, if marriage is viewed as a creature of the state, and if privacy inheres only in marriage, then privacy loses its footing as a substantive right. One would have it only when the state does something, namely, weds one. But one can speak, go to church, and conduct one's private affairs even if the state does not exist. The very nature of substantive rights does not allow substantive privacy rights to inhere in civic marriage. Were marriage viewed as neither a religious nor a state-created relation, but rather essentially as a natural institution, deserving, as a natural right, constitutional protection, then jurisprudence steps

---

9. *Eisenstadt,* 405 U.S. at 453.

10. See *Larkin v. Grendel's Den, Inc.,* 459 U.S. 116 (1982) (Establishment Clause bars the vesting of churches with the power to veto the issuances of liquor licenses).

straight back to the bad old days of Substantive Due Process and of reading into the Constitution whatever natural rights judges find lurking in the cosmos.[11]

As a constitutional principle, the right to marry is coherently understood only as part of the right to privacy and not vice versa. As such, it is a substantive right of *individuals*. Therefore, regulations not only of those who are married but of those who *would* marry are equally highly suspect as impinging on the right to marry. And indeed the two main right-to-marry cases in the last twenty years have correctly dealt not with rights within established marriages but with who may marry. Distinctions in racial mix and wealth among prospective spouses have been declared violations of the right to marry.[12] Yet the Court, standing uncomfortably at odds with these decisions, has refused to see a federal question involved in state bans to certain gender mixes in marriage.[13]

Nor can gay sex be distinguished from acts protected by the privacy decisions by claiming that the decisions protect only what has come to be called "family planning"—the decision *when* to have children. For openers, this claim fails to take into account *Stanley*.[14] One would be hard pressed to claim ingenuously that the right to possess pornography in one's own home, indeed to use it as one's sexual stimulation—even for a lifetime—was essentially a form of family planning. This claim would be mere formalism, a makeweight rationale. But even if granted, this interpretation of *Stanley* would do no harm to the assertion that privacy rights cover homosexual acts. The right to sexual privacy *has not* been doled out on the condition that one *eventually* make babies. Rights to contraceptives are not denied nongay couples who use them over a lifetime, as an alternative to voluntary sterilization. Similarly, viewing a life of exclusively homosexual sex acts bizarrely as an abiding choice not to have children—a sort of homosexual shakerism—should have no effect on the applicability of sexual privacy rights.

Moreover, since either privacy inheres in marriage or marriage in

11. See chapter 3, section VI A.

12. Respectively, *Loving v. Virginia*, 388 U.S. 1 (1967) and *Zablocki v. Redhail*, 434 U.S. 374 (1978).

13. *Baker v. Nelson*, 291 Minn. 310, 191 N.W.2d 185 (1971) (vague statute regulating marriage judicially construed to bar same-sex marriage and, so construed, upheld against Equal Protection challenge), appeal dismissed, 409 U.S. 810 (1972).

14. *Stanley v. Georgia*, 394 U.S. 557 (1969).

privacy, and the former has proven to be false, and since marriage is not morally or legally contingent upon the ability to have children (churches that claim the opposite are now simply laughed at), rights of sexual privacy cannot be viewed as limited simply to the temporary interruption of procreation. Consequently, sexual privacy rights cannot be viewed as limited to heterosexual lifestyles on the ground that they are the only *potentially* procreative ones—if in fact they are.

In any case, the Constitution does not protect lifetimes or even lifestyles. Rather it protects particular instances of actions from legal coercion. As in the case of associations, if a lifestyle is protected, it is so because an individual has rights to perform certain actions; a person does not have a right to perform certain actions because she has a certain lifestyle. When claims are made that marriage is protected, what must be meant is that actions, like weddings and sex acts, not a lifestyle or orientation per se, are protected.

Now, the state may have a legitimate *interest* in promoting reproductive lifestyles, for instance, an interest in providing a steady source of young recruits. But state *interests* do not *define* what rights exist or determine the types of actions protected by those rights. Rather, state interests weigh against the realization or the application in practice, in particular actions, of a right that one possesses. If sufficiently grave, the state interests may override the realization of an individual's right altogether. Therefore, society's interest in reproduction does not then define the scope of privacy, nor does it determine whether homosexual acts are in constitutional terms "private acts." The right to sexual privacy *cannot* be doled out on the condition that one is *eventually* going to make babies.

Further, though the Court has been chary to say so explicitly, the privacy decisions positively protect the right to have sex. It was not *Principia Mathematica* that the Court gave Stanley the right to use in order to gratify his senses and emotions.[15] And people do not buy condoms and morning after pills as *objets d'art*. The contraception cases do not provide simply the *opportunity* not to procreate. For everyone, save women raped by men, have that option through abstinence. Contraceptives are covered by privacy, then, *because* privacy covers in general one's ability to control one's sex life. The rationale for the right to

15. *Ibid.* at 564–65.

purchase contraceptives and own pornography must be derived from the right to *use* them—to guide one's sex life by one's own lights compatible with a like ability on the part of others.

In its currently guiding obscenity cases, the Court has tried unsuccessfully to distinguish *Stanley* from the rest of the line of privacy cases by viewing its protection simply as a "privacy of the home"—"restricted to a place."[16] Indeed, even the four-man dissent in *Bowers* adopts this same approach.[17] This analysis is wrong for two reasons. First, the fact that something occurs in the home does not even presumptively make it substantively protected.[18] It is not four walls that generate substantive protection for an activity. Rather the privacies of the home are those that are integral and distinctive parts of "the life which characteristically has its place in the home."[19] Now, sex does pass this test, while the possession of pornography does not—all the more so, if the possession of pornography is crabbedly viewed merely as part of a right to read, an activity as likely or better carried out at a library, in church or office, or on the Island of La Grande Jatte, and so an activity neither distinctive of nor (unfortunately) integral to the life of the home. Pornography is protected because sex is protected; pornography affords one mode of conducting one's sex life by one's own lights. Such conduct is what *Stanley* should be seen as protecting generally.[20]

16. *Paris Adult Theatre I v. Slaton*, 413 U.S. 49, 66 n.13 (1973) (upholding a bar to movie theatres showing obscene movies).

17. *Bowers*, 106 S. Ct. at 2852–53 (Blackmun, J., dissenting).

18. See chapter 4, section I.

19. *Poe v. Ullman*, 367 U.S. 497, 551 (1961) (Harlan, J., dissenting). Oddly, the four-man dissent in *Bowers* seems to reject this widely adopted test or at least view it as irrelevant, even though it would appear to help their case: "[P]rotecting the physical integrity of the home is more than merely a means of protecting specific activities that often take place there." *Bowers*, 106 S. Ct. at 2852 (Blackmun, J., dissenting).

20. The case also advanced an independent first amendment support for its result—a right to receive information. *Stanley*, 394 U.S. at 564. But this ground has been completely undercut in subsequent obscenity cases, for example, *United States v. Orito*, 413 U.S. 139 (1973) (upholding a federal law prohibiting an individual from transporting obscene materials *even* for private use). *Stanley* survived only as a privacy case up to the *Bowers* era. Nevertheless, the *Bowers* Court tried to distinguish the protection of gay sex from the protection afforded the owner of obscene materials in *Stanley* by claiming that *Stanley* is *only* a first amendment case. *Bowers*, 106 S. Ct. at 2846. This view conveniently overlooks that *Stanley* has been repeatedly cited as precedent for holdings in cases like *Eisenstadt v. Baird*, 405 U.S. 438, 453 (1972) and *Roe v. Wade*, 410 U.S. 113, 152 (1973), cases which could not by any stretch of the imagination be construed as first amendment cases. Further, despite Justice Stewart's claim in *Whalen v. Roe*, 429 U.S. 589, 609 (1977) (Stewart, J.,

Second, if it is the characteristic and distinctive activities of the home, not those that occur behind its four walls, that are protected, then the activities protected by a privacy right based on the home are not limited to the home's four walls. The protected activities travel, just as the rights of marriage may travel "to the hotel room or as otherwise required to safeguard the right to intimacy involved."[21] So the obscenity cases cannot consistently strait-jacket *Stanley* into having advanced a right entirely "restricted to a place."

Therefore, the protection of homosexual acts follows from the force of precedent; it ought not to be limited to the home but be extended to any place where there is a presumption of privacy.

concurring) (upholding drug registration against privacy challenge) that *Stanley* was only a first amendment case, the Court there flatly rejected this view. *Ibid.* at 599 n.25. Times change.

21. *Paris Adult Theatre I,* 413 U.S. at 66 n.13.

PART THREE

The State as Civil Shield

5. Four Millian Arguments for Gay Rights

I. INTRODUCTION: LAW FOR LIBERTY

This chapter provides four clustered arguments justifying the deployment of the coercive powers of the state to protect gays from discrimination in housing, employment, and public accommodations. Currently, protections from discrimination in these areas are provided by the 1964 Civil Rights Act,[1] the 1967 Age Discrimination in Employment Act,[2] the 1968 Fair Housing Act,[3] and the 1973 Rehabilitation Act.[4] These acts bar discrimination on the basis of race, national origin or ethnicity, gender, religion, age, and disability.[5] The arguments here tendered are

1. 42 USCS § 2000.
2. 29 USCS §§ 621 et seq.
3. 42 USCS §§ 3601 et seq.
4. 29 USCS §§ 701 et seq.
5. Gender is not protected in the area of public accommodation, and age and handicap protections cover only employment, and then handicap only in government-funded employment.
    In 1977, by administrative rule, the federal government held that homosexuality was not a handicap—even though the 1973 Rehabilitation Act wisely not only protects conditions that actually are handicaps but also those that are socially perceived to be handicaps. The American Psychiatric Association no longer considers homosexuality a mental illness and so (one might argue) for the purposes of this law homosexuality is not "objectively" a handicap. But the popular mind—as evinced by joke and slang—still clearly perceives homosexuality as a mental illness, and so, whatever the APA or other current mental "scientists" assert, homosexuality ought to be covered by the Rehabilitation Act's provision for the protection of perceived handicap. For the homosexual exclusion, promulgated without analysis by the Carter Administration, see 45 *Code of Federal Regulations*, part 84, appendix A, p. 310 (October 1, 1985 edition).

general with respect to the classes they would protect, though frequently they have a special application to gays as the result of the peculiar ways in which gays are socially treated and in particular because of the socially enforced closetude of most gays.

Throughout the long history of the enactment of the Civil Rights Act, from its original introduction in Congress with but one sponsor in 1942 to its final passage twenty-two years later, there was very little popular debate or even critical argumentation over its justifications. Popular support for the Act never got beyond the vaguest claims about the right thing or the righteous thing to do. And so sure were the Act's opponents that Southern Democrats could stall the bill into eternity by appeal to its *form*—an alleged violation of "states' rights"—that no one bothered advancing against the bill reasoned arguments that were tied to the *content* of the bill's provisions. In particular, no one advanced arguments of a libertarian stripe: no one claimed that it was not a proper function of government to coerce what businesses might do by limiting their ability to decide whom to hire and serve.[6] This style of argument, of course, was inconsistent with the obstructionist states' rights ploy, which implied that states might indeed properly pass such laws, just not the federal government.

So little discussed were the Act's provisions that women ended up being included under its employment protections as the result of a joke that backfired: A congressman, in an attempt to defeat the whole Act, offered an amendment adding women to the Act's list of protected classes, thinking this would either wake people up to the Act's true evil or at least throw so much flak into the path of the Act's liberal proponents, who were divided over the issue of women's inclusion, that its passage would be fatally disrupted. The motion, offered basically as a "dumb blonde" joke—and indeed greeted on the House floor with open laughter—became federal law, and in so doing was more influential in launching the women's movement as we now know it than the women's movement (fledgling at best in 1964) was in passing the chief law that protects women. Indeed it has stood them in better stead than the black men it was chiefly aimed at aiding.[7] Conversely, Jews, who were strongly

6. See Paul Burstein, *Discrimination, Jobs, and Politics: The Struggle for Equal Employment Opportunity in the United States since the New Deal* (Chicago: University of Chicago Press, 1985), p. 107.

7. See *ibid.*, pp. 23, 95. On the positive effects of the Civil Rights Act on women's

interested in, supportive of, and instrumental in the Act's passage, have, as it turns out, not had much occasion to use its provisions.[8] Political ironies played a more important role in the passage of the Act than did political ideas.

As America enters into an era of aggressive deregulation and begins to reexamine the role of free enterprise in society, it might well be worth examining what may be said generally for business restraint in this limited area—worth giving the arguments that no one thought to or bothered to, or perhaps could, give for civil rights legislation in 1964.

The arguments advanced here appeal for their motor concepts to the norms, dignity, self-sufficiency, general prosperity, and individual flourishing. The arguments will suggest that the passage of civil rights legislation is one of the rare occasions when government regulation can promote rather than destroy the conditions under which individuals develop and carry out their distinctive plans. The arguments are loosely inspired by the third and fourth chapters (especially the former) of John Stuart Mill's *On Liberty*, respectively entitled "Of Individuality, As One of the Elements of Well-Being" and "Of the Limits to the Authority of Society over the Individual."[9]

Now at first blush, Mill might seem an odd source for justifying state coercion. For usually and correctly Mill is thought of as the classical champion of *restrictions* on government powers as the chief mode of keeping in check the tyranny of the majority, and so in turn of promoting personal liberty. Constitutional immunities are the chief institutional check on such tyranny. Mill's constitutional principle holds that government may not protect individuals from themselves; it may properly restrict people only from harming others, where "harming" means that some distinct right of a specifiable individual is violated.[10] Mill, though, is thoroughly aware that the tyranny of the majority is not limited to the results of coercive social forces set in motion by tallies at the ballot box. He knows that even customs and conventions which do not register in law but which nonetheless are both socially pervasive and personally intrusive also tyrannize individuals. Indeed, at least in respect to freedom

employment, see *ibid.*, pp. 173, 175, 191–92. See also, Andrea H. Beller, "The Effects of Title VII of the Civil Rights Act of 1964 on Women's Entry into Nontraditional Occupations: An Economic Analysis," *Law and Inequality* (1983) 1:73–83.

8. See Burstein, *Discrimination*, pp. 7, 191–92.

9. John Stuart Mill, *On Liberty*, Elizabeth Rapaport, ed., (Indianapolis: Hackett, 1978).

10. Mill, *On Liberty*, chapter 4, especially pp. 73, 79.

of thought and expression, he thinks that social custom is an even more severe source of illegitimate restriction on liberty than is law.[11]

Mill, though, tells us little or nothing of how the tyranny of social custom which does not take the form of statute is to be confronted and overcome, though his strong promotion of freedom for the development and expression of ideas might help some. He never discusses what we would call civil rights legislation. (When *On Liberty* was published, in 1859, slavery was still a going concern on this side of the Atlantic; with that reality yet to be socially attended, it is perhaps understandable that Mill would not have thought so far down the pike of the future.) Constitutional immunities alone do little good in addressing social as opposed to governmental tyranny. For such immunities, as protections against government, do not even target the relevant source of oppression —The People—and so at best have indirect effects on social oppression, as is the case with first amendment protections for thought and speech. I wish to suggest that a chief means by which such nonlegal social tyranny can be overcome is through carefully justified and narrowly circumscribed legislation of the sort found in the 1964 Civil Rights Act.

Pure libertarians—who hold that the sole purposes of government are the defense of property and persons from theft and assault, and the enforcement of contracts, and so who see no occasion for the justifiable state coercion of relations between persons—may shriek, but I wish to suggest that the values of dignity, self-determination, and individual flourishing by which the libertarian's hero Mill defends his anti-paternalistic constitutional principle and the right of individuals to associate freely can actually sometimes be promoted by law, rather than always squelched by it. The conditions of individual flourishing required for his anti-paternalistic stance warrant more government action than the state merely serving as a night watchman who is called to active duty only when people's interactions are not wholly voluntary, are not mediated only by mutual consent. Paradoxically, certain very limited forms of state actions are required as the necessary preconditions for those very features of human experience that warrant general restraints on government. So if it turns out that, given certain social realities, civil rights legislation is in fact a necessary background condition for dignity, self-worth, self-sufficiency, the pursuit of happiness, and individual flourish-

11. Mill, *On Liberty*, chapter 2, especially pp. 29–31; for discussion see chapter 6, section III below.

ing, then civil rights legislation as coercive is justified by the very principles by which one would want to claim that government coercion is, in general, barred: that the individual knows better and is better situated than the government to get what is good for herself. This paradoxical arrangement, however, contains no contradictory elements. Such limited restraint for the sake of general nonrestraint here operates in much the same way that certain narrow restraints necessarily encumber democratic government, say, its ability to limit the franchise, if democracy is, in certain ways, to be justified as a general mode of government operation, say, justified as registering the popular will.

So quite generally, if my four arguments on the relation of civil rights legislation to individual well-being are sound, then such legislation can be justified both as a necessary precursor to the operations of the Millian constitutional principle and as a brake needed in Mill's system against nongovernmental social tyranny.

Such legislation can also be justified, though, as a remedy to direct violations of Mill's constitutional principle—properly understood. When an employer in his hiring practices discriminates against members of some group without regard to its members' individual merits or the requirements of the job, the employer is rarely indulging a whim. He is not typically aiming to gratify a personal desire to be arbitrary. His actions are whimsical and arbitrary when measured against the requirements of the job and the attributes of the applicant, but his actions are far from random or accidental from his own perspective. By so discriminating he is living out an ideology that holds certain types of individuals in contempt. He fails to show other individuals respect. The right of individuals to respect as an equal is not limited to immunities against government. It is a moral right at least on a par with the moral right not to be lied to. The right violated by the employer is clear and distinct and it is aways assignable since it is always some particular applicant that is rejected. The harm is not merely hypothetical, nor only statistically inferred.

Now, admittedly one does not usually think (and Mill does not require)[12] that the violation of each and every moral right should automatically trigger state coercion. The violation simply means that a threshold requirement for state coercion has been crossed, but many violations of rights are best handled by social opprobrium rather than

12. Mill, *On Liberty*, p. 73.

state coercion. Most lying, though a violation of its target's right to respect as an agent with plans of her own, is not thought to warrant state coercion. If, for instance, you negotiate a date with me in bad faith, I do not get to sue you for carfare when you fail to show at the agreed-upon meeting place.

Two factors, though, weigh in favor of treating violations against rights to treatment as an equal of the sort remedied in civil rights legislation not only as justified possible concerns of the state but also as evils of a degree and kind which the state should actively be engaged in remedying. First, it is exactly in the area of business dealings that people think that violation of rights ought to trigger state coercion. Lying in a business deal is considered actionable fraud. Therefore, though not every private insult to an individual that violates his desert for equal respect ought to engage state coercion, such disrespect in the business world, the world of public functions, should. If someone shouts "hey, nigger" at me from a speeding car, the shout is an insult, yet it is socially mitigated by the publicly perceivable cowardliness of the shouter and ought, in any case, to be protected by free speech rights. But if I, on the same grounds, am turned away with my family from a hotel lobby, the insult hurled at me because I am black is publicly affirmed; the social convention, not merely a personal insult, of racism is affirmed. In that circumstance, permissible state coercion should be actualized in law and is not trumped by any free speech consideration.[13] Where insult and disrespect

13. Unfortunately, gays, like some other traditionally oppressed groups, have shown an alarming tendency, when they get civil rights protections, to turn around and try to use them to violate other people's rights to free speech. The best known example is the lesbian and gay male majority on the city council of recently incorporated West Hollywood, California. In 1985 they used a gay rights ordinance they had just passed to force Barney's Beanery to remove a sign which had been posted there since 1933 and which read "Fagots [sic] Stay Out." The owner, under the city's threat of a civil fine, caved in and removed the sign simply to avoid the cost of prolonged, expensive, and divisive court battles. See *The Advocate* [Los Angeles], February 19, 1985, no. 414, p. 17. Those who claim that the sign's three words effectively prohibited gays from entering *even when* gays had knowledge that they could not be prohibited by the owner from entering can make out their claim only by having it layered over rather thickly with an unfortunate paternalism that views gays as mental and moral weaklings.

On another sad day for ideas, gays at Yale University managed, at least temporarily, to have a sophomore suspended for his posting antigay broadsides satirizing the campus' Gay Pride Week—a violation, so it was alleged, of the University's sexual harassment regulations. See "Yale Professors Backing Sophomore," *The New York Times*, September 28,

socially perpetuate further violations of the right to equal respect, state action is particularly well motivated. And this will almost always be the case in the public world of business, public accommodations, and housing.

Second, when animosity against a group is widespread, absent will be the social opprobrium that might usually be relied upon to address violations of moral rights sufficiently, as is the case with most lying. If you stand me up, word of that stand up may well get around and by your own actions you will have hurt your reputation and perhaps prospects for future dates with others. But if you insult me by not hiring me because I'm black in a world that is most often racist, the violation of my right will have little hope of rectification through usual moral forces in society. Therefore where violations of equal respect appeal to the socially despised status of some group, remedies through state actions will again be particularly well supported.

Therefore, direct appeal to Mill's principle will justify civil rights legislation if only one acknowledges that individuals have a right to equal respect and that this is a general moral right, not limited in its application just against government. Certain social realities will then warrant taking the violation of the right as a proper occasion for state coercion. The public nature of employment and the characteristics of discrimination which appeals to a socially despised group's status are two such sufficient social realities.

Where Mill is right and libertarians wrong is in his distinguishing and their collapsing two sorts of paternalism. Both Mill and the libertarian would reject a paternalism which holds that someone other than the individual—usually the state—knows better than the individual what is good for the individual and so is justified in imposing his "real," but unrecognized, best interests upon him—as upon a child. Where Mill and libertarians part ways is over a paternalism which does not claim to know better than the individual what is best for the individual, but which claims that the individual is sometimes unable on his own, even through maximum good efforts, to get what he reasonably wants and

1986, p. Y15. Gays are being naïve if they think that allowing sexual harassment codes to be used in this way will not also result in the codes' use against gays' speech. On sexual harassment codes as phony neutral rules, see below chapter 14. For cautionary notes on cases in which gay litigants try to protect their rights by inhibiting the speech of others, see Paul Siegel, "Lesbian and Gay Rights as a Free Speech Issue: A Review of Relevant Caselaw," *Journal of Homosexuality* (1988) vol. 15, in press.

might well be expected to get—but for circumstance. In this latter case, especially when the thing sought is constitutive of dignity or otherwise central to his well-being, one is correctly tempted to say that there is a role for the state to assist him, particularly when the imposition the state places on others in order for him to achieve dignity and well-being violates no rights of theirs and is inconsequential to their happiness. In these tightly circumscribed conditions, government provision is not demeaning nor condescending—the most objectionable features of objectionable paternalism—nor is it even likely inadvertently to promote these features in the long run, though constant vigilance is required to make sure that the proper motivating conditions do obtain for state coercion and that acceptable assistance does not in fact mask or degenerate into objectionable paternalism as many conservatives now argue is the case with welfare programs in the United States. But only an examination of actual social circumstances and individuals' experience as lived, not an *a priori* survey of human nature, can determine whether proper motivating conditions or seeds of degeneration obtain.

With a robust sense of the dangers of the state, as evinced in the preceding three chapters, I now turn to the four specific arguments warranting state coercion in the form of civil rights legislation as a means of promoting rather than destroying individual liberty. Indeed, to the extent that the arguments have particular application to gays for relief from the current tyranny of social custom, the arguments may in fact be collectively taken as a sort of case study for the general hypothesis that civil, and not merely criminal, law is sometimes a prerequisite for liberty.

II. DIGNITY IN AMERICA

Civil rights legislation, in important ways, promotes human dignity. The 1964 Civil Rights Act was passed out of the Senate *Commerce* Committee rather than, say, the Senate Judiciary Committee. The Commerce Committee, their nominal mandate notwithstanding, thought that the chief justification for the legislation was its promotion of individual dignity rather than some value properly promoted under the Interstate Commerce Clause. Regarding the Act's public accommodation provisions, the Committee claimed that the Act was not chiefly aimed at placing the travel of blacks, for instance, in the same category of possible legislative concerns as, say, the movement of cattle, fruit, coal, and steel across state lines, but rather was aimed at remedying "the deprivation of personal dignity that surely accompanies denials of equal access to public establishments."[14] The Senate Committee elaborated: "[I]n order to assure that the institution of private property serves the end of individual freedom and liberty, it has been restricted in many instances. The most striking example of this is the abolition of slavery."[15] The Committee though did not spell out its analogy between civil rights legislation and state-mandated emancipation. Instead it quickly moved on to claim that civil rights legislation is, in any case, not a very great intrusion into the affairs of business. This claim is true but irrelevant to the Committee's assertion about dignity. Can the Senate's assertion about dignity be made out? Can the Civil Rights Act be defended as proceeding in the same general moral orbit as the thirteenth amendment's abolition of slavery? I think so. For it reduces the circumstances in which a person may simply be a thing to or for another, while it makes possible and enhances the prospects that persons lead self-determining lives.

No one can have much self-respect nor can maintain a solid sense of self, if he is, in major ways affecting himself, subjected to whimsical and arbitrary actions by others and to the effective insults which such actions evince. Jobs, entertainments, and housing are major modes through which people identify themselves to themselves. Indeed in modern culture, after personal relationships and perhaps (for some) religion, it is jobs and housing that are probably the *chief* means by which people identify themselves to themselves and to others. Jobs are central to a person's conception of himself. A large but largely unrecognized, part of the misery of unemployment is not merely poverty and social embarrassment but also a sense of loss of that by which one identifies oneself to

14. *Senate Report* No. 872, 88th Congress, 2d Session (1964), pp. 16–17. Notwithstanding the Senate Report and the legislative history of the act more generally, the Supreme Court upheld the constitutionality of the Act only under Congress' powers to regulate interstate commerce and ducked the still unresolved issue of whether the enabling section of the fourteenth amendment gives Congress the power to promote equality in the private sector. *Heart of Atlanta Motel, Inc. v. United States,* 379 U.S. 241 (1964). In his concurrence, Justice Douglas thought this a needlessly timid way of proceeding, a way which in fact insulted blacks by tending to view them as commodities rather than as persons, and left open the possibility that many businesses might eventually be judicially construed as falling outside the stream of interstate commerce and so of the reach of the Civil Rights Act. *Ibid.* at 279 (Douglas, J., concurring).

15. *Senate Report* No. 872, pp. 22–23.

oneself, a loss which many people also experience upon retirement, even when their income and social esteem are left intact. People thrown out of jobs frequently compare this loss to that of a family member—in particular to the loss of a child.[16] Here the comparison is not simply to the intensity of the emotion caused by the loss, but to the nature of the loss: what was lost was a central means by which one constituted one's image of oneself.

Jobs also are the chief means by which people identify themselves to others. Indeed one's job is tantamount to one's social identity. Socially one finds out who a person is by finding out what she or he does. In normal social discourse, as at parties, asking after a person's job is the first substantive thing that one asks a person to whom one has been introduced. The singular exception to this social pattern is gay culture, in which it is considered a gross violation of etiquette to ask after a recently acquired acquaintance's place or even line of employment. Such perturbation of normal social discourse is, of course, a product, and a reinforcement through accepting acknowledgment, of the closeted status of gays, and should itself be taken as attesting to the breadth of discrimination against them and to its evil effects.[17] America is not a nation of

16. See Dorothy Gilliam, "Losing More Than a Job," *The Washington Post*, October 14, 1985, p. C3.

17. For empirical studies of the extent of employment discrimination against homosexuals, see Martin P. Levine and Robin Leonard, "Discrimination against Lesbians in the Work Force" in Estelle Freedman, et al., eds., *The Lesbian Issue: Essays from Signs* (Chicago: University of Chicago Press, 1984), pp. 700–10 and Martin P. Levine, "Employment Discrimination against Gay Men," *International Review of Modern Sociology* (July–December 1979) 9(5–7):151–63.

The most striking gay employment discrimination study, though, has been conducted by the American Sociological Association, which asked university department heads whether they thought they could hire an openly gay professor:

Sixty-three percent of the heads and chairs reported that hiring a known homosexual would produce serious problems or that it just could not be done. Difficulty in hiring gay rights' advocates is seen as being even more difficult; 84 percent of the heads and chairs said it would bring serious difficulty or could not be done. The proportion of heads and chairs who perceive barriers in promoting homosexuals also is high, 48 percent for promoting known homosexuals, 65 percent for promoting activists.

Among those most widely viewed as disapproving [of] homosexuals are the campus gatekeepers: recruitment/promotion committees (55%), higher administration personnel (63%), and trustees (74%).

Joan Huber, et al., "Report of the American Sociological Association's Task Group on Homosexuality," *The American Sociologist* (August 1982) 17(3):164. It comes as no surprise then that virtually all gays and lesbians in academe, especially graduate students,

contemplators and thinkers. It is a nation of doers. When job discrimination is directed at gays, it is a way of branding them as essentially un-American, as The Alien. It is a chief mode of expatriation and alienation from the national experience, imaging federal policies excluding gays from immigration and the armed forces.

Discrimination in housing similarly affects one's identification by and to others. Physical separation from and enforced concentration apart from the dominant social group are among the chief social means of marking a group as morally inferior, worthy of less respect, unclean, or even threatening—like prisoners or untouchables. Housing discrimination against a despised group is apartheid writ small, but not small enough to be morally acceptable.

Discrimination in housing also affects one's self-perception. It perhaps goes without saying that the conversion of a house into a home is one of the main ways that people identify themselves to themselves. Blocking or arbitrarily restricting the material basis of this conversion inhibits the development of self-respect and selectively disrupts the sanctities of private life. The common expression "keeping up with the Joneses," even in its mild censure or irony, attests to the role of housing in the way people identify themselves to themselves, in part, through the eyes of others. To be denied housing on the basis of some group status is a chief social mode of ostracism and exile.

That these major vehicles of character, personality, and identity can be taken away from a person without regard to any characteristic that is relevant to his possessing the vehicle is an outrage against personal integrity that deserves remedies from the state. To deny someone a job or to fire an employee on the basis of some characteristic that has no bearing on his ability to carry out the requirements of his job is one of the most sophisticated ways by which one can degrade a person or make him feel worthless. An employer who does so acts irrationally from the perspective of economic self-interest. This irrationality, though, makes the discrimination all the worse. For it means that what the discriminator is doing in his discriminating is expressing those of his values that are not for sale, his sacred values.[18] These values call for self-sacrifice. The discriminator is willing to sacrifice his economic well-being, as in a

---

are deeply in the closet, and even nongays studiously avoid doing gay research, lest they be viewed as gay. *Ibid.*, pp. 169–72.

18. For a discussion of sacred values, see chapter 10.

tithe, for the sake of his ideology—his commitment, say, to white or heterosexual supremacy. The protection which the nation has given religion from job discrimination correctly signals that damaging the dignity and hampering, in major ways, the lifeplans of others is not a proper channel for the symbolic expression of such ideological values. The sacred ideologist may express his values in religion, in private life, and in politics; and he may speak of them in any way he wants. But in his actions, though he may sacrifice his own dollars for the sake of these values, he may not properly sacrifice other people to them.

Looking for work and looking for a place to live are two of the most emotionally draining, anxiety-laden, fear-inspiring activities of life. Even in good times and societies, they are fraught with the prospect of humiliating and belittling treatment. For in these activities the sense that one is standing in judgment is all consuming. One feels exposed, stripped of the buffers of everyday patterns and familiarities. In these conditions, with their heightened sensitivity for insult, it is all the more important that indignities that can be screened away should be screened away.

Conversely, losing a job frequently turns on largely non-task-related factors, like personality conflicts, politics, or even changing times. Such sources of insecurity and the disquietude of spirit and dislocations of personality that attend it are bad enough on their own, without being further aggravated by worries that one is going to be the vehicle and victim of someone's motivation to insult a group of which one is a random example. Again here, indignities should, if indignities can, be kept from compounding already painful, already humiliating circumstance. The bigot ought not be allowed to act like the torturer who fills his victim's final gasp with piss.

Given widespread discrimination (actual or merely threatened) against gays in employment, housing, and other major modes of self-identity, it is not surprising that gays manifest many of the same self-destructive, self-deluding, self-oppressing patterns of behavior shared by other historically oppressed minorities.[19] The threat of job discrimination pre-

19. For a comparison of black, Jewish, and gay coping mechanisms, especially self-oppression, developed in response to widespread discrimination, see Barry Adam's excellent *The Survival of Domination: Inferiorization in Everyday Life* (New York: Elsevier, 1978), on gay self-oppression, see Adam's chapter 4; see also Andrew Hodges and David Hutter, *With Downcast Gays: Aspects of Homosexual Self-Oppression*, 2d ed. (1974; Toronto: Pink Triangle Press, 1979).

vents gays from having a properly moderate attitude toward employment.

On the one hand, gays frequently respond to the threat of employment discrimination by becoming workaholics. The reasons for overheatedly throwing themselves into their work are various. Their work becomes a mask by which they divert others from examining them too closely, while it serves as a distraction for themselves, to keep them from thinking too much about their own circumstance, lest they discover how awful it really is. Further, many are driven by a half-conscious belief that if they just show themselves productive enough, worthy enough, good enough, they will overcome the invisible stigma that lurks within them waiting to suppurate. But one can never work that hard, can never be that productive. The result of such misguided hyperactivities typically is further alienation from self and others.

On the other hand, many gays underidentify with their jobs. A sense that they have no security at the job prevents them from giving it a proper degree of commitment, a proper link to self, so they often engage in self-defeating behavior which results in poor performance and converts society's estimate of their capacities into a self-fulfilling prophecy. On either hand—whether the job becomes a mask or an occasion for failure—gay people are barred from experiencing their vocation as a mainstay of their existence and identity.

When gays are denied dignity through the usual social means to it, they contortedly seek it from other sources, from God or from worship of the dominant culture itself, and so become agents in their own oppression. It is not unusual for large companies to hire a personnel manager whose homosexuality is an open secret and to use him to keep "the fags" out. So pervasive is the social mangling of gay consciousness that closet cases, or more precisely homosexuals committed to the values of the dominant culture about homosexuality, are the most vicious oppressors of gays because the most pointed in their oppressing. They are like the Jewish police in the Polish ghettos during the holocaust. These police were more brutal in their handling of Jews than were the Nazis, who in their forced labor camps also found that the best prison guards were prisoners themselves. The mechanics of humiliation are quite capable of magnifying, multiplying, and perpetuating themselves by commandeering their victims to do their bidding. This capacity for the viral-like spread of indignity through the body politic makes it all the more important that such indignity should be ended as near its beginning as possible.

If, as here argued, the Senate Commerce Committee was right in seeing the protection of dignity as the chief justification for the Civil Rights Act, then a moral puzzle remains: why did Congress provide such meager legal remedies (somewhere between feeble and sickly) for discrimination? Injunctive relief is the only remedy available against discrimination in public accommodations. A judge may order a discriminator to stop the practice of excluding protected classes from his accommodation and hold him in contempt of court if he does not stop. But the victim of the discrimination gets nothing at all. The employment protections of Title VII also provide for injunctive relief. In addition, they provide for equitable relief—that is, the victim of discrimination can sue for what she or he would have gotten but for the discrimination, basically back pay and seniority (though only if that does not disrupt the seniority system itself). The victim may not seek compensatory or consequential damages to make him whole for losses caused by his loss of job, say, his subsequent loss of housing or family. And he may not seek punitive or exemplary damages. Yet if discrimination assaults dignity and is carried out intentionally or wantonly (as it is in virtually all gay cases), then the rationales for punitive damages apply in full force.[20]

20. Not all violations of the Civil Rights Act require a showing of intention to discriminate in order to establish the existence of illegal discrimination. Tests, hiring criteria, and the like which tend to exclude disproportionately or have a disparate impact against protected groups have also been held to violate Title VII if they cannot be shown to predict job performance accurately. *Griggs v. Duke Power Co.*, 401 U.S. 424 (1971) (requirement of possessing a high school diploma or passing standardized intelligence tests ruled violative of Title VII as having a disparate impact against black applicants without bearing closely on job performance). Most Title VII cases now are such "disparate impact" cases. By their very nature, disparate impact cases turn on the use of statistical arguments. Statistical arguments are also useful in establishing intentional discrimination. See Elaine Shoben, "The Use of Statistics To Prove Intentional Employment Discrimination," *Law and Contemporary Problems* (1983) 46(4):221–45.

Recent Congressional formulations of enforcement provisions for proposed federal gay civil rights protections exclude (at least some) uses of statistics to establish discrimination against gays: "No amendment made by this Act shall be construed to permit or require . . . the determination that discrimination exists to be based on any statistical differences in the incidence of persons of a particular affectional or sexual orientation in the general population as opposed to in the activity wherein such discrimination is alleged." "Civil Rights Act Amendments of 1987," *Congressional Record*, January 22, 1987, p. E211. Such a way of proceeding shows a gross ignorance of how discrimination cases are litigated

Exemplary damages are typically awarded in civil cases where the wrong done is aggravated by circumstances not only of violence or fraud but also of oppression, malice, or wanton disregard. The damages are intended to solace the plaintiff for "mental anguish, laceration of his feelings, shame, [and] degradation."[21] Criminal penalties might be morally appropriate in job discrimination cases, but are legally ill-advised, for they would require a standard of evidence—"beyond a reasonable doubt"—that would rarely be met in discrimination cases. Such cases are hard enough to litigate successfully even with the most relaxed standard of evidence—mere "preponderance of the evidence"—the standard that is used in civil rights cases.[22]

III. SELF-SUFFICIENCY

There is a general expectation in a nonsocialist, noncommunist society like our own that each person is primarily responsible for meeting his own basic needs and that the government becomes an active provider only when all else fails. I take it as a largely noncontroversial moral recognition that people ought to have their basic needs met. If argument for the recognition is needed, one can point out that meeting basic needs is a necessary material condition for one to carry out one's lifeplan, and so fulfillment of these needs is warranted up to the point at which the mechanics of their fulfillment defeat the very purposes for which they are met. If one aims in one's political theory at enhancing those conditions in which people are able to carry out their lifeplans in ways

---

and is little more than a sop to conservatives—one unlikely to be successful at that, but one likely to fix the final wording of future proposals. On the tendency of legislative language to calcify in the early stages of considering civil rights statutes—the power of the first draft—see Burstein, *Discrimination*, pp. 36–38, 94. If ever enacted, the bar on the use of statistical arguments as evidence of antigay discrimination may well have the effect of closing the barndoor before the horses are out.

21. See *Black's Law Dictionary*, 5th ed. (St. Paul: West, 1979), s.v. damages.

22. Title VII also allows for the recovery of "reasonable" lawyers' fees. Title VII cases typically drag on for years and years. In successful cases, lawyers' fees are virtually always higher than the equitable relief afforded by the Act. The morally dubious and legislatively unforeseen result is that lawyers' fees, which the Supreme Court has held are "reasonable" in civil rights cases even if calculated on an hourly basis rather than on a fixed percent of the take, are usually so high that they *de facto* serve as actual or threatened punitive damages directed against the employer who does or would discriminate. Such damages, of course, though, provide nothing to the victim of discrimination. On lawyers' fees, see *City of Riverside v. Rivera*, 106 S. Ct. 2686 (1986).

compatible with each other, then enhancing the conditions under which basic needs are met will be a high governmental priority and all the more capable of realization the less coercion its mechanics themselves place on lifeplans. Quite low, however, is the level at which government coercion directed at fulfilling needs reaches a point of diminished returns from the freedom which their fulfillment aims to enhance.

History should teach that the more government personnel are involved in fulfilling the domestic purposes of government, the more likely liberty is destroyed. In particular—as the Wannsee Conference and its efflorescences should have shown, and if not that any academic hierarchy would do—bureaucrats and administrators destroy freedom more thoroughly than do the police; for they are so much more pervasive in their meddling, penetrating in their probing, and avid in their pursuits. Explosion-accelerated lead may be the most effective way to kill the body, but committees—requiring, as they do, being nice to evil—are the most effective way to kill the soul. Administrators and administrative law grind down people more than tyrants and criminal law ever could. Bureaucrats are the shock troops of convention; committees the weak acids where individualism is inexorably dissolved and dispersed into community values.

Consider Barbara James. She received public aid to feed her child who otherwise had no source of food. When she declined to let the welfare brigades rummage through her apartment looking for evidence of child abuse and fraud—though there was no probable cause or even reasonable suspicion to believe that she was abusing her child or defrauding the state—the government cut off the child's food money. In 1971, the Supreme Court said it was all right for the government to so cut. For (1) the rummaging was not a search, (2) if it were a search, it was a reasonable one, and (3) even if it were an unreasonable search, by accepting the food money for her child, the mother had voluntarily waived any right against unreasonable searches—and all this at the heighth of the Court's liberal trajectory.[23] What the police could not have begun to think to do, socialist bureaucracy did with impunity. Two years later seven justices would hold that Ms. James' privacy would have warranted her killing the fetus that became her child,[24] but only three justices thought that she was warranted in feeding her child in private.

23. *Wyman v. James,* 400 U.S. 309 (1971).
24. *Roe v. Wade,* 410 U.S. 113 (1973) (held abortion covered by the right to privacy).

This state action and court case do not constitute a record which suggests that socialism and civil liberties are compatible—even where civil liberties are rather robust. Part of the problem here, of course, is that America finds it hard to see that America does not consider poor people to be real people.[25] But this is a problem unlikely to be addressed anytime soon, and not in any case with piecemeal and conflicting social programs that never quite return the poor to the position of being credible players in capitalist games.

Given all this, there is a highly desirable *tertium quid* between, on the one hand, pure laissez-faire, which holds out the prospect that some needs will go unattended and, on the other hand, rank socialism, which history has shown is incompatible with a robust sense of civil liberties because of the bureaucracy it necessarily entails. The middle way, which helps avoid both the failure of pure capitalism to meet needs and the tangles in the socialist's safety-net, is civil rights legislation. For it is chiefly through employment, in conjunction with access to certain public accommodations and housing, that people meet not only their needs for continued biological existence—those for food, shelter, and clothing— but also those culturally relative needs for the material and social conditions that are necessary to maintain people as credible agents in the going political, social, and economic systems. Civil rights legislation then helps people discharge their obligation to be self-sufficient in meeting their basic biological needs and the conditions for human agency. And it does so without placing any comparable burden on those who are restricted by the legislation (employers, retailers, and the like).

While civil rights regulations limit with whom one makes contracts, it does not limit at all the content of contracts. Compared with zoning ordinances, which thoroughly regulate the "what, where, when, how and why" of business, civil rights law is as nothing. Even in regulating the "who" of contracts, the law only screens out the use of non-job-related properties of prospective employees. Intelligence, character, talent, skill, and experience are all still legitimate business concerns left untouched by the Civil Rights Act. Civil rights legislation, then, does not limit the right *of* contract at all and it only shaves a sliver off the right *to* contract.

25. See *San Antonio Independent School Dist. v. Rodriguez,* 411 U.S. 1 (1973) (held that education is not a fundamental right and the poor are not a class deserving enhanced equal protections).

If gays were only barred from buying rocks at Tiffany's, eating truffles at "21," and holding seats on boards of trade, their inclusion under the Civil Rights Act on the grounds discussed in this section would not be very compelling. And indeed America holds a stereotype of gays as wealthy, frivolous, selfish, conspicuous consumers, and based on this stereotype some people claim that gays are not in need of civil rights protections. This stereotype has unfortunately been given a boost by the gay press itself, which, in a desperate but largely unsuccessful attempt to lure mainstream advertisers, conducts and reports on non-random, self-selecting, self-reporting, and so unverifiable surveys of their readers' incomes and buying habits. In Cuba and other Stalinist countries, this stereotype has been used to forge an alleged biconditional causal link between homosexuality and capitalism.[26] But the stereotype is a false one. Kinsey found more male homosexual behavior among the lower classes and the uneducated than among the wealthy and college educated.[27]

One of the little-sung heroes of the gay movement is John F. Singer. On June 26, 1972, Singer was fired from the Equal Employment Opportunity Commission—the government agency charged with enforcing federal civil rights legislation in America. He was fired for being gay. His case would take six years in front of courts and administrative panels before he was vindicated. Along the way it helped force the federal government to change its administrative policies toward gays in civil service jobs. When fired, he held the position of ribbon clerk.[28]

26. See Allen Young, *Gays Under the Cuban Revolution* (San Francisco: Grey Fox Press, 1981), chapters 1, 2, 5, 6.

27. For Kinsey on occupational and educational levels of those who engage in homosexual behavior, see Alfred Kinsey, et al., *Sexual Behavior in the Human Male* (Philadelphia: Saunders, 1948), pp. 357–62, 382–84.

28. *Singer v. United States Civil Service Commission*, 530 F.2d 247 (9th Cir. 1976), vacated, 429 U.S. 1034 (1977). On Singer, see Rhonda R. Rivera, "Recent Developments in Sexual Preference Law," *Drake Law Review* (1980–1981) 30(2):317–19, and "Our Straight-Laced Judges: The Legal Position of Homosexual Persons in the United States," *Hastings Law Journal* (1979) 30:822–23. Rivera observes and speculates: "It is interesting to note that the cases reviewed in this section [on government employment] mainly focus on clerks, typists, and janitors. Somehow one cannot help wondering why managers, lawyers, and other professionals are not the plaintiffs? Is it because only the relatively powerless are discharged under these [antigay] statutes and regulations? Or are higher ranking officials given the chance to resign rather than face dismissal?" (p. 822, n.135).

IV. GENERAL PROSPERITY

Civil rights legislation is also justified as promoting the general welfare. Such legislation tends to increase the overall production of goods and services in society, thus contributing to general prosperity. Perhaps the potentially wide appeal of this justification for civil rights legislation, paired with a perceived general lack of social sympathy for gays or perhaps even an inability of society to see gays as loci of dignity, has led Congressional sponsors of gay rights legislation to press this utilitarian justification as the main reason why they do and others should support their bill: gay rights are good for everyone.[29]

Civil rights legislation has the effect of maximizing social benefits chiefly in three ways. First, by eliminating extraneous factors in employment decisions, civil rights legislation promotes an optimal fit between a worker's capacities, talents, and skills and the bona fide occupational qualifications of his prospective work. Both the particular worker and her employer are advantaged, because a worker is most productive when her talents and the requirements of her job mesh. Across the business community as a whole, such legislation further enhances the prospects that talent does not go wasting and jobs are not filled by second bests.

Now, the Civil Rights Act allows, as it should, for exemptions from its provisions in cases where discriminations against an otherwise protected category can be shown to be necessary for the normal operation of a business. Discriminations in good faith are permitted.[30] But this exempting mechanism means that businesses cannot argue against civil rights legislation on the ground that they know better than Congress ever could what is good for business and so that businesses are more

29. For example, they point out: "A study by the National Institute of Mental Health . . . showed that over 16 percent of all gay people in this country have employment problems and over 9 percent lose their jobs solely because of their sexual orientation. . . . This [loss] robs the community of that individual's talents and productivity." *Congressional Record*, October 6, 1981, p. S11154, mentioning John M. Livingood, ed., *National Institute of Mental Health Task Force on Homosexuality: Final Report and Background Papers* (Rockville, Maryland: NIMH, 1972), p. 7, n.6. Subsequently congressional sponsors have dropped even this argument and instead have taken simply to cataloguing names of groups that support gay rights, oddly forgetting perhaps the forces their opponents might marshall in this same regard. See, for example, *Congressional Record*, January 22, 1987, p. E210.

30. For discussion of this provision and for an analysis of arguments which attempt to show that discrimination against gays is discrimination in good faith, see chapter 7.

likely to maximize productivity if free of government restraints than if bound by civil rights legislation. For if a business can show that a discrimination is reasonably related to its productivity or competitiveness then the discrimination is allowed. So the Civil Rights Act is a ratchet that turns only in the direction of productivity, for it promotes a fit between workers and jobs by screening out non-job-related factors while allowing bona fide occupational qualifications to override even its protections.

In response to prospective discrimination, gays are especially prone to take jobs which only partially use their talents or which squander them on trivial pursuits. Many gays take dead-end jobs to avoid reviews which might reveal their minority status and result in their dismissal. This trend is especially unfortunate for society since such reviews are likely to occur in the most specialized jobs, and so antigay policies or even just perceived prospective discrimination in these areas have the effect of artificially reducing the pool of job candidates just at the point where a large pool is the most desirable. Many gays go into small business because big business will not have them. In turn, many small businesses or dead-end occupations, like florists, hairdressers, male nurses, and female truckers and construction workers, have in society's mind become so closely associated with homosexuality that nongays who might otherwise go into these lines of employment do not, lest they be socially branded as gay. In these circumstances, the talents of people—both gay and not—are simply wasted both to themselves and to society. Gay rights *are* good for everyone.

Second, human resources are wasted if one's energies are constantly diverted and devoured by fear of arbitrary dismissal. This argument too has special import for gays. The cost of life in the closet is not small. In the absence of gay civil rights legislation, society is simply wasting the human resources which are expended in the day-to-day anxiety that attends leading a life of systematic disguise as a condition for continued employment.

Third, employment is a large constitutive part of what happiness is. Happiness itself, to a large extent, is job satisfaction.[31] Happiness stands to jobs as pleasure stands to sensation. When a sense organ is operating correctly, its operation itself is a source of delight—quite independent

31. See Richard Mohr, "A Platonic Happiness," *History of Philosophy Quarterly* (1987) 4:131–45.

of any particular object sensed or any particular sense datum received. So, too, when one's employment is of a favorable sort, one finds a delight in its very execution—quite independent of any object which the job generates, whether product or wage. People whose employment on its own counts as a personal flourishing—people, for instance, working in human services, academics, and other professionals, and people whose jobs entail a large element of craft—are indeed likely to view job satisfaction as a major constituent of happiness and rank it high both qualitatively and quantitatively among the sources of happiness. And even people who are forced by necessity or misfortune to take up employment which does not use their talents, or which is virtually mechanical, or positively dangerous, or which has other conditions that make the workplace hateful—even these people are likely to recognize that the workplace, if properly arranged, would be a locus of happiness, and this recognition of opportunity missed is part of the frustration which accompanies jobs which are necessarily unsatisfying to perform. And beyond the degradations laid upon the unemployed by social embarrassment and poverty is a spirit-crushing boredom.

For the unemployed, life is at best the somnolent droning on of the ascetic. More often, the unemployed are seized and seized up by a sense that there is nothing to be done, for they have nothing to do; and *that* nothing has the effect on them of making days feel like years, years eternities, and the future appear as an expanding void blotting out prospect and hope. To permit whimsical hiring practices to congest artificially the channel of happiness which employment provides, then, is to reduce happiness generally by barring access to one of its main sources. Because happiness is an analogue to pleasure, it is a property, unlike, say 'custom' and 'institution,' that necessarily attaches in the first place to individuals, and applies to groups or societies only derivatively. Promoting the general welfare, then, must take the form of promoting the welfare *of individuals*. In giving individuals, severally, greater access to the sources of happiness, civil rights legislation does just that.

V. INDIVIDUAL FLOURISHING

These three preceding general arguments—appealing to conceptions of dignity, self-sufficiency, and happiness—can be collectively pooled into a fourth. Government has a perceived obligation to enhance those conditions which promote the flourishing of individual styles of living. Thus, for example, the general rationale for compulsory liberal education is that such compulsion ultimately issues in autonomous individuals capable of making decisions for themselves from a field of alternative opinions. Analogously, civil rights legislation, though a somewhat coercive force in the marketplace, promotes those conditions in virtue of which people can begin to lead their lives guided by their own lights—to a degree compatible, of course, with certain obvious minimum requirements of law, including respect for other people's lifeplans. And because the activities protected by such legislation are so central to people's lives, it achieves this result again without any comparable loss on the part of those whom it restrains. The frustrated desire to act whimsically to a disfavored group or even to treat its members as sinners against one's religious values is easily outweighed by the frustrated desire of the disfavored minority to lead self-determining lives.

Such legislation withdraws the threat of punishment by social banishment, loss of employment, and the like from the arsenal of majoritarian coercion, so that individual lives need not be molded by social conventions and by the demands of conformity set by others. The result of such legislation is that the means by which one lives shall not be permitted to serve as instruments for the despotism of custom.

This justification for civil rights legislation also has special import for gays. With the lessening of fear from threat of discovery, ordinary gays will begin to lead self-developing lives. Imagine the lives of those gays who systematically forgo, say, the opportunity of sharing the common necessities of life and of sharing the emotional dimensions of intimacy—forced to seek out such intimacy as they are capable in environs the risks of which regularly include death—as the price for the means by which they place bread on their table. Love and caring could cost you your job—if you're gay—while sex and intimacy on the lam could cost you your life—felled by a virus or a queerbasher's bat.

Those homosexuals who come out view that experience as central to their existence. The transparency of the narratives of those who have gone through the coming out experience bear a stronger witness than even that of the recently religiously reborn to the centrality to self of what they have undergone. The recollection of the experience's position in the process of self-discovery and self-actualization can turn the staid and pinstriped unmeasuredly effervescent. Typical are the following statements of the first openly gay federal official in United States history, Representative Gerry Studds, made after his coming out speech given at age 46 on the floor of the U.S. House upon the revelation by the House Ethics Committee of an affair he had had a decade earlier with a male page:

> *How do you feel now that you have publicly declared you are gay?*
> Better than I've ever felt in my life. I suspect that's something that would be easy for your audience of gay people to understand. But I've found that in giving that response to the media in general, to folks who have not had this experience themselves, that it requires a great deal of explanation as to how in the midst of what for a lot of reasons appears to be a disastrous situation, one can candidly say, "I've never felt better in my life." Any person who has ever gone through the experience of coming out will understand that. I feel as if the remaining seven cylinders had just kicked in for the first time in 46 years. And that's a powerful feeling.[32]

> *Have you ever been in love before?*
> I don't think so. It's awkward, it's challenging in some very fundamental ways, to be both 46 and 19 at the same time. Maybe I shouldn't say that. . . . The world ought not to be such that anybody has to live 46 years the way I did, or the way most gay people did—and still do.[33]

Reflecting two years later on coming out, Studds would say:

> I feel comfortable and I feel well and I feel a vibrance, if that's the right word, for life. I have a strength and a calmness at the center that was not there before. I hope this is apparent to others, and hopefully it's a source of strength to others as well.[34]

In his coming out speech itself, Studds had begun:

> Mr. Speaker, all Members of Congress must cope with the challenge of initiating and maintaining a career in public office without destroying entirely the ability to lead a meaningful and emotionally fulfilling private life. It is not a simple task for any of us to meet adequately the obligations of either public or private life, let alone both. But these challenges are made

32. Larry Bush, "Gerry Studds—I," *The Advocate*, September 15, 1983, no. 376, p. 15.

33. Larry Bush, "Gerry Studds—II," *The Advocate*, September 29, 1983, no. 377, p. 21.

34. Pamela Glass, "Studds Savors a New Lease on Life," *Cape Code Times* [Hyannis, Mass.], November 10, 1985, p. 1.

substantially more complex when one is, as am I, both an elected public official and gay.[35]

In the absence of civil rights legislation, gays are placed in the position of having to make zero-sum tradeoffs between the components that go into making a full life—tradeoffs, say, between a reasonable personal life and employment, tradeoffs which the majority would not tolerate for itself even for a minute. But massive unfairness is not the only problem here.

There is something profoundly immoral—belonging to a vice without name—about a society that requires as the price of living in it that a person necessarily dissimulate all the time about himself in every dimension of the public, social, workaday world. Consider the coerced hypocrisy of a school teacher who instructs her pupils on the value of truth-telling but whose life before them needs must be a lie. Dan Bradley, former president of the United States Legal Services Corporation, speaks eloquently of life as lie:

> Always there was the coverup: Arranging for women with whom I was friendly and had shared my secret to brag about my virility to F.B.I. agents making a routine background check; keeping up a macho front with male colleagues; making sure I had a female escort for parties, and worrying about how to deal with homosexual issues in the legal services program. . . .
>
> Several homosexual House members I knew voted for the [McDonald] amendment [excluding gays from legal services funding. It was] something I could understand because I, too, had been a master of deception.
>
> The web of deceit I had so consciously and meticulously woven over the years made it possible for me to rationalize whatever I had to do to protect myself. You can rationalize the lies, the deceptions or whatever. There is no end of it.[36]

It is grandly immoral to force others to do that which, if voluntary, would be systematically immoral and it is to act in wanton disregard for human worth to force others to lead lives wholly of bad faith. Though

35. "Personal Statement of Representative Gerry E. Studds," *Congressional Record*, July 14, 1983, p. H5190.

36. Phil Gailey, "Homosexual Takes Leave of a Job and of an Agony," *The New York Times*, March 31, 1982, p. 24. (Those quotes which *The Times* here gives in indirect discourse have, for uniformity's sake, been in the text recast back into the first person.)

legislation will not alone open closet doors,[37] civil rights legislation at least would withdraw the imprimatur of law and social custom from this horrid grandeur and provide a model for private action among blood families, which are the other large latch on many closet doors.

These various arguments, if severally sound and collectively noncontradicting, should have a compelling cumulative force. What is needed is more courage on the part of gays to advance them to legislators and more courage on the part of legislators to rise above popular prejudices and cultivate a judicial state of mind, which is not only a virtue in the courts, but is also what, when present in legislatures, makes representational democracy superior to direct democracy and which is really necessary if in our cultural ideals minority rights are to be protected against social coercion, as well as government coercion.

When our culture talks of legal protections for minorities against discrimination in employment, housing, and public accommodations, it calls such legislation *rights* legislation—civil *rights*. This word choice is not accidental. It represents the moral insight that though such protections must be instituted through the mechanisms of majority rule, the justifications for such protections are, like those for Constitutional *rights*, anti-majoritarian. Virtually no other type of legislation has been given this special status in our culture's discourse. Therefore, if legislators treat such protections for gays as just one more political issue subject to the blandishments of the majority, then, against the background values of our civilization, they act immorally.

37. Norway, for instance, has the most "progressive" gay laws in the world, including admirable civil protections—the first of their kind in Europe—and (to my mind) objectionable gay antidefamation laws—also a first. Yet, the country's gays are the most closeted in Western Europe. See Robert Silver, "Norway," *The Advocate,* August 5, 1986, no. 452, pp. 28–29.

6. Invisible Minorities, Civic Rights, Democracy: Why Even Conservatives Should Support Gay Rights

---

I. INTRODUCTION

This chapter advances three related arguments for the inclusion of sexual orientation in such legislation as the 1964 Civil Rights Act as a characteristic on the basis of which a person may not be discriminated against in employment, housing, and public services. For gay men and lesbians, such protections from discrimination are necessary enabling conditions for their having reasonably guaranteed access to an array of fundamental rights—both civic and political—which virtually everyone would agree are supposed to pertain equally to all persons. For gays, these rights are eclipsed, it is here argued, in consequence of the *indirect* results which widespread discrimination has when it affects individuals who are members of invisible minorities.

The arguments here are not, then, general arguments for civil rights legislation based on the *direct* or immediate deleterious effects which discrimination in employment, housing, and public services would have on *any* person or even on society as a whole and which might on their own be sufficiently grave to justify a government ban on all but good faith discriminations in these areas—a ban which *per accidens* would catch gays within its broad protective reach. Such direct deleterious effects (as discussed in the prior chapter) include affronts to personal dignity, self-reliance, general prosperity, and individual flourishing.

Libertarians and other political minimalists tend to dismiss as irrelevant or inflated assessments of the nature and gravity of these possible direct effects and so have generally been unmoved by such arguments for civil rights legislation and its coercive intrusions into the private sector. But even if the direct effects of such discrimination were not as sufficient on their own as I think they are to warrant the state's deployment of its monopoly of preemptive coercive forces, still, if social realities are such that discrimination (actual or prospective) indirectly but determinately has the effect of denying access to certain universally recognized rights—the denial of which draws into doubt the very rule of law—then this effect does warrant state action on virtually any account of what constitutes legitimate state action.[1]

The arguments would apply equally well to other invisible minorities whose members are subject to widespread discrimination merely on the basis of their minority status rather than on the basis of their capacities, talents, or needs. By invisible minority I mean a minority whose members severally can be identified only through an act of will on someone's part rather than through the mere observation of the members' day-to-day actions in the public domain. Thus severely physically and mentally challenged people would rank along with racial classes, gender classes, and some ethnic and religious groups (like the Amish) as visible minorities, whereas diabetics, assimilated Jews, atheists, and released prisoners would rank along with gays as invisible minorities.

The arguments only presuppose the acceptability of a governmental system which is a constitutionally regulated representative democracy with a developed body of civic law. Such in broad outline is the government of The United States and its various states. The arguments, then, hold that gay civil rights are a necessary precondition for the proper functioning of this system. Specifically, they hold (1) that gay rights are necessary for gays having reasonably guaranteed access to judicial or civic rights, (2) that gay rights are necessary for gays having reasonably guaranteed access to the political rights of the sort found in the first amendment of the Constitution and (3) that gay rights are necessary if democracy is consistently and coherently to be given a preference-utili-

---

1. For libertarian argument against the 1964 Civil Rights Act generally, but for some government involvement in assuring access to courts and political processes, see for example Anne Wortham, "Individualism versus Racism" in Tibor R. Machan, ed., *The Libertarian Alternative*, pp. 403–7 (Chicago: Nelson-Hall, 1974).

tarian rationale—that is, if democracy is at least in part justified as the form of government that tends to maximize goods and services in society by registering people's overall preferences.

II. MAKING CIVIC RIGHTS COHERENT

This section argues that civil rights legislation for gays is warranted as being a necessary precondition for gays having equitable access to civic rights. By civic rights I mean rights to the impartial administration of civil and criminal law in defense of property and person. In the absence of such rights there is no rule of law. An invisible minority historically subjected to widespread social discrimination has reasonably guaranteed access to these rights only when the minority is guaranteed nondiscrimination in employment, housing, and public services.

For an invisible minority, possessing civil rights has the same ethical justification as everyone's having the right when on criminal trial to have a lawyer at government expense. A lawyer through her special knowledge and skills provides her client with *access* to the substantive and procedural rights of the courts—rights to which a layman left to his own devices would not have reasonably guaranteed access. Without the guarantee of a lawyer, judicial rights are not equal rights but those of the well-to-do.[2]

All would agree that everyone ought to have judicial rights, and moreover—as in the case of having a lawyer at state expense—ought to have in that strong sense of rights by which an individual can make demand claims based on them. All individuals must be assured the right to demand from government access to judicial procedures. Judicial rights ought not to be debased to the level where government may simply be prevented from prohibiting judicial access, but need not guarantee it. This debasement would give judicial access the same status that abortion now has in the U.S.; it cannot be prohibited, but is not guaranteed for those who want or even (in most cases) need it. Civic rights ought not to be mere immunities and they ought not to be restricted only to certain classes.

Imagine the following scenario. Steve, who teaches math in a suburban high school and coaches the swim team, on a weekend night heads

2. See *Gideon v. Wainwright*, 372 U.S. 335 (1963) (held that the sixth amendment requires that states provide defendants in criminal trials with a lawyer).

to the city to try his luck at Up and Coming, a popular gay cruise bar. There he meets Tom, a self-employed contractor, who in his former life sired two sons by a woman who now hates him, but who is ignorant of his new life. Tom and Steve decide to walk to Tom's nearby flat, which he rents from a bigot who bemoans the fact that the neighborhood is going gay and refuses to rent to people he supposes to be gay; Tom's weekend visitations from his sons are his cover.

Meanwhile, at a nearby Children's Aid Home for teenagers, the leader of the Anglo gang is taunting Tony, the leader of the Latino gang, by calling him a faggot. After much protestation to the contrary, Tony claims he will prove to the Anglos once and for all that he is not a faggot, and hits the streets with his gang members, who tote with them the blunt and not so blunt instruments of the queerbasher's trade. Like a hyena pack upon a wildebeest, they descend on Tom and Steve, downing their victims in a blizzard of strokes and blows. Local residents coming home from parties and others walking their dogs witness the whole event.

Imagine that two miracles occur. One, a squad car happens by, and two, the police actually do their job. Tony and another of the fleeing queerbashers are caught and arrested on the felony charges of aggravated assault and battery, and attempted murder. Other squad cars arrive and while witnesses' reports are gathered, Steve and Tom are taken to the nearest emergency room. Once Steve and Tom are in wards the police arrive to take statements of complaint from them, complaints which will engage the wheels of justice in what appears to be an open and shut case. But Steve knows the exposure of a trial will terminate his employment. And Tom knows the exposure of a trial would give his ex-wife the legal excuse she desires to deny his visitation rights and he knows he will eventually lose his apartment. So neither man can reasonably risk pressing charges. Tony is released, and within twelve hours of attempting murder, he returns to the Children's Aid Home hailed by all as a conquering hero. Gay rights are a necessary material condition for judicial access.

Any reader of gay urban tabloids, like Chicago's *Windy City Times*, San Francisco's *Bay Area Reporter*, Boston's *Gay Community News*, Toronto's *The Body Politic*, or *The Washington Blade*, knows that the events sketched here—miracles excepted—are typical. Every day gays are in effect blackmailed by our judicial system. Our judicial system's threat of exposure prevents gay access to judicial protections. The example given above of latter-day lynch law falls within the sphere of criminal justice. Even more obviously, the same judicial blackmail occurs in civil cases. Nor are the offending parties always outsiders to the group whose civic access is thus limited:

> Similarly, lesbians can be sexually harassed by other lesbians. Some lesbians may foist sexual attentions upon other lesbians who already have lovers, for example. To a large extent lesbians who are victims of nondiscriminatory [i.e., peer-on-peer] sexual harassment will be on their own. A lesbian will tend to reject any suggestion that she initiate a civil suit against her female harasser. Fearing that she will be laughed out of court, or doubting the wisdom of publicly proclaiming her sexual preference, the lesbian is apt to handle her problem in informal ways.[3]

These "informal ways," however, are bound to be unsatisfactory. For insofar as they try to circumvent the law and yet require for their warranted success the sort of justified coercion which is the exclusive preserve of the state's police powers, they will at a minimum result in violation of the law,[4] and more likely end in attempted usurpation of the law.[5]

3. Rosemarie Tong, "Lesbian Perspectives," in *Women, Sex, and the Law* (Totowa, N.J.: Rowman & Allanheld, 1984), p. 187.

4. Example: in December 1982, the only two women's bars in NYC—unwilling, not without reason, to rely on police protections—initiated a "women only" door policy to protect patrons from persistent harassment from nongay males. This action, of course, violated state liquor codes (among others) which bar gender discrimination. The result: both establishments lost their licenses and were closed by the state (Tong, *Women*, p. 186). I leave here as open questions whether such a door policy could be justified as a private sector affirmative action program or whether, given the historically central role of bars in the development and maintenance of lesbian and gay male culture and politics, the license revocations should be subject to successful challenge as violations of the constitutional right to (political) association. On this role, see John D'Emilio, *Sexual Politics, Sexual Communities: The Making of a Homosexual Minority in the United States, 1940–1970* (Chicago: University of Chicago Press, 1983), pp. 30–33, 49–51, and especially 97–99, 107, 186.

Caveat emptor: usually, though not always, such Constitutional challenges to civil rights ordinances have worked against rather than in favor of gay male and lesbian interests, especially when religious rights have been invoked. See, for example, *Walker v. First Presbyterian Church,* 22 F E P Cases 762 (Cal. Super. Ct., 1980) (Free Exercise Clause voids application of municipal gay employment protections to gay church organist).

5. For a grisly example of such vigilantism—a case of revenge over an alleged violation of personal rights in which the avenger is in no position to seek recourse in the law—see Tong, *Women*, p. 189; for further examples and analysis, see "Lesbian Battering" *Gay Community News*, January 14, 1984, 11(25):13–17, and Kerry Lobel, ed., *Naming the Violence: Speaking Out About Lesbian Battering* (Seattle: The Seal Press, 1986).

It is unreasonable to expect anyone to give up that by which he lives, his employment, his shelter, his access to goods and services and loved ones in order for judicial procedures to be carried out equitably, in order to demand legal protections. Even if one were tempted to follow the libertarian and say that these are in fact reasonable expenses to pay for making the choice of living an open lifestyle, that a person always makes tradeoffs among his necessarily limited options, and that this condition does not warrant the state coercing *others* on his behalf—even if one believed all that, one would not, I think, go on and say that these costs are a reasonable price to pay to see one's assailants dealt justice or to enter a court of equity.

Now what is bitterly paradoxical about this blackmail by the judiciary is that it is a necessary concomitant of two major virtues of the fair administration of justice. The first is that trials are not star chamber affairs, but are open to scrutiny by public and press. The second is that defendants must be able to be confronted by the witnesses against them and have compulsory process for obtaining witnesses in their favor, while conversely prosecutors must have the tools with which to press cases on behalf of victims. In consequence, determinations of guilt and innocence must be based on a full examination of the facts. The result of these two virtues is that trials cast the private into the public realm.

The Supreme Court itself has recognized that public exposure of the private realm necessarily attends the workings of justice; thus wrote Chief Justice Burger for a unanimous Court in *United States v. Nixon:*

> [A]ll the values to which we accord deference for the privacy of all citizens . . . . must yield. . . . to our [nation's] commitment to the rule of law. This is nowhere more profoundly manifest than in our view that "the twofold aim [of criminal justice] is that guilt shall not escape or innocence suffer." We have elected to employ an adversary system of criminal justice in which the parties contest all issues before a court of law. . . . The very integrity of the judicial system and public confidence in the system depend on full disclosure of all the facts.[6]

That trials cast the private into the public realm puts the lie to those condescending (would-be) liberals who claim that what gays do in private is no one else's business and should not be anyone else's business, so that on the one hand gays do not needs rights, and on the other hand they do not deserve rights, lest they make themselves public. If the

6. 418 U.S. 683, 708, 713, 709 (1974).

judiciary system is to be open and fair, it is necessary that gays be granted civil rights. Otherwise judicial access becomes a right only for the dominant culture.

In being *de facto* cast beyond the pale of civic procedures, gays, when faced with assaults on property and person, are left with only the equally unjust alternatives of the resignation of the impotent or the rage of man in a state of nature. Societies may remain orderly even when some of their members are denied civic procedures. Many tyrannies do. But such societies cannot be said to be civil societies which respect the rule of law.[7]

In October 1984, the governor of California signed a bill making actionable as civil suits assaults on gays which are motivated by an animus against gays.[8] In March of the same year, he had vetoed a civil rights bill which would have protected gays from private employment discrimination. Given the lived experience of gays, the former legislation will prove virtually pointless in the absence of the latter.

7. I have not here intended to address a complementary problem of criminal justice for gays: whether, when gays stand accused of crime or pursue civil litigation, they get fair treatment from police, bench, and jury. For some eye-opening examples of patently prejudicial and abusive treatment of gays from the bench, see Rhonda R. Rivera's magisterial "Our Straight-Laced Judges: The Legal Position of Homosexual Persons in the U.S.," *Hastings Law Journal* (1979) 30:799–955 and for a history of police abuses of criminal procedures against gays, see D'Emilio, *Sexual Politics*, pp. 14–15, 30, 49–51, 70, 110–11, 120–21, 157, 182–84, 187–88, 193–94, 200–1, 202, 206–7.

To the extent that civil rights legislation for a group tends to legitimate that group in the eyes of society as a whole, gay civil rights legislation would in fact increase the likelihood of gays getting fair trials. The issue is complex, but I doubt that this benefit outweighs the general inappropriateness of government throwing its weight behind one or another lifestyle or class. There is no guarantee that the government's symbolic actions are a ratchet that turns only in the direction of the good, so gays would do well to remember that what government may bless government may curse. I am inclined to agree with neoconservatives that gay civil rights legislation is not warranted *if* its main purpose and effect is simply a symbolic legitimizing of gays. See Jean Bethke Elshtain, "Homosexual Politics: The Paradox of Gay Liberation," *Salmagundi* (1982–1983) 58–59:255.

8. While I think that all assaults (or at least highly aggravated ones, as queerbashings almost always are) should *qua* assaults be actionable as civil suits, I do not think that they should be actionable (especially with punitive damages) *simply in virtue* of some political dimension of the assault, such that the only distinguishing feature between actionable and nonactionable assaults is simply the assailant's social or political beliefs and attitudes. Indeed, to the extent that a law draws a distinction based solely on the political dimension of some violent act, the law should be declared unconstitutional on first amendment grounds.

III. MAKING POLITICAL RIGHTS COHERENT

In the same 1938 case in which the Supreme Court programmatically withdrew its attention from the field of economic legislation, it set forth an agenda for itself in the area we now call civil liberties. The Court recognized *inter alia* that "legislation which restricts those political processes which can ordinarily be expected to bring about repeal of undesirable legislation" might need "to be subjected to more exacting judicial scrutiny under the general prohibitions of the Fourteenth Amendment than are most other types of legislation."[9] Even more perceptively the Court recognized that social, as opposed to legal, forces also might have the result for some groups of effectively excluding their participation in the political life of the nation: "Prejudice against discrete and insular minorities may be a special condition, which tends seriously to curtail the operation of those political processes ordinarily to be relied upon to protect minorities."[10]

Here it is argued that widespread *social* prejudice against gays has for them this very effect about which the Court, at the level of principle, so perceptively worried—the virtual eclipse of political rights. In the absence of gay civil rights legislation, gays are—over the range of issues which most centrally affect their minority status—effectively denied access to the political rights of the first amendment, that is, freedom of

9. *United States v. Carolene Products Co.*, 304 U.S. 144, 152 n.4 (1938).

10. *Ibid.* In this circumstance, laws affecting discrete and insular minorities "may call for correspondingly more searching judicial inquiry." *Ibid.* To date, race, alienage and, to a lesser degree, gender and illegitimacy have in the Court's eyes marked out discrete and insular minorities warranting special judicial protections from the political process.

If this section is correct, gays also ought to be considered a discrete and insular minority *on the very ground* that the Court gives in establishing the classification, namely, that prejudice tends to push the minority group out of the political process. See John Hart Ely, *Democracy and Distrust* (Cambridge: Harvard University Press, 1980), pp. 162–64. See also Justice Brennan's dissent from denial of certiorari for *Rowland v. Mad River Local School District*, 470 U.S. 1009 (1985).

If given the status of a "suspect" class with attendant Constitutional protections under the fourteenth amendment, gays would be largely spared legislation that is targeted specifically against them. They would be guaranteed rights as *immunities* or certain negative freedoms, but this protection alone is nowhere near a sufficient guarantee of gay social justice. For as long as gays, even with immunity rights, still remain outside the political system, they will not be able to register their *interests*, however well protected their (immunity) *rights* may be. At a minimum, gays require for social justice that public policy take their interests into account.

speech, freedom of press, freedom of assembly, and freedom to petition for the redress of grievances. Further, gays are especially denied the emergent constitutional right of association—the amalgam of the freedoms of speech and assembly—which establishes the right to join and be identified with other persons for common (political) goals.[11]

This eclipse of political access is most evident if we look at gays severally. Put concretely, does a gay person who has to laugh at and manufacture fag jokes in workplace elevators and around workplace coffee urns, in order to deflect suspicion from himself in an office which routinely fires gay employees, have freedom to express his views on gay issues? Is it likely that such a person could reasonably risk appearing in public at a gay rights rally? Would such a person be able to participate in a march celebrating the Stonewall Riots and the start of gay activism? Would such a person be able to sign, let alone circulate, a petition protesting the firing of a gay worker? Would such a person likely try to persuade workmates to vote for a gay-positive city-councilman? Would such a person sign a letter to the editor protesting abusive reportage of gay issues and events, or advocating the discussion of gay issues in high schools? The answer to all these questions is "obviously not!" Such a person is usually so transfixed by fear that it is highly unlikely that he or she could even be persuaded to write out a check to a gay rights organization.[12]

In the absence of 1964 Civil Rights Act protections, the vast majority of gays are effectively denied the ability to participate equally in first amendment rights, which are supposed to pertain equally to every citizen, and moreover pertain to every citizen *qua* individual. First amendment rights, like other such rights, apply directly to citizens or persons as individuals. They do not apply directly to groups and only derivatively to individuals.[13] It will not do then to suggest that some, or even

11. See Lawrence Wilson and Raphael Shannon, "Homosexual Organizations and the Right of Association," *Hastings Law Journal* (1979) 30:1029–74 and Donald Solomon, "The Emergence of Associational Rights for Homosexual Persons," *Journal of Homosexuality* (1979–1980) 5(1–2):147–55.

12. Some organizations, like National Gay Rights Advocates, desperately aware of this last problem's magnitude, set up fund-raising account "fronts" with innocuous-sounding names, like "Legal Foundation for Personal Liberties," in an attempt to ease money, if not persons, out of the closet. Many organizations simply dissimulate, lying by omission or vagueness in assuming for themselves closeted names; thus the national gay political action committee baptizes itself "The Human Rights Campaign Fund."

13. See chapters 3 and 4.

most, gays' inability to participate in politics is unproblematic on the alleged ground that other gays—those who *are* open about their minority status—may voice the interests of those who are not. This position simply confuses individual rights, like first amendment rights, with group "rights." The position further naïvely assumes that gays uniformly have the same interests and espouse the same views on any given gay issue, so that one simply needs to know one sociological fact—the percent of gays in the general population—to know the extent to which some publicly espoused gay interest is held.[14]

If further, for a moment, gays are viewed collectively as a potential political force, it should be clear that for a group that—fanciful contagion and recruitment theories of causation aside—is a permanent minority, it is hardly fair to be further encumbered by having the majority of its members absent through social coercion from the public workings of the political process.

If first amendment rights are not to be demoted to privileges to which only the dominant culture has access, then invisible minorities that are subject to widespread social discrimination will have to be guaranteed protection from those forces which maintain them in their position of invisibility. Civil rights protections are a very long step in that direction.

Now, it might be argued that first amendment rights are to be construed as mere immunities, that they merely prevent the government from interfering with certain types of actions, so that as long as the government and its agents do not, say, refuse parade permits to gays, smash up the gay press, deny the formation of gay student groups on state university campuses, and the like, then in fact gays do have first amendment rights just like everyone else.[15] In these circumstances, it

14. The "Letters" columns of gay tabloids are regularly littered with frequently vituperative but always anonymous contributions of those who claim that open gays do not represent their interests, indeed positively destroy their interests. These authors though are in a nearly hopeless position politically; the column is their only outlet, an incredibly narrow one at that, and readers reasonably enough are going to doubt the convictions and the courage of conviction of those who resort to anonymity. Such doubt is the reason most mainstream tabloids decline publication of anonymously submitted letters.

More generally, as D'Emilio, writing of the years bridging 1980, claims: "the [gay] movement itself shows no unanimity as to the social rearrangements that equality would require," *Sexual Politics*, p. 247.

15. For the *status quaestionis* of gays and the first amendment, see José Gómez, "The Public Expression of Lesbian/Gay Personhood as Protected Speech," *Journal of Law and Inequality* (1983) 1:121–53, and Paul Siegel, "Lesbian and Gay Rights as a Free Speech

would be reasonable to say that gays are *free from* active government interference in their political designs. Nevertheless, gays would still remain effectively denied the *freedom to act* politically.

Whatever else first amendment rights might be, they have as one of their chief rationales and purposes not merely *not making impossible* the procedures of democracy, but also actually promoting, enhancing, and making likely the proper working of democratic processes. To this end, then, first amendment rights need somehow to be construed not merely as immunities, as the mere absences of government interference, but as somewhat stronger rights. Indeed, they need to be realized as powers which place the government under a certain liability.

Democratic government should operate under the liability not only of removing its own possible interference with the dissemination of political views but also of removing those forces in society in general which block the *potentially effective* dissemination of political views.

At a minimum, potentially effective political activity requires that the political position espoused is widely and pointedly disseminated. Only with the widespread and lively dissemination of political ideas is it possible for a minority political position on social policy to have a chance of becoming the majority opinion and so of becoming government policy and law. If the majority of people never has the occasion to change its opinions to those of the minority, political rights would be otiose. It would seem incumbent upon government, then, to militate against those social conditions and mechanisms by which majority opinion perpetuates itself *simply by the elimination* of the hearing of alternative possible policies, or what is as good, *the reduction* of alternatives to the mere slogans of strawmen.

Now it is not a requirement for democratic process that minority opinions must at some point carry the day and become the majority opinion, as a sign that the system is working correctly. It is required only that minority opinions have their day in the court of the body politic, that majority opinion should not be allowed constantly to win out *by default*.

Issue: A Review of Relevant Caselaw," *Journal of Homosexuality,* (1988) vol. 15, in press. See also *National Gay Task Force v. Oklahoma City Board of Education,* 729 F.2d 1270 (10th Cir. 1984) (law permitting the dismissal of a teacher for advocating or encouraging homosexuality in a way that might come to be known at the teacher's school ruled unconstitutional on its face), aff'd mem. by an equally divided Court, 470 U.S. 903 (1985).

To this end, government must prohibit nongovernment agents from interfering with the political activities of individuals and groups. Thus, for instance, because we consider the freedom of assembly to be a power rather than merely an immunity, we not only insist that political rallies, say, should be immune from government interference but we also deem it a major obligation of government and its police actions to make actual as a power the rights of people to hold rallies by prohibiting goon squads and hecklers from disrupting political rallies. The goon performs an act considerably worse than simply assault when he strikes a speaker; the assassin worse than murder. A special need for police action against the goon and assassin arises over and above normal police activities of protecting civic rights.[16] Analogously, bigoted employers are the goon squads and hecklers that, when unrestrained by law, deny gays access to political rights. Civil rights legislation for gays should be considered an essential part of the police activities of the state.

Only when the government protects gays against discrimination in housing, employment, and public accommodation will gays have first amendment rights as powers. For all potentially effective political strategies involve *public* actions. More specifically, all the actions protected by the first amendment are public actions (speaking, publishing, petitioning, assembling, associating). Now, a person who is a member of an invisible minority and who must remain invisible, hidden, and secreted in respect to her minority status as a condition for maintaining a livelihood is not free to be public about her minority status or to incur suspicion by publicly associating with others who are open about their similar status. And so she is effectively denied all political power—except the right to vote. But voting aside, she will be denied the freedom to express her views in a public forum and to unite with or organize other like-minded individuals in an attempt to compete for votes which would elect persons who will support the policies advocated by her group. She is denied all effective use of legally available means of influencing public opinion before voting and all effective means of lobbying after elections are held.

16. Meting out greater penalties to the goon or assassin than to a typical assailant or murderer does not punish the criminal simply on the basis of his political views, as it does in the case of the queerbasher (see note 8 above). Rather the criminal here is given a greater punishment because the result of his action is a greater offense—the disruption of legitimate government. It is true that but for his political views he probably would not have committed the greater offense, but that is irrelevant.

Such denials to minorities of first amendment rights as powers differ in kind depending upon the minority affected, and remedies vary accordingly. Blacks, for instance, though constituting a visible minority, nevertheless, as the result of being in general poorer than whites, are effectively denied first amendment rights as powers, since blacks are, for financial reasons, effectively denied the political use of such expensive mass media tools as purchasing television time and newspaper space.[17]

For gays, it is not poverty *per se* which effectively denies them first amendment rights. Indeed gays are, as Kinsey showed, dispersed nearly homogeneously throughout all social and economic classes. Rather it is the recriminations that descend upon gays who are publicly gay that effectively deny them first amendment rights. Maybe such recriminations deny to them these rights even more effectively than poverty denies those rights to blacks, since the poor but visible at least have available to them such inexpensive but limited methods of public communications as sit-ins, marches, and demonstrations. Gays—as long as job discrimination is widespread—are effectively denied even these limited modes of public access.

On the one hand, the closeted condition of most gays has meant that nothing remotely approaching the widespread dissemination of views on gay issues necessary for any potentially effective political strategy has occurred in this country or any other. The condition has caused gay political organizations to be small, weak, inbred, ill-financed, impermanent, and subterranean. It greatly curtails any outreach to the nongay world, leaving such organizations largely "to preach to the converted." Membership tends to stand in inverse proportion to an organization's public profile; thus memberships in gay religious and other largely hermetic social organizations far outstrip those in gay political organizations.

In consequence, any widespread portrayal of gays and gay issues has been left entirely to the mercies of the mass media, which, however much they may preempt political discussion and activity, are no substitute for them. The general media have their own agenda, which includes politics largely to the extent that politics is entertaining. Regarding gays, the mass media have been able to see little beyond the titillation of fear and

17. For a general defense of first amendment rights as powers and for an application of the view to blacks, see Alan Gewirth, *Human Rights* (Chicago: University of Chicago Press, 1982), pp. 310–28.

death. Such titillation after all is largely what keeps the mass media massive. It would be fanciful to say that hidden amongst the columns devoted to AIDS, Congressional scandals, and serial murderers is something like a robust national debate of gay issues. Little in this regard has changed in the last thirty years. Writing of the mainstream press during the period 1956–1960, historian John D'Emilio could summarize: "When articles did find their way into the press or periodicals, they tended to focus on scandal, tragedy, or stereotypical images of homosexual and lesbian life. Gay women and men rarely enjoyed the opportunity to express in print their own views about their lives."[18]

Can the liberal press serve as a proxy for gays in the discussion of gay issues? In December 1984, the Berkeley city council passed domestic partner legislation which gives gay couples the same city employment benefits as legally married couples. This was the first successful piece of domestic partner legislation in the country and so a major gay news story. Yet *The New York Times* thought this beacon worthy of but twenty-three words and failed even to mention that the law applied to and was designed for gays, choosing rather to focus its three-inch article on Eldridge Cleaver's presence at the council meeting.[19] Subsequently, Clever's presence was made a feature in *The Times'* Sunday "Ideas and Trends" column—where, however, no mention at all was made of the domestic partner legislation.[20]

It is ironic that the antigay polemics of the conservative press have done a better job of covering gay issues than the liberal press. The January 1985 issue of *Moral Majority Report* contains three articles on

18. D'Emilio, *Sexual Politics*, p. 109.

19. "Berkeley Council Backs Friendship Benefits," *The New York Times*, December 7, 1984, p. Y12.

20. "The Trials of Cleaver," *The New York Times*, December 9, 1984, p. D7. See also note 44 below.

Paul Burstein summarizes the role of the mass media in the black civil rights movement thus:

> Media coverage had no independent effect on the outcome [of the civil rights movement]. That is not to say that the media were not important. It is very plausible, as so many have suggested, that media coverage of the activities of the civil rights movement was necessary if the movement was to succeed in getting the public concerned about the issue. But the media did not play an independent role. Coverage followed upon events; it did not, in the aggregate, precede them.

Paul Burstein, *Discrimination, Jobs, and Politics: The Struggle for Equal Employment Opportunity in the United States since the New Deal* (Chicago: University of Chicago Press, 1985), p. 95.

176 STATE AS CIVIL SHIELD

gay issues, the March issue four, covering AIDS, first amendment issues, privacy rights, CIA employment, gay parents, and domestic partner legislation. The cover of the February issue features a photograph of two gay men in affectionate embrace. In context, such reportage is but editorial fodder. Even so, to an extent, it inadvertently defeats itself in two ways. First, just the mention of gays begins to break down the taboo that has previously surrounded even the mention of homosexuality.[21] Second, what is intended to shock the reader and elicit an immediate sense of revulsion also, as a side-effect, informs and desensitizes the reader. He who sees men kissing in an image accompanying a conservative funding solicitation will be less surprised when he sees the original on the street. The more conservatives discuss gay issues, the less they can rely on automatic social responses which are fueled by fear of the unknown.[22] If a group's greatest political enemies are the best media aides it has available, the media can hardly be an adequate proxy for the wide dissemination of the group's views.

On the other hand, local dissemination of views is also impeded. Indeed, the closeted condition of gays blocks the most effective sort of political communication in which gays in particular might engage with others—personal conversation. Social reality is such that many people do not know or think they do not know any gay people firsthand. Such widespread ignorance is a breeding ground for vicious stereotypes. Problems compound when misunderstanding is added to ignorance. Many people *sort of* think they know that someone, say, a workmate is gay. But given the way the workmate acts, especially in avoiding certain topics, in being selectively "absent" from social intercourse or in confusingly broadcasting mixed messages, others think the gay person is embarrassed about his or her status and so do not initiate any discussion of

21. On this important role of antigay polemics, see D'Emilio, *Sexual Politics*, p. 52.

22. Conservative attention to gay issues runs another risk as well. For many people the traditional taboo on even discussing gay issues may be one of the chief mechanisms by which homosexual desire is kept from waxing into consciousness and act. See Michael Slote's "Inapplicable Concepts and Sexual Perversion" in *Philosophy and Sex*, Robert Baker and Frederick Elliston, eds., 1st ed., pp. 261–67 (Buffalo: Prometheus, 1975). See also Renaud Camus' forward to *Tricks: 25 Encounters* (New York: St. Martin's, 1981), p. xi: "Still other [homosexuals], and doubtless they are even today the majority, are unaware of such tastes because they live in such circumstances, in such circles, that their desires are not only for themselves inadmissible, but inconceivable, unspeakable. They possess no discourse of accommodation with which [they might] assume such desires and could change lives only by changing words."

it, and so further they are left with the impression that there is something wrong with gays because gays themselves seem to act as though there is. The nongay person oddly fails to realize that the gay person may have or—what comes to the same—may *suppose* he has solid prudential reasons for his skittish behavior.

When this widespread ignorance and misunderstanding combines with gut reactions to gays of fear and loathing or even just queasiness and discomfort, mere reportage (even accurate reportage) about gays or mere abstract discussion (even insightful discussion) of gay issues has little chance of success in changing the attitudes by which people conduct their lives. When people's attitudes are informed by deeply held emotional responses—ones perhaps central to their conceptions of themselves—reason's hope is slight. The most effective way of changing nongays' views about gays is for nongays to interact personally with some openly gay people.[23]

Such interaction is almost the only way to cut through stereotypes and fears, which when left unchecked tend mutually to aggravate each other into dangerous frenzy. At a minimum, personal contact generally reveals as sheer paranoia much of the fear some people have of gays. And yet such personal outreach of gays to the nongay person is not likely to occur, however willing the nongay person, as long as a gay person has to put her job and other major interests on the line to make the contact. It is after all at the job site and in certain public accommodations that people tend to have the sorts of contacts with others, initially strangers, which might lead to personal conversations. And yet it is exactly in these locations that a gay person is most likely to encounter discrimination if open about his status. And so the most effective avenue of communication for gays about the issues of importance to them as gays is effectively blocked in the absence of civil rights protections.

The California Supreme Court has taken cognizance of the adverse impact that employment discrimination has on political participation by

23. The State of Oregon conducted a study of gay employment discrimination and found that positive attitudes toward gays in the workplace index closely to the degree of workers' firsthand acquaintance with gays. State of Oregon, Department of Human Resources, *Final Report of the Task Force on Sexual Preference* (Portland: State of Oregon, Department of Human Resources, 1978), pp. 73–87. For a review of the empirical literature on stereotyping of gays, see Alan Taylor, "Conceptions of Masculinity and Femininity as a Basis for Stereotypes of Male and Female Homosexuals," *Journal of Homosexuality* (1983) 9(1):37–53, especially 37–44.

gays. Prior to 1979, Pacific Telephone and Telegraph had an explicit company policy of firing gay employees. No systematic measures were taken by the company to find out who its gay employees were, but "manifest homosexuals," that is, gays who said they were gay or "made an issue of" being gay, were regularly fired. In a groundbreaking case, *Gay Law Students Assoc. v. PT&T Co.*,[24] the court ruled that such firings of 'manifest' gays violated the plaintiffs' political freedoms in violation of the sections of the California Labor Code which forbid employers from preventing employees from engaging or participating in politics.[25] The court recognized, for the first time in U.S. legal history, the special political plight of gays as an invisible minority. It acknowledged that if gays are to have political rights, they must be free to be open about who they are. After holding that the struggle for gay rights is political activity covered by the Code, the decision reads, in relevant part:

> A principal barrier to homosexual equality is the common feeling that homosexuality is an affliction which the homosexual worker must conceal from his employer and his fellow workers. Consequently, one important aspect of the struggle for equal rights is to induce homosexual individuals to "come out of the closet," acknowledge their sexual preferences and to associate with others in working for equal rights. In light of this factor in the movement for homosexual rights, the allegations of the plaintiffs' complaint assumes a special significance.[26]

Here the court recognizes that the ability to be openly gay is a necessary prerequisite for gays, *qua* gay, having any effective political rights. The California Labor Code, in its political dimension, stands to the first amendment as the 1871 Civil Rights Act, with its civil remedies for procedural abuses to equal protection, stands to the fourteenth amendment. These very general legislative acts turn the immunities of the amendments into effective powers.

Now, in the absence of such legislation the courts themselves should not take the step of construing constitutional guarantees as powers rather than as mere immunities,[27] by ruling, say, that first amendment

24. *Gay Law Students Assn. v. Pacific Telephone and Telegraph Co.*, 24 Cal. 3d 458, 595 P.2d 592, 156 Cal. Rptr. 14 (1979).
25. Cal. Lab. Code, §§ 1101, 1102 (West 1971). These sections were passed in 1937.
26. *Gay Law Students Assoc. v. PT&T Co.*, 24 Cal. 3d at 488 (1979).
27. Exceptions are those few rights in the Constitution that explicitly are powers,

rights entail rights to welfare and education as necessary enabling conditions for the equitable realization of first amendment rights. As long as the courts merely say in what ways the government *may not deploy* its monopoly of coercive forces against individuals and systematically avoid mandating (except as compensation for violations of constitutional immunities) that the government *must deploy* its monopoly on coercion in some way, then the courts, while retaining the legitimate capacity to construe constitutional rights broadly, avoid the conservative's common charge that in dilating constitutional guarantees, the courts mistakenly act like Platonic Guardians and usurp the proper power and function of legislatures.[28] But, the very last thing that Plato's Platonic Guardians do is to dispense to individuals immunities from state coercion. Their core activity, *like that of legislatures,* is essentially to deploy coercive force against individuals by either prohibiting or compelling acts in the private sector. If courts avoid coercing the private sector, they systematically avoid intruding into the essential activity of legislatures.

If, however, civil rights protections are to remain creatures of legislatures rather than the courts, the problem arises that the majority is left as the judge of its own fairness to minorities. Those most in need of such protections seem the least likely on their own to acquire them. Here the California case is instructive to political strategists. The labor code covers gays without explicitly mentioning them. Yet the omission is neither a ruse nor an oversight. Rather, the labor code appeals to general principle and general social realities, and in doing so is broad enough in scope that many people will find it attractive legislation. For many can imagine themselves as potential beneficiaries of it. And so the likelihood of enacting such legislation is greatly enhanced.

---

namely, a defendant's right to compulsory process at criminal trials for producing witnesses on his behalf and thirteenth amendment rights against slavery and involuntary servitude.

28. See for example Chief Justice Burger's dissent in *Plyler v. Doe,* 457 U.S. 202, 242–43 (1982): "The Constitution does not constitute us as 'Platonic Guardians' nor does it vest in this Court the authority to strike down laws because they do not meet our standards of desirable social policy. . . . The Court employs, and in my opinion abuses, the Fourteenth Amendment in an effort to become an omnipotent and omniscient problem solver." This view simply confuses immunities and powers.

That nonlegal social forces hinder robust political life to an even greater extent than does government coercion has been eloquently stated by John Stuart Mill:

> It is [social] stigma which is really effective [in stopping] the profession of opinions which are under the ban of society. . . . In respect to all persons but those whose pecuniary circumstances make them independent of the good will of other people, opinion . . . is as efficacious as law; men might as well be imprisoned as excluded from the means of earning their bread. Our merely social intolerance roots out no opinions, but induces men to disguise them or to abstain from any active effort for their diffusion.[29]

Mill probably underestimated the effects of social intolerance in rooting out or even inverting opinions. He shows virtually no awareness of the possibility that members of a despised group may so thoroughly absorb the values of their culture regarding them that they become unwitting participants in their own oppression. Gays seem particularly prone to this mangling of their beliefs about themselves.[30] However, Mill is certainly correct in his general assessment of the effects of social ostracism and job discrimination in blocking the diffusion of unpopular beliefs and forcing their holders into lives of disguise. And though Mill never mentions homosexuals here or elsewhere in *On Liberty,* he could not have picked a clearer illustration for his general thesis.

Up to the AIDS crisis, the meager energies and monies of the gay rights movement had been directed almost exclusively at trying to get 1964 Civil Rights Act protections for gays.[31] Without these legislated rights, which would begin to bring gays into the procedures of democracy, gays have not even been able to begin thinking seriously about the substantial issues on which gays reasonably would want to exert influence in democratic policy making—issues, for instance, concerning sex and solicitation law, licensing, zoning, immigration policy, judicial and prison reform, military and police policy, tax law, educational, medical

29. John Stuart Mill, *On Liberty,* Elizabeth Rapaport, ed., (Indianapolis: Hackett, 1978), pp. 30–31, cf. p. xv.

30. See Andrew Hodges and David Hutter, *With Downcast Gays: Aspects of Homosexual Self-Oppression,* 2d ed. (1974; Toronto: Pink Triangle Press, 1979) and Barry Adam, *The Survival of Domination: Inferiorization and Everyday Life* (New York: Elsevier, 1978), especially chapter 4.

31. Successes have been few in number and their effects minimal. Municipal protections, in particular, tend to be limited in scope, have weak enforcement provisions, have frequently been voided by popular referendum, and have been successfully challenged as unconstitutional violations of state charter provisions which grant powers to cities.

and aging policy, affirmative action, law governing living associations and the transfer of property, and 'family' law. By being effectively denied the public procedures of democracy, gays are incapable of defending their own interests on substantial issues of vital concern.

It is important to remember that the 1964 Civil Rights Act and similar legislation reasonably enough contain exemption provisions that allow for employment discrimination on the basis of an otherwise protected characteristic, *if* a business can show that the discrimination is reasonably necessary to the operation of the business—that is, that the discrimination is a discrimination in good faith. So, for example, it is reasonable for a bank to discriminate in its hiring practices against the invisible minority that consists of repeatedly convicted embezzlers, even though this minority may be organizing politically to try to reform embezzlement laws. However, given exemption provisions for discriminations based on *bona fide* occupational qualifications, ex-convicts, as an invisible minority subject to widespread discrimination, should be, as they are in a few jurisdictions, included within the reach of civil rights protections on the basis of the arguments advanced here. It is also important to note that the arguments for the inclusion of gays as an invisible minority within the reach of the 1964 Civil Rights Act hold good independently of whether gay sex acts are legal in any given jurisdiction.

IV. MAKING DEMOCRACY COHERENT

The previous section argued that the absence of civil rights protections for gays draws into doubt the fairness of current political *procedures* surrounding democratic voting. This section suggests that the same absence also draws into doubt the adequacy of certain *justifications* for democracy.

Perhaps the strongest argument for democracy is that democracy is justified on utilitarian grounds. Those who try to justify democracy as the institution which most directly gives expression to individual dignity simply overestimate the significance of political activity and voting in people's lives. The *consequences* of democratically enacted statute may be great for an individual, but for the vast majority of people, an individual's *contribution* to the democratic system—unless she is political by profession—is slight in her overall pattern of life. Campaigning and voting are sporadic activities. They are neither activities by which individuals sustain their day-to-day lives nor are they activities in which everyday activities culminate. At least one never hears anyone say "I work that I might vote" or "I live that I might vote." And so politics and voting are not integrative principles nor even integral parts of day-to-day life. They are not activities in terms of which any but a few do or should define their lives. The childless curmudgeon who religiously votes against school levies is no more dignified than the social worker who, caught up in a flurry of commitments, fails to vote. The resident alien is not deprived of essential human dignity by his inability to participate fully in the mechanisms of democracy.[32]

This is not to deny that many, even most, of the things that individuals do in their day-to-day lives do have political overtones. Since nearly all of everyday discourse is devoted to persuading people of this or that, or asserting to others the value of this or that, an individual's day-to-day activities will tend to shape other people's views in ways that may well register at the ballot box, but this registration is usually an entirely incidental and unconscious spinoff effect of day-to-day activities and not what motivates them or gives them importance in individuals' lives.

To make democratic politics the paradigmatically human activity is also to place it uncomfortably at odds with soundly held beliefs that voting should be restricted in what it may achieve. If one views voting as the paramount human value, and if voting is not to be made a merely formal activity, a hollow ritual, in virtue of having its effects voided, then one will be committed to a pure, direct democracy operating without substantive constitutional restraints and holding out the prospect that law can be the mere amassing of prejudice—a position virtually everyone would reject.[33]

Further, the right to vote ought not to be viewed even as a value on a moral par with other constitutional rights. The Court has persistently claimed for a century that voting if not *the* fundamental right is at least *a* "fundamental right" on the ground that voting is "preservative of all

32. For a critique of the view that politics represents the central medium for dignity and human value, see Gerald Doppelt, "Rawls' System of Justice: A Critique from the Left," *Nous* (1981) 15:259–307.

33. So correctly Ronald Dworkin arguing against John Hart Ely's *Democracy and Distrust* (note 10 above), which interprets constitutional rights essentially as only procedural rights. See Ronald Dworkin, *A Matter of Principle* (Cambridge: Harvard University Press, 1985), pp. 58–69.

rights"[34] or, put somewhat more modestly, because voting is "preservative of other basic civil and political rights."[35] The Court, however, in these cases simply is conceptually confused. For democratic voting and its deployment of the state's coercive powers by majority rule are how fundamental constitutional rights, including "political" rights like speaking and assembling, are impinged and trampled. At best, the right to vote is how *legally* engendered rights, not constitutional rights, are preserved. That which is the vehicle for the destruction of rights cannot itself be viewed as on a par with them. Therefore, voting is a fundamental right not as other constitutional rights are fundamental, but in consequence of whatever role democracy properly plays in the constellation of just political institutions.[36]

In sum, democracy is a better registrar of desire than it is a vehicle of dignity. And as such, democracy is best justified in utilitarian terms.

It is reasonable to suppose that the policies that overall represent the wishes of the most people will be the policies which will most likely maximize utility. For given the complexity of *predicting* precise consequences of social policies for large and complex populations, relying on the *preferences* of the people in general rather than on the *predictions* of social engineers as likely indicators of future utility seems eminently reasonable.[37] It is precisely in the area of economics and areas which are

34. *Yick Wo v. Hopkins,* 118 U.S. 356, 370 (1886).

35. *Reynolds v. Sims,* 377 U.S. 533, 562 (1964); cf. *Harper v. Virginia Board of Elections,* 383 U.S. 663, 667 (1966).

36. The Court is vaguely aware of this contingent status of what is fundamental about voting, even though the awareness stands at odds with the Court's "preservative of rights" analysis. Thus the Court correctly holds that "the right of suffrage is a fundamental matter *in a free and democratic society"* (*Reynolds v. Sims,* 377 U.S. at 561–62 [1964], emphasis added) and more fully, that "though not regarded strictly as a natural right, but as a privilege merely conceded by society according to its will, under certain conditions, nevertheless [voting] is regarded as a fundamental political right" (*Wick Yo v. Hopkins,* 118 U.S. at 370 [1886]).

The value of the role which democracy plays in any system of just institutions will more than sufficiently warrant bars to most democratically generated restrictions and regulations of the franchise—even if voting is not given the same rank of importance as those other constitutional rights which are implicit in the idea of ordered liberty. *Textually* the right to vote may be derived from the overall structure of the Constitution. See chapter 3, section VI C. *Reynolds v. Sims* reaches the right result: infringements on the right to vote must pass the highest constitutional standards.

37. For a related argument to this end, see Ronald Dworkin, *Taking Rights Seriously* (Cambridge: Harvard University Press, 1977), p. 233.

productive of public goods—ones which each person wants but cannot get (or get efficiently) without the coercive coordinations of the state— that democracy is going to be the most accurate guide for social policy and least justifiably accused of irrationally burdening liberty.

However, if preferences pure and simple were the whole rationale involved in establishing social policy, social policies could be determined simply by direct democracy, as manifest in referenda and plebiscites.

For democracy coherently to have a preference-utilitarian justification, though, requires that a distinction be drawn between an individual's internal and external preferences. A person's internal preferences are her preferences for goods and services *for herself*. Her external preferences are preferences that she has for things *for persons other than herself*. To be *coherent* preference-justified democracy must discount and disregard a person's external preferences. For the person who has external preferences and who would have society act upon them is assuming for himself the role of social engineer—a role discredited by the very premises of the argument justifying democracy in terms of preferences.[38] Further, if democracy is to be an *accurate* gauge of likely utility maximization, it must for this reason also discount external preferences. For in general it is unlikely that anyone other than a person himself is going to know what is best for himself; hardly anyone will hold another's interest in the same regard that he holds his own.[39]

38. This argument is similar to an argument that Dworkin makes only in passing to the effect that in many cases counting a person's external political preferences (say, for some group not to get some scarce resource, when the person does not want or need the resource for himself) will simply be self-defeating from a utilitarian standpoint (*Taking*, p. 235 middle). I do not wish to commit my argument to Dworkin's assumptions that the right to treatment as an equal is the most fundamental of rights (*Taking*, p. 273) and that taking external preferences into account in social policy is wrong as violating that right (*Taking*, pp. 234–35, 275–76).

Even the necessary proviso in any utilitarian justification for democracy that each person's preferences are to count for one can be justified in purely utilitarian terms without appeals to general principles of equality. For, given the presumption that we are only considering conscious *homo sapiens* as voters and are not including in the franchise, say, comatose individuals or especially sensitive creatures from space, and given that people are more equal than unequal in their sensitivity and in the volume of their desires, then it seems likely that assigning one nonweighted vote to each will be a more accurate gauge in general of overall preference than if we try to establish some (unimaginable) mechanism to weight votes for small variations in either sensitivities or intensities of preferences.

39. See Mill, *On Liberty*, pp. 74–75.

If, in consequence, external preferences are to be disregarded in the calculus of preferences, then direct democracy cannot be the instrument for this measurement. For referenda and plebiscites give equal weight to internal and external preferences; they give equal weight to the views of bigots and non-bigots. The remedy—where the distribution of powers rather than immunities is concerned—is a form of representative democracy in which it is hoped the elected official is rational enough and impartial enough to rise above popular prejudices and to take into account in her own voting only the internal preferences of her constituents. A legislator who discounts external preferences is not to suffer the accusation of moral elitism, for she is acting in accordance with sound democratic principles.[40]

Now, there are two sorts of external preferences which the rational legislator must discount. He must, on the one hand, discount the crass egoist's preferences for disutilities to be distributed to others and discount the possible attendant sadistic pleasures which the egoist might take in seeing other people's plans defeated.[41] On the other hand, the legislator must disregard the preferences of the altruist, who wishes to see the utilities of others promoted, and must discount the possible

40. So correctly Dworkin, *Taking*, p. 255, but contrast p. 276 bottom, where it is claimed that the mechanisms of democracy are incapable of winnowing internal and external preferences. In the latter passage, though, Dworkin simply runs together the mechanisms of direct democracy and representational democracy. The numerous cases in which city councils have passed gay civil rights legislation only to have it overturned by vast margins in referenda would suggest that legislators can on occasion rise above the prejudices of their constituents. The solution to the problem is not to abandon all hope that legislatures might effect a refined utilitarianism, opting instead for a democratic system awash in prejudices and checked only by constitutional immunities. The solution is for the Court to dust off the Guarantee Clause of the Constitution with its requirement that the federal government guarantee a *republican* form of government in the states (article IV, section 4), resurrect it from the deadletter status to which it was assigned in the original reapportionment case, *Baker v. Carr*, 369 U.S. 186, 224 (1962), and with it void that decidedly nonrepublican mode of governance: the referendum. Cf. *Fortson v. Morris*, 385 U.S. 231, 249 (1966) (Fortas, J., dissenting).

41. I disagree with Dworkin that external preferences are no "less a source of pleasure when satisfied and displeasure when ignored, than purely personal preferences" (*Taking*, p. 276). The pleasure of external preferences satisfied is illusory in intensity. For such pleasures are parasitic upon a mere perceived *contrast* of one's situation to that of another —and are not consequences of anything one has done or experienced on one's own. Such pleasures have a similar status to mere absences or cessations of pains. One can discount such pleasures *even on a utilitarian account*. Again, one need not resort to a theory of rights to rid the utilitarian calculus of external preferences; see n. 38 above.

masochistic pleasures which the altruist might take in seeing the plans of others succeed.[42]

The rational legislator will sift through his mail, public debates, editorials, letter columns and all the other modes of public discussion of social policies and will winnow out external preferences. The legislator in this scheme is as justified in disregarding the altruistic opinions of the well-intended heterosexual (or would-be heterosexual) do-gooder who writes him supporting gay-positive legislation, as he is to disregard the opinion of the religious zealot who desires state persecution of gays.

If this system of justifications for democratic procedures is to work, it presupposes that people can present publicly their opinions on social policy as desires for things for themselves. They must be able to present themselves publicly as members of classes of which they in fact are members, so that they can promote legislation which benefits them as members of their classes.

For preference-utilitarianism to be a coherent rationale for democracy, everyone must be permitted to present himself in public debate as what he is. For preference democracy to be coherent, gays must be free to present themselves publicly as gays; and gays are effectively precluded this option, if the means by which they live can be removed from them at whim for being publicly gay. Civil rights protections for invisible minorities are a necessary prerequisite for coherent democratic processes.

V. POLITICAL PARADOX AND POLITICAL DECENCY

Current society puts gays in the queer position of not being able to fight for gay rights unless gays are already "out" and gays cannot be "out" unless gays already have gay rights. Paradoxically, gays cannot get gay rights, unless they already have them. This "particularly vicious circle" was noted over thirty years ago by an author himself closeted. Little has changed:

> On the one hand, . . . the social punishment of acknowledgment [of one's homosexuality is] so great that pretense is almost universal; on the other

42. See Dworkin, *Taking*, pp. 235, 277 top. Whatever the moral worth of the altruist's acts and their masochistic pleasures, the intensity of the pleasures is again illusory based not upon anything that one's self has accomplished or experienced directly.

hand, only a leadership that would acknowledge [its homosexuality] would be able to break down the barriers . . . of discrimination. Until the world is able to accept us on an equal basis as human beings entitled to the full rights of life, we are unlikely to have any great numbers willing to become martyrs. . . . But until we are willing to speak out openly and frankly in defense of our activities and to identify ourselves with the millions pursuing these activities, we are unlikely to find the attitudes of the world undergoing any significant change.[43]

The author perhaps overestimates the potential effectiveness of martyrs;[44] but his main point is sound. As an invisible minority, gays cannot fight for the right to be open about being gay, unless gays are already open about it; and gays cannot reasonably be open about being gay, until gays have the right to be openly gay. One would hope that once society was made aware of this paradox, if society had any sense of decency and fair play, it would on its own move to establish civil rights for gays.

43. Donald Webster Cory [pseud.], *The Homosexual in America* (New York: Greenberg, 1951), p. 14. For the strange history of "Donald Webster Cory," subsequently the antigay polemicist Edward Sagarin, see D'Emilio, *Sexual Politics*, pp. 33, 57, 98, 139, 167–69.

44. Thus during the 1985 nationally televised Academy Awards, a seemingly ingenuous presenter could describe a documentary movie on the assassination of a gay activist elected official—*The Times of Harvey Milk*—merely as "a film about American values in conflict." *GayLife* [Chicago] March 28, 1985, 10(39), sect. X, p. 1. Had the film not won the "best documentary" award, no one in the audience of millions not already in the know would have learned that the film even had a gay content. As it was, the award recipients made mention only of their subject's pride, not his death, while those in the know were left with the suspicion that the Academy supposes that killing gays is an "American value."

7. Can Antigay Discrimination Be Noninvidious?

This chapter argues that there are no good moral reasons for exempting gays as a class from the protections against discrimination in employment which Title VII of the 1964 Civil Rights Act affords racial, gender, ethnic and religious classes.

For the range of issues discussed here, it will be assumed that the elimination of arbitrariness with respect to the persons with whom one makes business contracts is a reasonable government function. The justifications for such legal rights against discrimination are diverse and were discussed earlier.[1] All but the most hardened of libertarians would accept this, and even hardened libertarians are likely to hold that consistency demands that if some classes are afforded such protections, all relevantly similar classes should also be afforded the same protections. And I take it that it is not in general the claim that one's sexual orientation is dissimilar in relevant respects to one's protected properties (race, religion) that forms the core of possible reasonable objections to the inclusion of gays within the protections of the Civil Rights Act.

For, on the one hand, if sexual orientation is something over which an individual has virtually no control, either for genetic or psychological reasons, then sexual orientation becomes relevantly similar to race, gender, and ethnicity. Discrimination on these grounds is deplorable because it holds a person accountable without regard for anything *he himself* has done. And to hold a person accountable for things over which she has no control is a central form of prejudice. A similar argument from nonprejudicial consistency would seem persuasive for also including most of the physically and mentally challenged within the reach of the Civil Rights Act. And indeed Congress has extended such protections to these groups in the Rehabilitation Act of 1973.[2]

1. See chapters 5 and 6.
2. The Rehabilitation Act, 29 USCS §§ 701 et seq., Pub. L. 93–112, 87 Stat. 359 (1973).

On the other hand, if acquiring one's sexual orientation is a matter of individual choice or, more generally, of individual responsibility, sexual orientation would seem relevantly similar to religion, which is a protected category. Importantly, too, the protections of the 1973 Rehabilitation Act make no distinction between the *sources* of the handicaps they cover: the person whose handicap is willfully or negligently inflicted upon himself is as protected by the Act as is the person whose handicap is of irreversible, congenital origin. It is not simply conditions beyond the reach of the individual will that are protected by civil rights legislation.

Frequently, however, popular debate on the proper scope of civil rights protections takes no note of or conveniently forgets the cases of religion and negligent or even willful handicap as having such protections. Claims then by some politicians and religious leaders to the effect that civil rights provisions should not be extended from the protection of *status* to the protection of *behavior*—under the latter of which they suppose being gay falls—are simply mistaken about the current reach of civil law. This oversight is particularly bizarre in the case of religious leaders—or at least those who fail to call for the revocation of protections for religious behavior, such as religious observances and practices. The 1964 Civil Rights Act specifically requires that employers make arrangements "reasonably [to] accommodate . . . an employee's . . . religious observance or practice."[3]

Foreseeing the possible difficulty which the case of religious protection poses for religious objectors to gay protections, some religious advocates have claimed, oddly enough, that religion is not a matter of choice but the result of social conditioning, coercive family tradition, or the like. But since every day of the week people do freely and sincerely change their religions, and indeed are even encouraged by religions to convert, this claim seems to be, as a simple matter of fact, false. Further, the claim is conceptually incompatible at least with Christian religions, for which acceptance of the savior must be voluntary in order to be meaningful and for which man's free will with its attendant prospect for evil actions explains how it can morally be that there is evil in God's world though he is omnipotent and good: providing man with free will maximizes good in the world even though it means that there also will necessarily be some evil in it.

3. 42 USCS § 2000e, Title VII, § 701(j).

In the alternative, it has been suggested that the first amendment requires that the government view religious behavior as involuntary even if it is not: "For the state to classify such a belief [that is, a belief that 'all of one's beliefs are ordained by God'] as voluntary is in fact to deny freedom of religion to all its holders."[4] This claim misunderstands constitutional rights. For constitutional immunities, like those of the first amendment, require only *tolerance* of that which they protect, including actions and behavior, whether political marches or religious advocacy; they do not transform voluntary behavior into something it is not. Government may require, on nonpolitical grounds, parade permits for political marches and even bar the sidewalk distribution of religious literature by children,[5] exactly because the parades and distribution are *behavior* and not merely *states* of belief. It would be silly to say that the first amendment required that a parade not be treated as action and behavior even if the marchers sincerely believed that they had no choice in holding the belief that what they were doing was not an action or behavior. Religious attempts to remold religion as a form of "race" in order to escape from having consistency force an admission that behaviors and lifestyles are protected by the Civil Rights Act will not work.

Now, one would say that a personal moral choice, such as that of one's religion, is not a reasonable ground for discrimination *even when* the private belief in and practice of it has very public manifestations, as when a religious person becomes involved in politics with a religious motive and a religious intent. And to claim that gay sex is in some sense immoral will not suffice to establish a relevant dissimilarity here. For the nonreligious and the religious may consider each other immoral in this same sense and various religious sects will consider each other immoral, and yet all religious belief is protected. Indeed the point of protecting religion in the Civil Rights Act at least in part appears to be to insulate religious beliefs, practices, and observances, as a paradigmatically private affair or personal matter, from the judgments and social pressures of others so that at least one's material circumstances do not depend

4. Samuel McCracken, "Are Homosexuals Gay?" in Burton Leiser, ed., *Values in Conflict: Life, Liberty and the Rule of Law*, pp. 301–10, quote from p. 302 (New York: Macmillan, 1981), reprinted from *Commentary* (January 1979) 67:23–28.

5. *Prince v. Massachusetts*, 321 U.S. 158 (1944) (upheld, against challenges based on the free exercise of religion and parental rights to substantive due process, a bar on children distributing religious literature on the streets even when they are accompanied by their parents).

upon conformity to someone else's religious beliefs and practices. The same justification holds equally well for protecting gays, their sexual orientation (even if chosen), and behavior in accordance with it: to insulate paradigmatically private activity from the effective judgment of others so that at least one's material circumstances do not depend upon conformity to someone else's beliefs regarding sexual behavior and orientation.[6]

So it appears that consistency by itself generates a strong prima facie case for including sexual orientation within the ambit of the 1964 Civil Rights Act. For sexual orientation is relevantly similar to either race or religion. Now, the Civil Rights Act reasonably enough has an exemption clause which allows for discrimination on the basis of a protected category when the discrimination against an otherwise protected category represents a "bona fide occupational qualification reasonably necessary to the normal operation of that particular business or enterprise."[7] This explicit exemption applies to religion, gender, and national origin, *not* to race,[8] but the courts have allowed an affirmative "business necessity" defense for discrimination based *even on* race.[9] Such exemptions when tied to the specific nature of the business in question are reasonable since they mean that discrimination carried out under the exemptions cease to be whimsical or arbitrary, cannot arguably be construed as degrading members of protected classes, and do not promote social inefficiency. Such discriminations are discriminations in good faith.

Two obvious examples of good faith discrimination are the following. First, it seems obvious that a sperm bank can legitimately limit offers to buy only to males and need not go through all the initial screening tests on anyone, regardless of gender, who might walk in through the door. Second, even if Laurence Olivier may play Othello satisfactorily, it is good faith discrimination for the director of the movie *The Life of Martin Luther King Jr.* to consider only black male actors for the title role. Such a movie would not have the degree of artificiality which

---

6. For arguments that gay sexual behavior is indeed paradigmatically private, see chapter 4.

7. Title VII, § 703(e).

8. *Ibid.*

9. See, for example, *Robinson v. Lorillard Corp.,* 444 F.2d 791 (4th Cir. 1971) (permitting as an affirmative defense against Title VII challenge the claim that an otherwise protected discrimination is a business necessity; in the case at hand—that of a racially based seniority system—the defense, however, was found wanting).

allows Jessye Norman to sing Elsa without a hitch and requires a mezzo soprano to sing Octavian. Race discrimination in the *King* movie would seem necessary to its artistic success yet that success would not depend upon racist beliefs nor would the discrimination tend to perpetuate racial discrimination and racial stereotypes—far from it. Indeed the racial distinction made in the movie would seem necessary to keep the movie from appearing to be the painful and insulting joke on blacks that Al Jolson's singing in blackface was.

It appears that the one possibly reasonable attempt to argue that gays should not be afforded civil rights protections is that in their case such exemptions swallow the rule—that is, nearly all discrimination against gays is discrimination in good faith, so that it would be disingenuous to include gays within the compass of protected classes. The rest of the chapter argues that virtually all attempts to justify discrimination against gays as discrimination in good faith fail, so that there is nothing remotely approaching a general case to be made for exemptions of gays from civil rights protections. It will emerge that attempts to justify discrimination against gays fall into fairly clear recurrent patterns, all of which have some obvious moral flaw or which have been rejected as grounds for discrimination in the case of other protected groups. Examples of attempted (and all too frequently successful) discriminations against gays —discriminations defended as discriminations in good faith—will be here drawn from the public sector, where, thanks to even the weakest interpretation of the fourteenth amendment's Equal Protection Clause, there is already a general presumption against antigay discrimination and where such discrimination is permissible only if it is rationally related to a legitimate government interest.

When trying to give an account of what constitutes good faith discrimination, one enters murky territory. In current practice, there is no widely recognized and accepted taxonomy of what constitutes good faith discrimination, nor is there any obvious sufficient set of general principles governing what constitutes a good faith discrimination. Is it, for instance, a good faith discrimination for the new management of a bar that has gone gay to fire all the nongay union employees of the former management, claiming that only gay waiters will make the bar's new clientele feel comfortable? This is an actual case that occurred in the late 1970's in Toronto. The outcome of a legal challenge to the firings was that the same court which had ruled earlier that the new management of what was to become an Irish bar could fire all the previous non-Irish employees, ruled against the new gay management, claiming that "being gay is not as substantially different as being Irish." So stated, we seem to have here bad grammar, dubious metaphysics, and liberal condescension all masking bigotry; but, I wish to contend that for whatever bad reasons the court used for this ruling, it was nevertheless the correct one.

For I suggest that the following is a valid general principle governing the establishment of good faith discriminations. The principle is that simply citing the current existence of prejudice, bigotry, or discrimination in a society against some group or citing the obvious consequences of such prejudice, bigotry, or discrimination can never constitute a good reason in trying to establish a good faith discrimination against that group. Let us call this principle oscar wilde. Wilde tells us that stigmas which are entirely socially induced shall not play a part in our rational moral deliberations. I suggest, for instance, that a community could not legitimately claim that a bylaw banning blacks from buying houses in the community was a good faith discrimination on the grounds that whenever blacks move into a heretofore white area, property values plummet. This is illegitimate, since it is only the current bigotry in the society that causes property values to drop—as the result of white flight and the subsequent reduction in the size of the purchasing market.

In general, the *fact* that people discriminate can never be cited as a good reason for institutionalizing discrimination. But even more clearly, the current existence of discrimination cannot ethically ground the continuance of the discrimination, when there are reasonable prima facie claims against discrimination. To hold otherwise is to admit the validity of the heckler's veto: to hold that it is acceptable for the state to prevent a speaker from speaking when a heckler in advance threatens disruption if the speaker does speak.

If wilde is intuitively obvious (once attention is drawn to it), it has a direct bearing on almost every case where people try to justify discrimination against gays as discrimination in good faith. A recent antigay prison ruling offers an especially pure example of the successful invocation of the heckler's veto. The Sixth Federal Circuit has allowed the barring of the national gay Metropolitan Community Churches from holding religious services in prisons although it allows all other denominations to do so. The Court bought without examination the state's contention that "permitting the [gay] Church's congregate worship services was unacceptable because it would increase the opportunities for identification of homosexual inmates" and so "expose innocent inmates, who might choose to attend the Church's group meetings, to violent and predatory prisoners" and so "innocent inmates would become victims of rapes, intimidation, extortion and personal abuse."[10] Phony paternalism aside, here the heckler's veto becomes the rapist's veto—threats of the violent are allowed to morally ground restrictions on the liberty of the wholly innocent.

The reach of wilde is wider still. For one of the obvious ranges of its application is cases where some joint project is a necessary part of a job. It is in this category of cases that good faith discriminations against gays are most often attempted.

Bans against gays in the armed forces and on police forces are classic cases of the attempt to establish such good faith discrimination against gays. The armed forces, after losing a series of court cases at the turn of the decade, have abandoned the strategy that gays make incompetent soldiers as the basis for their systematic discrimination against gays. In light of the Matlovich case, the Beller case, and others[11] in which gay soldiers were shown to have sterling performance records, the armed forces no longer rest their policy on such contentions as the claims that all faggots have limp wrists; limp wrists cannot tote and fire M16's; and therefore gays reduce combat readiness. Instead the Pentagon has placed renewed emphasis on the contention that gays cause a drop in morale and for this reason reduce combat readiness. As of January 16, 1981, the Pentagon has seven, official, articulated reasons for banning gays:

> The presence of such members adversely affects the ability of the armed forces [1] to maintain discipline, good order and morale, [2] to foster

10. *Brown v. Johnson*, 743 F.2d 408, 412 (6th Cir. 1984) (upholding a bar to gay church services in a prison where church services conducted by all other denominations are permitted).

11. See *Matlovich v. Secretary of the Air Force*, 414 F. Supp. 690 (D.D.C. 1976); *benShalom v. Secretary of Army*, 489 F. Supp. 964 (E.D. Wis. 1980); *Beller v. Middendorf*, 632 F.2d 788 (9th Cir. 1980). For the current depressing status of gay military law, see Rhonda R. Rivera, "Queer Law: Sexual Orientation Law in the Mid-Eighties—Part II," *University of Dayton Law Review* (1986) 11:287–324. In February 1988, however, a divided three-judge panel of the Ninth Federal Circuit, in the most intelligent gay-related opinion on record, held that exclusions by the armed forces based on sexual orientation are violations of the Equal Protection Clause, which the panel interpreted as giving homosexuals the same degree of protection as it gives to blacks. *Watkins v. United States Army*, 837 F.2d 1428 (9th Cir. 1988).

mutual trust and confidence among servicemembers, [3] to insure the integrity of the system of rank and command, [4] to facilitate assignment and worldwide deployment of servicemembers who frequently must live and work under close conditions affording minimal privacy, [5] to recruit and retain members of the armed forces, [6] to maintain the public acceptability of military service, and [7] to prevent breaches of security.[12]

Claims 1 through 6 form a group. Claim 7 is discussed in a separate context below. What all the first six claims have negatively in common is that none of them is based on the ability of gay soldiers to fulfill the duties of their stations. More generally, none of the claims is based on gays *doing* anything at all. So whatever else may be said for the policy, it lacks the virtue of being a moral stance, since it is a minimum requirement of a moral stance that people are judged and held culpable only for *actions* of their own doing. What the six reasons have positively in common is that their force relies exclusively on current widespread bigoted attitudes against gays. They appeal to the bigotry and consequent disruptiveness of nongay soldiers (reasons 1, 2, 3, and 5) who apparently are made "up-tight" by the mere presence of gay soldiers and officers, and so claim that they cannot work effectively in necessary joint projects with gay soldiers. The reasons appeal to the antigay prejudices of our own society (reason 6), especially that segment of it which constitutes potential recruits (reason 5), and to the antigay prejudices of other societies (reason 4). No reasons other than currently existing widespread prejudice and bigotry of others are appealed to here in order to justify a discriminatory policy. So all six reasons violate wilde and are illegitimate.

Gay soldiers are being discriminated against on current Pentagon policy simply because currently existing bigotry and prejudice are counted as good reasons in trying to establish good faith discrimination. To accept such a reasoning process as sound is to act like a right-wing terrorist who produces social disorder through indiscriminate bombings and then claims that what is needed is a police state. Clearly the social

12. The current exclusion of gays from all branches of the military is contained in Department of Defense Directive 1332.14, *Federal Register,* January 29, 1981, 46(19):9571–78. The whole slew of rationalizations offered in the Directive has been accepted as reasonable, indeed endorsed as "common sense," by the federal courts. *Dronenburg v. Zech,* 741 F.2d 1388, 1398 (D.C. Cir. 1984). See though, *Watkins v. United States Army,* 837 F.2d at 1448–51, which rejected the armed forces' rationales, correctly viewing them as irrational prejudices.

problem created by the bigoted soldiers and the terrorist is not solved if society accedes to their demands. It is soldiers who do not cease to be bigoted, not gay soldiers, who should be thrown out of the armed forces. Practically, of course, the solution to the problem is for the armed forces to re-educate its bigots and to expel those who are incorrigible. It should be remembered that until 1948 the U.S. armed forces were racially segregated on exactly the same grounds as those adduced now for barring gays, and especially on the ground that whites could not work with blacks. That year, by Presidential executive order, the forces were racially integrated and the skies did not fall. The West German armed forces have been integrated with respect to sexual orientation in noncommissioned ranks and the skies have not fallen there either. The Dutch forces are integrated at all levels, and even the Israeli army has integrated forces, though the Israeli army treats gay men as the United States forces treat women: they are prevented from filling combat roles.[13]

It is perhaps worthy of note that the current Pentagon policy on gays is simply a mirror image of the long-standing antigay policy of the International Association of Chiefs of Police, a policy which for the same reasons is equally illegitimate. That policy reads:

> Whereas, the life-style of homosexuals is abhorrent to most members of the society we serve, identification with this life-style destroys trust, confidence and esteem so necessary in both fellow workers and the general public for a police agency to operate efficiently and effectively; now, therefore, be it resolved, that the IACP reaffirm[s] its position established in 1958 . . . and thereby endorses a no hire policy for homosexuals in law enforcement.[14]

Despite the bogus appeal to "life-style," gays are here again being discriminated against not for anything they *do,* or on the basis of their ability to carry out police duties, but solely on the basis of the bigoted attitudes of others. If, as is quite possibly the case, the majority of society

13. For gay military policy around the world, see International Association of Lesbians, Gay Women and Gay Men, *IGA-Pink Book: A Global View of Lesbian and Gay Oppression and Liberation* (Amsterdam: COC-magazijn, 1985); for West Germany, see p. 142, on the Israeli army, see pp. 70–73. On the Dutch armed forces, see *The Advocate* [Los Angeles], January 5, 1988, no. 489, p. 11: "Dutch army recruitment brochures note that applications from gays are encouraged and if gays encounter problems, they should contact . . . the agency Homosexuals and Military, an officially recognized advisory service for Dutch gay soldiers."

14. International Association of Chiefs of Police, *The Police Yearbook 1978* (IACP, Gaithersburg, Md.), pp. 346–47.

lacks trust and confidence in and finds abhorrent blacks, Latinos, women, and Jews *as* police officers, the argument would hold equally well against these groups, and yet the argument singles out only gays. So aside from being a bad argument, based entirely on violations of wilde, the policy fails to treat relevantly similar cases similarly.

I wish to give three other, I hope now obvious, examples of bad faith parading as good faith. The U.S. Civil Service Commission has ceased as a matter of policy to discriminate against gays,[15] but discrimination against gays is still systematic in the State Department, the CIA, the FBI, and the armed forces, on the alleged good faith discrimination that gays are security risks, since they are, it is claimed, subject to blackmail.[16] That gays are subject to blackmail, though, is simply the result of

15. See *The Federal Personnel Manual*, S3-2a. (3)(c), subchapter 53, Guidelines for Applying Specific Factors, United States Civil Service Commission, Federal Personnel Manual Systems, FPM Supplement 731-1, Inst. 2, July 31, 1979, p. 8; see also *Memorandum, Policy Statement on Discrimination on the Basis of Conduct Which Does Not Adversely Affect the Performance of Employees or Applicants for Employment* (Office of Personnel Management, May 12, 1980). On gays in federal employment, see Rhonda R. Rivera, "Queer Law: Sexual Orientation Law in the Mid-Eighties—Part I," *University of Dayton Law Review* (1985) 10:483–86.

16. On security clearances for gays, see Rivera, "Queer Law—Part II," pp. 275–87; in theory and in practice, but not in policy, the armed forces have dropped, as a rationale for the exclusion of gays, the belief that gays are security risks. Rivera concludes her exhaustive analysis of military cases crossing into 1986: "Finally, the Army's varying reasons for excluding gay people have at last been refined to only one reason—the problems allegedly created by the 'social intolerance of peers.' No longer are gays erroneously portrayed as incompetent or security risks. Now the justification is clear and simple" (*ibid.*, p. 313). Subsequently, the Department of Defense has reaffirmed its policy of gay exclusions from security clearances on grounds that are unintelligible or cagey or both. 32 *Code of Federal Rules*, Part 154.7 (1987); the whole set of security regulations is published in *Federal Register*, April 8, 1987, 52(67):11219-56. In these new rules, the final criterion for exclusion from security clearances—criterion "q"—is "Acts of sexual misconduct or perversion indicative of moral turpitude, poor judgment, or lack of regard for the laws of society." *Ibid.*, p. 11222. However, disregard for *any* law and poor judgment about *anything* are independent grounds for exclusions—respectively, criteria "g" and "i" (*ibid.*) —so the rationale for mentioning sexuality at all here reduces to the contentless and job-irrelevant pleonasm "moral turpitude." More mysterious still: when one turns to the Department's interpretation of criterion "q," as bearing on gays, in the Department's legally binding "Adjudication Policy," one finds that the interpretation has nothing to do with "turpitude." The problem now, we learn, is one of "disorder." The severally sufficient "disqualifying factors" for the application of "q" include: "Deviant or perverted sexual behavior which may indicate a mental or personality disorder (e.g., transexualism, transvestism, exhibitionism, incest, child molestation, voyeurism, bestiality, or sodomy)." *Ibid.*, p. 11254. Leave it to a government bureaucracy to use the modal "may" in a restrictive subordinate clause. This is garble, nothing more.

currently existing prejudices and bigotries in the society, some of which are enshrined in law and government practice; so this argument violates wilde. Further, since the fact that one will be thrown out of the CIA (or any of the other organizations mentioned above) if exposed is what leads to the potential for blackmail, the argument also looks as though it is verging on being circular; for the government policy establishes the situation the government is trying to avoid, and then the government uses this situation as a reason for its policy. The rational government policy would be to encourage gays to be open about their sexual orientation, especially to their families, so that the agency would have the widest possible pool of candidates from which to select personnel to fill what it admits to be highly specialized roles. The more highly specialized the task, the more reasonable it is to maintain the widest pool of potential candidates. In any case, the rationale for the policy of exclusion, circularity of argument aside, can hardly be claimed of those who are already open about their sexuality. These people surely cannot be blackmailed. The practical solution is for the President to issue an executive order banning discrimination on the basis of sexual orientation for all those who are out or are willing to come out upon the government's discovering "their little secret" and to promote those social programs, including civil rights legislation, which will promote the openness of gays.

All this aside, there is good reason to believe that the whole worry over sexual security clearances is a giant red herring—concocted for the sake of heterosexual ideology alone. For, on the one hand, the government has never come up with even a single instance of a gay American soldier, sailor, or spy who was successfully blackmailed. The only example the government ever uses is an Austrian closet-case from the First World War.[17] A federal district judge recently summed up the government's evidence for the blackmail of gays with security clearances:

> There is simply no evidence of either a gay applicant for a security clearance having been tempted by blackmail or any lesbians or gay men who have obtained industrial clearance having transmitted classified information to anyone unauthorized to receive it. At the Senate Permanent Subcommittee

17. See "Employment of Homosexuals and Other Sex Perverts in Government," U.S. Senate Committee on Expenditures, Interim Report, 81st Congress, 2d Session (December 15, 1950), p. 5, reprinted in Jonathan Katz, ed., *Government Versus Homosexuals* (New York: Arno, 1975).

on Investigations hearings of April 1985, the FBI and the Defense Intelligence Agency produced no evidence of persons being blackmailed because of homosexuality. Of the approximately 40 "significant" espionage cases, two involved gay people; neither of these involved blackmail.[18]

Further, empirical study has shown that gays can be found in the armed forces at nearly the rate that they are found in the general population and that the armed forces is very poor at weeding out gay soldiers, even though the vast majority of them are sexually active while in the services.[19] So the national security establishment can hardly claim that the reason that there are no blackmail cases of record is because the policy of exclusion based on prospective blackmail has been so successful.

Yet, on the other hand, we are bombarded almost daily with press reports of heterosexuals whose selling of our country down the river has been heterosexually enhanced—as the result either of procreation, as in the case of the Walker family spy ring,[20] or of sexual liaisons with foreigners, as when Sargeant Clayton Lonetree and other confessed heterosexual U.S. Marines escorted their communist paramours around the parts of our Moscow embassy which they were supposed to be securing from spies.[21] Had these Marines been sleeping with each other rather than with communists, our national security would be ever so much better off. But it has never crossed the mind of the security establishment that heterosexuals pose a serious threat to America and the security establishment keeps right on recruiting them—at our documented peril.

Take as another example of bad faith discrimination the arguments used in lesbian child custody cases. In no other area has socially en-

18. *High Tech Gays v. Defense Industrial Security Clearance Office*, 668 F. Supp. 1361, 1375 (N.D. Cal. 1987) (holding gays a quasi-suspect class under Equal Protection Clause and so giving them rights similar in strength to those of women and illegitimate children) (citing *Federal Government Security Clearance Program: Hearings Before the Permanent Subcommittee on Investigations of Committee on Governmental Affairs United States Senate*, 99th Congress, 1st Session [April 16, 1985], pp. 171–87, 913–26).

19. Joseph Harry, "Homosexual Men and Women Who Served Their Country," *Journal of Homosexuality* (1984) 10(1–2):117–25.

20. See "Two Walkers Plead Guilty to Spying: Chance to Debrief Ring's Mastermind Called 'Essential' " and "A Loyal Son's Path into Espionage," both in *The Washington Post*, October 29, 1985, p. 1; "Father and Son Get Spying Terms: John Walker Is Told To Serve Life and Michael 25 Years for Roles in Navy Ring," *The New York Times*, November 7, 1986, p. Y14.

21. "Third Marine Guard From U.S. Embassy in Moscow Arrested," *The New York Times*, April 1, 1987, p. 1; "Marine Convicted by Court-Martial of Embassy Spying: Guilty on All 13 Accounts," *The New York Times*, August 22, 1987, p. 1.

dorsed stereotyping been so flatfootedly appealed to in forming social policy.[22] Despite some recent positive developments in legal theory, legal practice in nearly all jurisdictions operates on a strong presumption in favor of giving custody to the mother, *unless* the mother is a lesbian, in which case the presumption of parental fitness shifts sharply in the direction of the father. Sometimes the argument for this sharp shift is merely a statement of bigotry. It runs: lesbians are evil; lesbians cause their children to be lesbians; and therefore, lesbians cause their children to be evil.[23] In attempts to justify this shift as a good faith discrimination, the argument runs as follows: there is nothing inherently evil about mother or child being lesbian, but nevertheless, since, while the child is growing, there will be strong social recrimination from peers and other parents against the child as it becomes known in the community that the mother is a lesbian, only by discriminating against lesbian mothers are their children spared unnecessary suffering.[24] This argument, I take it, is an obvious violation of wilde. Currently existing bigotry and its consequences are cited as the only reason for perpetrating and institutionalizing discrimination. Note that if one does not think such discrimination

22. For recent developments in lesbian and gay child custody cases, see Rivera, "Queer Law—Part II," pp. 327–71. For horror stories, see any issue of *Mom's Apple Pie: Newsletter of the Lesbian Mothers' National Defense Fund* [Seattle].

23. Thus, for example, a recent lesbian child custody case out of Missouri held:

> [M]orality is always a factor in child custody cases. . . . The wife and [her lesbian] lover show affection toward one another in front of the children. They sleep together in the same bed at the family home in Union. When [the] wife and four children travel to St. Louis to see Airrow [the lover], they also sleep together there. All of these factors present an unhealthy environment for minor children. Such conduct can never be kept private enough to be a neutral factor in the development of a child's values and character. We will not ignore such conduct by a parent which may have an effect on the child's moral development.

S.E.G. v. R.A.G., 735 S.W.2d 164, 165, 166 (Mo. App. 1987).

24. The same Missouri case provides a star case of this line of thinking as well:

> Since it is our duty to protect . . . the best interests of the minor children, we find [the w]ife's argument lacking. Union, Missouri is a small, conservative community with a population of about 5,500. Homosexuality is not openly accepted or widespread. We wish to protect the children from peer pressure, teasing, and possible ostracising they may encounter as a result of the "alternative life style" their mother has chosen.

Ibid. at 166.

Empirical study has shown that children in the custody of lesbian mothers indeed do not suffer. See Richard Green, et al., "Lesbian Mothers and Their Children: A Comparison with Solo Parent Heterosexual Mothers and Their Children," *Archives of Sexual Behavior* (1986) 15(2):167–84. See also the movie on lesbian child custody cases *In the Best Interest of the Children* (Berkeley: Iris Films/Iris Feminist Collective, 1977).

is illegitimate *exactly because* it violates wilde, one would seem equally obliged to argue for the sterilization of interracial couples; for only then would their "progeny" be spared the needless suffering created by the strong social recrimination directed against mixed-race children in current society.

Another bad faith argument is the widely held *Time* magazine argument for discriminating against gay teachers.[25] It runs as follows: though openly gay teachers do not cause their students to become gay, an openly gay teacher might (inadvertently or not) cause a closeted gay student to become openly gay; the life of an openly gay person is a life of misery and suffering; therefore, openly gay teachers must be fired, since they promote misery and suffering. It seems that the second premise—life of misery—if true in some way peculiar to gays is preponderantly the result of currently existing bigotry and discrimination in society of the very sort which the argument tries to enshrine into school board policy. So the argument violates wilde. But further, one cannot legitimately try to justify a social policy based on the consequences it is supposed to have, by first attaching punishments to violations of the policy and then citing as evidence that only behavior in conformity with the policy is producing good consequences. Stated more formally: it is illegitimate to give a rule-utilitarian rationale for law, attach sanctions to the law, and then show that one was correct in one's moral ground for the law by observing the consequence of implementing the sanctioned law. Sanctions make rule-utilitarian justifications self-fulfilling prophecies. If one passes sanctions against openly gay people, then obviously if one observes openly gay people beset by these sanctions one is going to claim that one wouldn't want one's children to live that way. The solution, though, is to eliminate the sanctions which turn discriminations, based on alleged consequences of being openly gay, into self-fulfilling prophecies.

It should be noted that highly generalized claims that gays are immoral or religious claims to the effect that gays are wicked seem to bear no weight at all in establishing good faith discriminations. First, it is not clear for what sort of job being a non-sinner or simply being generically moral is an essential job qualification. Second, if one takes morality here simply to mean popular or positive morality—what the majority of folk take to be moral—and casts that as a job qualification, one violates

---

25. *Time*, January 8, 1979, p. 51. On the current depressing legal status of gay teachers, see Rivera, "Queer Law—Part I," pp. 514–35.

wilde directly: abiding by raw popular prejudices is allowed to be a legitimate job qualification. Finally, Title VII explicitly exempts "religious organizations" from the strictures of the act "with respect to the employment of individuals of a particular religion to perform work connected with the carrying on by such corporation . . . of its religious activities."[26] Having been exempted from obeying the Civil Rights Act, religions cannot base their objections for extending its protections to gays on grounds of self-interest or morality as they themselves define that; they can base their objections only on a belief, quite un-American, that it is all right to impose one's religious beliefs upon others.

Where certain moral qualities or character traits are clear and specific, they may well be properly tied to jobs; for instance, the virtues of conscientiousness and trustworthiness are bona fide occupational qualifications for quite a number of jobs. But there is no reason to suppose that the spelling out and defining of such specific virtues would make any reference to sexual orientation. (It is true that in Attic Greek the word for the virtue courage is a paronym of the word for male, but that, I fear, tells us more about Greek culture than it does about courage.)

Nor, aside from appeals to insidious stereotypes of gays variously as dizzy, flighty, unreliable, self-indulgent, sex-crazed plague-bearers,[27] is there any reason to believe that heterosexuals have an exclusive or even preponderant purchase on these specific job-related virtues. But even if heterosexuals were more likely than gays to possess some relevant virtue, this possession would still not be a sufficient warrant for allowing sexual orientation to be a decisive marker for the virtue. For if one of the rationales behind the Civil Rights Act is to blunt stereotyping so that each person's own merits are given a chance to carry the day, then it is reasonable to expect that an employer should be required to make a particularized determination of whether a gay or nongay person indeed does possess a legitimate job-related virtue rather than merely let statistical probabilities over groups determine who is hired. Just as race may not legitimately be taken as a marker for job-related intelligence, even though blacks (for whatever reasons) do poorer than whites on standardized intelligence tests, so too being gay cannot legitimately be taken as a marker for reliability, even though gay men (for whatever reasons)

26. Title VII, § 2000e-1, § 702, as amended, Pub. L. 92–261, effective March 24, 1972.
27. See chapter 1, section II.

are much more likely to have been arrested, booked, and convicted than nongay men.[28]

Indeed the Supreme Court has held not only that such particularized determinations must be made if at all feasible in cases where a protected category has been used as a marker for a job-related characteristic, but also, conversely, that if an employment test or qualification has a disproportionate statistical impact on a protected group (as disqualification on account of an arrest record would have on both black and gay men), then, to be sustained as legal, the test or qualification must be validated —that is, the employer is burdened with demonstrating that the test accurately predicts successful performance on the job.[29] Such validation is virtually never established.

This double action of the Court in neither allowing protected categories to be markers for other, legitimate job-related characteristics nor letting stand as controlling unsubstantiated business claims and policies that disproportionately exclude otherwise protected groups is both wise and important, for it helps eliminate not only the effects of false stereotypes (by requiring that the individual be taken into account as an individual, with her own accomplishments, talents, and character) but also the bad effects of "true" stereotypes. The latter are statistical claims about a group's members that, while factually correct (e.g., blacks smell differently than whites, and gay men get arrested more than nongay ones), are nevertheless given a normative implication or weight that is unwarranted (blacks are unclean, gays unwholesome) or, more specifically, in employment, given an import that is irrelevant to the job at hand.

Nevertheless, most jurisdictions do require "good moral standing" for state and city licensing for a vast number of professional jobs ranging from doctors and lawyers to hairdressers and morticians—and will

28. See Alan P. Bell and Martin S. Weinberg, *Homosexualities: A Study of Diversity Among Men and Women* (New York: Simon and Schuster, 1978), p. 191: "[T]he homosexual men as a whole were significantly more likely than the heterosexual men ever to have been arrested, booked, or convicted for any reason."

29. The principle was laid out in *Griggs v. Duke Power Co.*, 401 U.S. 424 (1971) (ruled, as violating Title VII, the requiring of a high school education or passing of a standardized general intelligence test as a condition of employment when neither standard is shown to be significantly related to successful job performance, both requirements operate to disqualify blacks at a substantially higher rate than white applicants, and the jobs in question formerly had been filled only by white employees as part of a longstanding practice of giving preference to whites).

count almost anything as establishing that gays lack it. Though the federal government in 1975 dropped "immoral" behavior from its list of conditions which disqualify one from employment as allegedly hurting the efficiency of the civil service, it has maintained "infamous or notoriously disgraceful conduct" as such a ground for dismissal.[30] How these requirements of morality, fame, and grace are held to be reasonable or even desirable qualifications for these jobs is, as we have seen, unclear. After all, one wants as a lawyer someone who is shrewd, not someone who is pious. In particular, it is unclear how a determination of "morality" without more, or of "infamous and notoriously disgraceful conduct" could be made that did not violate wilde.

One might hope that eventually the courts will rule that these sorts of moral qualifications are so *vague* as to be incapable of fair application and so violate the Due Process Clause of the Constitution.[31] In the meanwhile, these requirements are abused in the most outrageous ways against gays. For in states which do not have consenting adult laws, gays are selectively discriminated against as systematically violating the laws and so, allegedly, as necessarily lacking in good moral character.

"Morality" unanalyzed also arises as a statutory requirement for child custody, adoption, and fostering in virtually all states and so too gay men and lesbians in states with sodomy laws are denied custody, adoption, and fostering on the alleged good faith ground that they lack good moral character.[32] Now, these applications of such moral qualifications against gays should also count as a violation of wilde. For unless one is going to count the breaking of parking laws and getting traffic tickets as a ground for denying custody and the like—which is not the case—the mere claim that violating some law was the ground for good faith

30. 5 *Code of Federal Rules,* § 731.202(b) (2) (1980); see Rivera, "Queer Law—Part I," pp. 484–85.

31. See *Coates v. City of Cincinnati,* 402 U.S. 611 (1971) (ruled void for vagueness, under the Due Process Clause, an ordinance making it a criminal offense for three or more people to assemble on sidewalks in a manner annoying to persons passing by).

32. One of the first legal consequences of the Supreme Court's upholding the constitutionality of sodomy laws, in *Bowers v. Hardwick,* 106 S. Ct. 2841 (1986), was that the Arizona Court of Appeals, citing *Bowers,* held that the state's sodomy law justified the blocking of a bisexual man from adopting an elementary school child, because possible past, present or future violations of the law made him an immoral role model—and more: "It would be anomalous for the state on the one hand to declare homosexual conduct unlawful and on the other create a parent after that proscribed model, in effect approving that standard, inimical to the natural family, as head of a state-created family." *Appeal in Pima County Juvenile Action B–10489,* 727 P.2d 830, 835 (Ariz. App. 1986).

discrimination would be legitimate only if the moral ground of the law turned out to be, independently of the enshrinement of the law's content into statute, a good ground for a good faith discrimination. And on examination arguments against consenting adult laws turn out to be mere statements of popular distaste or prudery, or merely religious or aesthetic claims.

Indeed the Supreme Court's sole expressed reason in *Bowers v. Hardwick* for upholding Georgia's sodomy statute from Equal Protection challenge was that the law expressed a legitimate state purpose in that it promoted "morality."[33] The Court made clear that what it meant by "morality" was simply "the majority sentiments about . . . morality," the positive or merely descriptive morality of the nation.[34]

This position errs along several dimensions. First, as the four-man dissent in *Bowers* pointed out, the Court has repeatedly rejected the mere expression of raw majority power as generating a legitimate state interest.[35] Thus in a 1974 case, *O'Connor v. Donaldson,* a unamimous Court inquired:

> May the State fence in the harmless mentally ill solely to save its citizens from exposure to those whose ways are different? One might as well ask if the State, to avoid public unease, could incarcerate all who are physically unattractive or socially eccentric. Mere public intolerance or animosity cannot constitutionally justify the deprivation of a person's physical liberty.[36]

Yet in *Bowers* the Court upheld the rationality of a ten-year prison sentence for sodomy by an appeal to public intolerance without more.

Not only are the *Bowers* Court's brief claims about morality inconsis-

---

33. *Bowers,* 106 S. Ct. at 2846.
34. *Ibid.*
35. *Bowers,* 106 S. Ct. at 2855 (Blackmun, J., dissenting).
36. *O'Connor v. Donaldson,* 422 U.S. 563, 575 (1974) (held, on vague Substantive Due Process grounds, that a state cannot confine, without more, a nondangerous individual, declared by the state "mentally ill," who is capable of surviving safely in freedom by himself or with the help of willing and responsible family members or friends).
A year earlier the Court had claimed:

> [I]f the constitutional conception of "equal protection of the laws" means anything, it must at the very least mean that a bare congressional desire to harm a politically unpopular group cannot constitute a *legitimate* governmental interest.

U.S. Department of Agriculture v. Moreno, 413 U.S. 528, 534 (1973) (emphasis in original) (held, even under a weak Equal Protection analysis, that "hippie households" cannot be denied federal food stamps merely as the result of social hostility to "hippies").

tent with precedent, they are inconsistent with what a constitutional right is. A constitutional right is a justified immunity claim by minorities against majorities, who, but for such rights, get their way through the ballot box. The Court's claim in *Bowers* that "majority sentiment" is enough to fulfill a legitimate state interest in upholding morality where morality has as its sole criterion that it *is* the majority sentiment means, patent circularity aside, that *all* laws have legitimate ends, for all laws register majority sentiment—through the ballot box. Further, since the coercive threats attached to legal sanctions against an activity might conceivably lead to a reduction in the occurrences of the proscribed activity, it turns out that by the very act of making an "immoral" act illegal, legislatures will have established a rational relation between the law and its legitimate purpose—the promotion of "morality." So the *Bowers* Court renders completely vacuous both prongs of the right to Equal Protection as it applies to all law—a requirement that all laws both have a legitimate goal and, as means, are rationally related to that goal. For, on the *Bowers* account, all laws have legitimate purposes simply because all laws register majority sentiment and all laws are rationally related to this purpose simply because all laws have threats of penalities or at least stigmas attached to their violation.[37] The *Bowers* Court entirely lost track of what rights are. If equal protection of the law is a right, the determination of its scope cannot be left to the mercies of majority rule.

What makes it all the more amazing that the Court should be so blind here is that, but two years earlier, it had given an even more sophisticated analysis of prejudice than that given in *O'Connor v. Donaldson*. Indeed, the Court gave every appearance of having elevated wilde to a constitutional principle. The case is *Palmore v. Sidoti*.[38]

Palmore and Sidoti are white. They had a child—then a divorce. The

---

37. Even if the coercive threats attached to the prospective violations of laws which are "designed" to promote morality caused an *increase* in the proscribed behavior, the Court on its weak Equal Protection analysis would still uphold the law, for the standard for "rational" fit between means and ends is that "[a] statutory discrimination will not be set aside if *any* state of facts reasonably may be *conceived* to justify it." *McGowan v. Maryland*, 366 U.S. 420, 426 (1961) (upholding Sunday closing laws) (emphasis added). Therefore, "*X* is rationally related to *Y*" means only "In some possible world—however remote from the actual one—*X* could produce *Y*."

38. 466 U.S. 429 (1984).

mother was given custody. Then she married a black man. Then in light of this change of circumstance alone, Florida's highest court transferred custody to the natural father. On appeal, a unaminous Supreme Court reversed.

On the surface, the Court, in its announced analytic, treated the case as though its result turned on the issue of what rights there are. And it gave, on the surface, the answer that what the case presented was simply a straightforward example of race discrimination, thus triggering the highest constitutional standards for Equal Protection. In order for the discrimination to pass constitutional muster, it would have to be found to be a necessary means to a compelling state interest.[39] But on this reading, the Court's own reading, it is arguable that the ex-husband should have won and that the Florida court was right. His winning claim with the lower court had been that social recriminations falling on the child of a mixed race marriage would damage the child. Now, the Supreme Court itself had repeatedly claimed that the promotion of the welfare of children, even just of one specifiable individual child, is a compelling state interest.[40] Further, the relevant finder of fact in the case had found that the harm coming to the child of this mixed-race marriage was "inevitable."[41] It would appear then that the change in child custody would not only be in the best interest of the child but moreover, in what is the constitutionally relevant respect, would be necessary to a compelling state interest, and so ought to override any constitutional right. Perhaps subconsciously sensing this difficulty, perhaps operating completely at random, the Court in any case paid no attention to the ordinary high-tier equal protection analytic it nominally had set out for itself.

Instead, the Court unwittingly framed an entirely different question, a question about whether there are not some means themselves which,

39. *Ibid.* at 432–33.
40. Most notably in its child pornography case, *New York v. Ferber*, 458 U.S. 747, 756–57 (1982) (the state's self-evidently compelling interest in safeguarding the physical and psychological well-being of a minor, when paired with the police's incompetence in using child pornography to prosecute the case of child abuse depicted in the child pornography, makes the banning of the distribution of non-obscene but lewd representations of children necessary to a compelling state interest and so overrides the representations' first amendment protections).
41. *Palmore*, 466 U.S. at 430–31 (1984).

even if necessary to compelling ends, are nevertheless beyond the pale of acceptance—are illegitimate means. Its answer correctly is "yes" and is wilde:

> The question . . . is whether the reality of private biases and the possible injury they might inflict are permissible considerations. . . . We have little difficulty concluding that they are not. The Constitution cannot control such prejudices but neither can it tolerate them. Private biases may be outside the reach of the law, but the law cannot, directly or *indirectly,* give them effect.[42]

The illegitimacy of the law taking into its calculus the consequences of prejudices and so giving them indirect effect means that prejudices or the obvious consequence of prejudice cannot be taken as good reasons in trying to establish good faith discriminations. The means by which the state calculates and executes its ends are themselves constitutionally circumscribed and are not to be constitutionally judged simply with reference to their degree of fit to their purposes. This principle was a long time in coming, but in a constitutional scheme that puts brakes on (direct calculations of) utility, it ought to be a constitutional principle that not every end, however important, will justify any means.

The question in *Palmore* was not what enhanced equal protection rights there are, but what permissible means the state may use—what are its legitimate instrumentalities? Here the claim is that the perpetuating of stigmas is not something that the state may legitimately do even if in being forced to disregard them, the state (or as here, the Court acting as the executor of law) likely or even inevitably permits harms to befall known individuals.

Note that, so construed, the principle here enunciated has nothing particularly to do with race. It applies equally well to all cases where social stigmas either prospectively or actually generate harms which the state then claims it may legitimately stop or avert. And indeed the Court has taken the *Palmore* principle out of the racial context of its origin and applied it to discrimination against the handicapped, even when they are viewed as having no special enhanced equal protection rights. The Court, the year after *Palmore,* claimed that even on the weakest Equal Protection grounds, calling only for a finding of a statute's having a rational relation to a legitimate state interest, the *Palmore* principle—

42. *Ibid.* at 433 (emphasis added).

that the law cannot give private biases either direct or indirect effect—is sufficient to bar zoning laws that give voice to mere "negative attitudes" toward or "fears of elderly residents" over having a group home for the mentally challenged nearby.[43] Such attitudes and fears "are not permissible bases" for distinguishing the treatment of the mentally challenged from other groups.[44]

However, if the Court, the next year in *Bowers,* could not see that it is illegitimate, even on a weak equal protection analysis, for the state to give private biases *direct* effect in sodomy laws, then one cannot hold out too much hope that the Court will see that in all the cases discussed above—gay teacher cases, lesbian child custody cases, gay military and police cases—the state is discriminating against gays on what it alleges to be good faith grounds but which are in reality nothing more than the law giving to private biases illegitimate *indirect* effects—the same illegitimate *indirect* effects the Court so perceptively noted and voided in *Palmore.*

Courts more consistent and wise than the current Supreme Court should strike down all these discriminations against gays as violating even the weakest of equal protection standards, which now should be seen as having a new third prong—a requirement of legitimacy of means, not just of ends.

Such courts, I suspect, will be rare. For five years after *Palmore,* I am aware of only one case where a court has correctly seen the relevance of *Palmore* to antigay discrimination and then gone ahead and correctly applied *Palmore* in a gay context. It is a lesbian child custody decision by the Alaska Supreme Court, which, citing *Palmore,* refused to follow the usual pattern and change custody to the father when the mother's lesbianism came to light: "Simply put, it is impermissible to rely on any real or imagined social stigma attached to [the] mother's status as a lesbian."[45]

Instead of following this constitutionally warranted and morally required path, court after court keeps right on accepting violations of the

43. *City of Cleburne v. Cleburne Living Center, Inc.,* 473 U.S. 433, 448 (1985) (there quoting *Palmore v. Sidoti,* 466 U.S. at 433).

44. *Cleburne,* 473 U.S. at 448.

45. *S.N.E. v. R.L.B.,* 699 P.2d 875, 879 (Alaska 1985). Subsequently, a divided panel of the Ninth Federal Circuit correctly saw the application of *Palmore* to all of the military's rationalizations for its exclusion of gays. *Watkins v. United States Army,* 837 F.2d 1428, 1449 (9th Cir. 1988).

wilde-palmore principle as "common sense" when directed against gays and holding them as legitimate and reasonable grounds for discrimination against gays. The typical judicial strategy now is to say, even in national security cases, that homosexuality is not *per se* a bar to some opportunity for a gay litigant (say, custody or a security clearance), but then, in the end, to find the litigant's homosexuality fully dispositive anyway—even going so far as to pose dilemmas with no escape for the gay litigant.

Take lesbian custody cases again. On the one horn of judicially con-cocted dilemma, if a lesbian mother, say, does not have a lover—because she finds (reasonably enough) that social discrimination makes that very difficult or impossible—then she is found by the court to be unstable and so a bad influence on the child. If, on the other horn, she does have a live-in lover, this publicly recognizable love is found to be a flouting of community standards and so, too, a bad influence on the child.

Or again, take security clearance cases. In one and the same federal circuit, two panels of judges, with two of the three judges on each panel overlapping, can in the very same month claim of gay security clearances that, on the one hand, if a gay person does not have a lover, he can legitimately be branded as emotionally unstable, unreliable, and so, unfit,[46] and on the other hand, if a lesbian does have a partner, though the lesbian herself may be open about her sexuality and so not subject to blackmail, her very attachment to the partner, who may not be open, may cause her to be subject to blackmail.[47]

Here are classic cases of damned if you do, damned if you don't. I suggest that the ability to concoct such exitless dilemmas entirely out of violations of wilde-palmore reveals what is bad about the arguments as arguments and shows that wilde-palmore is sound principle. For its opposite generates contradictions, like the recommendation both to have and not to have a lover. But what is more important is that such dilemmas tip their authors' hands and strongly suggest that the argu-

46. See *Doe v. Weinberger*, 820 F.2d 1275, 1277–78 (D.C. Cir. 1987) (a gay worker at the National Security Agency wins a tiny procedural battle in a way that guarantees he will lose the substantive war).

47. *Padula v. Webster*, 822 F.2d 97, 104 (D.C. Cir. 1987): "It is not irrational for the [FBI] to conclude that . . . the general public opprobrium toward homosexuals exposes many homosexuals, even 'open' homosexuals, to the risk of possible blackmail to protect their partners, if not themselves."

ments are not even tendered in good faith, or perhaps, to be less harsh, are advanced in a bad faith born of gross intellectual negligence: they are cases, all too common in gay public policy, of willfully ignorant bigotry.

My hunch is that all antigay arguments that are cast as good faith discriminations violate wilde or are circular or are illegitimate self-fulfilling prophecies, but I do not presume to outguess human ingenuity in generating rationalizations for its hatreds and fears. The bigot's mind, even if floating above judicial robes, is receptive to the sheen of argument without its substance, and as we have seen in the dilemma cases, bad arguments with the sheen of respectable rationality are a nickel a dozen. The clever bigot's mind—the concocter of bad arguments fit for a ready audience of less clever bigots—is more sinuous and enduring than Proteus. It is never caught. The bigot's mind, without being particularly modern, is capable of dancing even after the music of reason has stopped.

PART FOUR

The AIDS Crisis: Ethics in Dark Times

8. AIDS, Gay Life, State Coercion

"Sperm to worm!"—Tony (regretting his impatience) in "Tonight" from Stephen Sondheim's *West Side Story*.

"Who wants to suck a dick with a rubber on it?"— Fred, 46, a self-described reformed reprobate.

I. ALARUMS AND EXCURSIONS

Of those dead and dying from AIDS two-thirds are gay men.[1] Government funding for both preventive medicine (basically the discovery of a vaccine) and patient care (especially hospice care) is, I shall argue, something society owes to gay men. The former is a necessary condition for

1. "Articles on AIDS Risk Are Criticized by Koop," *The New York Times*, February 20, 1988, p. Y7: "As of Feb. 15, there were 53,814 cases [of AIDS] reported to the Federal Centers for Disease Control. About 65 percent were homosexuals or bisexual males."

basic human goods—freedom from terror and the capacity to realize central personal values; the latter is a matter of compensatory justice. Many will find these claims shocking; to most they may seem little more than special pleading. I suggest, however, that such views depend upon ignorance or misconception of how gay people live.

As things stand, there is virtually no specific government AIDS funding for patient care and preventive funding has risen significantly only as AIDS has come to be thought a threat to the dominant, nongay culture. Preventive AIDS funding, I fear, is being defended for wrong and dangerous reasons, ones which raise the specter of government coercion.

Funding to prevent harm to potential innocent victims is largely noncontroversial. No one objects to the funding of necessary or well motivated deterrent and interventive police actions. But if preventive medicine is justified on grounds of self-defense, so it would seem are many other, much uglier things. For the defense of individuals from substantial harms from others is precisely the chief warrant for governmental coercion of individuals.

State-mandated discrimination against groups at risk for AIDS has already begun in employment and access to services, allegedly on medical grounds but in pointed contradiction to the judgments of the very medical institutions to which society has entrusted the determination of such grounds (the Department of Health and Human Services, the Centers for Disease Control [CDC], and the National Institutes of Health).[2] This contradiction is especially significant in that the heads of these institutions, political appointees subject to political pressures, in cases of possible error might well be expected to err on the side of the social majority.

Government's disregard for medical opinion in dealing with medical policy strongly suggests that prejudicial forces are at work. There is of course nothing new in this, but it grows alarming when one remembers that prisons and quarantines are conceptually distinguished only by the respective presence or absence of an intent to (or a reckless disregard for) harm on the part of those from whom society would protect itself.

2. See particularly the guidelines of the Centers for Disease Control (CDC) for preventing transmission in the workplace, "Recommendations for Preventing Transmission of Infection with Human T-Lymphotrophic Virus Type III/Lymphadenopathy-Associated Virus in the Workplace," *Morbidity and Mortality Weekly Report (MMWR)* November 15, 1985, 34(35):682–95, and "Recommendations for Preventing HIV Transmission in Health Care Settings," *MMWR*, August 21, 1987, 36:2S–18S.

Prisons and quarantines make no distinction between the harms from which they would protect society nor between the harms they themselves inflict on "offenders." As leper colonies have shown, it is silly to suppose that internments do not stigmatize those interned—that simply not calling internment "punishment" counts for anything. And as internment of Japanese-Americans in World War II showed, the losses of property, opportunity, and freedom are the same however one names the concentration.

The armed forces have already established quarantines of those at risk for AIDS on some bases.[3] With state-mandated discriminations installed and calls for civilian quarantines circulating, it is clear that the AIDS crisis is testing the country's mettle. Not since the Supreme Court affirmed the Japanese internments has so live a danger existed to America's traditional commitment to civil liberties. And again the danger is created by hysteria and not a reasoned necessity.

The hysteria, when not simply an expression of old antigay prejudices, is based on the presumption that the disease is spread indiscriminately. This presumption permitted Jeane Kirkpatrick to begin a syndicated column by using AIDS as a metaphor for international terrorism—"it can affect anyone"—in the serene belief that her audience, educated America, already thought this about AIDS and might even be ready for extreme measures.[4]

II. ALLEGED HARMS TO OTHERS

For public policy purposes, however, the most important fact about AIDS is not that it is deadly but that, like hepatitis B, it is caused by a blood-transmitted virus. For the disease to spread, bodily fluids of someone with the virus must directly enter the bloodstream of another. In

3. *The Washington Post*, October 19, 1985, p. A12; *The Advocate* [Los Angeles], March 18, 1986, no. 442, p. 14.

4. *The Washington Post*, October 13, 1985, p. B8. If a *Los Angeles Times* poll of 2300 Americans is to be believed, the country indeed has been ready for extreme measures for some time: 51 percent favored quarantines of people with AIDS, 48 percent the closing of gay bathhouses, 42 percent closing gay bars and 14 percent tattooing people with AIDS; 28 percent thought AIDS was God's punishment for homosexuals and 23 percent thought AIDS victims were "getting what they deserve" (December 19, 1985, p. 1). For discussions of civil liberties issues raised by the AIDS crisis, see for example "AIDS and Individual Rights," *The New York Times*, December 15, 1985, p. E6 and "Quarantines Considered to Combat AIDS," *The Washington Post*, December 16, 1985, pp. A1, 26–27.

order to infect, the virus must be virtually injected into the bloodstream. And among bodily fluids, "only blood, semen, vaginal secretions, and possibly breast milk" have been implicated in the transmission of the virus.[5]

That the virus is blood transmitted means first and foremost that groups at risk for the disease are clearly definable—more so than for virtually any other disease known—with 99 percent of cases having clearly demarcated modes of transmission and cause. And now that blood supplies are screened with a test for antibodies to the AIDS virus, the number of these groups is indeed dropping. Hemophiliacs not already exposed and blood transfusion recipients are no longer groups at risk.

Attempts to use Africa's much greater and diverse incidences of AIDS in order to predict the United States' future overlook numerous relevant factual differences between the two areas.[6] Perhaps a quarter of the Third World suffers from hepatitis B, which in the U.S. infects the same groups that are at risk for AIDS. Though hepatitis B has always been around, it has not been a threat to the general U.S. population and has never caused much social or government concern, despite its severe symptoms and effects, which fall almost entirely on gay men and intravenous drug users. Indeed, the very close epidemiological modeling of AIDS to hepatitis B is both what first led medical investigators to hypothesize that AIDS was caused by a blood-transmitted virus, long before the virus itself was discovered, and what continues to be the chief basis of the CDC's guidelines for AIDS prevention.[7] Those who take Zaïre as their vision of AIDS contagion in the U.S. conveniently fail to weigh these facts or even mention them.[8] Fear of general, indiscriminate contagion by AIDS is unwarranted—though it makes for terrific press.

The July 1985 cover of *Life* informed the nation in three-inch red letters that "NOW NO ONE IS SAFE FROM AIDS." The magazine used as its allegedly compelling example a seemingly typical Pennsylva-

5. *MMWR* August 21, 1987, 36:3S.

6. See "Revising the Risk Assessment for Heterosexuals: Why the Course of AIDS [in U.S.] Is Defying Africa's Precedent," *The New York Times,* February 21, 1988, p. E6.

7. For a comparison of AIDS virus transmission to that of the hepatitis B virus, see *MMWR* November 15, 1985, 34(35):682–83.

8. For example, Mathilde Krim, "AIDS: The Challenge to Science and Medicine," in *AIDS: The Emerging Ethical Dilemmas, A Hastings Center Report Special Supplement,* August 1985, p. 8.

nia family all but one of whose members has the disease. But it turns out that all those members with the disease were indeed in high risk groups. The father was a hemophiliac, his wife had sex with him, and she conveyed the virus to a child in the process of giving birth. No one got the disease either mysteriously or through casual contact. The family example in fact was evidence *against* the article's generic contagion thesis. Equally irresponsible journalists, lobbyists, and elected officials have compared AIDS to airborne viral diseases like influenza and the common cold.[9]

The case for general contagion cannot be made.[10] In consequence government policy which is based on that fear is unwarranted. The extraordinary measures—including the suspension of civil liberties—which government might justifiably take, as in war, to prevent wholesale slaughter simply do not apply here. In particular, quarantining the class of AIDS-exposed persons in order to protect society from indiscriminate harm is unwarranted.

III. HARMS TO SELF

The disease's mode of contagion assures that those at risk are those whose actions contribute to their risk of infection, chiefly through intimate sexual contact and shared hypodermic needles.[11] In the transmis-

9. For an irresponsible analogy of AIDS to airborne disease, see Dr. Richard Restak's widely reprinted op-ed piece "Worry about Survival of Society First; Then AIDS Victims' Rights," *The Washington Post*, September 8, 1985, p. C1. For claims of casual transmission, see Tom Johnson, "Congressman AIDS," *Los Angeles*, January 1986, p. 125 and especially p. 199. For a history of irresponsible and hysteria-pandering reportage in the mass media, see Simon Watney, *Policing Desire: Pornography, AIDS, and the Media* (Minneapolis: University of Minnesota Press, 1987).

10. In particular, fears that swept the country in 1986 based on a belief that the heterosexual transmission of AIDS would explode into the general population and not remain tethered to intravenous drug use have proven unwarranted. The increased recorded rate of heterosexual transmission was the result largely of the redescription of old cases rather than the occurrence of new ones. See "AIDS Not Spreading Fast Among Straights," *San Francisco Chronicle*, March 24, 1987, p. 1; "Anxiety Allayed on Heterosexual AIDS," *The New York Times*, June 5, 1987, p. Y11.

11. A small exception is those whose well-being and life chances are already substantially at the mercy of the person who infects them—newborns of infected mothers. For this set of cases social policy should be whatever it already is for cases of parents who pass fatal congenital disease to their children. Society has never required or even thought to require preparental or premarital testing for known inheritable fatal illnesses even where such tests are readily available. Therefore those who try to justify mandatory premarital

sion of AIDS, it is the general feature of self-exposure to contagion that makes direct governmental coercive efforts to abate the disease particularly inappropriate.

If independence—the ability to guide one's life by one's own lights to an extent compatible with a like ability on the part of others—is, as it is, a major value, one cannot respect that value while preventing people from putting themselves at risk through voluntary associations. Voluntary associations are necessarily examples of people acting in accordance with the principle of independence, for mutual consent guarantees that the "compatible extent" proviso of the independence principle is fulfilled. But the state and even the courts have not been very sensitive to the distinction between one harming oneself and one harming another—nor has the medical establishment.[12] It appears to all of them that a harm is a harm, a disease a disease, however caused or described. The moral difference, however, is enormous. Preventing a person from harming another is required by the principle of independence, but preventing someone from harming himself is incompatible with it. While no further justification is needed for the state to protect a person from others, a rather powerful justification is needed if the state is to be warranted in protecting a person from himself.

In the absence of such a justification, the state sometimes tries to split the moral difference and argue that state coercion *may* be used when the harm to others is remote and indirect. A common example of argument from indirect harms runs as follows: state-coerced use of, say, seatbelts and motorcycle helmets is warranted, for helmetless motorcycle crashes and seat-beltless car accidents harm even those not involved in the accidents, by raising everyone's insurance costs and burdening the public

---

testing for AIDS antibodies as an attempt to protect third parties—children—are, at best, concocting principle, not applying it. Such justification is, in any case, wildly over-and-under-inclusive, since many who get married do not have children and many who do not do. On marital testing, see chapter 10.

12. For instance, Mervyn F. Silverman, former Director of Health for San Francisco, shows no cognizance of the distinction in his argument for his unsuccessful 1984 attempt to close that city's bathhouses. Mervyn F. Silverman and Deborah B. Silverman, "AIDS and the Threat to Public Health," in *Special Supplement* (see n. 8 above), pp. 21–22. Nor does Randy Shilts even once draw the relevant distinction between harms-to-self and harms-to-others in his 600 page critical commentary on AIDS public policy issues, *And The Band Played On: Politics, People, And The AIDS Epidemic* (New York: St. Martin's, 1987).

purse when victims end up in county hospitals. Here state coercion comes in through the back door.

This line of argument has been used with increasing frequency even by self-described liberals like New York's Governor Cuomo, and it is beginning to be heard in AIDS discussions. This is not surprising, for the cost of AIDS patient care from diagnosis to death is somewhere between $35,000 and $150,000. Often, private funds are quickly exhausted, and the patient ends up on the dole—harming everyone, and so allegedly warranting state coercion of the means of possible AIDS transmission.

J. S. Mill's rule-of-thumb for appraising such appeals to indirect harms is exactly on target: an indirect harm counts toward justifying state coercion only when the harm grows large enough to be considered a violation of someone's right. This understanding of harm to others is necessary in order that independence is not rendered nugatory and that, *as a right,* it is outweighed only by something comparable to it. Now, while it is nice if products (like car insurance) are cheap and taxes low, the considered opinion of society is not that one's rights have been violated when taxes or the price of milk goes up. Indeed, in the case of taxes, the considered opinion is cast as a constitutional provision. So arguments that smuggle coercion in through the back door of indirect harms are not successful.[13] Whether it is legitimate for the state to condition, for instance, motorcyclists' access to county hospitals upon the wearing of helmets, cannot be determined independently of an assessment of the arguments for such free health care in the first place.

---

13. A wife who contracts AIDS from a bisexual husband does not have a right that has been violated by the bathhouse where he may have been exposed to AIDS. Rather if she has a legitimate plaint, it is against the direct harm caused by the husband or against the institution of marriage itself if it has kept her in a position of enforced ignorance. But, it should be remembered that traditional marriage vows pledge the participants to joint risk taking and place commercial and medical risks on a par. The institution of marriage itself, then, acknowledges what is independently true: it is as little a good reason to shut down bathhouses to protect "innocent" wives as it is to shut down stockmarkets to spare them lost spousal income.

Further, it is wholly unfair to coerce one institution because of the patent immoralities of another. The immoralities which occur within marriage (lying, cheating, promise-breaking, willful ignorance) or which are endemic to it (enforced ignorance, indenture) cannot ground the coercion of gay bathhouses. For an excellent discussion of the procedural and substantive abuses inherent in traditional, legal marital arrangements, see Sara Ann Ketchum, "Liberalism and Marriage Law," in Mary Vetterling-Braggin, et. al., eds., *Feminism and Philosophy,* pp. 247–76 (Totowa, N.J.: Littlefield, Adams, 1977).

(The arguments advanced below for AIDS patient funding bar any such conditioning of relief upon conformity to behavior that reduces costs.)

In general, heed should be given to Justice Douglas' warning in his dissent to *Wyman* that the welfare state is gradually being allowed to buy up rights. In *Wyman* the Court ruled, among other horribles, that an indigent woman in accepting welfare for her child had simply waived her fourth amendment rights.[14] Actions infringing upon rights are most likely to go unnoticed or be misperceived, and so be most insidious when they are performed for an end that is good. Many addressing the AIDS crisis seem to be operating with bad motives, and can generally be easily spotted: appeals to consistency are usually enough to trip them up. But those with good motives yet anxious to do something quickly are those most likely to effect policies which destroy rights. The problem identified by Justice Douglas is part of a wider problem detected in Justice Brandeis' vindicated dissent in *Olmstead*: "Experience should teach us to be most on our guard to protect liberty when the Government's purposes are beneficent. Men born to freedom are naturally alert to repel invasion of their liberty by evil-minded rulers. The greatest dangers to liberty lurk in insidious encroachment by men of zeal, well-meaning but without understanding."[15]

IV. STATE PATERNALISM CONSIDERED

The important question remains whether AIDS warrants paternalistic state coercion to prevent those not-exposed from harming themselves, through banning or highly regulating the means of possible viral transmission. Usually, paternalistic arguments cannot be made sensible and consistent. For example, federal AIDS funding for FY 1986 in the House came with a paternalistic rider giving the surgeon general a power he already has—to close bathhouses (gay social institutions) if they are determined to facilitate the transmission or spread of the disease, which indeed they do. (So do parks and bedrooms.)[16] The sponsor of the rider

14. *Wyman v. James*, 400 U.S. 309, 328 (1971) (Douglas, J., dissenting): "The central question is whether the government by force of its largesse has the power to 'buy up' rights guaranteed by the Constitution. But for the assertion of her constitutional right, Barbara James in this case would have received the welfare benefit."

15. *Olmstead v. United States*, 277 U.S. 438, 479 (Brandeis, J., dissenting).

16. A directive from New York's Governor Cuomo in late 1985 mandated the closing

argued that it was "a small step to help those who are unable or unwilling to help themselves."[17] Cast so baldly, the argument simply denies independence as a value. For it is consistent with the presumption that the majority gets to determine both what the good life is and to enforce it coercively. The argument could as well be used to justify compulsory religious conversion—those who are unable or unwilling to see the light are helped to see it.

Governments that have written off the value of gay sex altogether by having made it illegal, largely on religious or other grounds that do not appeal to harms caused to others, should be viewed as especially suspect when they make paternalistic arguments on behalf of gays. For they have already clearly shown that they do not respect gays as independent beings.

<hr />

of public accommodations where oral or anal sex occur. But the distinction between a public accommodation and a private dwelling, given the nature of the disease, is medically irrelevant. So is the distinction between providing for profit a location for sex and providing one for free. Public accommodations, private clubs, parks, and bedrooms—even marital ones—are medically all equally suspect. The line of thought that has led to bathhouse closings, if carried out consistently, would require shutting down realtor's offices that make a profit from selling homes to gays.

Further, the directive curiously enough omits banning vaginal sex. Though there is some reason to believe that anal sex is extremely risky, there is no evidence that vaginal penetrations are any less likely a mode of transmitting the virus than oral sex. Cuomo's directive disingenuously recriminalizes sodomy in New York. *The Washington Post*, October 31, 1985, p. A1. New York City's corporation counsel has argued that restrictions on oral and anal sex do not discriminate against gays because the restrictions also apply to nongays. *The New York Times*, December 15, 1985, p. D6. One could as well argue that a law against sleeping under bridges does not discriminate against the poor because it also bars the wealthy from sleeping there.

In applying the directive both the Governor and New York City's Mayor Koch claimed that their acts were not to be construed in any way as assaulting the gay community. But instead of showing good faith in this regard by doing something that would be politically unpopular (like first shutting down, say, a marriage with an AIDS-exposed hemophiliac member), they chose instead to shut down as their very first target a central part of gay male mythology—a notorious private membership sex club, The Mineshaft. *The Washington Post*, November 8, 1985, p. A7.

Subsequently, New York state's health commissioner reported that "his investigators will enter hotel rooms if necessary to stop sexual activities linked to the spread of AIDS." *The Washington Post*, November 18, 1985, p. A4. His office has assured gays that the free enterprise system will preclude discrimination against gays in hotel accommodations. *The Washington Blade* [DC], November 22, 1985, p. 12. New York, like forty-eight other states, has no legislation that would bar such discrimination against gays.

17. *The Washington Blade*, October 4, 1985, p. 1.

A. Reason Assured

Occasionally, to be sure, the case for paternalism can be made to work. One legitimate way to justify paternalistic coercion is to claim as warrant a lack of rationality on the part of an agent (say, a child). By "rationality" here I mean having relevant information and certain mental capacities, including the ability to reason from ends to means, but I do not presume that making the best possible assessment of means to an end is a requirement for rationality—error is compatible with rationality.

A presumption of an agent's rationality is a necessary condition for the very respect which is owed to her making her own decisions and guiding her life by them. Thus, paternalistic interference is warranted when a person is operating at risks which she is unable to assess due to diminished mental skills or lack of information. But education, not coercion, is the solution which is tailored to, and so appropriate for, such incapacities. Coercion in such cases is warranted only temporarily, to permit a check of whether a person indeed knows the risks she or he is taking. Thus (to borrow an example from Mill) it is justified forcibly to detain someone about to cross a structurally compromised bridge just long enough to inform him of its condition. Dilated to an extreme, this line of argument permits paternalistic labeling of possibly dangerous products and other means of placing a decision-maker in a reasonable position to make decisions for himself.

But far from justifying major paternalistic coercion of gay institutions, say, closing gay baths, the argument from rationality here indeed suggests that paternalistic arguments surrounding AIDS are not even being advanced in good faith. For though education is one of government's highest spending priorities, governments have made no serious attempt to educate people about medically informed risks of AIDS and of safe alternatives to high-risk sexual practices. Five years of the AIDS crisis had passed before the federal government even put out bids for studies of ways in which programs of AIDS education might be effected.[18] The government then stalled in releasing the funds and finally barred their use for sexual messages that would be explicit enough to be effective. James Mason, the director of the CDC, which administers the grants,

18. See *Federal Register,* July 25, 1985, 50(143):30298.

claimed "We don't think that citizens care to be funding material that encourages gay sex lifestyles."[19]

Local governments in many cases have positively hampered private attempts at such education. In Los Angeles and Philadelphia, for instance, government sponsorship of private-sector distribution of safe-sex literature was denied or withdrawn when some officials branded the literature as pornography—neofeminists take note. Thus one is probably justified in seeing as disingenuous any governmental argument for the coercion of gay institutions on paternalistic grounds. At most the argument from rationality warrants placing warning labels on baths as they are placed on cigarettes, the use of which also threatens death.[20]

B. Self-Indentured Gays?

The other legitimate argument for paternalistic coercion is that one should be protected from ceding away the very conditions that enable one to be an independent agent. Thus one cannot legitimately contract to become a slave or to sign away rights to the fair administration of the enforcement of contracts or more generally the equitable administration of justice. Sometimes justifications of social and legal coercion against suicide are attempted on the ground that a suicide has chosen not to be independent—in spades. However, in some circumstances, as when one's options have become so limited by, say, natural causes that being an independent person loses all significance, this justification for paternalism will fade away, indeed at the same rate that suicide becomes a prudential choice. At its extreme, this line of justifying paternalistic coercion is used to support legislation mandating seatbelt use: it's good for you, since it preserves you as an independent agent (though usually politicians cast the argument in terms of indirect harm to others). How does putting oneself at risk for AIDS weigh into this conceptual scheme?

19. *The Advocate*, January 7, 1986, no. 437, p. 20.

20. Whether warning labels *should* be placed on bathhouses turns on considerations of consistency: some dangerous products are labeled, others not. What gets labeled should not depend on ideology, prejudice, or politics. Getting right on this point is particularly important in the case of bathhouses since such labeling, even when carried out in good faith, will have the side effect of saying to most people that gay sex is bad. The relevant question, one for which I do not have an answer, is whether bathhouses present the same degree of risk to the user as other products that are already so labeled.

Does AIDS, at least virtually always fatal, rise to a level of seriousness to warrant on these paternalistic grounds a state-imposed bar to putting oneself at risk for it?

Admittedly, minimally good health is a central personal concern and its possession a necessary condition for being viewed seriously as an independent agent. So at first blush the AIDS case may seem relevantly similar to the contracting-to-slavery case. It differs, however, in two significant, severally decisive ways.

First, slavery *by definition* is a condition of lost independence. However, as with other venereal diseases, not every sexual encounter with a virus-exposed person exposes one to the AIDS virus, and even exposure to it is nowhere near a guarantee of actually contracting AIDS, since only some portion of those exposed actually get the disease.[21] Because the risk is high but the results not invariably catastrophic, putting oneself at risk for AIDS becomes less like contracting into slavery and more like being a race car driver, mountain climber, or astronaut. In the absence of inevitability, the assessment of risk should be left to the individual, and indeed—as the examples of space flight, mountaineering and race car driving show—this is the considered standard of society as well. Deviations from the standard in other similar cases are likely to be motivated by something other than honest paternalistic concerns.

Second, it is hard to imagine even dispassionately and impartially that the momentary gain—say, some psychological thrill—from submitting to slavery could be reasonably balanced against the value *to the individual* of independence permanently lost. This differs significantly from "slavery" in sex play where the thrill to the "slave" lies in continuous voluntary submission. To imagine the pure case, however, is as hard as trying to imagine (Mishima aside) someone seeing suicide as the culmination and chief organizing principle of his life rather than as an exit from a life that has become incapable of significance.

Sex is one of the central values of human life: as the chief portal to ecstasy, as a recurrent natural need, and as the near occasion of, undergirding for, and necessary prompt to love.[22] The centrality of sex to life means that it may have to be balanced with the value of continued independence—all the more so if independence is chiefly, like health, a

---

21. For summaries of ten-year longitudinal studies, see *The New York Times*, June 30, 1987, Y23.

22. On the importance of sex, see chapter 4, section IV.

generalized means to individuals' ends rather than an end in itself. Independence is not the only value of life, or one prior to all other values.

Further, central values are not equally central for all—some people indeed do not find sex very important and yet do not appear repressed. These people seem to be missing something, not to be morally lesser beings but somehow, like Gertrude Stein's Oakland, to have less there there. It would be silly for them to take high sexual risks, for the balance for them is so clearly tilted in one direction, and little would be lost if the state nudged them that way. But this tilt will in general not be so clear. The balancing in cases of conflicting personally affecting values is not a decision that the state could reasonably make the same for all. The state is not capable of the probings of the soul that would be necessary for such a decision. Individuals, not the state, must make the difficult choices where values centrally affecting the self come in conflict.

That such choice falls to the individual is generally recognized where religious commitment and health come in conflict. The state cannot legitimately make the tradeoffs that an informed adult will make between religious values and health by, say, coercing a person—for the sake of preserving his own independence—to have a blood transfusion against his belief that a transfusion, even a coerced one, will damn him for all eternity. Sexual attitudes and acts in accord with them are at least as central to a person as religious beliefs and acts, and so they too are not fit subjects of state coercion for the individual's own good, even when that good is the continued ability to make choices.[23]

23. Some medical experts, in an attempt to justify the use of coercion to stop the spread of AIDS, compare a person who knowingly exposes others to the AIDS virus to a drunk driver or to someone shooting randomly in a theater. For example, see the comments of Dr. M. Roy Schwarz, an AMA vice president, in "Privacy of AIDS Patients," *The New York Times,* July 30, 1987, p. 1. But the requirement of self-exposure for the transmission of the disease makes its mode of transmission relevantly dissimilar to either of these analogies. Acts of will on the part of a theatergoer struck by a bullet or a sidewalk bystander hit by a drunkenly driven car are not directed toward, nor actively participate in, nor contribute to, the course of events that harms them. One would not say that their actions *caused* them to be shot or run over. Fault here lies entirely with the drunk driver or the sniper. The people they fell are correctly thought of as victims.

But the person who gets AIDS through sexual contact or shared needles actively participates in the very action that harms him and his deeds are properly said to be a contributory cause of the harms that come to him. He is not a victim.

So too, the mode of AIDS transmission is relevantly dissimilar to the circumstances in which the California Supreme Court proclaimed that there exists a third party legal duty

228 THE AIDS CRISIS

V. JUSTIFIED PREVENTIVE FUNDING

A. Central Values Assured

The centrality of sex to individual lives, however, is a chief justification for state funding of preventive AIDS research. People ought not to be in the position where they have to make tradeoffs between the components of a complete life. Ending the conflict of central personal values will be especially attractive when the means to it place no nearly comparable burden on others. The case at hand requires tax dollars for both basic immunological research and applied viral research. Yet, given the ends likely to be achieved and assuming an equitable tax system, taxation places no comparable burden on those taxed. For while taxation coerces to some degree the *extent* to which one may realize one's choices, it places no burden at all on the *types* of choices one may make. Libertarians who equate taxation with slavery simply miss the relevant distinction between extent and kind. Taxation is the ideal form of nonpunitive government coercion.

Now not every sort of medicine, even preventive medicine, ought to be subsidized with tax dollars. The burgeoning field of sports medicine, addressing as it does the foibles of luxury, should not come knocking at

---

to warn: a man told his psychiatrist that he was going to kill a specified person—his girlfriend—and then did so. The Court allowed the victim's family to sue the psychiatrist because he had failed to breach patient-doctor confidentiality and warn the eventual victim of the danger she was in. See *Tarasoff v. Regents of the University of California,* 131 Cal. Rpt. 14, 551 P.2d 334, 17 Cal. 3d 425 (1976). Many medical ethicists suppose that this ruling justifies a doctor telling a wife about her husband's exposure to AIDS if the husband will not tell her himself. See *ibid.* and "The HIV-Positive Patient Who Won't Tell the Spouse," *Medical Aspects of Human Sexuality,* March 1987, p. 16. The California Court's novel and controversial decision is a conceptual muddle, crying out for an emergency philosopher to explain the basics of causation and for an emergency grammarian to explain the preposition "by," but even given the case as is, it should not be taken as controlling in the context of AIDS. For only the most compelling state interest could justify overriding the right to privacy exampled in the patient-doctor relation. Yet saving people *from themselves* is necessarily a weaker state interest than saving people *from each other.* The privacy right in the AIDS case is therefore not properly overridden by a state interest in protecting a wife from herself. The doctor would be justified in informing the wife about how AIDS is transmitted and even to do so coercively (as in the earlier example of the compromised bridge) but he may not do even that in a way which violates a third party's rights—in this case, the husband's. That popular support for the doctor telling the wife is so overwhelming—see "Privacy of AIDS Patients"—suggests that America still does not view wives as people.

the doors of state treasuries. If AIDS funding were aimed simply at preventing the deaths of intravenous drug users, it would not be nearly as well motivated as it indeed is. For drug use is not for anyone a central personal value. In this regard, drug addiction and tennis elbow have about the same standing. Nor should the state be subsidizing preventive medicine for those who gratuitously put themselves at risk—that is, where the very experiencing of risk generates a large part of the risky activity's attraction. If gay men were in general, as mountain climbers are, mere seekers of beauty or sensuous pleasure because the pleasure has been enhanced by risk taking, then again AIDS funding would not be as well motivated as it is.

B. The Avoidance of Terror

A second argument for preventive AIDS funding is that no one should have to live in a condition of terror. Imagine a prisoner who is never actually tortured but who daily witnesses the torture of others. His witnessings are not merely unpleasant concomitants of prison life, on a par, say, with tasteless food. Rather, both the torture victims and he himself have experienced cruel and unusual punishment. Constantly expected but uncertain pain and destruction seizes up the mind, destroying the equanimity necessary for thinking, deciding, and acting, and grotesquely turns the mind against itself, punishing itself as a way to avoid uncertainty and to produce the appearance of order and progression—a consistency forged of pain. Human dignity on pretty much any account is here destroyed.

Gay men now live in such a condition of generalized terror. When there were few cases of AIDS and its horrors seemed personally remote, gay men understandably dealt with it as the mind can do with forebodings on the horizon—they avoided it through denial, a typical coping mechanism of the already beleaguered. But as the number of AIDS cases has risen exponentially, spreading from cities to towns and leaving nearly everyone with the memory of lost acquaintances, the terror of constantly expected but uncertain destruction and its attendant contortions have become quite general. It turns out, for instance, that gay doctors, who cannot easily sustain the denial stage, are experiencing more anxiety and mental disturbances over AIDS than people who actually have the disease.[24] Not a day goes by now when the typical gay man does not several times check himself over for the telltale signs of the onset of disease, feeling for swollen glands, wondering whether the blemish there will become a zit or a lesion. Many such signs are ordinary daily events—a dry cough, headaches. At a minimum gay men are experiencing the equivalent of the V–2 bombings of London.

The case, though, is much worse. Londoners and Britain were after all on the same side. As AIDS hysteria sweeps the land, bringing with it threats of discrimination and other harms, the terror is considerably magnified. Quite independent of any view one may have on moral guilt or innocence in the spread or acquisition of AIDS (the prisoner in the example was, let's say, tenured deadwood, a mass murderer, or a communist), no one, however scrupulous or dastardly, deserves the terror that has filled the everyday reality of gay men. Indeed, everyone exposed to terror has a positive claim that it be ended.

VI. FUNDING PATIENT CARE

A. The Innocent Attended

Though AIDS is a disease caught in a condition where one has put oneself at risk, nevertheless gay men in general ought in consequence of certain natural and cultural forces to be viewed as morally innocent in its contagion and spread. The disease should not be viewed as a matter of paying the piper, as suffering from a mountain climbing accident might be, where the costs of the effects of one's negligence are to be borne by oneself. And so even in the absence of justifications for perfectly general government health-care plans, funding should nevertheless be provided for the care of those whose life chances in civil society have been permanently destroyed by natural catastrophes that elude the protections of civil defense—so that their dying might at least avoid unnecessary suffering and the indignity to which this disease in particular tends to expose patients.

The general case for innocence is one to be made from an accumulation of factors. Consider, first, that the incubation period for the disease is indeterminately long. The disease had not come to light anywhere in

---

24. *The Advocate*, July 23, 1985, no. 425, p. 31.

the U.S. until July 1981, when it was shrouded in mystery, its nature unknown. This means that there are people who even under maximal conditions of risk avoidance—totally swearing off sex on first hearing of the disease as potentially contagious—could still even now be coming down with the disease. Social policy has no way of telling who these innocent victims are. Second, as mentioned, educational material that would make people aware of their risks has only recently even begun to be discussed by governments. And the mass media continue to be more than a little reluctant to provide details of safe-sex practices. So many people even now are taking risks in situations of constrained information. These people too should be viewed as innocent.

Yet, even in conditions of complete information, most individuals are not very good at risk management. So even with a knowledge of the likelihood of contagion per sexual contact, together with some accurate weighing of expected utilities, many people would still make mistakes. Such errors, however, are not the product of negligence: it's just that most human beings have very poor intuitions about statistics and probabilities.[25] The average person, for instance, thinks it as likely that eight hundred of a thousand tossed coins will come up heads as that eight of ten will. That such intuitions are so poor makes a big difference in assigning fault to individuals. Successful choice and guilt do not jointly exhaust the moral field. The high value society places on choice *despite* a significant propensity of people to make poor choices creates a zone of the failed innocent.

Further, there are a number of reasons why the gay sexual agent, even with complete knowlege and clear capacities, might be led to take risks which many would think extraordinary. First, sex drive is not something over which one has an unrestrained control. One truth that the AIDS crisis seems likely to confirm is that sexual orientation is not something over which one has strong control. If that were the case—something from which conservatives could make political mileage—every gay male cognizant of the health crisis would have tried to switch orientations long ago.

25. Daniel Kahneman and Amos Tversky, "On the Psychology of Prediction," *Psychological Review* (1973) 80:237–51; Kahneman and Tversky, "Subjective Probability: A Judgment of Representation," *Cognitive Psychology* (1973) 3:430–54; Tversky and Kahneman, "The Framing of Decisions and Psychology of Choice," *Science* (1981) no. 211, pp. 453–58.

If orientation is fairly fixed, the only relevant question becomes how much sex is okay. For several years, the chief advice of safe-sex manuals —to reduce the number of one's sexual partners—was based partly on the now discredited hypothesis that the disease was caused not by a virus but by some sort of immune system overload. (This advice was still given, though with less confidence, by those holding the viral hypothesis.) But acting on that information (the best information available) was inadequate to assure not getting the disease; indeed, given the rate at which exposures to the virus have spread among gay men, it proved no effective protection at all. Thus many gay men who were operating on the best information and medical advice available are now dying.

The Centers for Disease Control now recommend that gay men simply be celibate—unless they have lived in completely monogamous, long-term relationships. This advice seems remote from reality and quite oblivious to the cussedness of sex and culture. On the one hand, the recurring and intrusive nature of sexual desire guarantees that in general gay men, like others, will not be celibate. On the other, past long-term gay relations, if not as rare as adamant, are at least as rare as rubies. And necessity is a particularly poor forge for working the most delicate of human bonds with a view to future domestic continence (which is not to say that all shotgun marriages fail).

Those who espouse safe-sex guidelines also seem to bump up against reality. Though in midcrisis it is politically injudicious to say so, safe-sex is poor sex—as likely to frustrate as satisfy. The much recommended use of condoms seems particularly blind. For those for whom sensation and not just will and fantasy is requisite for the transition from arousal to orgasm, condoms fail. Further the vast majority of gay sex is oral sex. And for oral sex condoms are (well) distasteful—as unsatisfying as unappetizing. This leaves masturbation, which, as Masters and Johnson have shown, produces the strongest orgasms of any sexual activity but which lacks the invasive yet ecstatic intimacy for which I suspect people have sex together in the first place, and which makes sex the natural symbol of union projected into the future.

Worse still for the likely escape from risk is the layering over of sexual drive with certain cultural forces. Sex is the core of gay male culture. Gay male culture is largely a system of highly efficient sexual delivery systems. Not surprisingly so, for the dominant culture allows no public presence to gay culture or institutional leeway for gay sex. Social forces are such that young men even in the blush of first love do not so much as hold hands in public. The casting of gay culture to the outer margins of society means that gay culture will do little more than produce means of satisfying powerful physical drives.

Even now most men who have gay sex are not gay self-identified and, in order to keep jobs, preserve marriages and children, and otherwise accommodate the dominant culture as a condition for social life, they necessarily have sex on the run. Many of these men consciously do not have safe-sex, lest that, paired with the dominant culture's virtual identification of AIDS and "queers," force them to a recognition that they themselves are after all "queer."[26]

These facts ensure that, with the exception of a few gay community centers and churches, gay turf consists of sex arcades: cruise bars, backroom bars, parks, alleys, piers, tearooms, adult book stores, gloryhole shops, truckstops, sex clubs, porn theaters, and bathhouses. To be the least bit openly gay is constantly to breathe a sexually charged atmosphere not conducive to prudential judgments.

More importantly, given social reality, it is only in these institutions and the sex acts they facilitate that gay men are able to affirm themselves as gay. And yet for the gay male, his sexual orientation is the chief factor of his existence, just as for blacks, due to social realities, being black is the chief factor of existence. Society, in focusing its concerns exclusively on the single characteristic by which an individual deviates from the norm, makes that one characteristic into the whole person: the homosexual, the faggot.

Forthright gays, however, in the process of reappropriating for themselves that very characteristic by which the dominant culture transfixes them, indeed reinforce (reasonably enough) its very centrality to themselves. As the result, something more than just pleasure and the fulfillment of need is wrapped up in sex for gays. With some slight exceptions like the gay choral movement and (sure enough) AIDS support groups, sex is the only mode in which gays in current culture are allowed to identify themselves to themselves. Self-respect, such as it is, for gays in our culture is the product of a robust sex life.

Even so, it is likely that the core of that respect is poisoned. One

26. See "AIDS Specter for Women: The Shadowy Bisexual," *The New York Times*, May 3, 1987, p. Y10: "[People closeted to themselves] may not practice safe sex because that would be an admission that it is high risk, homosexual behavior."

cannot completely prescind oneself from one's culture, in this case a culture that takes gays to be worth less than nongays and very likely worthless *simpliciter*. In the absence of ordinary familial or other everyday institutional arrangements that militate against this cultural despising of their very existence, gays are even more apt than other minorities to feel self-hatred. Gays will eventually come to realize, as feminists have, that no amount of consciousness raising and politically correct behavior ever completely undoes this damage. And for gays as an invisible minority, this damage or its threat produces a deadly paradox.

To the extent that one tries to avoid culture's despising of gays by disguising one's identity to others (and so also to a degree denying it to oneself) and bracketing and isolating one's sex life in one's conception of oneself, one is less likely to be able to make wise decisions about one's sex life. However, the more one is openly gay, the more one is exposed to being despised—not merely through increased exposure to day-to-day taunts and assaults but also through a heightened awareness of the ways culture transmits its hatred of gays and so of the breadth and intensity of that hatred.

In this latter circumstance, self-hatred and sexual desire tend to become fused. Just as violence—even against oneself (as in the "rough trade" phenomenon)—can be an especially effective object of sexual arousal, so can death—even one's own. The desire need not be conscious to be effective. Few people with such desire ever achieve even the level of consciousness of the characters in Yves Navarre's 1973 novel *Sweet Tooth*, who are somewhat aware that their sexual love is for death —their own—but who do not consciously seek it out; rather they simply drift into situations where the desire will be fulfilled.

AIDS is such a situation. Many gay men are drifting into it in part as the fulfillment of the dominant culture's appraisal of them, in part as a spinoff from the search for self-respect in a society that thwarts it. This is not idle speculation: it turns out that the same gay doctors who have extreme anxieties over the AIDS crisis have proven to be particularly unable to live by the sexual guidelines they prescribe to others.[27]

In light of these facts, it looks as though the chortling "we told you so" of some conservatives should in fact be seen as contributing to the very problem they would seek to end through police powers. It also seems that some gay strategists who aim at political expedience are

27. *The Advocate*, July 23, 1985, no. 425, p. 31.

misguided in their attempt to detach AIDS issues from gay social issues in general. The AIDS crisis is destroying the gay civil rights movement, but as that small edifice falls, it should be observed that the crisis is in significant part the product of that movement's lack of success.

To some, these alarming facts may suggest that gays are acting so unreasonably that state intervention is warranted on legitimate paternalistic grounds. But even if the irrationality claim could be made out (and I do not think it can), the argument still does not work. For the source of the alleged irrationality in these cases, when it is not a matter of poor education, is the indirect but determinate result of social and governmental stigmatizing of gays. In consequence, paternalism is here smuggled in through the back door, and again illegitimately so. Simply citing the existence of prejudice, bigotry, or discrimination against some group or the obvious consequences of such bias does not count in trying to establish a "good faith" discrimination against that group. Just as the state must not allow hecklers threatening disruption to determine what a speaker may say, so too social stigma cannot be alleged to be a legitimate ground of public policies. Otherwise one must believe, for instance, that in order legitimately to force—for their own good—the conversion of Jews to Christianity, it is sufficient simply to persecute them to the point where any refusal to convert appears severely irrational. Stated starkly, the historical persecution of gays by society waives any claim that society has to be acting on gays' behalf.

B. Deathbeds and Families

The first residential AIDS hospice in the nation's capital is named after a gay doctor who died of AIDS—The Robert Schwartz House. Doctors cure, but there is no cure. Rather, AIDS patients chiefly require routine nursing and hospice care. The disease is typically characterized by a progressive loss of energy and bodily control, punctuated by opportunistic infections which bring with them debilitating pain, disorientation, incontinence, and an inability to perform even basic functions without assistance. Historically, routine nursing and hospice functions have been performed by family members, and long-term disabilities were thus not major public policy concerns. Even now in the standard nursing home this tradition is carried on in its own unsatisfactory way: it falls to the patient's family to arrange for the "home," pay the bills, and provide whatever emotional support the patient is to receive.

I wish to suggest that hospice and nursing care is owed to gay patients by the state as a matter of compensatory justice for society's and government's prohibition against the creation of gay families. If society barred a motorcyclist from wearing a helmet he would otherwise have worn, he would certainly be owed compensation from society for any injury a helmet could have prevented. So too society owes gays the protections and comforts which it, by forbidding gay families, prevents them from acquiring on their own.

Fifty percent of nongay marriages fail even though they are given society's highest imprimatur and luxuriate in many material benefits from the state. It is surprising, indeed amazing, therefore, that any gay relationships survive. Some do; most do not. Most never even get off the ground.

Hatred of gays as internalized by gays—a condition magnified and darkened by the AIDS crisis—is probably the leading cause of the failure of gay relations to materialize and mature. If one does not take oneself seriously as a gay person, it is hard to take another seriously—as the object not of desire but of an abiding love, a patient tendance crafted something out of nothing and tendered for the long haul. Unqualified acceptance of the beloved is an ideal in matrimonial love. Few, if any, relations achieve it, but in gay relations the taint of self-hatred makes it likely that the ideal is not even in sight. Such acceptance will hardly be possible should the lover perceive the beloved as stained by a potion which they mutually share and which is the very catalyst and medium of their attraction. Gay men now scurrying for relations as a hedge against the health crisis are largely unaware of how ill-equipped they are for the journey.

Further, in a society where discrimination against gays is widespread, it is unlikely that gay couples will flourish. For acting as a couple tends, as much as anything short of saying one is gay, to project one's affectional preferences into the public realm and so target one for discrimination. (Members of nongay couples are here asked to imagine conducting their relationship for even just a week in such a way that no one could guess their orientation.) More generally, discrimination or its threat promotes for gays as an invisible minority a pervasive anonymity. This in turn both encourages high-risk sex and discourages social contacts that might lead to more lasting relationships. In nongay parlance a date is who you go out with; in gay parlance, it is who you come in with. The perils of anonymity are another way in which the lack of gay civil rights has aggravated the AIDS crisis.

For those who do establish bonds but must for job-related or familial reasons remain closeted about their relation, the bond frequently becomes an emotional pressure cooker. The relation typically is asked to bear more than is reasonable. The burden on the simple dyad is further weighted down by the myth, both romantic and religious, that one finds one's completion in a single other. White knights and messiahs never come in clusters. The myth has a special attraction for gays, by whom frequently and increasingly the lover is naïvely viewed as savior.

People would be lesser beings if they were so simple that complete life were but a two-piece puzzle. Fortunately, the myth gets nothing more than lip service in typical families, as they exist with multiple members in complex relations, embedded in supportive institutional networks. Typical socially acceptable families are matrices with a certain amount of open texture and play at the joints. In gay families, however, closetude holds the myth to one's head like a gun. One person is made to bear all of another's considerable emotional weight. Relations which are normally distributed among several people and expectations usually to be filled diversely are cast onto but one. It used to be that external sexual relations were the typical venting mechanisms for pressures and tensions in male relations. Gay males have never had much of a problem with spousal battering—but such venting is now deadly.

Another sign of and attempted solution to the pressurecooker effect in male bonding is a marked tendency among gay couples to "exteriorize" their relation in some way, treating it as though it were a third member to be given a concrete manifestation in, say, a house or a business. Cynics see these and the ferns and the pets as mere child substitutes— heterosexuality *manqué*. But in reality they are a (sometimes desperate) attempt to create psychic spaces and to avoid being consumed by the relation—to spike the myth. The very exteriorizing of the relation, however, usually tends to cast it into the public realm. Even Mary Hartman's ditsy mother, Martha Shumway eventually figured out that the guys next door were gay. But then the specter of discrimination returns. Successful family structures paradoxically are both crucibles of intimate privacy and gateways to the wider world. At nearly every turn, discrimination or its threat tends to so diminish the quality and impede the progress of gay relations that they falter. And the comfort from one's knowing friends in the bars is "what did you expect?"

It perhaps goes without saying that attempts of gays to create blood relations and extended families of their own have been blocked by society and now increasingly by the state. States have recently been codifying into statute and regulation what has been the reality in practice all along—the exclusion of child custody, adoption, and fostering by gay couples, even those couples who—but for gender mix—have in every other dimension a probity unquestioned even by the state. Founded on an overlay of several invidious stereotypes, these policies simply waste a rich lode of human resources. They systematically, yet needlessly, block the creation of gay familial units and indirectly contribute to the decay of gay relations by appealing so directly to an alleged wickedness of gays as corruptors and an alleged worthlessness of gays as role models.

One of the sadder moral side effects of the AIDS crisis is the number of men, stricken in their prime and deprived of medical insurance by forced unemployment, who have had to return to their frequently bewildered mothers and alien environments to be nursed through the final months of their suffering. Effectively denied the possibility of creating his own nurturing family, the son experiences the final humiliation of being treated again as a child, accepted, if at all, not for himself but in spite of himself. Thus is wrought even the corruption and inversion of the traditional family. Those in their prime taking care of those in old age becomes those in old age treating those in their prime as children.

Compassion would suggest, and compensatory justice should require, that the day-to-day care of the final-stage AIDS patient be provided in lieu of the care he would have likely had but for society's blocking his creation of his own family.

VII. PUBLIC HEALTH AND TOTALITARIANISM

Arguments offered so far by the medical establishment against quarantines and bathhouse closings have largely adopted the terms of mere practicality, appealing to such facts as the large number of people involved, the permanence of the virus in those exposed, and the possibility that the sexual arena may simply shift away from bathhouses where some educational efforts may be possible.[28] I have suggested to the contrary that quarantines and closings should be opposed, not because they are impractical (though they may be), but because they are immoral. Doctors have also tended to see the warrant for blanket funding of research and patient care as simply obvious—the only problems being ones of strategy. Again to the contrary, I have argued for funding on specific moral grounds, ones which differentiate what should and should not be funded—stopping well short of universal open-ended government funding for research and care.

Doctors tend to hold these unrefined views because they, not surprisingly, tend to see health as a trumping good, second to none in importance. This is a dangerous view, especially when coupled with their idea that the virtue of health is an undifferentiated one. They fail to distinguish between my harming my health and my harming your health. Behind this oversight lies the further (sometimes unarticulated) presumption that you and I both are absorbed into and subordinated under something called the public health—a concept that tends to be analyzed in inverse proportion to the frequency with which it is used when trying to justify coercive acts.[29]

No literal sense exists in which there could be such thing as a public health. To say the public has a health is like saying the number seven has a color: such a thing cannot have such a property. You have health or you lack it and I have health or lack it, because we each have a body with organs that function or do not function. But the public, an aggregate of persons similarly disposed as persons, has no such body of organs with functions which work or fail. There are, however, two frequently

28. For examples, see Kenneth H. Mayer, "The Epidemiological Investigation of AIDS," in *Special Supplement* (see n. 8 above), p. 15 (against both quarantines and bath closings) and Silverman and Silverman, "AIDS and the Threat to Public Health," p. 21 (against quarantines).

29. For a signal example, see "Additional Recommendations to Reduce Sexual and Drug Abuse-Related Transmission of HTLV-III/LAV," *MMWR* March 14, 1986, 35(10):154, recommending the closing of bathhouses "on public health grounds." No definition, elaboration, or analysis is offered of the notion "public health." The recommendation stands in marked contrast to the CDC's employment recommendations (see n. 2 above), for which elaborate analysis and argumentation are offered. Even the usually astute National Academy of Science could publish a whole book of AIDS recommendations (including many coercive ones) based on appeals to "the public health" without giving one word of conceptual or normative analysis to the notion. See Institute of Medicine, National Academy of Science, *Confronting AIDS: Directions for Public Health, Health Care and Research* (Washington: National Academy Press, 1986).

used metaphoric senses of public health that do have a reference: one is a legitimate use but largely inapplicable to the AIDS crisis; the other, when used normatively, is the pathway to totalitarianism.

The legitimate sense places public health in the same conceptual scheme as national defense and water purification. These are types of public goods in a technical sense: they are not what most people want and thus what democratic governments give them nor are they what tend to maximize by state means some type of good (pleasure, happiness, beauty); rather they are what everyone wants but cannot get (or get efficiently) through voluntary arrangements, and which thus require coercive coordinations from the state, so that *each* person gets what she wants. Thus, the private or voluntary arrangements of the market system do not seem likely to provide adequate national security, because a defense system that protects those who pay for it will also protect those who do not; everyone (reasonably enough) will tend to wait for someone else to pay for it, so that national security ends up not being purchased at all, or at least far less of it is purchased than everyone would agree to pay if there were some means to manifest that agreement. The coercive actions of the state through taxation are then required to achieve the public good of national defense.

For exactly the same reason, the state is warranted in using coercive measures to drain swamps and provide vaccines against airborne viruses. But the state is not warranted by appeal to the public good in coercing people to take the vaccine once it is freely available, for then *each* person is capable on his own—without further state coercion—of getting the protection he wants from the disease. The mode of AIDS contagion, makes it relevantly like this latter case. Each person on his own—without state coercion—can get the protection from the disease that he wants through his own actions, and indeed can get it by doing himself what he might be tempted to try to get the state to force upon others—say, avoiding bathhouses. As far as the good of protection is concerned, it can be achieved with no state coercion.

Is there a public good involved simply in reducing the size of the pool of AIDS-exposed people? I see just one, the one I argued for—the ability to have access to sex without fear of death. But this good does not permit every form of state coercion. Not every public good motivates every form of coercion. The public goods mentioned so far could all be achieved by *equitable* coercion (e.g., universal conscription, taxation, compensated taking of property). When equitable coercion is the means, the public good can be quite slight and still be justified (as in government support for the arts). But when the coercion is inequitably dispersed, the public good served must be considerably more compelling than the means are intrusive. Thus, dispersed coercion against select individuals that involves restricted motion and physical suffering is warranted only by unqualifiedly necessary ends: when the individuals coerced have harmed others (as in punishment), or when it is necessary to the very existence of the country (as a partial military draft may be for a nation at defensive war). The public good of an unencumbered sex life, however, fails this weighted ends-to-means test if the means are a dispersedly coerced sex life. For the intrusion and the good are on a par—on the one hand encumbered sex, on the other unencumbered sex. And so it appears that only equitably coercive means are available to achieve the end of reducing the pool of AIDS-exposures—taxation for preventive measures like vaccine development, but not coercive measures that affect some but not others, like closing bathhouses, or banning or regulating sex practices selectively, or mandating antibody tests where the social consequence of testing positive are significantly worse than the consequences of testing negative.

Those who do not find the possibility of carefree sex a public good—probably the bulk of those actually calling for state coercion—will find no legitimate help in the notion of public health for state coercion of sexual practices here. Those who do will find it justifies only equitable measures.

The other metaphoric sense of public health takes the medical model of the healthy body and unwittingly transfers it to society—the body politic. But his transfer (when it has any content at all) bears hidden and extremely dangerous assumptions. Plato in the *Republic* was the first thinker systematically to press the analogy of the good society to the healthy body. The state stands to the citizenry, and its good, as a doctor stands to the body and its health. Society, so it is claimed, is an organism in which people are mere functional parts, ones that are morally good and emotionally well off only insofar as they act for the sake of the organism. The analogy is alive and well today and calling out for extreme measures. Thus former Director of Health for San Francisco,

Mervyn S. Silverman, claims in defense of his failed attempt to close bathhouses: "Much as a physician treating one organ must consider the effects on the entire organism, a public official has the community as the patient and must attend to all factors in seeking the greatest overall good."[30] In this view, the individual, however harmed, cannot fulfill his or her role. A damaged organ, the spleen for example, can simply be cut out. By comparison, quarantines and coerced sex lives might appear as mild remedies. But something has been lost here—persons.

The medical model of society is the conceptual engine of totalitarianism. It presumes not that the goods of individuals are final goods but that individuals are good only as they serve some good beyond themselves, that of the state or body politic. The state exists not for the sake of individuals—to protect and enhance their prospects as rational agents —but rather individuals exist for the state and are subordinated to society as a whole, the worth of which is to be determined only from the perspective of the whole. The individual, thus, is not an end in himself but exists for some social good—whether that good be some hoped-for overall happiness or some social ideal—like, purity, wholesomeness, decency, or "traditional values." Unconscious obedient servicing is dressed up as virtue.

The worst political consequence of the AIDS crisis would not be simply the further degradation of gays. Gay internments would not be anything new to this century. In the European internment camps of World War II, in addition to Jews' wearing yellow badges, gypsies wore brown triangles, Jehovah's Witnesses purple, political prisoners red, race defilers black, and gays pink triangles. Worse than the further degradation of gays in America would be a general, and not easily reversed, shift in the nation's center of gravity toward the medical model and away from the position, acknowledged in America's Constitutional tradition, that individuals have broad yet determinate claims against both general welfare and social ideals. The consequence of such a shift would be that people would come to be treated essentially as resources, sometimes expendable—a determination no less frightening when made by a combined father, colonel, and doctor than by a fearful mob.

30. Silverman and Silverman, "AIDS and the Threat to Public Health," p. 22.

VIII. A RUNE AT H.H.S.

The north portal to the U.S. Department of Health and Human Services Building is decorated with a monumental WPA-era granite intaglio of a shovel, a staked sapling, and two men holding hands, gazing into each other's eyes and smiling.

9. AIDS, Gay Men, and the Insurance Industry

"I ought to punch your face in, you faggot bastard."—
physician working for American Founder's Life Insurance Company to a California applicant questioning the legality of the company's required test for antibodies to the AIDS virus.[1]

California, Wisconsin, and the District of Columbia have passed laws barring insurance companies from using tests for AIDS antibodies to screen applicants for health insurance policies. A number of other states, including Massachusetts and New York, have done so by administrative regulations issued by their executive branches.

Are such laws and regulations warranted and just?[2] Though the relevant issues have been misunderstood on both sides, governments can legitimately and should bar insurance companies from using the AIDS antibody test.

The gay side tries to play down the ability of the test to predict the likelihood that someone will come down with AIDS. And as long as one sticks just to an examination of the individual case, this is true. After all, not everyone who smokes heavily will come down with lung cancer or die of heart disease. But the individual case is irrelevant to the determination of actuarial tables for insurance purposes. What are relevant are statistical probabilities *over groups*. And there is no denying that people who have AIDS antibodies revealed by the test are much more likely to come down with AIDS than those for whom the test is negative, just as

1. "Insurance Company Doctor Threatens Violence," *National Gay Rights Advocates Newsletter* [San Francisco] (Summer 1987), [p. 3].

2. For opposing points of view on the issue, see Benjamin Schatz, "The AIDS Insurance Crisis: Underwriting or Overreaching?" *Harvard Law Review* (1987) 100:1782–1805 and Karen A. Clifford and Russel P. Iuculano, "AIDS and Insurance: The Rationale for AIDS-Related Testing," *Harvard Law Review* (1987) 100:1806–25.

smokers are much more likely to come down with lung cancer than nonsmokers. That one cannot say which individual smoker or which antibody carrier will become ill is irrelevant to the determination of insurance rates.

The insurance industry, however, is equally misguided. It claims that banning the use of the antibody test is unfair because the rates of the majority of people will go up even though they are not at risk for AIDS. It is true that rates will go up, but this does not establish that the government policy is unfair.

To establish that the law is unfair, the insurance industry would have to show that the rate increase would violate some right or legitimate claim of its clients. And this it cannot do. While it is nice if costs, like taxes or the price of beans, go down as the result of some government policy, no one's rights have been violated if some legitimate government purpose has the effect of raising taxes or the price of beans. Similarly, though it may irk the majority (and the insurance industry is counting on this), the simple raising of insurance premiums does not violate anyone's rights, any more than the use of credit cards violates anyone's rights, even though their use drives up the price of goods for everyone—those who use cards, those who have them but do not use them, and those who are refused the use of them.

To make the point concretely: does an individual policy holder have a legitimate complaint against his insurance company if the insurance company has not pursued a policy of trying to screen out every imaginable risk group for every imaginable disease that might cause a rise in insurance rates, should some of the insured come down with it? The answer is obviously not.

A person's rights against his or her insurance company have not been violated if it fails to ask women whether they have had multiple sex partners and thus have put themselves at increased risk for fatal cervical cancer. There is nothing wrong therefore—no rights are violated—if the government, for some legitimate reason, deflects insurance companies from asking that question. And it does have such a legitimate reason: to protect privacy. So too, then, if the government bars the industry from asking after a person's antibody status, no individual policy holder's rights have been violated. And the government does have a legitimate reason to do so: to help raise gay people out of their refugee status, a status that has been aggravated by the AIDS crisis.

Insurance companies come to the AIDS crisis with dirty hands. Traditionally, they have, as a matter of policy, discriminated against gay people both in issuing policies and in employment opportunities.[3] And they have, as a matter of practice, been especially effective at such discrimination—because they snoop. They make their money from the statistical norm, and so they suppose that it is also the moral norm. They mistakenly think they are promoting something normal, something American, when they discriminate against gays. It is therefore especially appropriate—a matter of compensatory justice—that the insurance industry should shoulder some of the burden in the move toward social justice for gays.

3. The National Association of Insurance Commissioners in the mid-1980s adopted a guideline that "sexual orientation may not be used in the underwriting process or in the determination of insurability." However, a 1988 study by the Congressional Office of Technology Assessment found that underwriters at many insurance companies indeed do screen out gay applicants for health insurance and use "indirect approaches or inspection agencies to confirm 'suspicions of homosexuality.'" Of 61 insurance companies responding to a survey by the Congressional agency, 18 *admitted* to violating the industry guidelines. So much for self-regulation. For quotes and numbers, see "Study Finds Most Health Insurers Screen Applicants for AIDS Virus," *The New York Times,* January 18, 1988, p. 1.

10. Policy, Ritual, Purity: Mandatory AIDS Testing

"There is not a good word to be said for anybody's behavior in this whole mess."—Larry Kramer, *The Normal Heart*

I. A TALE OF THE SOUTH AND A THESIS

Well after *Brown v. the Board of Education,* Jackson, Mississippi maintained racially segregated public swimming pools, claiming that only through segregation could violence and social chaos be avoided there.[1] The federal courts saw through this stratagem, noting that it was a variant of the heckler's veto thinly masking racial animus.[2] But they did not tell Jackson to integrate its swimming pools—only that it could not maintain segregated ones. Did Jackson integrate its pools? No. The city council voted instead to close them all. This time out, the courts were not so wise.

In 1971, the Supreme Court upheld the constitutionality of the pool closings.[3] The Court was snookered by the surface similarity of the

1. This paper was written for and delivered to the Chicago Area AIDS Task Force, a private-sector, umbrella organization of the various public and private Cook County agencies and organizations addressing the AIDS crisis, July 14, 1987.

2. *Brown v. Board of Education,* 347 U.S. 483 (1954); *Clark v. Thompson,* 206 F. Supp. 539 (S.D. Miss. 1962), aff'd, 313 F.2d 637 (5th Cir), cert. denied, 375 U.S. 951 (1963).

3. *Palmer v. Thompson,* 403 U.S. 217, 219–21, 226 (1971).

policy's treatment of blacks and whites—neither could, after all, use the swimming pools. The practice appeared to treat similar cases similarly. And indeed the pool closing statute did not refer in any way to blacks. However, shallow formalism aside, the pool closing was an even more inequitable treatment of blacks than was the original policy of segregation. Segregation merely perpetuated custom, but the closings were a social ritual that elevated pervasive custom to the level of a sacred value. For the white city council's action told blacks that whites view them as so disgusting and polluting that white social solidarity will be maintained even if to do so requires of whites the loss of comfort, joy, and the pleasures of the season. Happiness is as nothing when social identity is challenged—racial purity is not a value that the South was willing to sell; it was priceless. The Court could not see that the point of the legislative act of closing the swimming pools was to stigmatize blacks, even though the act made no mention of them.[4]

Similarly, I will argue here that the point of mandatory AIDS antibody testing is the degradation of gays and the reconsecration of heterosexual supremacy as a sacred value, even though mandatory testing, to date, has not been directly aimed at gays nor indeed has made any mention of them. AIDS testing legislation is not to be understood as business-as-usual public policy making aimed at maximizing overall social utility or realizing public goods;[5] it can be adequately understood only in terms

4. The Supreme Court has made little progress on this front. See McCleskey v. Kemp, 107 S. Ct. 1756 (1987), in which the Supreme Court rejected as constitutionally irrelevant statistical evidence—twice as strong as that causally linking smoking to heart disease—showing that the lives of white murder victims are valued many times more than the lives of black murder victims. Both the equal protection of the laws and the bar to cruel and unusual punishment require (so the Court declared) particularized showings of an intent to discriminate against a specific individual—showings which, given speech taboos now covering racism, can never be met.

5. Examples of the "public goods" which I mean here include national defense, water purification, and equal opportunity. By "public good" I mean a good which everyone wants but cannot get or get efficiently through voluntary arrangements and which thus for its realization requires coercive coordination from the state—typically to circumvent "free riders"—so that *each* person gets what he wants.

Public health can be a public good in this sense, when for instance a measure carried out in the name of public health takes the form of the funding of research for vaccines against airborne viruses. But in this paper I use "public health" in an operational, nonnormative, adjectival sense simply to designate people, actions, institutions, and the like which are typically referred to in ordinary English usage as elements of the public health community and its behavior.

of the nature and function of social rituals, in particular, purification rituals.

II. SOME SOCIAL STRUCTURES

Six years into the AIDS crisis the nation's civic leader and moral pater-familias gave his first speech on AIDS. Without ever mentioning gays, he entrusted the moral evaluation of the disease's possessors to the future estate and its judgment of God, while resting present judgment in an awkwardness-dodging silence.[6]

In marked contrast, the speech carefully attended to recommended statute, administrative policy, and government practice, which he announced ought chiefly to take the form of mandatory testing for AIDS antibodies among certain segments of society: marriage license applicants, prisoners, and immigrants applying for permanent U.S. residency.[7] Subsequently, the latter two forms of testing were formally instituted at the national level through administrative rule[8] and the Illinois legislature has passed mandatory marital testing—the first state legislature to do so.[9] Other groups already subject to mandatory federal AIDS testing are military recruits and active duty personnel, Foreign Service officers, and employees of the Job Corps.[10]

6. *The Advocate* [Los Angeles], July 7, 1987, no. 476, p. 11.

7. "President Calls for Widespread Testing," *The New York Times*, June 1, 1987, p. 1.

8. "AIDS Test Ordered for U.S. Prisoners and Immigration," *The New York Times*, June 9, 1987, p. 1.

9. "Illinois Backs AIDS Tracing," *The New York Times*, July 1, 1987, p. Y9; "Veto of AIDS Bills Urged in Illinois," *The New York Times*, July 7, 1987, p. Y11. Illinois was the first state to have its legislature pass mandatory marital AIDS-antibody testing. Between the passage of the bill and its signing by Illinois' governor several months later, Louisiana's legislature passed and its governor signed such legislation; the bills in both states went into effect on January 1, 1988. "Broad Laws on AIDS Signed in Illinois," *The New York Times*, September 22, 1987, p. Y15; "AIDS Bills Focus on Education," *Chicago Tribune*, September 22 1987, p. 1.

When the implementation of the Illinois testing law proved socially unwieldy, its senate sponsor claimed that "the cost of implementing the law was not a consideration in creating it." "Prenuptial AIDS Screening a Strain in Illinois," *The New York Times*, January 26, 1988, p. 1.

10. "AIDS Test Ordered for U.S. Prisoners and Immigration," *The New York Times*, June 9, 1987, p. 1. Popular support for all forms of testing is overwhelming. A Gallup poll shows that 90 percent of people favor testing immigrants, 88 percent federal prisoners, 83 percent military personnel, 80 percent marriage license applicants and 52 percent all

Doctors, social workers, government health agencies, medical ethics thinktanks, AIDS support groups, gay and other civil rights groups and the like have done a passable, if mixed and modest, job—sometimes marred by phony patriotism[11]—in showing that mandatory testing policies are not justified on traditional public health grounds. They have shown in particular that coerced testing is unlikely to do much to stop the spread of the disease but is likely to drive the disease underground. They have also shown it to be a very poor investment of social dollars, incapable of justification on a cost-benefit analysis, and having consequences that are tragic when producing false test results and absurd considering that the funds for the tests' administration could be going into desperately needed research and patient care.[12]

However, this public health community, in showing that mandatory testing is nonsensical from the point of view of social utility and in opposing it on that ground, has completely missed the social point of the statutes and rules mandating antibody testing; indeed in its very claims (though true) that the laws are inefficient, it actually sustains the evil of the laws' real purposes. For legislative and administrative actions mandating AIDS testing are not miscalculations, merely misdirected attempts to maximize utility, nor are they failed attempts to provide the things that everyone wants but can only get through the intervention and coercive coordinations of the state—the admitted aims of most legitimate legislation. Rather they are social rituals through which the nation expresses and strengthens its highest values, its sacred values—the values, that is, for which it will pay any price.[13]

Such rituals and their values are the means by which and the forms in which the nation identifies itself to itself, and through which it maintains, largely unconsciously, its group solidarity. But group solidarity comes with a price—or as the anthropologist and social theorist Mary

---

Americans. "Widespread Tests for AIDS Virus Favored by Most, Gallup Reports," *The New York Times*, July 13, 1987, p. Y11.

11. The American Medical Association, for example, is on record as supporting testing of prisoners and immigrants. "Doctors' Panel Suggests Limited AIDS Testing," *The New York Times*, June 21, 1987, p. Y19.

12. "Need to Widen [Voluntary] AIDS Testing Seen as Health Forum Ends" and "Homosexuals Applaud Rejection of Mandatory Test for AIDS: Advocates Express Relief over Consensus," *The New York Times*, February 26, 1987, p. Y13.

13. For an analysis of sacred or priceless values in government deliberations, see Douglas MacLean "Social Values and the Distribution of Risk" in Douglas MacLean, ed., *Values at Risk*, pp. 85–93 (Totowa, N.J.: Rowman and Allanheld, 1986).

Douglas has summarized the main finding of her lifework: "Solidarity is only gesturing when it involves no sacrifice."[14] The social inefficiency of AIDS testing demonstrated by the public health community is the sacrifice that society has accepted to express and reconfigure its solidarity around its central sacred value. An examination of cases—especially that of marital testing—will show that the chief sacred value wrought by various AIDS testing laws is what Adrienne Rich has called compulsory heterosexuality.[15]

Mandatory AIDS antibody testing laws are social purification rituals through which, by calling for sacrifices of and by the dominant culture, that culture reaffirms the sanctity of compulsory heterosexuality and rededicates heterosexuality's central and controlling place in society. The imprecatory counterpoint of such sanctification is the degradation of gays, even though in part for social convenience and moral salve the laws make no mention of them.

But even setting aside attempts to skirt possible political ugliness and taboos on speaking of sex, it is still probable that gays would not be mentioned in AIDS legislation—at least for now. For typically, especially when all goes passably well, a society does not have a foreground cognition of what its highest values are. They are not the object of its active concern but a filter through which all social structures are projected and, in turn, through which social behavior is perceived.[16] The latter filtering explains, for instance, the leaden density of most people's inability to see even openly gay people.

Paradoxically, then, in the case at hand, that which is most degraded —the gay person—goes entirely unmentioned, while the most carefully articulated values and best justified actions—those of the public health community—actually contribute to overall social evil.

If I am anywhere near the mark, then we shall unhappily have broached

14. Mary Douglas, *How Institutions Think* (Syracuse: Syracuse University Press, 1986), p. 4.

15. Adrienne Rich, "Compulsory Heterosexuality and Lesbian Existence," *Signs: Journal of Women in Culture and Society* (Summer 1980) 5(4):631–60.

16. Mary Douglas explains:

For Fleck, the thought style [of society] sets the preconditions of any cognition, and determines what can be counted as a reasonable question and a true or false answer. It provides the context and sets the limits for any judgment about objective reality. Its essential feature is to be hidden from the members of the thought collective.

How Institutions Think, p. 13.

a justifiable skepticism about the nature and existence of human good-
ness and the worth of democracies, even constitutionally restrained ones.

III. CASES IN POINT

A. Marital Testing

The most obvious case for my general thesis is mandatory testing as a
condition for getting a marriage licence—remember gays need not apply.

Courts have done backflips in order to uphold cases of the legal
existence of marriages even when the formal requirements (like age) and
procedural requirements (like solemnization) for entry into marriage
have been wholly absent or blatantly violated.[17] They have done so to
such an extent as to draw into doubt the rule of law in this area. The
one spot, though, where they have balked at allowing access to marriage
is access for gays. The courts have used every legal contrivance to block
the recognition of gay marriages.[18] These paired legal patterns showing
a systematic and uniform warping of supposedly impartial and rational
judicial judgment clearly suggest that here we have reached the bedrock
and fundamental stuff of society—the thing that will not be budged, the
thing that cannot be remade.

Now, when absolutes are challenged, beware. And that is what is
happening in the AIDS crisis, in part because it has thrown gays more
prominently and more threateningly into social consciousness than ever
before and in part because of the transfiguration of sexual values wrought
by it, a change that would be comical if it were not so scary in what it
tells us about people's ability to distinguish means and ends.

AIDS has caused people to confuse the merely instrumental virtue of
prudence with the final goods for the acquisition of which one would

17. For cases and discussion, see Harry D. Krause, *Family Law*, 2d ed. (St. Paul: West,
1983), pp. 31–74.

18. See, for example, *Singer v. Hara*, 522 P.2d 1187, 1194–95 (1974), in which
Washington's supreme court held that the requirement that men marry one but not the
other gender was not a requirement that triggered a state constitutional bar on distinctions
made with respect to gender. See also *Adams v. Howerton*, 486 F. Supp. 1119, 1124–25
(C.D. Cal. 1980) in which the court claimed that even if gays did have a fundamental right
to marry, a bar on gays marrying would still be upheld because necessary to a compelling
state interest.

want to be prudent. AIDS has certainly upped the ante on the means to a robust sex life; promiscuity unguarded is not now prudent. But rather than seeing AIDS as merely raising prudential concerns, weak minds, including most gay ones, have looked for deeper meanings and unwittingly transferred the badness of means—high costs—to sex as an end. Sex is now a final bad, to be tolerated and redeemed, if at all, only within an abiding relation for which it serves as a token or symbol—a relation not merely of monogamy (for one can, after all, be monogamous with a stranger) but a relation of exclusive marriage. Those who have bought into this romantic reformation, though using a somewhat different rhetoric, are conceptually indistinguishable from those who believe that AIDS is the judgment of God. For all the wrong reasons, AIDS has applied practical pressures to the heterosexual purchase on marriage.

Now, marriage is the central institution of heterosexuality. In a culture where religion, sports, and political affiliation have become a matter of personal taste, heterosexuality is the standard form and standard bearer of social cohesion. If, under pressures exterior to the institution of marriage but interior to the society which it is supposed to epitomize and valorize, the institution is to be maintained in its traditional form, it must be purified and reannointed. Simply perpetuating the old bar to gay legal marriages is not sufficient to new circumstances. A new ritual is called for and it is handily supplied by the AIDS crisis itself, since there is a virtual identification in the mind of America between AIDS and gays, as revealed most clearly in acronymic jokes and AIDS graffiti, those distillates of popular morality. The new ritual that, within the configuration of marriage, will do the requisite work is to test those who are to be married to make sure that they are not polluted with the very stigma that challenges the institution itself. Here a social policy, perfectly absurd when viewed in terms of social utility, makes perfect sense when viewed as a social purification ritual.

The cost of the policy is the social sacrifice the dominant culture is willing to make in order to worship fully its final values, just as Abraham is willing to sacrifice his own son to show his praise of and obedience to God. A willingness to sacrifice someone else's child, as in Aztec blood sacrifices, will not do the same moral work. That is merely negotiating with the gods. It does not express or generate sacred values. Similarly poisoning one's enemies' wells with the corpses of their dead degrades the enemy not so much as when oneself is there wanting for water. So too, degrading gays by purifying marriage of their taint does not count as much, does not register and express value as much, unless some sacrifice is incurred by those who do the degrading.

The practical or policy-oriented rationalizations that have been tendered for marital testing are quite bad. The President's rationale is that such testing would help in tracking the natural history of the disease: "AIDS is surreptitiously spreading throughout our population, and yet we have no accurate measure of its scope. . . . And that is why I support . . . testing."[19] Now, this research agenda is very bad science, for it appeals even on its face directly to a self-selecting sample, the members of which, moreover, may have some doubts about or inklings of how the results may eventually be put to use. But even this rationale is perhaps not so crazy after all, if again viewed not as public policy but as part of social ritual. For such selective testing might approximate a showing of the incidence of AIDS exposure among those who *really* count, if to "really count" means to participate in the institution by which society defines itself. The real people are those who are allowed to marry and indeed usually do.

More sophisticated arguments for marital testing are based on paternalism, but also fall stillborn from the mind. They are concocted out of the materials mined from the quarry of public health and so lack even the hidden ritualistic value of the President's rationale. A pragmatic paternalism compares AIDS testing to testing for syphilis. But this is a misguided analogy. For, unlike syphilis, AIDS currently has no cure. Jack can't go off and get cured before he marries Jill. Note that on the syphilis-based testing model, the one partner need never know the other's test results; they must each simply come up clean to the state before the license is issued.

Some feminists, focusing on Jill, have advanced as a ground for mandatory marital testing a paternalism of enforced shared knowledge: the test gives a woman knowledge that is relevant for making a rational decision on whether to go ahead and get married.[20] But this argument comes too late in the day. The legal institution of marriage is shot

---

19. "President Calls for Widespread Testing," *The New York Times*, June 1, 1987, p. 1.
20. Julien S. Murphy, "Women with AIDS: Sexual Ethics in an Epidemic," in Inge Corless and Mary Pittman-Lindeman, eds., *AIDS: Principles, Practices and Politics*, pp. 67–71 (New York: Harper and Row, 1988).

through with regulations, legal commitments, binding obligations, and risks affecting major life components about which the partners typically know nothing and about which indeed they are socially and legally encouraged to stay in ignorance.[21] This paternalistic argument played out consistently then draws into doubt the whole institution of marriage as a legal entity.

Standard public policy gambits directed at social efficiency make no sense as explanations of AIDS marital testing. An interpretation of the phenomenon as social purification ritual makes much better sense.

It should not be surprising that Illinois—Northern in gesture and form, Southern in substance and sincerity—should be the first state to pass marital testing. AIDS has replaced abortion as the issue of choice on the state assembly's social agenda. Illinois has done for abortion litigation what New York has done for the Interstate Commerce Clause and Georgia for obscenity law. Session after session, the Illinois legislature has passed abortion restrictions, even though they have already been struck down as unconstitutional and even though it costs the state a great deal of money to see them so declared. In 1987, however, no coercive abortion legislation was passed. Instead, the legislature enacted a host of coercive AIDS measures. This transfer of attention, though, should not come as a surprise, for the passing of abortion bars too should be viewed not as standard public policy making but essentially as rituals of sanctification. And the value these rituals develop and express is the same value as the AIDS testing rituals—compulsory heterosexuality.

Abortion restrictions have almost universally been taken as a women's issue by liberals, who construe the error of such laws chiefly as that of gender discrimination, even though the laws are struck down on grounds of privacy, rather than equal protection. Here again means and ends are confused. Abortion bars, though they control and coerce women, do not have the control or degradation of women *qua* women as their end. The end is to force women to have babies—the central heterosexual event. Indeed most social and legal discrimination against women does not have the stigmatization of women as women as its end, but is directly parasitic upon or analogically derivative from the roles that women are forced to play within the structures of heterosexuality. The casting of

21. On formal and substantive failings of marriage as a contract, see Sara Ann Ketchum, "Liberalism and Marriage Law" in Mary Vetterling-Braggin, et al., eds., *Feminism and Philosophy*, pp. 247–76 (Totowa, N.J.: Littlefield Adams, 1977).

women into clearly subordinated service roles, for instance, as nurses, is parasitic upon the role of women within heterosexuality as wives and mothers—the ultimate, paradigmatic service roles.

This order of things means that battles for women's equality in aiming simply at eliminating legally and socially enforced gender distinctions have targeted the symptoms of the problem rather than its cause—compulsory heterosexuality. The women's movement's usual embarrassment over and sidestepping of lesbian issues—at best treating lesbians as a fifth wheel in the movement—then, explain why the movement's successes to date have not been very deep ones. When conservatives argued that the Equal Rights Amendment, if passed, would necessarily permit homosexual marriages, just as the Equal Protection Clause had resulted in the states' necessarily having to permit miscegenation,[22] the women's movement's advertised response was simply to deny the whole thing. The ERA failed.

Because compulsory heterosexuality is so pervasive in society as to be its persistent and uniform background phenomenon, it goes as unnoticed in our thinking about society as air at a constant skin temperature goes unnoticed as we walk around a room. Though we are completely engulfed in it, we are completely oblivious to it. Though it is essential to our motions and we constantly adjust to it, it never enters our forethought. Hardly anyone looking at the advertisements and comics in the dailies thinks "hey, where have all the lesbians and gay men gone?"

It is only within such wider, revisionary social thought on AIDS—thought in which public health categories play no role—that coercive AIDS legislation begins to make sense. Marital AIDS testing reconsecrates the temple of marriage—and the cosmic canopy of heterosexuality—largely by the careful exorcising of demons.

B. Immigration and the Military

Other categories and forms of mandatory AIDS antibody testing can be treated in shorter compass. Immigration policy and military policy are nominally designed to defend the nation, but the history of both institutions, their racial histories, for instance,[23] shows that their chief function

22. *Loving v. Virginia*, 388 U.S. 1 (1967) (held that the Equal Protection Clause bars anti-miscegenation statutes).
23. See Bernard C. Nalty, *Strength for the Fight: A History of Black Americans in the*

is not so much defending what the nation is but determining what the nation is. This is the real reason that mandatory AIDS testing has been instituted in these two areas.

The military's own rationales are two. One is paternalistic: knowing a soldier's antibody status will allow the army to better take care of him. This paternalistic argument is wholly bogus. In no other area is the army suddenly concerned with the better care of its personnel. Indeed it has recently fought to the mat for—and won—an uncontestable right to feed soldiers LSD under false pretenses.[24] The other Army rationale is nominally strategic: soldiers are supposed to be walking bloodbanks, but this rationale is simply so statistically overinclusive as to be an intellectual ruse. The National Academy of Science study of the AIDS crisis showed that such battlefield transfusions virtually never occur, thanks to the extensive use of much safer blood-volume expanders.[25] One normally does not, and indeed the armed forces do not, make policy based on the oddball case. Rationally self-interested people do not spend huge sums to increase their safety only marginally, and the armed forces certainly do not spend large sums to guard against every eventuality to personnel who after all are not even there, in the army's eyes, for their own good. Yet an oddly wide spectrum of people including some nominally activist gays have bought this military argument for testing simply in order not to appear unpatriotic.

What tips the military's hand to reveal its true motives is its actual practice. Even though Congress has barred the armed forces from using

Military (New York: The Free Press, 1986) and Elizabeth Hull, *Without Justice for All: The Constitutional Rights of Aliens* (Westport, Conn.: Greenwood Press, 1985), chapter 1.

24. *United States v. James B. Stanley*, 107 S. Ct. 3054 (1987).

25. Institute of Medicine, National Academy of Science, *Confronting AIDS: Directions for Public Health, Health Care and Research* (Washington: National Academy Press, 1986), p. 122. The Army's own study and account of blood transfusions in the Vietnam War makes no mention at all of any battlefield transfusions other than the extensive use of plasma expanders. The study concludes that "from the standpoint of methods used to wound—mines, high-velocity missiles, and boobytraps—as well as the locale in which many were injured—in paddyfields or along waterways where human and animal excreta were common—Vietnam was quite a 'dirty' war." Nevertheless "the availability of whole blood, which had been a problem early in each major war to date, was not a problem in Vietnam. An efficient distribution system kept pace with the increasing requirements for whole blood; in no instance was blood unavailable when, where and in the types and amounts needed." Major General Spurgeon Neel, *Medical Support of the U.S. Army in Vietnam, 1965–1970* (Washington, D.C.: Department of the Army [Vietnam Studies], 1973), pp. 49–50, 55–56, 66, 114–26, 172–73, quotes from pp. 49, 172–73.

a soldier's antibody status as a reason for demobbing him, in practice the military simply badgers the antibody positive soldier until he admits he's queer and then discharges him on that ground—so much for care and concern.[26] Antibody testing is the physical correlate for heterosexuality that the military has long been seeking in order to purge itself of pogues. Recent empirical studies have shown that the military's past record of discovering even its sexually active gay males has been very poor indeed.[27] In the World War II era, it used a tongue depressor test to discern queers. If a recruit failed to gag on the depressor when it was stuck suddenly to the back of the throat, then in the army's mind that meant that other things less savory had likely been there and the recruit would be rejected.[28] With AIDS testing the army now thinks it has found the tool for which it has long hankered. The purpose of AIDS antibody testing in the army and its twin, immigration policy, is the purge of gay people in order to keep pure the institutions by which the nation defines itself.

C. Of Walls and Vampires

Prison testing is a convoluted yet particularly telling case. Here the nominal public health rationale for such testing, pushed for instance by the American Medical Association, is that sex in prison will spread the disease, so that body-positives have to be segregated from the general population to prevent its spread. This argument shows a certain forgetfulness about the mode of the disease's transmission and an ignorance of prison life. Given that in men's prisons no one is transmitting the virus perinatally, a prisoner, unless coerced, has to expose himself to the virus in order to get it. Nonviolent positives are being put in "protective custody"—basically, solitary confinement, something than which nothing greater can be conceived—because *other people* may be violent

26. See Rhonda R. Rivera, "The Military," in Harlon Dalton, Scott Burris, and the Yale AIDS Law Project, eds., *AIDS and the Law: A Guide for the Public*, pp. 221–34 (New Haven: Yale University Press, 1987).

27. See Joseph Harry, "Homosexual Men and Women Who Served Their Country," *Journal of Homosexuality* (1984) 10(1–2):117–25.

28. See Allan Bérubé, "Gays at War," *Mother Jones* (February-March 1983) 8(11):23–29, 45, and "Marching to a Different Drummer," *The Advocate*, October 15, 1981, no. 328, pp. 20–25, reprinted in Ann Snitnow, et al., eds., *Powers of Desire: The Politics of Sexuality*, pp. 88–99 (New York: Monthly Review Press, 1983).

toward them or coerce them into having sex. Here the health rationale makes sense only if one accepts as sound the heckler's veto argument— and in a form elevated to a level that permits the utter crushing of human dignity, a commodity already rare in gang-run U.S. prisons. Is America in the AIDS crisis suddenly so concerned about the health and well-being of its prison populations? If you are naïve enough to believe that one, you are naïve enough to believe that when prison guards use with the press the studied ambiguity "homosexual rape," it is the homosexuals that are doing the raping.[29]

The Justice Department spokesman who announced the beginning of mandatory testing in federal prisons gave two rationales for it: "the testing [is] designed to gauge the extent of AIDS infection among prisoners and the department's ability to conduct routine testing."[30] Note that neither of these rationales has anything specifically to do with prisons and prisoners; they might as well have been claimed on behalf of Boy Scouts or blondes or indeed any group. The second rationale ought to have sounded alarms, but has not: why learn how to do routine testing on a large scale unless one has big plans for its use. In any case, the rationales offered for prison testing fail to justify the vigor with which the policy is being pursued nationally and locally.

No, the real reason for prison testing is provided by a remark, cryptic on its surface, made by the U.S. Attorney General, the man to whom America has entrusted the realization of justice. He claimed that prison testing is necessary because when prisoners are released many of them gravitate toward jobs in daycare centers.[31] I take it that this dense remark, when unfolded, entails something like the following concatenation of ideas: one, gays should be in prison and some actually are put there; two, homosexuality is a corruptive contagion, so that even if one was not queer going into prison, one likely is when coming out; three, all gays are child molesters, who, if unchecked, will destroy civilization through the corruptive contagion of its most tender link, its children, its future.

A corruptive contagion is a disease that reproduces itself from one

29. See Wayne Wooden and Jay Parker, *Men Behind Bars: Sexual Exploitation in Prison* (New York: Plenum, 1982).

30. "AIDS Test Ordered for U.S. Prisons and Immigration," *The New York Times,* June 9, 1987, p. Y22.

31. *Ibid.*

person to the next simply and sufficiently through its symptoms. The myth that homosexuality is a corruptive contagion—that one gets it from someone performing homosexual acts upon or near one—runs very deep in our culture. In 1978, Associate Justice, now Chief Justice, Rehnquist, while protesting the Supreme Court's declining to hear a successful gay student case, went out of his way to hold that a gay student organization's claim to campus recognition is "akin to . . . those suffering from measles [claiming they] have a constitutional right, in violation of quarantine regulations, to associate together and with others who do not presently have measles, in order to urge repeal of state law providing that measles sufferers be quarantined."[32]

AIDS too is mistakenly thought by America to be a corruptive contagion: irrational fears of casual contagion and the mistaken but popular comparison of it to airborne diseases, like influenza,[33] suggest that it is a disease the symptoms of which are the proximate cause of its transmission, where in fact, since it is a bloodborne disease, the actions of the person who gets the disease are the proximate cause of its transmission. It is the clustering of these two errors of taking gays and AIDS as each a vampire-like corruptive contagion, together with a statistical overlap between the two on a par with that of poverty and color, that has led to the virtual identification of AIDS and gays in the mind of America: they are taken as a tandem of invisible lurking evils, lying in wait to get you.

Gays then would do well to remember that in 1987 the Supreme Court first upheld the preventive detention of those who are innocent yet deemed by the courts a danger to society[34] and then the very next week punted on an opportunity to overturn the World War II Japanese internment case.[35] *Korematsu* is still good law: all U.S. citizens of Japanese descent can be indefinitely interned because the government cannot determine who, if any, of them might actually be dangerous.[36]

32. *Ratchford v. Gay Lib*, 434 U.S. 1080, 1082 (1978). Though the genre of dissent from a denial of certiorari requires Rehnquist to have stated the position as a hypothetical, his immediately preceding discussion of the facts of the case make it clear that he does indeed accept the hypothesis as true.

33. For a mainstream piece of influential hysteria, see Dr. Richard Restak's widely reprinted op-ed piece, "Worry About Survival of Society First; Then AIDS Victims' Rights," *The Washington Post*, September 8, 1985, p. C1.

34. *United States v. Salerno*, 107 S. Ct. 2095 (1987).

35. *United States v. Hohri*, 107 S. Ct. 2246 (1987).

36. *Korematsu v. United States*, 323 U.S. 214 (1944). Justice Jackson warned in dissent

The social thinking revealed in the real rationales for antibody testing in prisons, with its companion concentrations, applies just as well to gays who are not in prison, whether testing positive or not. The ritualistic purpose of prison testing is to assert the social validity of the purging of gays from the general population. Gays might well remember here too that the 1942 immurement of the Warsaw ghetto was promulgated as a public health measure—to stop the spread of typhus. It made no reference to Jews. And gays would do well to remember that FDR's executive order 9066, which set up America's concentration camps, made no mention of Japanese-Americans; rather it authorized the military to exclude "any and all persons" from designated areas to protect national security.

Antibody testing of hospital personnel and patients appeals so obviously to the blood stigmas which in the past have been hurled against blacks and Jews that their resurrection in time of "the gay plague" to help search out invisible lurking evils perhaps needs no comment to be seen for what it is. Note that the policy's marginal health utility comes into play only when health care personnel are doing their jobs poorly, so any public health rationale for it is in fact immoral: the bad, in this case the incompetent, are the prompt for imposing coercive policy upon the innocent.[37] Again we have not public policy but purification ritual at work.

IV. PROGNOSIS

Testing discovers and divides. Testing discovers the invisible and mysterious and it divides "us" from "them." It is the perfect vehicle for a civilization in need of reasserting its most basic values under challenge.

---

that "the principle [that the innocent, the merely potentially dangerous, may be put in concentration camps] . . . lies about like a loaded weapon ready for the hand of any authority that can bring forward a plausible claim of an urgent need." *Ibid.* at 246. Gays ought to be more than a little leery of the war metaphors that have been circulating amongst governmental officials addressing the AIDS crisis and surely ought themselves to cease using as names for their own efforts such violence-evoking metaphors as "The New Manhattan Project" and "Stamp Out AIDS"—especially given the social mind's perception of a virtual identity between gays and AIDS.

37. See "Three Health Workers Found Infected by Blood of Patients with AIDS," *The New York Times*, May 20, 1987, p. Y1.

It casts lurking threats into the light so that they may be exiled or committed to the flames. At the same time, testing regroups the dominant culture by showing that it is willing not only to sacrifice others *to* its values but sacrifice itself *for the sake of* them as well.

This sacrifice by and of the dominant culture may be understood on an analogy to civil disobedience in which an individual sacrifices his interests or at least puts them imminently at risk for the sake of his central values, his personal integrity. With AIDS testing and other purification rituals the body politic sacrifices its interests for the sake of a higher goal, that of preserving and solidifying its identity and integrity. The difference between civil disobedience and social purification rituals of course is that in civil disobedience the state is resisted, while in purification rituals the state is blindly affirmed and strengthened as the instrument and vehicle of the purification.

When a government uses coercion to express a society's deepest values and establish or rededicate them as sacred, there will be no stopping it however odious and immoral its acts, for these values are already or come to be embedded in a pre-institutional social knowledge which serves as a lens through which all else is judged. The pairing of coercion and sacred values will simply short circuit the usual procedures that put limits on tyranny. Through the filter of sacred values, what is zany as social policy and might be discovered as such through, say, careful legislative hearings, will be seen rather as natural, necessary, and good —not in need of any articulated or particularized justification. And any hint of attack on the values themselves must and will be dealt with as through expiation—prayer in action, holy war—a cleansing of taint and a rededication through self-sacrifice of purity restored.

If we now ask what is to be done and what is to become of things, I fear my social interpretation of AIDS testing counsels little, if any, hope —and perhaps it will be resisted for that very reason. As we have seen in the transfiguration of sexual values worked by the AIDS crisis, people yearn for purpose in their lives to such an extent that they will even scan the universe looking for it when they fail to find it in themselves or hereabout. This tendency of the human mind, while in a way admirable —for it shows a certain intrepidness of the human spirit even among human weaklings—is nevertheless scary—for it means that people will try anything and they rarely, especially if weak, just stop at trying it on and for themselves. One sees this in people who have voluntarily taken the antibody test, come up negative, and then mount a pretty high horse calling for coerced testing of others. The political right is counting on the large number of recently married body-negatives to serve as the advance troops for universal mandatory testing.

Even if mandatory testing were to take its most severe forms, the Supreme Court, which Martin Luther King Jr. always paired with God and which in our society is structurally the chief dispenser of rights, will be of no help in blunting the coercive state.[38] Compulsory heterosexuality need not have been mentioned in the nation's constitution, for all that is in it would be interpreted through that filter. Thus the Supreme Court could rule that gays have no privacy right to have sex, without even discussing gays or privacy or sex.[39] Under the filter of heterosexuality, the configuration of gays, sex, and privacy was completely invisible, not even a mote on the field of rights. Yet when glitches in custom have legally burdened traditional family structures, the Court has come to the rescue with the constitutional magic of Substantive Due Process—voiding laws in order to assert and restore familial sanctity as beyond calculations of social utility.[40] The Courts will be no help in addressing mandatory AIDS testing for similar reasons. The legislation in its social function—as the expression of sacred values—asserts the very values that make up the Court's interpretative lens.

The picture is gloomier still. If the courts will not work, what of trying to educate society? If my interpretation is anywhere near the mark, then many liberals (and I include myself here) have been mistaken to suppose that society's response to the AIDS crisis is a panicked response caused largely by ignorance. Rather the coercive legislation which society is

38. See Deborah Jones Merritt, "Communicable Disease and Constitutional Law: Controlling AIDS," *New York University Law Review* (1986) 61:739–99.

39. *Bowers v. Hardwick*, 106 S. Ct. 2841 (1986).

40. See, for example, *Meyer v. Nebraska*, 262 U.S. 390, 399–401 (1923) (giving parents a constitutional right of Substantive Due Process to have their children taught German), *Pierce v. Society of Sisters*, 268 U.S. 510, 534–35 (1925) (Substantive Due Process used to strike down a Ku Klux Klan inspired Oregon law requiring parents to send their children to public schools), and *Moore v. City of East Cleveland*, 431 U.S. 494 (1977) (Substantive Due Process used to void a zoning ordinance barring grandchildren from living with their grandparents). *Moore* provided the constitutional standard that was used in *Bowers*, 106 S. Ct. at 2844, to claim basically that gays have no place in the constitutional scheme of the United States: "Our decisions establish that the Constitution protects the sanctity of the family precisely because the institution of the family is deeply rooted in this Nation's history and tradition. It is through the family that we inculcate and pass down many of our most cherished values, moral and cultural." *Moore*, at 503–4, footnotes omitted.

now enacting in response to AIDS is simply the expected working out of the country's governing social knowledge as it has become aware of new facts. Mary Douglas might as well have had the AIDS crisis specifically in mind when she wrote quite generally:

> The conclusion [is] that individuals in crises do not make life and death decisions on their own. Who shall be saved and who shall die is settled by institutions. Putting it even more strongly, individual ratiocination cannot solve such problems. An answer is only seen to be the right one if it sustains the institutional thinking that is already in the minds of individuals as they try to decide.[41]

Society's response to the AIDS crisis could be changed only if the culture itself were changed, and that is not going to occur, if ever, twixt now and Vaccine Day, should it come. Societies are even less likely than individuals to change behavior through education and we have seen that traditional educational efforts have had no significant effect in stopping the spread of AIDS among gays; urban centers where educational efforts were most intense now have AIDS-saturated gay male populations.[42] Such change as has occurred in gay male behavior patterns is not the result of safe-sex pamphlets broadcasting, as they do, mixed and confusing messages about sex and sexuality. No, the educator was death. And we know from the history of war that death wins no teaching awards. And we should remember too that when death is the social educator, society responds not with new ideas and liberality but with fear and retrenchment.

Still less likely are educational efforts going to be effective because AIDS social coercion has become a body accelerated under the gravitational pull of our anxieties over nuclear destruction. Doing anything significant to alleviate the prospects of the collective death of everything that can die is effectively out of the reach of any ordinary individual and indeed of any political group now in existence. So individuals transfer the focus of their anxieties from nuclear omnicide to AIDS, by which they feel equally and similarly threatened, but about which they think they can do something—at least through government. AIDS coercion is doing double duty as a source of sacred values and as a vent for universal

41. Douglas, *How Institutions Think*, p. 4.
42. "Five-Year Plan to Fight AIDS Drafted by New York," *The New York Times*, May 25, 1987, p. Y11.

anxieties over universal destruction. Against this daunting combination, no educational efforts will have any significant effects.

What of the public health community? Here the paradox is that the more the public health community points up the irrationality of mandatory testing by its own criteria, the more it underscores and contributes to the true public function of the testing, which is the assertion of group solidarity through self-sacrifice. In this crisis, the good intentions, good will, sometimes good arguments, and even some good actions of the public health community all inadvertently contribute to evil. Theodicy is here inverted. The public health community in the crisis is the lone lit candle in Kafka's cathedral: its singular flame simply makes the darkness darker.

Well-intended gay leaders and theorists, particularly of a socialist stripe,[43] have, I fear, also inadvertently contributed to this evil. Gays—for reasons as diverse as self-hatred and hoped-for social collegiality—have played a shell game of statistics in order to claim that AIDS is not a gay disease. In doing so, they simply misunderstand the operative social dynamics of the crisis and reinforce irrelevant public health thinking on AIDS. As gays indulge the discomforts of nongays in the crisis by denying these dynamics, they act as abused children do who try to comfort their parent even while he is beating them. When gays fail to oppose marital testing, because they think it does not affect them, and hope thereby to score a few social points by appearing patriotic, they are as aware of social realities as European Jewry of the 1930s allowed itself to be when it failed to oppose anti-miscegenation laws on the ground that Jews were supposed to marry Jews anyway.

When gays are not busy indulging worldly heterosexuals, they are scampering off to God, the big heterosexual in the sky. Instead of thus shooting into the void their ability to generate value through reverence, gays should begin to establish rituals by which they value and honor themselves. Some recent gay AIDS burial rituals, though marred by religiosity, have been a step in the right direction.[44] The ritualistic dimensions of old-fashioned consciousness-raising groups are another. Finally, by laying hearthstones together, gays would help return sacred

43. See, for example, Dennis Altman, *AIDS in the Mind of America* (Garden City, N.Y.: Doubleday, 1986), chapter 3.

44. "New Rituals Ease Grief as AIDS Toll Increases," *The New York Times*, May 11, 1987, p. C11.

values to their most proper place, the sanctities of the home and the privacies of life.[45] And instead of pinning their hopes on answered prayer from Masses or on compassion from the masses, gays should prepare to resist. Now when The Good is receding from gays with all the speed and brilliance of quasars, it is time to stop looking for silver linings.

I fully expect though that gay self-hatred, exacerbated as it has been by the AIDS crisis and its concomitant transvaluation of sex and sexuality, will defeat both efforts—not a promising picture, but then it should be beginning to become clear that we have grossly underestimated the evil of men and the cussedness of things.

45. I do not think that rituals and sacred values have no role in public life or even government actions. The use of public funds for government-sponsored voluntary initiatives that enhance the value which people in general place on the particularized lifeplans of individuals is quite unobjectionable and actually will tend to put breaks on governmental tyranny, by asserting the value of the right of individuals to live out their own distinctive lives and not to be viewed socially and legally as merely filling socially assigned functions. Rescue missions are clear cases of such admirable social ritual:

> Startling examples of ritualized behavior are common in our dealings with hazard and risks. We need only to consider our willingness to engage in rescue missions when identified individuals are involved: saving crash victims, fliers lost at sea, or an astronaut; retrieving the wounded or dead in battle; diverting resources from making mines safer in order to mount rescue missions for trapped miners; or even supporting individual medical treatment rather than more public health research. These actions and policies defy economic or even risk-minimizing sense.

MacLean, "Social Values," p. 87.

11. Noyade

"There was no help for it then:
but now it is worse."

This is how Antigone at Colonus describes Thebes as its plague years bleed into internecine wars.[1] She could as well have been speaking of our present as her own.

The thesis which I wish briefly to bruit here, not by argument but through three short, yet I hope telling, stories—stories of a philosopher with AIDS, a doctor with AIDS and a university with AIDS—is not a happy one. I suggest that ideas, thoughts, reason, and argument will have no significant role to play either in the formation of public policy or in changing individual behavior in the AIDS crisis. I do not mean to be advancing a general skeptical thesis on the role of reason in private life and public policy. There have been startling instances where it has made a difference—after all we live daily in the terror that has emanated from Marx scribbling away in the British Museum.

The thesis was suggested to me, I suppose, by reflection on my own experience. The crisis from the beginning has caused me to feel acutely and increasingly alienated from my body—oddly, just as I felt in the period immediately before I came out. The crisis has caused me to experience a continuous background drone of depression punctuated only by hate and rage; if my soul had an image now, it would be the bodies of Richard Avedon's sun-baked, sand-blasted, crizzle-faced, vacant-eyed drifters, and I live with a sad sense beyond tears unnamed but which stands to mourning as dread stands to fear—and stands to dread as mourning stands to fear. The great symphonies of death and annihilation—Mahler's 10th, Shostakovich's 11th—no longer work on me their former homeopathic magic. I thought that writing on the crisis might give me some distance from it, from these feelings and fissures, as

1. Sophocles, *Oedipus at Colonus*, l. 1745. This paper was written for and delivered to the University of Illinois' Unit for Criticism and Interpretive Theory, March 2, 1987.

writing usually gives me distance and respite from my subjects—and besides so many people were saying so many stupid things—but it didn't make a difference either to me or, it seems, to others. I suspect the AIDS crisis has unusual properties, appealing to intractable features of individual and social existence, ones which will continue not to be pretty as they and the crisis unfold. There was no help then, and now it is worse.

My husband says I whimper here, but I think rather that my cursor is just one more victim of the necessary truth in Yves Navarre's refrain: "one cannot *be* sincere and *appear* sincere."[2] In any case, my three stories: one takes place in New York and Paris, one in Chicago, and one in the washrooms of the University of Illinois' graduate library.

In the summer of 1983, two years after the first cases of AIDS came to light in New York City and well after condom dispensers began appearing in leather bars there, Michel Foucault gave a seminar at New York University's Humanities Institute. Every night of the seminar, he would go, I am told by the philosopher who served as his guide, to the gay baths which he enjoyed enormously. A year later, on June 25, 1984, Foucault died, brain-shriveled, in Paris from AIDS.[3] Inverting Plato's Orphic maxim, Foucault had told us that the soul was the tomb of the body. And I suppose for him it was.

There are two major strands of Foucault's thought that do not sit comfortably with each other. One from his penology, one which I think essentially correct, is that power in the modern era does not manifest itself in the hamfisted but discrete and isolated forms of tyrant or king, but is ever more diffused and permeating, ever more ramified and sinuous but all the more penetrating and powerful for pulsing at the capillary level.[4]

The other strand from his sexology, one which I think essentially false, is that in sex there are no essences: the categories of sex are at heart products of social convention, in particular products of the unfolding structures of discourse.[5]

2. Yves Navarre, *Cronus' Children*, trans. Howard Girven (1980; London: John Calder, 1986).

3. On Foucault's death, see *The Advocate* [Los Angeles], March 4, 1986, no. 441, pp. 30–32.

4. Michel Foucault, *Discipline and Punish: The Birth of the Prison*, trans. Alan Sheridan (1975; New York: Random House, 1977).

5. Michel Foucault, *The History of Sexuality: Volume I: An Introduction*, trans. Robert Hurley (1976; New York: Random House, 1980).

The problems here are two. First, that which is ever more diffuse in form cannot create or even maintain the architecture needed to constitute a system of categories. Second, the model of the metastasizing filaments of power cannot explain how, once a person no longer has a sexual essence or core desires, the person nonetheless falls into some but not others of the sexual categories that society has hollowed out.

Sometimes the categories are portrayed as toys for the choosing—just take your pick from the pleasure chest. Sex is a game the value of which lies in its opportunities for creativity. During his 1983 U.S. tour, Foucault was giving interviews in which he would claim in seeming oblivion to the current sexual realities swirling around him and without irony that "sex is not fatality; it's a possibility for creative life" and that what the "gay movement needs now is an art of life [rather] than a science of what sexuality is. We have to create a gay life. To *become.*" And there is much talk of possibilities. But he has no answers whatever when asked after the content and manner of his proposed new institutions of creative sexuality.[6] He is also known to have made the most cavalier of comments about AIDS as a personal threat: "How can I be scared of AIDS when I could die in a car. If sex with a boy gives me pleasure. . . . Oh, [d]on't cry for me if I die."[7] Yet, like Liberace, he tried to deflect public attention from his own sexual orientation, lest it damage his reputation among Americans, a breed to whom he apparently thought it worth pandering his self-esteem.[8]

Those are the facts. What is one to make of them? They invite speculation. I suspect that for Foucault the cubicles that are the central fixture of American bathhouses were a resolution by intersection in local practice of the two strands of his thought that were conceptually irreconcilable and incapable of joint instantiation on a broader canvass.

I suggest that the cubicles were for him, on the one hand, the prison cells of his central penal image, the Panopticon—a Benthamite proposal in which stacked prison cells are laid out in circular array such that their solid sides completely partition off each prisoner from all others while their barred sides face a central tower from which a single guard can,

6. See Bob Gallagher and Alexander Wilson, "Michel Foucault, An Interview: Sex, Power, and the Politics of Identity," *The Advocate,* August 7, 1984, no. 400, pp. 26–30, 58, quotes from p. 27.

7. Philip Horvitz, "Don't Cry For Me Academia," *Jimmy & Lucy's House of "K"* [Berkeley, CA], August 1984, no. 2, p. 80.

8. See *The Advocate,* March 4, 1986, no. 441, pp. 30–32.

though unobserved by the prisoners, watch their every move. Here power is diffused to the atomic level, the level where finally persons are individuated, unique each in their own private yet thoroughly observed cell, reduced each to a body subjected to and living out someone else's —society's, culture's, the state's—invisible vision.

On the other hand, I suggest that the bathhouse cubicles for Foucault were the institutional form of the social categories of gay sexuality: the socially marginalized, fragmented, and dispossessed. The power transfixing him there and causing him reactively, passively to perform there would not be the penetrations of the unobserved observer but of, how to say, the other prisoners there, for whom the social vision controlling them is invisible because it itself has become a category through which they see each other. As consistency really required, the tyrant-guard too had become diffused—or, as we have learned from concentration camps and maximum security prisons, the more severe their conditions, the more their prisoners themselves are the enforcers of order there.

Contrast to this diorama, the sexually aroused prisoner of Jean Genet's movie *Un Chant d'Amour*. While he gives, half out of desire, half compulsion, a blowjob to a Luger which his wavering and confused guard stuffs in his mouth, he can at least dream of the prisoner "next door," who dances for him to smoke puffs which he blows through a haystraw poked along an illicit peeptunnel between their cells. For Foucault, pinned at the intersection of the diffusion of power and the hollowing out of sexual categories, there could be no such transcendence, only dose loads. The soul is the tomb of the body. And the more general bad news appears to be that the view that sex is malleable has no more to recommend by way of prudence than its opposite.

My second story deals with the state as healthcare provider, educator and pupil. On February 2, 1987, the Cook County Board, which oversees Chicago's Cook County Hospital, temporarily suspended a doctor with AIDS from patient contacts, pending a recommendation from the hospital's medical review board. Two days later, this twenty-five member medical board, concurring with guidelines of the Centers for Disease Control for such cases,[9] voted unanimously to reinstate the doctor, who then worked for four more days till the County Board, disregarding the

9. On the guidelines of the Centers for Disease Control for doctors, see its publication *Morbidity and Mortality Weekly Report,* November 15, 1985, 34(45):682–95 and especially, April 11, 1986, 35(14):221–23.

medical recommendation it had sought, voted 12 to 2 for the doctor's permanent suspension. The reason for the suspension as told by the hospital's director was not a medically informed one; rather he claimed that there "was a need to prevent this from frightening the community at large."[10] Now one would have thought that if there was one settled ground rule in contemporary social thought, it is that a heckler's veto does not count as a legitimate reason for the establishment of any public policy. In the only Supreme Court case in the history of the nation to be signed by all nine justices, they declared that "extreme public hostility" cannot be given any weight in the execution of public policy.[11] Yet here that illegitimate factor is allowed to exhaust the whole rationale for public policy. The doctor now must seek out justice, if he is to have it, either in the labyrinth of the 1973 federal Rehabilitation Act, which the Attorney General has ruled allows even completely unsubstantiated fears to ground good faith exemptions to the act's protections,[12] or in the night and fog of current equal protection law. Both courses, whether ultimately successful or not, typically take years and years to work their way through the courts; if the doctor is an anywhere near typical person with AIDS, he's got but one.

Just as prudence is not going to infect individual sexual behavior, so too reason more generally is not going to have much role in sexual politics. The problem is not just that the justice department has given irrationality a green light. Though that is bad enough, things get worse. What was not reported in straight-press accounts of this story and what makes it such a particularly telling one is that Cook County Hospital has had, from even before the existence of AIDS, a permanent, openly gay-operated, gay-oriented STD clinic—for a state institution, to my knowledge, a unique occurrence. It's the Sable-Sherer Clinic, named in half after one of its openly gay founding doctors, whose titular other half would eventually serve as the head of the governor's task force on AIDS. Now if such a clinic cannot educate its own administrators about medically relevant facts and dispel from them dangerous myth, who could?

10. On Cook County Hospital, see *The New York Times*, February 5, 1987, p. Y14; February 10, 1987, p. Y18; *Windy City Times* [Chicago], February 12, 1987, pp. 1, 18.

11. On the role of hostility in public policy, see *Cooper v. Aaron*, 358 U.S. 1(1958) (heckler's veto cannot be used as a reason to suspend school integration).

12. For the U.S. Department of Justice on AIDS, see *The New York Times*, June 23, 1986, p. Y1. For full text, see *Daily Labor Reporter* (BNA), June 25, 1986, no. 122, pp. D1–16.

Further, the heckler's veto "argument" used here and in other success-ful attempts to restrict AIDS-exposed persons, as in current foreign service policy, is the classic argument that has been used as successfully as it is illegitimate in trying to establish good faith discriminations against gays—from child custody cases, to teachers cases, the police and military service. I suggest that this is not an accidental correlation and that whatever the mainstream press may now be claiming of America's mind, the nation continues to perceive, as AIDS jokes and graffiti con-firm, that AIDS is essentially a gay disease and so America's view of gays continues as the unacknowledged center of gravity around which AIDS public policy is developing. This configuration explains why arguments that have been shown illegitimate everywhere except when applied to gays are being allowed to succeed in the AIDS crisis—and that, by explicit appeal to amassed irrationality as sufficient justification for public policy.

My third story takes place in the johns on the fourth floor of the University of Illinois Library, where gay men have ritualized sex, three of some ten or eleven such tearooms scattered across the campus.[13] The intrepid, noble, local Gay Community AIDS Project (GCAP) daily re-stocks these johns and other area cruising spots with safe-sex literature and has pasted up there their elegant but reserved "Fight Fear with the Facts" posters, which give a contact number but no facts or safe-sex information.

The posters have become bulletin boards for the thoughts and hearts of America's future leaders. My two favorite graffiti there of late deserve mention, for they are more telling than anything one reads in the press about America and AIDS. The first reads:

AIDS Kills Gays.

[then a second hand adds:]

The more, the better.

[and a third:]

I would too, if I could get away with it.

The second graffito is a member of that most frequent genre of AIDS jokes, the acronym (like: "What does GAY mean? Got AIDS Yet?" and conversely, "What does AIDS mean? Adios, Infected Dick Sucker," or

13. On University of Illinois tearoom locations and policies, see *People Like Us* [Cham-paign-Urbana], December 1986, no. 6, p. 3 and February 1987, no. 8, p. 6.

"Anally Inserted Death Sentence"). Generally, such acronymic jokes, and also the spate of Rock Hudson jokes, view gays simply as ridiculous because hapless creatures, but not as a threat. They are like Helen Keller jokes, that way. But this graffito presages a new wave of AIDS jokes and falls into that venerable American tradition, the joke of genocide.[14] It reads "What is AIDS? America's Initiative Defense Strategy." This play on and inversion of the Reagan administration's "Star Wars" abbreviation, SDI, suggests that AIDS is to be praised as being of a piece with the government's past policy of giving smallpox-infected blankets to immuneless native peoples. It bests the typical genocidal joke, which also typically views its target as hapless, by holding that gays are a positive danger, indeed, a national hazard on a par with a preemptive Soviet nuclear strike.

As is, the safe-sex brochures aimed at saving lives are themselves tossed about, many are ruined, trashed, thrown in the toilets or otherwise rendered unusable. To help circumvent these problems, GCAP wants the library to install plastic racks for their tastefully gay-brown literature. But the library has balked. Its refusal is tendered on the moot ground that the pamphlets might clog the toilets. The real reason, of course, is that the library—that font of reason, facts, enlightenment and truth—does not wish to acknowledge the existence of the rituals older than Pompeii that take place there. The library is willing, though, to shut down a public AIDS forum by installing plexiglas covers over the GCAP posters. But the posters have a proven track record of failure. When they appeared earlier on local city busses, virtually no one called the contact number to get the information that was to help people save their lives. Indirection and circumspection don't work.

And so the University, in a balance between, on the one hand, the lives of its gay males and, on the other, avoiding what it perceives as an embarrassment, has decided to plump for embarrassment avoided. It is hard not to conclude that the University, by effective omission, basically agrees with the graffiti, and, in any case, that to the University the life of a gay man is worth less than a fart. *Homo sapiens,* what a species.

14. For AIDS jokes, fag jokes, Rock Hudson jokes, Helen Keller jokes and genocide jokes, see Blanche Knott, *Truly Tasteless Jokes I-VI* (New York: Ballantine, 1982–1983; New York: St. Martin's, 1984–1986).

PART FIVE

A Liberal's Education

12. Gay Studies in the Big Ten: A Survivor's Manual

In what follows I shall describe a gay issues course which I taught in an intersession format during May of 1981 at the University of Illinois, where I was then an assistant professor in an all-white, all-male, seventeen member philosophy department.[1]

In the Fall of 1980 two other assistant professors in my department got the bright idea of putting on a show. They wanted to try to raise the department's campus and community profile, the lowness of which had been a source of frequent administrative complaint. Now, when the state pays you just to think, it's not that easy to dazzle the public's imagination. Nevertheless, the two young professors decided to hold a series of public lectures by philosophy faculty on current 'pop' topics. Only assistant professors rose to the occasion and three initially signed up: one paper on computers, one on fetuses, and one on animals. I thought it might be refreshing if someone did a paper on people. And though heretofore I had written only on souls dead for over two millennia, I wrote and delivered, as a fourth member of the series, "Two Arguments for Gay Rights." Eventually this paper, several revisions later, would appear as two papers on the program of the American Philosophical Association's 1981 Eastern Division meetings. I was pleased at this upshot, for in fact the public lecture was a bomb, with a disappointingly low turnout of only about 40, where the others had been rousing successes with average audiences of 150. It's hard to beat computers and animals at a science-oriented land-grant college, and fetuses, well. Undaunted, I decided that, if I was going that public, I might as well also

1. This chapter appears here virtually as it was written in July 1981; it was slightly revised in June 1983 prior to its first publication, and I have made a few changes in diction for this printing. Several paragraphs stand in tension with the tone, and two sentences stand at odds with the content, of passages from the book's Introduction and chapters four and fourteen. Since the chapter is autobiographical, I have felt it better to let the tension and odds be, rather than edit and erase my past. Where later ideas contradict earlier ones, they should be taken as superseding them.

put in a course proposal on gay issues. The University's experimental three-week intersession format seemed an ideal initial target. And the department already had the perfect rubric, Philosophy 280: Current Controversies. Further, one of the course's possible topics as enumerated in the University Calendar, though never previously used, was "Human Sexuality." Now, since I did not know the first thing about heterosexuality, I figured I would just leave that part of human sexuality out.

Proposals for intersession courses had to be submitted early in the Fall and I didn't hear the final word on my proposal until just before Christmas. During this period I worried a lot and wrote less than usual. If I had known just how much I was going to worry, I probably would not have submitted the proposal in the first place. A spy told me that the proposal was voted through the department's executive committee in utter and atypical silence. The department chairman insisted that the silence did not signal embarrassment, but admitted that he had no idea what might become of the proposal as it went up the pipe; several tiers of approval were needed beyond the departmental level. One embarrassed deanlet sounded like a choked-up Santa Claus in his attempt to pronounce the word "ho-ho-homosexual." The course was approved, though I never got any report on what anyone actually thought of the proposal. Mere tolerance without support is almost as emotionally exhausting as being closeted; it is certainly more exasperating.

Anyway, the University was to have its first-ever gay studies course— enrollments willing. Given the poor turnout for my public lecture, the enrollment minimum of ten students had me a bit worried through the Spring term. The other departmental intersession offering was titled Religion and Science (Jesus v. Galileo and Darwin). The final enrollments for the two courses were Gay Issues 34 and Religion and Science 56, which shows that you can't beat Jesus either.

I had designed the course with the expectation that the vast majority of the class would be gays in various stages of the coming-out process. This expectation was based on the few things I'd been able to read about gay-studies courses elsewhere and on an analogue with black studies and women's studies courses. Further I had done a fair amount of direct advertising to the local student-centered gay community.

My expectation turned out to be entirely false. Less than a third of the class was gay, with only one up-front lesbian. Fortunately, I guess, only one student seemed to be taking the class as an attempt to sort out his

turbid sexual life. About a third of the class were suburban white females, most of whom claimed never to have met a gay person. And
about a third of the class were black football players.

The course was designed such that during the first week we would
discuss ethical principles and sexual concepts. The second week we
would discuss what constitutes responsible sex, centering on the hot
topics of impersonal sex, pornography, S&M, romance, and intergener-
ational sex. The third week would deal with sexual politics, centering on
gay rights, gay political strategies, and self-oppression.

The first day, I was quite nervous. I feared the much-resurgent campus
neo-Christians might pack the house. Some students signing up for the
class had told me that they had heard rumors this was in the offing. And
the week prior to the class an evangelical group, Brothers and Sisters in
Christ (BASIC), had plastered antigay handbills all over the building in
which the philosophy department is located. Fortunately, the born-agains
never showed up.

The degree of my apprehension about the class could be measured by
the number of handouts I had for it. I viewed them as psychological
shields. Usually I go into an introductory class, say something outrageous, and we are off and rolling with a minimum of organization and
prepackaged direction. For this class, not only did I have a detailed day-
by-day syllabus (a first for me), but also a bibliography (another first),
copies of the first readings, detailed instructions about how to locate the
other readings, and a handout on the right to privacy.

The first hour of the first day I went over the syllabus; and without
the benefit of first having given a lecture on what-is-philosophy, I tried
to explain that the course would be a course in applied ethics. This was
not successful; more background preparation was needed. I explicitly
told them a few things the course would *not* be: that it would not be a
history course (Was Alexander the Great gay?); that it was not a literary
course (Does *Orlando* demonstrate a gay sensibility?); that all the readings for the course were nonfiction works, even though many were
written by authors best known as novelists (Rita Mae Brown, John
Rechy, Jane Rule); that the course was not a sociology course (How
many gays live in Cleveland?); that it was not a psychology or medical
class (What causes homosexuality? Do poppers cause cancer?). I tried to
impress upon the class that the sort of questions with which we would
be dealing—Is gay sex moral? Natural? Should gay sex be legal? What

responsibilities do we have to sex partners? Do gays have rights? And what are rights anyway?—these were not the sort of questions that could be answered by appeals to facts as we normally conceive of facts and we would hardly be dealing with facts at all in the course.

This sermonette apparently did not sink in. I'm certain that the majority of the class was expecting the course to be basically sociological in outlook and that the gays thought it would be a gay-culture course (What's it like to live at Castro and Market Streets?).

At the end of the first hour, I told the class that I was gay and laid out one initial ground rule, namely, that the classroom for the hours of the class was a gay space, and that though the contours of this space would evolve with the class, minimally "gay space" meant that I would use the powers of my office to make the gays in the class comfortable enough to be openly gay without fear of recriminations from other class members. Talk is cheap, I would learn.

The second hour, I showed the forty-five minute version of the documentary *Word is Out*, sixteen lesbians and gay men talking about growing up and coming out.[2] The University's Film Center, though it has 15,000 documentary movies for classroom use, did not have this movie or indeed any gay movies. Fortunately, some good soul in Medical Sciences had recently ordered it for their audio visual collection. My purposes in showing the film were first a naïve hope that it would do all the consciousness-raising activity that needed to be done for the nongay members of the class before I could reasonably begin the substantive discussion of God, Nature, and Ethical Methodology with which I hoped to start the next day, and second that it would be a celebration for the gay members of the class and so make them comfortable enough and encourage them to feel free enough to talk about themselves, as do the people in the film. I had made popcorn for everyone in an attempt to lighten the atmosphere.

After the screening, I began discussion by asking whether there was anything in the film that had made anyone feel uncomfortable. The lesbian was quick out of the blocks with a condemnation of the one weirdly dressed male in the movie. She claimed that he was in drag and that drag oppresses women by pandering to damaging stereotypes. I was

2. Mariposa Group, *Word is Out: Stories of Some of Our Lives* (New York: New Yorker Films, 1978).

quite pleased with this response. Not that I agreed with it, but it hinted that the level of debate in the class might be good. I was again mistaken.

For after pointing out to her that, in fact, the fellow was not in drag but was doing gender-fuck (the class wanted the term written on the board and explained) and that as such he was Politically Very Correct, the discussion quickly devolved.

The nongay women in the class were upset at the couple of slight expressions of physical affection displayed in the otherwise accommodatingly sterile film. The women claimed this was sick, disgusting, unnatural, and made them nauseated. I parried the best I could by forcing them to define terms like "unnatural" and "sick," by drawing parallel cases, and by appealing to consistency and coherency of beliefs, all moves which we would, by the end of the week, try to formalize into a view of what constitutes minimum requirements for a reasonable moral opinion.

I was now doing fairly well with the whites, especially by drawing parallels between black and gay oppression. But this strategy served only to outrage the blacks in the class who did not want to be reminded that they were part of an oppressed minority. Near chaos ensued as the blacks mounted a unified frontal attack against gays on the basis of every stereotype that has ever been thrown at gay men: gays want to be women, gays molest children, gays destroy the family, gays are sex-crazed maniacs and fuck animals (they were mortified when I told them that at the time bestiality was legal in Illinois). They used the term "fags" with impunity and referred to themselves as "just regular guys, man." Mostly they hated gays, they said, because gays were always trying to "rub on them." It was never coherently explained, though, why this was the dreaded threat: Fear that this meant they were effeminate looking? Fear of gay cooties? Guilt by spatial association? A lot of it boiled down, though, to mere sexism: only 'real' men were to have the cultural privilege of initiating sexual activity.

By this time, everyone in the class was yelling at everyone else. Multiple conversations were spontaneously spouting up all around. I feared physical violence might break out between the gay men and the football players. The class was as near the verge of being out-of-control as any I had ever taught.

I was literally saved by the bell, but only after having offended the women in the class by citing the Kinsey Institute statistic on gay males to the effect that by the average age of 37, 43 percent of gay men had had over 500 sexual partners.[3] Cries of "sick," "disgusting," "immoral" rose from bodies that were slumping under their desks, as others fled with the sounding of the hour buzzer. No one bothered getting out paper and pencil: 37 years minus, say, 18 years equals 19 years, which equals 988 weeks, which equals much less than one sexual partner per week, a number rather modest, I thought in that era before AIDS.

The two gay politicos in the class spoke with me for two hours after the first class about how much they had hated it. They said that I had given the class members an even worse impression of gays than they had had coming into the course, that I advanced my own views as though they were the views of all gays and that they didn't like my modified clone outfit. So I had managed to alienate all three-thirds of the class. I was depressed.

In addition, my lover was out of town coping with a personal crisis that could conceivably have ended our relation of several years. Further unknown to me at the time, I had, right here in the middle of no where, contracted the trinity of enteric diseases then new to urban gays. These were draining away my strength. I was exhausted, demoralized, and felt like cancelling the class. I was only getting paid one ninth of my regular salary for the course, not enough to make any appreciable difference in the quality of my luxuries. I had offered the course out of a sense of duty to my people, rather than for the bucks. And now "my people" were telling me they hated the course and that I was a jerk. It was only because cancelling out would have been an acute embarrassment to my department that I didn't go through with it.

If the class was to continue, I figured something had to be done to reduce the racial tensions which were running so high at the end of the first class. Installing a metal detector or talking things through seemed to be the options. So I shelved my original plans for the second day. Instead, we discussed the relation of blacks to gays inside and outside of the black community. I suggested that gays are more hated by blacks than by whites as the result of a pecking-order phenomenon. The blacks were outraged at this analysis and said rather that a black man's pride flows from his control of his family, that gays somehow challenge this

3. Alan P. Bell and Martin S. Weinberg, *Homosexualities: A Study of Diversity Among Men and Women* (New York: Simon and Schuster, 1978), p. 308, cf. pp. 70, 298.

arrangement and so gays are despised for this reason. I countered by suggesting that such a strategy, even if correct as an *explanation* of the phenomena, when viewed as a *justification* of the phenomena, simply grounded heterosexism in mere sexism. This move did not make much of an impression on the football players, though I think it got through to the three black women in the class. In any case, after a couple of hours the black males calmed down, apparently satisfied that they were free to speak, and would be treated with equal respect even if I thought their views were evil. They stopped using the term "fag" and started referring to themselves as "nongays."

And so I finally managed to get the class off to its substantive start with a lecture which ran quickly through the three standard theistic arguments for the existence of God, suggesting that, even if the arguments were good arguments, they failed to establish God as a likely candidate for the position of author of morality, and that people who base their morals on religion do so from a position of faith rather than reason. The class was mesmerized. I've never understood why metaphysics classes aren't more popular.

Only two days into the class, I was already a day behind schedule. Perhaps it was a mistake to have shown the film, but I think not. If people had as much bigoted garbage in their souls as was demonstrated in our "consciousness-raising" sessions during the first two days and it were left unexpressed, overlooked, or merely repressed, I don't think anyone would have been open to learning anything in the class. New ideas, I think, would have simply bounced off the class's high defenses.

To get back on schedule, I simply dropped the day we were to analyze systematically the notions 'contrary to nature' and 'perversion' and moved directly to an analysis of what conditions the use of such terms would have to satisfy in order to qualify as reasons for claims of immorality. The central reading for the first week was Ronald Dworkin's "Liberty and Moralism," a counterattack on Lord Devlin's attack on the 1957 Wolfenden Report and its recommendation to legalize gay sex in Britain.[4] The central tenet of the Dworkin piece is that for a moral opinion to count as an opinion which must be taken seriously (not agreed with, but taken as worthy of debate), it needs to fulfill certain basic requirements. The opinion must have a reason and the reason cannot be preju-

4. Ronald Dworkin, *Taking Rights Seriously* (Cambridge: Harvard University Press, 1977), pp. 240–58.

dicial, cannot be a personal emotional reaction, cannot be a rationalization which dips below standard rules of evidence and inference, and cannot simply be someone *else*'s reason. Further, the person giving the reason must be willing to apply consistently the moral principles which inform and give substance to his reason, once the relevant principles are pointed out. Finally, the moral principles themselves must not be so specialized as to be arbitrary (e.g., if someone were to claim that it is self-evident that photography is immoral). A person whose claims fail to pass these requirements is a bigot. Although the article was elaborate and required for its exposition a detailed mapping out of arguments and counter-arguments, students basically got its main thrust and became much more cautious about the sorts of criticisms they would make of *outré* positions and would even catch each others' opinions failing one or more of the Dworkin tests. Many reported trying out Dworkinian moves on their parents when discussing the class with them on weekend trips home. I was pleased. This is the sort of success that, when it occurs, however rarely, keeps philosophy professors from becoming cynics.

For the last day of the first week, I had the class read the case *People v. Onofre,* in which the highest court of New York State declared New York's sodomy laws unconstitutional on the basis of the right to privacy.[5] The class was a disaster, for the students didn't know even enough basic American civics to be able to follow the case, even though it is written in ordinary, nontechnical English. No one in the class, with confidence, could tell me what it meant for a law to be declared unconstitutional. None of the blacks in the class knew what *Brown v. the Board of Education* was. And so for this day I merely lectured on the history of the right to privacy and mapped out the court case. People found this dull, especially since it was a gloriously sunny spring day outside.

The second week, in which we discussed what should be the role of sex in our lives, what constitutes responsible sex, and hit on all the hot topics, like pornography and S&M, was the most successful part of the course. Overall, I argued an anti-romantic line: sex can stand on its own feet without need of justifications outside itself; it is a prima facie good simply as being pleasant and a compelling good insofar as it answers a basic personal human need. Good sex will not successfully bear much of

5. *People v. Onofre,* 51 N.Y.2d 476, 415 N.E.2d 936, 434 N.Y.S.2d 947 (1980), cert. denied, 451 U.S. 987 (1981).

the freight with which we usually burden it: neither is it a product, token, or embodiment of love, nor does it lead to worthy emotions. Indeed we would do well not to talk of love, but rather should dissolve this notion into other, concrete relations—those of mutual life planning, cuddling, and lust. I have distilled some of these themes into a slogan which I use part as catalyst and part as springboard when I begin discussions of matters sexual. I announced to the class my Motto of Personal Life:

> Love is ideology,
> Caring is paying the rent,
> Affection is body-heat,
> Sex is sex.

The class, abounding with neo-romantics (both gay and straight), was a bit taken aback. A certain class spirit developed as everyone attacked what appeared to them as steely views. By the end of the week many class members, no doubt, thought I took my pleasures from drowning kittens in bleach.

During the first week I had, along the way, mapped out some standard ethical stances, like libertarianism, utilitarianism, Marxist humanism, and liberalism. I proceeded in the second week to show how a person holding certain general ethical principles was committed to certain specific stances on the various hot topics. This was the 'applied' part of the course. Many people had expressed great sympathy with libertarianism the first week, but then felt a little uncomfortable when this view turned out to commit them to saying that pretty much all pornography (even violent pornography) and S&M were morally unobjectionable.

I began the week by showing, for voluntary attendance, four fifteen-minute sexually explicit gay and lesbian movies, which were also owned by the Medical Sciences library. My purpose was two-fold. First, I wanted to desensitize the class, so that students could talk about sex acts without giggling and being squeamish. It is for this reason that Medical Sciences owns the films for use in sex-education classes. The second reason was that we were going to devote a large part of the week to discussing pornography and I wanted the class at least to have seen something sexually explicit, so they wouldn't be talking in complete ignorance. The films were a huge success on both counts. The films themselves were a bit on the romantic side (lots of kissing and foreplay, and lots of artsy, distracting montage photography). Nonetheless, explicit they were—the last ending with a male fist-fucking sequence. The class was mesmerized. The men, both gay and straight, were fascinated by the fist-fucking sequence and asked a lot of technical how-to questions. The women, again, admitted to being made queasy by some of the goings-on. But only one had actually left the room, and even she regrouped and returned.

Reason was, momentarily at least, reigning in the class. For the people who admitted to being made queasy said that they were not able to use the same epithets which they had used of the affection expressed in the film *Word is Out*. Their considered feeling was that it was illegitimate to call the films sick and disgusting.

No one complained at having seen the films, either orally or in anonymous course-evaluations which I had the class write toward the end of the course. Many nongay members of the class admitted that heretofore they had been unable to visualize gay sex acts. They were able to think cock-in-hairy-ass but had been completely unable to draw a mental image of this with any degree of vividness. I mentioned this phenomenon to some 'mature' Kinsey-zero friends and they also admitted to having the same incapacity. Surely there is a political point here. If nongays cannot even imagine what a gay sex act is like, then clearly the majority is holding gays accountable on the basis of some perceived *status* rather than on the basis of anything gays actually *do*. And such an accounting is one of the central forms of prejudice.

Loosened up by the films, people were able to talk quite freely about John Rechy's *The Sexual Outlaw* with its copious, and graphic, autobiographical accounts of and glowing praise for sexual exploits set in parks and alleys of Los Angeles.[6] The universal reaction to the book was initial horror and disgust, followed by reading it cover to cover in a single sitting, and then leaving it around on coffee tables for roommates and friends to pick up innocently. After surfacing from both shock and titillation, though, most people viewed Rechy as a figure to be pitied rather than feared. By now, the class was so taken with libertarianism that few were willing to brand Rechy as immoral. I, for once, turned out to be the real conventionalist, suggesting that even on the impersonal sex circuit one has some moral obligation to try to meet one's partners'

6. John Rechy, *The Sexual Outlaw: A Documentary* (New York: Grove Press, 1977).

reasonable sexual needs, and that self-centered Rechy was systematically immoral in that respect.

Rechy, though praising sex without emotion, admits in unguarded moments to a great deal of fear, self-doubt, and even desperation. And indeed he cuts a sad figure. The romantics in the class thought that all this was clear evidence that my sex-is-sex view must be wrong and therefore that good sex and good emotions must be mutually enhancing in some fashion. I deflated this move by pointing out that it was simply Rechy's overweening narcissism—not the 'impersonal' nature of his encounters—that systematically prevented him from making significant connections with others. I explained that I was certainly not committed to the view that people should be narcissistic, or that sex without emotion necessarily or even probably entails a narcissism which seals one's world off from others. I had, for instance, met my lover whilst park cruising. What one gets out of the impersonal sex circuit depends in significant part upon the attitudes one takes into it. If one is consumed by self-love and simply uses others for ego-gratification, as does Rechy, then it is not at all surprising that one has trouble meeting people, and that one experiences more than the usual pendulum swings of self-esteem.

When I would make moves like this the class was quite willing to think that they didn't have to take them too seriously. They supposed that someone (perhaps a white knight) could come up with the correct counter-counter-argument, even if they could not, and that somehow I had won the argument not because I was right, but because I'd thought about these matters in advance and had a merely clever answer ready at hand—the sort of thing that *does* make cynics out of philosophy professors. After having thought we had established that not all opinions are of equal worth, such a move on the class's part could be taken only as an unthinking retreat to skepticism. But they were unmoved even by this charge. You can't beat the masses either.

I had invited the local contingent of Womyn Confronting Pornographic Media to give their slide-show and talk to the class. But they declined the invitation, citing as their reasons lack of energy and a rumor in the women's community that the class was "suspect," even before the class had started. So I used their brochure instead, which was like shooting fish in a barrel, since it was so poorly written, leaving its crucial terms like "degrading," "objectification," and "unnatural" entirely undefined and unanalyzed.

The pornography debate in the class divided uniformly along gender lines, with the exception of one gay male politico who had learned, by rote and slogan, the Standard Feminist Line: "Pornography is violence against women." The debates were so heated that some of my best points went entirely unnoted in student papers on the topic. I had suggested that, issues of rights aside, even pornography that portrays violence is (potentially) justified *if* it has the effect of isolating and organizing into manageable form various psychic poisons produced by sexual repression and frustrations and so of keeping them from permeating the whole psyche. A similar therapeutic interpretation for S&M is given by Edmund White in *States of Desire*.[7] By the time we got to S&M, though, people were either tired or blasé. It did not produce the fireworks of the pornography discussions. This surprised me, since during the first week students had regularly cited S&M as an evil as obvious as any evil could possibly be.

The third week, dealing with political issues, I feared would be a disaster, since this was the part of the course the design of which had been most influenced by my unrealized expectation that the bulk of the class would be gay. Even so, and despite flagging energies on everyone's part, the week worked out well, though there was more lecturing and less discussion than before.

I began by covering my arguments for gay rights. I was amazed to discover that most of the nongay members of the class did not realize that gays regularly lose their jobs just for being gay and have no legal recourse against such discrimination. Some even initially viewed with suspicion my claims of the extent of such discrimination. But the general outrage expressed by the vast majority of the class that *any* such discrimination occurs was cheering. Even the blacks in the class who hated gays outright thought such discrimination was outrageous.

Another day, I mainly just gave a history of the gay rights movement, centering around the Stonewall Riots and the White Night Riots as paradigms for political action. I'm afraid I don't have much optimism for legislative, educative, executive or even judicial political strategies. The correct political strategy for gays is what I call "gay presence." For gays, coming out is the ultimate political act, for it confronts others'

7. Edmund White, *States of Desire: Travels in Gay America* (New York: Dutton, 1980).

unconsidered fears, breaks the deadening silence surrounding gay issues, and begins to create a space in which gays may begin to flourish. The gay rights movement does not need to be clean, respectable, and unified as much as it needs to be up-front. The gay movement would do well to take up as its Motto of Political Life a bit of advice which Rhett gives to Scarlett: "If you had enough courage, you wouldn't need a reputation."

And gays should not place too much hope on traditionally political liberals. Gays should always remember that the liberal who penned the Declaration of Independence, with all of its cant of consent and catalogue of government abuse, nevertheless thought gays should be castrated by the government.[8]

It has never even crossed the minds of liberals to give up the privileges of the dominant culture as a good-faith gesture: to stop getting married, to stop taking family rates, to stop getting insurance, and to come and drink at the niggers' fountain.

I was pleasantly surprised that these notions did not freak out the straights in the class. Rather, they freaked out the gays in the class, most of whom thought that being 'out' meant going to a gay bar and telling two straight friends, usually women. The message got through in part, though: almost all of the gay males in the class chose to write their term papers on David Hutter and Andrew Hodges' pamphlet *With Downcast Gays: Aspects of Homosexual Self-Oppression*, an analysis of how gays, in pathetic attempts to assimilate to the dominant culture, are accomplices in their own oppression.[9] We discussed the pamphlet toward the end of the course. Many gays treated the book as something on the order of St. Paul's trip to Damascus. The straight whites couldn't make much of the book. And the blacks simply, and surprisingly, did not believe such a thing as self-oppression exists. They, for instance, seemed honestly to believe that, in prior decades, when blacks straightened their hair, this was an act of artistic creation rather than an act of pandering to the values of the dominant culture. That Bo Derek did her hair in corn rows at the time was somehow viewed as decisive evidence for this belief. I was disarmed.

The best success of the last week was a guest speaker. I managed to

8. On Thomas Jefferson, see Johnathan Katz, *Gay American History: Lesbian and Gay Men in the U.S.A.: A Documentary* (1976; New York: Avon, 1978), p. 19.

9. David Hutter and Andrew Hodges, *With Downcast Gays: Aspects of Homosexual Self-Oppression*, 2d ed. (1974; Toronto: Pink Triangle Press, 1979).

get a local lesbian-separatist to talk to the class. She is a professor at a local community college. She spoke for about a half an hour, mostly giving a political autobiography, and then took questions. We had read some heavy-duty lesbian tracts by Andrea Dworkin and Adrienne Rich, stretches of which I found obscure and puzzling, so *I* had lots of questions to ask.[10] The speaker had expressed the importance of the concept of motherhood to her development, and both A. Dworkin and Rich treat the relation to the mother as the paradigm, perhaps also the cause, of all female-female bonding. I admitted that it struck me as bizarre that lesbians would take as their standard of identification that ultimate heterosexual act which is motherhood. She told me that I was too stupid to understand and basically that I should fuck off. The whole class spontaneously broke into gales of applause at this challenge to my tyrannical ways. I shook a grandmotherly finger at them, telling them they were all going to get F's. Lamentably, three of the jocks did get F's —for plagiarism.

And so gay studies came to this sleepy Republican university in a little Republican town in the tired Republican state of Illinois.

———

The course has had some cheering upshots, some visible, some, I hope, invisible. I have subsequently offered the course twice in a regular-term format. My hope is that the course is gradually creating some gay space for other local academics. But one's expectations in this regard must be moderate. For one thing, the gay faculty here is deeply closeted. There is only one other professor in the whole University who is really out. By "really out" I do not mean "goes to the local gay bar and is selectively out to departmental colleagues," but "is known to be gay open-endedly to the countless administrative tiers above the departmental level."

For another, the coming out process unfortunately confirms Aristotle's views on how we acquire virtues. One does not acquire the courage to come out by seeing others do so or from hearing about others doing so; one does not become virtuous by example or education. Indeed the initial response of a closet case to an acquaintance's coming out is

10. Andrea Dworkin, "Lesbian Pride," in *Our Blood* (New York: Harper and Row, 1976); Adrienne Rich, "Compulsory Heterosexuality and Lesbian Existence," *Signs* (Summer 1980) 5(4):631–60.

typically to become increasingly tense, withdrawn, and sometimes even vicious. One gains the requisite courage by doing small courageous acts and discovering that one's fears were exaggerated; this discovery in turn emboldens one. The creeping pace at which most people come out is a constant source of irritation to gay politicos, who overestimate the mind's control of the rest of the soul. And in this respect the mind of the academic is no better than that of your Average Joe.

It does look like eventually the English department will actually offer the gay-literature class it keeps threatening to mount, though only a graduate student rather than a gay faculty-member will likely be teaching it. Overtures have been made to other departments. Peace has been made with Women's Studies, who, in a bizarre spate of antigay hyperventilation, originally condemned my course for alleged lesbian tokenism, even though half of the readings for the course were written by lesbians and even though in the seventy-one courses which Women's Studies itself had offered in the three prior terms, lesbianism did not arise even once in their detailed course syllabi. There is now a librarian in charge of systematically acquiring gay materials and organizing gay materials now scattered through the Byzantine library system here.

There are two things, though, of which I am most proud about the course—that is—beyond my actually having given it. First, many members of the class, especially the women, claim to have acquired a more robust sense of reality as a result of taking the course. They no longer fear, so much, the real world. For them the bogey men have lost their substance. One woman confided that if she could sit through the porno flicks, there wasn't anything she couldn't do.

Second, the course had a completely unexpected spinoff effect. One of the most up-tight suburbanite women in the class, someone who made dramatic strides through the three weeks in shedding mental and social encrustations, works part-time at a local shelter for runaways. She told them that she was taking the course, described it to them, and told them how it was changing her views. Apparently her convictions were taken as authentic, for many of the runaways came out to her. Previously they were completely closeted to the shelter's authority figures, even though their being gay was the cause of their being on their own. For, as applied to gay youth, "runaway" is usually a complete misnomer; usually it's a case of "beaten up and thrown out." Now these 8-to-17 year-old 'runaways' meet Wednesday evenings for gay rap-sessions supervised by my ex-student. That these gays, completely unknown to me, have ended up in a gay support group in a little Midwestern town rather than staring vacantly around the New York Port Authority Bus Terminal, reduces to insignificance the class's mentioned and unmentioned disasters, and increases my sense of pride and hope.

13. The Ethics of Students and the Teaching of Ethics: A Lecturing

"There [the students'] curiosity ends. Because, basically, they don't give a shit"—Christopher Isherwood, *A Single Man*, emphasis omitted.

———

I hate students. They are not the death of spirit, they are its malaria. I hate students.[1]

At university the best teachers I had, the men from whom I learned how to teach, hated their students too. They are Charles Wegener and the late Richard McKeon of the University of Chicago, and R. E. Allen then of the University of Toronto. To Allen we students were just so many rocks in his path. We impeded his research. He knew the truth that the only legitimate reason for someone to do college teaching is so that he might have time to write. Real universities, from Plato's Academy to the Rockefeller University and Institute for Advanced Study, have no students. I regret not being good enough to work for one. When in the mid-430s Aristotle returned to Athens and set up the Lyceum complete with subjects and courses, class notes and students, things went down hill fast. Plato's research institute, The Academy, could nurture the curiosity, brilliance, and originality of a Eudoxus, Aristotle, Speusippus, and Arcesilaus or even just the imagination of a Xenocrates or a Crantor. But with a curriculum and students, Aristotle could do no better than produce epigones and hacks like Theophrastus and Aristoxenus. Things have not improved. Real universities stand to the fake ones we teach in as an understanding of quantum mechanics stands to Chernobyl.

McKeon in social settings was amiable enough with students, but he

1. This lecture was written for and delivered to a conference on "Teaching Philosophy and Public Policy" held at The Catholic University of America, June 19, 1986 and sponsored by The Center for Philosophy and Public Policy of The University of Maryland. It appears here in only slightly revised and expanded form.

hated them in the classroom. We were dumb, for the most part incorrigibly so, and further largely unaware or unconcerned that this was so. While we bridled in secret sympathetic embarrassment when he made women students cry, we also did not know the answers to his questions, even though sometimes the questions did have them. McKeon knew the truth that to teach well one has to have a line to push. He was not shy about this and so did not need to dissimulate, as so many weaker creatures do, that this was not what he was doing. Like Allen, he had something to say, and was not laboring under the comforting illusion, so frequently trotted out by unproductive faculty, that they like teaching because they learn things from their students. Allen and McKeon simply admitted honestly to the asymmetries of knowledge and power that exist between teachers and students, and which are the very reasons why there is a need for and the possibility of teaching to begin with. It is probably because we are so largely deluded about what our colleagues actually are—deluded that we get something from them of academic value, even though all they really are are our friends—that by transference we more often than not mistakenly suppose that faculty and students are part of a joint project, one that has the same end for both.

Now, it is perhaps misleading to say that Wegener hated students; he just seemed to have no idea what they were doing in the classroom with him; he seemed honestly puzzled by our presence, as though someone had without explanation left an empty box in the back seat of his car. He was not disturbed by our presence, for everything was either this way or that way and both this way and that way (with appropriate gestures of rocking hands and a great deal of admirable pacing and pipe puffing). He did not have a line to push, but he did know the most basic truth about academe: thinking is something one does with oneself and the blackboard, and since in the end the chalk marks are usually illegible or mere doodles, ultimately by oneself alone.

In the *Theaetetus* (190a) and *Sophist* (263e), Plato says that thinking is simply an inner dialogue. But this nostalgic reminiscence of the early Socratic dialogues has things exactly backwards. The content of talking and so of discourse is rather the making exterior of what one comes up with on one's own. Plato oddly seemed to have been seduced by the behaviorist's error into thinking that since the materials of thought—language—are necessarily of public origin, thought made from the materials is as well. But this belief is like holding that because the materials of marriage come from nature that marriage is a natural institution.

Now, it is true that we may not know our own thoughts clearly or firmly until we articulate them, but when we talk with others to clarify our thought, we do no more than when we get a second opinion on whether the soup needs more chervil. Discourse is not analogous to the creation of a recipe or even the execution of it. Professors who are worth anything are therefore by nature and necessarily absent minded. Thought is incompatible with committees—the sinkholes of the moral landscape, the mass graves of ideas. Thanks to their capacity for generating variation rapidly, word processors are obviating even the need for soliciting a second opinion about the spicing, so that the writer, the real teacher, can finally be free from the kindness of strangers, those colleagues who are too busy drinking gibsons, selling real estate, being taught by students, and ingratiating themselves to other deadwood and to deadwood heaven —administration—to read drafts.

I hate students. They are bad for universities. In his book, *The Ivory Tower,* Anthony Kenny correctly points out that "in recent decades, in many countries, some of the worst attacks on academic freedom have come from the students who are the primary beneficiaries of the academy."[2] By academic freedom he means the making of academic decisions based on academic criteria. What he has in mind as its student violations, however, are simply the interruption of lectures and seminars, the persecution of unpopular teachers, and the use of force and threat as a way of making academic decisions. These forms of "direct action" are however relatively rare, at least in my ken, and may even cancel each other out in the long run. At my home university, for example, the presence of an anti-apartheid shantytown was, after much turmoil and partisan violence, permitted on campus grounds by the administration, only then to be, while occupied, razed by pro-apartheid fraternity members, who by doing so seem to have completely routed from campus the militant anti-apartheid group, which had been disrupting board of trustees' meetings and the like. These various destroyers of academic freedom at least show a little spunk.

More insidious in their workings and effects are student dullards, who

2. Anthony Kenny, "Academic Freedom," in *The Ivory Tower* (Oxford: Basil Blackwell, 1985), p. 129.

determine what departments shall exist and courses be given not by violence but by the way they drive enrollment-driven financing. One of my colleagues recently offered an experimental intersession course on utopias. In a sad commentary on the times, it got, at a school of 35,000 students, an enrollment of four. You can bet it will not be given again. Students also determine who will get tenure and promotion through anonymous computer-read ballots on their favorite teachers. At my home university—as though a prom queen were being picked—such popularity polls are required by the administration for all tenure and promotion decisions. Now "academic criteria" is admittedly a bit vague, but I doubt that any plausible conception of it includes as an integral part the confusions and desires of the B-minus student. By their feet and by their number-two pencils, B-minus students determine who shall teach and what shall be taught.

They also manipulate research agendas in obvious ways—and in some subtle ways as well. If it is to be done even passably well, research is a full-time job. So if one is forced to teach, one can really be doing research on only the subjects that one is forced to teach. Conversely, one cannot really teach well if one does not do research on the subjects taught. So if students rather than academics largely determine what is taught, they doubly manipulate research agendas.

Now one might claim that students in these insidious forms of academic oppression are, in ways they obviously are not in Kenny's examples, largely innocent. For these forms, though not Kenny's, require complicity and even planning by administrators. But this is too quick. For administrators are simply giving students what the students and their parents want; administrators are here, as usual, followers not leaders. And for students, the university exists to get them not an education but a job—a university function to which academic criteria cannot be applied.[3]

The other current chief enemy of academic freedom simply complements and extends this oppression from students. It is the burgeoning direct entanglement of universities with industry. The evil of this problem is the same as that of the student problem: commercial standards replace academic ones. This trend takes a particularly insidious form at

3. "A recent campus survey of University of Illinois freshmen showed that 78 percent of them are going to school mainly to get a good job." *News-Gazette* [Champaign, Illinois], May 24, 1987, p. 1.

research universities. For increasingly research funds are available from companies rather than governments—not that governments are ever wholly impartial (one need only think of the half politicized, half Alexandrian National Endowment for the Humanities of the 1980s for evidence). But how much less likely than even government are profit-created, profit-directed companies to use neutral academic criteria in assessing research proposals? Admittedly again, administrations are complicitous. It is they who have increasingly placed emphasis on the acquisition of "outside" research dollars as a mark of successful scholarship and use it rather than actual scholarship as a key criterion for tenure and promotion.

The entanglements have other insidious forms as when they produce a business mentality among administrators who begin to see things in business-like ways. One mark of this is the search for pseudo-objectivity in numbers—as in student popularity polls and in numbers of outside research dollars. My home university offers another good example. There one of the three chief criteria, and in the end the only one that really counts, for salary raises is what administrators call "marketability"—people who might get swept away by business or other universities are to get the goodies. Now this policy simply flaunts academic oppression: if you want a raise, don't do research on unpopular or unusual topics—topics for example that traditionally have excited discrimination at universities. Allowing the purchasing power of other universities to determine who and what shall be supported is not basing academic decisions on academic criteria, it is viewing universities as commercial enterprises and applying commercial criteria.

These insidious entanglements pale, however, when compared to the increasingly explicit entanglements of business and universities. My home university is setting up a huge cognitive sciences "enterprise zone" in which people from industry will work literally side-by-side with academic appointees. Industry will be footing much of the bill. The same is occurring with the university's new super-computing center. It is fatuous to suppose that the university will be able to maintain academic freedom when it has virtually signed away its academic character. Industrialists rather than academics will determine who shall teach, what shall be taught, what topics researched, and who rewarded. For the employment prospects of its students (who with engineering degrees for the most part leave the state anyway), and for the state's economic betterment (for which it vainly hopes), the university has become an indenture to an industrial park.

I hate students. They are bad for professors. When the classrooms around my office are taken over on weekends by chanting, stomping barbarians practicing routines for Mom's Day Weekend, the police tell me that they can't throw them out for disturbing the peace since the Office of Space Utilization has given them permission to be there. The police seem honestly puzzled when I ask whether the same reasoning would apply to rape and murder. The Office of Space Utilization tells me that it is tough beans that I can't work in my office on weekends, that tryouts are an integral part of Mom's Day Weekend, that Mom's Day Weekend is an integral part of campus life, and that I should try working during what they call "normal hours," whereby—if there were any doubts—administrators tip their hand to show that they are not professionals.

Just as to the smoker the world is an ashtray, for students the world is their private sandbox, to play and piss in at will. Like tenured deadwood, students are in the academic community but not part of it. Like tenured deadwood, they drain the academic community pale. Like tenured deadwood, they are parasites on campus life, because they are parasites on social life in general. They run down housing and neighborhoods and don't care—after all, they'll be moving on in June. They steal my irises, peonies, apricots, roses, even oddly day lilies and hollyhocks. They drink a lot and drink a lot together; then they use my yard as a pissing trough. When I ask them to leave they call me faggot. When in the village's Fourth of July parade I march with my people, they throw firecrackers at me and through my ringing ears I hear them calling out for my death from AIDS.

Drinking reveals the true nature of students. Drinking for them is not cocktails and laughter with Noel Coward or even the fearsome possibilities of a drunken Alcibiades. Drunkenness shows their essential greed. They are simply out to use professors in any way they can. If not showing up for an appointment they've set serves their purposes, they don't show up. If accusing you of rape fits their purposes, they accuse you of rape. They may look like people but in general they are not, for in general they are incapable of respecting others as creatures with ends of their own. The institutional arrangements of the university promote this exploitation of professors by students, for the student has no direct contractual relation with professors. In the student's mind, the professor has simply been subcontracted out by their parents or the state or, in any case, someone else. Usually students aren't even footing a significant part of the bill, so they have all the worst characteristics of children. They are all desire and expectation with no sense of obligation, developed respect, or responsibility. They are the ultimate gimme, gimme, gimme generation. If virtue can be taught, let it be Javert's aqueous courage.

For now, those among us with steely courage will recognize the situation as hopeless, but more frequently professors, unwilling as usual to face reality, try to rationalize the teacher-student relation, fantasizing it into something it isn't, into something not horrible: the relation of parent and child or of master and slave or, worse, of friend and friend. The student-teacher relation lacks and should lack the degree of intimacy necessary for the first and last fantasies and the necessary power asymmetry for effective slavery. Kenny describes the relation as "pastoral";[4] which sounds nice, but he fails to tell us whether he is viewing students as sheep or as those in need of God. The former is both too kind and too vicious, the latter inappropriate whatever we may think of our divine talents. To claim the student-teacher relation is *sui generis*—that of master-teacher and protege—is just to throw in the towel. All this simply suggests that people generally go into teaching for the wrong reasons. The only legitimate reason for being an academic is curiosity, a trait usually flagging in graduate school and virtually always dead by tenure.

I hate universities too. Universities have come to have three social functions in contemporary American society: one an entertainment function, one matrimonial, and one commercial. Academic values have no place in any of these roles, so it is not surprising that they have virtually dropped out of the American academic scene.

Colleges are, as much as anything, hatcheries for professional athletes. At first it might seem silly to call this one of the chief functions of the contemporary university. But during periods between wars, it is chiefly in athletics that we as a nation worship and instill value in masculinity. The triviality and practical irrelevance of Title IX aside, athletics are the rituals by which we express, maintain, and enhance the value we place on masculinity pure and simple. This expression and enhancement has to occur in a quasi-religious or game-like setting, for men are valued as ends in themselves, rather than for what they do or produce. Play or

4. Kenny, *Ivory Tower*, p. 128.

entertainment here is not a mere matter of relief or distraction, but is how we express our highest cultural values. Women are valued only for functions they serve—mom and apple pie—rather than as having any value on their own as persons. Colleges are therefore one of the chief guarantors of sexism in society.

The second chief social function of the contemporary university is to marry off the middle class to itself. The state university is a cotillion for middle white trash. This function largely explains the virulence of heterosexuality on campus. The dominant culture can hold marriage in exclusive reserve as its pure social form only if it can crush out others who could as easily attain the form or worse ring changes on it. If universities are chiefly coming-out parties for ersatz debs, there won't be much room tolerated for other sorts of comings-out.

The move to co-educational colleges in the last quarter century has had little to do with gender equality. Rather it is an attempt to buttress compulsory heterosexuality and class purity. The target had to be moved nearer the archer, lest the whole sport be lost in distraction. But then it could not be too close either. Thus, radical polarity in dress according to gender is encouraged by universities and their vision of campus life, and so too are maintained gender-segregated dormrooms.[5] Such gender-seg- regation, like the wider maintenance of gender-segregated washrooms, has nothing to do with the avoidance of violence—universities' cavalier attitudes toward and attempts to suppress the reportage of rape deci- sively gainsay that possibility—nor is gender-segregation prompted by respect for privacy. Like racial segregation, it is wholly social in func- tion. Its purpose is not to degrade women but to enhance heterosexual mystique. The gender-segregated dormroom in the civilizational mar- riage factory that is the university specifically serves the same ritualistic purposes of male initiation rites in other cultures, where typically fe- males are totally excluded until the male initiate is fully incorporated in the society as a possessor of women. This ritual is explicit in contempo- rary marriage ceremonies. On the wedding day, the groom is barred from seeing the bride until she comes resplendent down the aisle to be

5. On the contemporary focusing of socially maintained gender distinctions on style, mien, and dress as a vehicle for compulsory heterosexuality, see Sandra Bartky's excellent "Foucault, Femininity, and the Modernization of Patriarchal Power" in Irene Diamond and Lee Quimby, eds., *Feminism and Foucault: Paths of Resistance* (Boston: Northeastern University Press, 1988).

had by him to whom she pledges obedience. The university in a society so infantile that its offspring take forever to grow up serves essentially as society's belated and benighted puberty rituals. The co-ed university is the modern social crucible for compulsory heterosexuality.

At my home institution, two chancellors in as many years vetoed even minimal civil protections for gay students in university housing. Excuses tendered aside, the chancellors simply collapsed under pressures from sororities and fraternities, which are distinctive there in that many are the founding chapters and head offices for their various national affiliates. To have gays accepted at the University of Illinois might just destroy the nation, or so it goes.

Eventually, a sit-in and a committee later and just before the second chancellor skipped town, the university took gays out of that exalted class of angels, blondes, cats, and other persons for whom it has no civil rights policy and made the second-class status of gays official—by confecting a legally unenforceable statement just for gays to the effect that it does not discriminate against them. Now, since the university is a governmental agency subject to the Due Process Clause, had it an articulated policy of nondiscrimination against gays, it would, in accordance with settled principles of administrative law, be *legally* bound by the policy and be subject to civil suits under it. The University's nondiscrimination "policy" for gays, as opposed to its protections for all other classes explicitly covered in its nondiscrimination statutes, banks on people's ignorance of this finery of law and is cagily worded to deceive gays into thinking they are protected from discrimination when they are not. Its two sentences read:

> Among the forms of invidious discrimination prohibited by University policy but not law is sexual orientation. Complaints of invidious discrimination based solely upon policy are to be resolved within existing University procedures.[6]

Now, what the second sentence here says legally is that the "policy" in the first sentence is not a policy at all—otherwise the University would be legally bound by it. If this is the *policy,* you can imagine the *practice.* Only a university would be so cleverly depraved to think to use a statement nominally opposing invidious discrimination as an official

6. "University of Illinois at Urbana–Champaign Nondiscrimination Statement," *Code on Campus Affairs and Regulations Applying to All Students* (August 1987), p. [ii].

means of individiously discriminating against gays and degrading them into second-class status. Colleges are one of the chief guarantors of gay oppression.

The third function of universities, their commercial function, mentioned earlier, is to see that America's middle class can be self-sufficient and gainfully employed when finally unleashed upon the world. Like the other two functions, this function is, as a side-benefit for civilization, intended to keep ephebes not only off their parents' backs but also safely off the streets. In its formal mode, this function basically comes down to job training, an activity to which academic criteria cannot be applied and which is at loggerheads with the academic enterprise of nurturing curiosity and exploring ideas. The result of the attempt to blend trade schools with academic ones is an inefficient grotesquery. At the University of Illinois to get a bachelor's degree in dietetics one has to take twenty-five hours of organic chemistry. Of these perhaps two minutes at most would ever be useful in actually performing the job of institutional meal planning for which the degree is supposed to be a union card. Or consider law schools: their three years of classes are not sufficient for anyone to pass state bar exams, yet any intelligent person who took Stanley Kaplan or any other summer bar review course could pass the exams. The contortions of organic chemistry courses and law courses cannot be justified on teaching or employment grounds. Lawyers don't need to know much, if any, constitutional law and dietitians don't need to know genetic engineering. The existence of such courses is an obvious ruse to keep law schools and chemistry departments afloat. It is silly to suppose that those who carry out a craft or even those who teach it need to know its principles and causes. Only those who do research in the field need be bothered with them, so it is silly to be wasting time and energy teaching them to people who are largely incapable of appreciating and who will in any case never use them.

What is needed for youth employment in America is not the American university but, if anything, government subsidized on-site job-training. Law schools should largely be replaced with articling programs and working up through the ranks, as is normal in any normal business and which was normal practice even in law until this century.

We should try to blunt the myth that universities somehow legitimate and make glamorous what are basically just crafts. America should cut back the size of universities considerably while greatly expanding less pretentious and more efficient community colleges, where job-training is unabashedly what is going on—and what ought to be going on. The newly reduced universities—basically research institutes—ought to have the sort of place in society that museums used to have before the King Tut show transformed them into the visual equivalents of the Boston Pops. In such properly poorly attended groves, there would be some room for the curious to roam in, roam around and even become part of the institution. Such institutions could be easily run on the money now wasted on tenured deadwood alone. Purged of contradictory criteria and divided attention, the new universities would likely be much more efficient though existing on a scale miniature by current standards.

It should be plain that I think that there is no proper role for the teaching of ethics and public policy either in the university as currently conceived by society or even in the ideal university. I also have grave doubts that it has any proper place in the community college system, like some Kennedy School writ small. We have all seen friends turn into monsters when they get a little bit of legal training. If you want to see what people do when they get a little bit of public policy training, you might wish to read Plato's autobiographical *Seventh Letter,* where philosophy and power join hands to produce, best of intentions notwithstanding, carnage all round.

But all is not lost. There is a function for the teaching of normative issues within the current imperfect university—a remedial function, the proper place for which is high schools. The proper function of high schools and compulsory public education in general—one that by default must be carried out by colleges—is the saving of students from their parents and their religion. Because of privacy conventions properly valued in society, parents pretty well get to manipulate their children in any way they see fit. This "education" virtually always takes the form of forcing the parents' imagined values and usually unreasonable hopes upon the child. As a logical possibility these values might be the appreciation of such "second order" values as freedom or independence but, the Mills senior and junior aside, these imposed values are virtually always some particular expected lifeplan, some particular religious tenets, sexual mores, expected line of employment, and pattern of social relations including political, racial, and gender relations. All of these views on how one ought to live abide pretty much unchanged throughout public schooling—where, however, they are frequently layered over with the crudest sort of patriotism. The views of culture on all of these matters, save religion, are uniform enough to be regularly plumped for in text and class—often unconsciously. And with religion, it turns out most often that students have only the vaguest notions of what their religion actually commits them to. Practicing Catholics turn out in general to know diddley-squat of the catechism and cannot even name the sacraments. The result, when students come to college, is that they have deeply inculcated beliefs on how they and others are to live, but these beliefs are crude, unexamined, and perhaps unconsciously held. Any chat of liberty and justice for all has been lipped so automatically—indeed in rituals that typically gainsay their very sense, like compulsory flag salutes, school assemblies and the like—as to render the notions as meaningless as the twirling of a Tibetan prayer wheel. Our aim should be to correct this failing and it is by the very crudity of their beliefs, if at all, that students may be saved.

The purpose of a liberal education is not to make students well-rounded individuals, who can speak intelligently on a wide range of acceptable topics at mixed cocktail parties because they have learned a little of this and a little of that. The purpose of a liberal education is not to know 15,000 fun facts about Western Culture. The purpose of liberal education is not to generate the perfect faculty spouse. It is to generate liberals—or persons, if you like a different rhetoric—creatures who are in a position to guide their lives by their own lights and who can respect others in doing the same. This end chiefly entails two educational tasks for which the philosophic teaching of ethics and policy issues is especially well suited—one methodological, one substantive.

The first is to develop students' intellectual skills to appraise policies and practices so that one's beliefs become freely chosen and appropriated as one's own. The other is to attack petrified social norms so that one can come to see alternatives, which then might be tested as being suitable to oneself. The purpose of public education is to provide, to the extent that the word can, Mill's prerequisites for self-realization: freedom and a variety of situations.

My sense is that intellectual freedom or the development of critical intellectual skills is more likely to be successfully achieved in applied philosophy classes than in courses specifically labeled "critical thinking" or "informal logic"—the courses that unfortunately are increasingly the bread and butter which sustain philosophy departments in the face of enrollment-driven financing. These courses thrive on the clever example and tend to trivialize the power and importance of critical thinking. Since it is really the formalism that is being taught, course names notwithstanding, content simply gets lost. For the rote-learned rules to apply and fifteen fallacies neatly to be discovered, the content of such courses has to be simplified to the point of distortion and etiolated to the point of insignificance. Nothing that is worth knowing fits neatly into the patterns that even informal logic can discern. As a result, these courses generate a certain glibness about thinking—just apply the right rule to the cute example and you can think critically and carefully about anything.

In a way the courses become a denial of the very ambiguity they are carefully trying to get their students to be able to discern. Thinking has been reduced to a parlor game, imaging in its fun the "bread and circuses" atmosphere in which these courses are typically taught. The importance of discerning ambiguities in arguments is more likely to be noted and remembered by students if, for instance, in the course of debate on abortion, one points out that the slogan "right to life" is ambiguous than if students are taught a limerick on rare rubies and rare steaks. And in ethics and policy courses the point about ambiguity turns out not simply to be the negative one: avoid using ambiguous terms as the middle term in syllogisms. The point becomes a positive one—that we make intellectual progress when we are able to make relevant distinctions. If one believes that there is a right to life and means thereby merely a right not to be killed unjustly, that will commit one morally to one thing; if, on the other hand, one believes there is a right to life and means thereby a right to sufficient means for continued biological existence, that will commit one to something quite different. Not only is glibness avoided if critical reasoning is taught in practice, it is only there that it has its full import.

The other half of proper public education for which the philosophic teaching of public policy issues is also uniquely suited is pedagogically more sticky—the provision of a variety of situations. For the way to do this is to push a specific line and to push the line that is, most often, at odds with the received opinions of our culture, the ones the students already have. In teaching ethics and policies, such pushing means that the class will carry a high political charge. Courage, which thanks to the tenure system is the rarest academic virtue, is required for such good teaching and even in its presence success is not likely, given the extent to which the metastasizing filaments of the ordinary have already deadened student minds, but this course is the one we should be pursuing.

One needs to push a line in order to be intellectually honest and to do what philosophers indeed do. It would be odd, after teaching in critical thinking classes that it is worth arguing about arguments, to find in the end that all arguments are equally good, equally bad, or mere dilemmas, paradoxes, or antinomies. If we are to teach students how to think, we must be willing to show them how to draw conclusions. One does that by playing out some line of argument to its end. In any case, one will be pushing a line whether one is explicit about it or not. Why not just be forthright about it from the start? In classes that are allowed to be all discussion and no conclusion, cynicism holds the reins while skepticism rides shotgun.

Further, if we wish students to have access to a variety of life's situations, it is not enough just to discuss classical liberalism as a general philosophical position, though it is useful to point out what its commitments are. One must also, if one is going to free up the students, persuasively introduce them to specific positions contrary to the ones they likely hold; otherwise the old ways will win out by default. The balancing of views (touted by some as a way for all sides to be equitably heard), when carried out wholly within the limits of the classroom, results again in a skepticism in which none of us actually believes. Such balancing ought to occur rather against the general background of the culture. With this point of reference, one is able to argue for a specific position and yet to have all sides be aired for sake of fairness—the culture itself will be airing the one side it always has. But this pedagogical stance entails arguing for positions like the right to abortion, gay rights, for pornography, euthanasia, and affirmative action, and against the death penalty. All but the last are actually going to affect the way the people in the class live and all are issues where feelings run deep. Further, rudimentary arguments on these issues have been sounded by The Right and, to a lesser degree, in the popular press, so students may not only feel strongly on these matters, they may also think they know what they are talking about. Set against explicitly politicized instruction, the combination can be explosive. Most teachers, already bored and burnt out, take a safe course and try to avoid potential, soul-saving controversy. Like a Rogerian psychiatrist, they just let students talk their minds, themselves not plumping for one side or another. And the result is usually what my C-minus students claim when they complain at course's end, having missed its entire point: "I thought it was just an opinions course." After all, nothing matters.

Alternatively, for lack of courage professors will back whatever position will least rock the boat politically. Courses end up being politicized this way too, only insidiously so. At Catholic University of America, the theologian Charles Curran has published extensively in religious ethics holding, at the horizon of Catholic thought, that contraception, abortion, and homosexual marriages are to be encouraged in some circumstances. Over the recent years the Vatican has threatened him to recant or lose his position here. When last I was tracking the story, the worst possible combination of results had occurred. Curran had agreed to stop teaching his views if the Vatican agreed not to revoke his theological credentials. So we have, on the one side, courage abandoned, and on the other, the complete destruction of academic freedom. One could, of course, properly call an institution such as this a parish school, ordered, as it is, by liturgical rather than academic criteria, but one ought not to call it a university, and it should not be accredited as such.[7]

Pressures on others are more likely to be subtler than the blunderbusts of the Catholic Church, but effective nevertheless. Yet assuming one has the requisite courage and that one teaches at a university, not a church, there are a number of precautions that one can take to enhance the prospects that explicitly political teaching will nevertheless be fair to students, even when one has a low regard for their talents. Perhaps mentioning some of these might encourage others to take the plunge and teach explicitly political courses.

First, be forthright about your prejudices. This likely involves waving some of your privacy, but as in politics such a loss comes with the turf. Students should be told up-front what one's general political orientation is, what one's religious beliefs are generally, what one's sexual orientation is, and to what sort of political and social organizations one belongs. The purpose of such revelation is not to get chummy with them

7. Eventually the Vatican would boot Curran out of his teaching position at Catholic University of America by withdrawing his theological credentials. "Vatican Silences U.S. Theologian," *The Chicago Tribune*, August 19, 1986, p. 4. On gays and Catholic educational institutions, see Timothy F. Murphy, "The Sinner from the Sin: Catholicism in the Age of AIDS," *Christopher Street* [New York] (1987) 10(5), no. 113, pp. 25–33.

and there should be no expectation that they should reciprocate; indeed, that generally should be discouraged. The reason for such disclosures is the same as for high-level politicians putting their finances in blind trusts: so that one cannot manipulate the affairs of an unwitting public for one's own benefit. The effect of such disclosures is to assure the students that nothing is being put over on them. The cards are on the table. There are no hidden agendas, as is the case in virtually all other classes they take, where subtlety all too often is a ruse for intellectual seduction.

Second, offend everyone. Anyone with opinion appropriately strong enough to be teaching adequately should have no problem with this. A classical liberal position which argues strongly for individual rights especially against government but also sees a role for government in enhancing the circumstances in which and out of which independence may be realized will usually offend everyone in the right degree. Those who but for boredom and ignorance would be Nazis will be offended by the degree of individual choice advocated in this view. Commies—there are always a couple—will think that government has not gone far enough on this model and possibly will attack the very notion of individual rights as a bourgeois conspiracy, while libertarians—there are usually a couple Randians too—will think the state has gone too far. Now it's hard to offend everyone equally, but if people see all others getting shot down now and then, they will realize that one is not playing favorites. During discussions in a politicized class, though tempting, it is especially important not to let the brighter students, the ones who have twigged to your points, lecture other students, for it smacks too heavily of favoritism and unfair teaming-up or conspiracy. The students, while being given the one, must not be given the one-two. I've been unusually fortunate never to have attracted groupies.

Third, provide students some time to express their opinions, though don't hold out much hope for their worth and don't indulge views that are clearly off the wall (students in general are surprisingly sensitive to the latter and are unhappy if you let it eat up much time). I find a pseudo-socratic method or directed discussion works best for me. Both argument and objection are expounded by asking students questions. They in turn get to ask questions and raise objections along the way. Straight lecturing, though it admittedly makes for cleaner exposition of arguments, tends to leave them brittle, and it fails to engage students, fails to pique their curiosity—at least beyond the point of wondering whether this is going to be on the examination. Too often, teaching is like inquisitorial torture: it tries to get at the truth but instead simply gets the victim to say whatever the perpetrator wants to hear.

I call my method socratic, for when a student advances a position by submitting it to series of questions, I will run it through the standard philosophical gauntlet to see how it stands up. Sometimes admittedly the student feels badgered or bulldozed. When that happens, it is useful to stand back and reflect on what has occurred, not indulging the student specifically, but summarizing how the position or argument has been clarified or elaborated in the testing of it. Thereby, the examination is shown not to be mere browbeating or one-upmanship. One can try to strengthen the student's own position by indicating on its behalf distinctions, principles, and connections which the student has not noted, but such a move even when carried out in good faith will as likely as not be viewed suspiciously as a sleight of hand. To a degree, the suspicion will be justified. I call the method "pseudo-" for I, the questioner, don't pretend not to be advancing a position.

Fourth, admit failure and ignorance. Teachers are supposed to be authority figures—or so we are told. And we are supposed to be the teachers, not the students, chiefly 'cause we know more stuff than they. And as far as it goes, this is true. But many teachers over-generalize and act as though they know everything or at least think it too embarrassing to admit failure as somehow undermining their authority. Of course, if they really are faking it and resting their authority merely on their office, they will, like tenured deadwood, have a lot of gaps to try to hide. The good teacher admits error when he has made a mistake in an argument or when a student correctly points out that he has just contradicted something he said three weeks ago. More often, the opportunity arises simply when a student asks a question to which one does not know the answer. Even if it's a largely irrelevant query after some factual matter, an admission of ignorance is to most students a breath of fresh air. It shows that the politicized teacher, as pushy and self-assured as he may appear, is not speaking *ex cathedra* and honestly believes, as he has been claiming all along, that there are better and worse arguments and better and worse reasons.

Fifth, take the argument one more step. If you're teaching an article with which you basically agree, it is helpful if you can tease out some problematic feature that has not been fully elaborated in the piece but that nevertheless does have a solution within the general framework assumed by the paper. This strategy involves doing research—either original thinking or at least following the literature. No research, no good teaching. This strategy is especially effective in dispelling skepticism and cynicism. For it shows that there can be progress in ideas. The political teacher is not committed to final solutions; she claims only that there are better positions and worse ones, and what better way to show this than to show that positions can get better and better.

Sixth, and finally, don't grade politically. Be sure to have enough graded assignments early on so that students can be assured that they are not being judged by their degree of conformity to the teacher's views, but on how well they can argue for a position, whatever position it may be. The student must be allowed to advance her or his own position in exams and papers. Don't degrade your students in the name of efficiency by giving them multiple choice, true false, or short answer exams. Such testing is a terrible thing to do normally, for such an exam assumes by its preemptive structure that students have nothing worth saying, and it is intolerable in a politicized class, for the student is then left entirely to second-guess the professor's motives in so-called objective questions.

In general, I find grading a self-correcting procedure. The students who get buffeted and cuffed the most in class almost always come through with A's. Those who have come to the course with an explicit political ideology, basically the commies and Randians, if they struggle through to the end, do very well. For the positions they espouse did not arise in civilization by accident; each captures some political reality and, in offering comprehensive political agendas, they invariably provide the basis for the students to make some observation that had not been made in class and so score points for (relative) originality. Students who come to the class with deeply held but inchoate conservative beliefs usually by the end of it have put in the time to learn how to defend their positions better. The students whose positions are closest to my own frequently do poorly, for they have the least room in which to come up with something original. Those who do worst are students who simply ape my positions, for they invariably get them wrong. Taking me as a model is noisome enough, and then to be gotten wrong, I find causes me to become impatient; and they pay for it, if it is fairly clear that they're just trying to snooker me.

With these dogma-dispelling safeguards installed in classroom controversies, one can at least feel confident that one is doing the best one can
in handing to students the intellectual possibility of liberty. The effort
will largely go unappreciated. They're there, remember, for all the wrong
reasons. You are too. "The class has got to listen to George because, by
virtue of the powers vested in him by the state of California, he can
make them submit to and study even his crassest prejudices, his most
irresponsible caprices, as so many valuable clues to the problem: How
can I impress, flatter, or otherwise con this cantankerous old thing into
giving me a good grade?"[8] And the lessons which the institution is busily
teaching them, insidiously in their unreflective ritualized form, are the
exact opposite of what you're teaching them. And it will reward you
accordingly. In any case, few students have the stuff of change and
improvement. Few have enough curiosity even to be nourished by ideas.
You won't get any teaching awards. You will have done what is right.

"The silly enthusiastic old prof, rambling on, disregarding the clock,
and the class sighing to itself, He's off again! Just for a moment George
hates them, hates their brute basic indifference, as they drain quickly out
of the room. Once again, the diamond has been offered publicly for a
nickel, and they have turned from it with a shrug and a grin, thinking
the old peddler crazy."[9] Good teaching is just like that.

I am sometimes asked whether I haven't ever had any students who
amounted to anything, of whom I was proud. Yes, two. One went on
from being an undergraduate to whom I taught his first Plato class to
getting a PhD from Princeton in only three years, writing his thesis on
Plato. He then became an assistant professor of classics at the University
of Texas-Austin; he then became a fellow at the prestigious Center for
Hellenic Studies in Washington; he then threw it all in and resigned—to
try to become a rock star. The other took my gay issues course, became
a gay activist, became a gay passivist, became a gay accommodationist,
got on committees, and finally played me Judas.

8. Christopher Isherwood, *A Single Man* (1964; New York: Lancer Books, 1968), pp.
50–51.
9. *Ibid.*, pp. 60–61.

PART SIX

Sullen Voices, an End and an Agenda

14. Dignity *vs.* Politics: Strategy When Justice Fails

Gay justice does not exist and does not nearly exist. The nation's institutional means for establishing justice—the courts—have completely failed in their duty when it has come to the plight of gays. Indeed, they have now become a major part of the mechanisms of gay oppression. The problem is not merely that the courts are now regularly upholding antigay laws—that alone would be reason for pointed protest. The problem chiefly is that the very procedures which the courts have adopted to address—or more accurately, to fail to address—gay issues reinforce the social view that gays are not worthy of equal respect.

In its 1986 decision *Bowers v. Hardwick,* the Supreme Court, by upholding Georgia's unenforced sodomy law, allowed the state to use law as invective against gays.[1] It allowed governments to shout "faggots" at gays. The problem with unenforced sodomy laws is not so much that they cause harm to gays but that they assault the dignity of gays—they attack persons as persons. First, unenforced sodomy laws, like other forms of group-directed invective, focus importance on a largely irrelevant characteristic of the group attacked and so attack persons as repositories of deserved fair treatment and equal respect. Second, unenforced sodomy laws, as holding people morally accountable without regard for anything they have done, show disrespect for persons as moral agents.[2] Such results are deplorable enough.

What is more disturbing is that the Supreme Court reached its conclusion that the Constitution does not "confer[ ] a fundamental right upon homosexuals to engage in sodomy" without addressing, entertaining, or considering any gay issues. It reached its conclusion that the state may bar gays from having any sex life at all without even discussing gays, or

1. For a detailed analysis of the nature and import of the Supreme Court's sodomy decision—*Bowers v. Hardwick,* 106 S. Ct. 2841 (1986)—and of its other privacy cases, see part two.

2. For elaboration of this point, see chapter 2.

privacy, or sex. Concerns of gays simply did not merit any attention from the Court. The case was not one where gays and their issues were given a hearing, their circumstances examined, and their argument found wanting; rather their concerns were simply dismissed out of hand by the Court. It could not be bothered. The Court failed to fulfill its role as the forum in which, unlike rough-and-tumble, popularly biased electoral politics, the best argument is supposed to carry the day. The Court simply did not address any arguments. In one sentence—with no analysis—it dismissed past privacy precedents as irrelevant and in one more sentence—again with no analysis—it assimilated gay sex to incest, child molestation, and drug use. The Court, in its rush to let the state insult gays, could not be bothered with argumentation and ideas.

As a result the case is short and dull. Claims in the gay press and fundraising brochures to the contrary, the case contains none of the openly prejudicial and inflammatory language found in past cases which insult socially despised groups. But this silence itself is all the more scary than vitriol, for it means that even before gays have any rights, society has already learned how to discriminate against them subtly. Perhaps the New Right has learned more from the civil rights movement than gays have—has learned how not to tip its hand. The Court contributed the insult of the snub to the legislative insult of legal invective. At least invective is directed at what one openly acknowledges as existing, while one snubs what one holds below contempt, acting toward it as toward shit—acting, if one can, as though it did not exist.

Unfortunately, this compounded insult of gays by the Court in *Bowers* has not been an isolated incident. It is a pattern. In 1987 the Court heard and decided a gay case which, unlike the *Bowers* case, was completely trivial, wholly symbolic. The issue: may the Gay Olympics call itself the "Gay Olympics"? The Court answered: "No."[3] Now, the gay side had already lost this case in lopsided, nasty opinions at every lower level. There was no issue of national importance involved. There was no split on the issue (as there had been in *Bowers*) among the various federal circuit courts calling for a higher finality. The case presented none of the usual reasons for the Supreme Court to decide to hear a case. It is hard therefore to believe that the Court is not now out gunning for gays.

3. *San Francisco Arts and Athletics, Inc. v. United States Olympic Committee,* 107 S. Ct. 2971 (1987).

Again the Court found no gay issues here. It used two strategies of avoidance. First, the Court claimed the use by gays of the term "Olympics" was simply a crass attempt to make money and so was to be given only the very weak protections afforded commercial speech.[4] This interpretation of gay speech suggests that the Court simply was viewing gays stereotypically as greedy, exploitative manipulators. Second, though the gay side was seeking to speak and print a noun both descriptive and normative, the Court interpreted such speech and press as simply posturing and gesturing, and so to be afforded only the comparatively weak protections it gives symbolic *actions,* as though gays' speaking the word "olympics" were relevantly like burning draft cards.[5] This interpretation of speaking and printing "gay olympics" suggests that the Court was viewing gays again simply through stereotypes, viewing gays as poseurs, frauds, and deceivers, but not as possibly having a message to convey, certainly not any serious political message. Only two justices saw that the denial to gays of the use of the term denied gays an important political means to the important political goal of dispelling one of the most severe of antigay stereotypes—that gays are limp-wristed wimps incapable of prowess or anything noble.[6] Indeed the Court aggravated this stereotype by completely giving itself over to it. Again by failing to engage gay concerns, the Court snubbed gays and treated them as below contempt.[7]

4. *Ibid.* at 2980.
5. *Ibid.* at 2981.
6. *Ibid.* at 2998 (Brennan, J., dissenting): "Here, the SFAA [i.e., the Gay Olympics] intended, by the use of the word 'Olympic,' to promote a realistic image of homosexual men and women that would help them move into the mainstream of their communities."
7. The "Gay Olympics" case also raised the important fifth amendment issue of the scope of the actions which will trigger constitutional protections. Did the special trademark which Congress gave to the United States Olympic Committee (USOC) make the discriminatory act of the USOC against gays a "state action" and so subject to the constitutional restraints of Equal Protection? Only four justices thought that it did—that there was a close, symbiotic, mutually beneficial relation between the federal government and the USOC which made the USOC's action relevantly similar to constitutionally forbidden discrimination against blacks by a privately owned restaurant operating in a government owned parking structure. See *ibid.* at 2987 (O'Connor and Blackmun, JJ., dissenting in part and concurring in part), at 2991–93 (Brennan, J., dissenting). A black case was used to establish the constitutional doctrine of symbiotic relations as generators of "state actions." *Burton v. Wilmington Parking Authority,* 365 U.S. 715 (1961). A gay case has been used to undo the doctrine. The Court's opinion fails even to mention the restaurant case, but by implication seems to suggest that the government would have had to be directing and controlling the restaurant's operations for them now to count as state

In the lower courts, there is more of the same. Every federal circuit court that has been faced with a claim of gay equal protection has summarily rejected it. Not one federal circuit court has made even a remotely good faith effort to determine whether the standards that the Supreme Court has laid out for affording enhanced protections to groups —racial groups, ethnic groups, women, illegitimate children, legal aliens, and illegal alien children—also apply to gays.[8] And now, in the wake of *Bowers,* the lower courts claim that if gay sex itself can be illegal, then society cannot be treating gays in unjust ways that trigger enhanced equal protections—failing to recognize that society's treatment of the *status* of being gay has virtually nothing to do with the sexual *acts* that gays perform.[9] Such a recognition would require the courts' having some

---

actions. Contrast *San Francisco Arts and Athletics,* 107 S. Ct. at 2985 n.27 with *ibid.* at 2991 n.12 (Brennan, J., dissenting).

8. For summary rejections of gay equal protection claims, see for example *Rowland v. Mad River School Dist.,* 730 F.2d 444 (6th Cir. 1984), cert. denied, 470 U.S. 1009 (1985); *Dronenburg v. Zech,* 741 F.2d 1388 (D.C. Cir. 1984), rehearing en banc denied, 746 F.2d 1579 (D.C. Cir. 1984); *Padula v. Webster,* 822 F.2d 97 (D.C. Cir. 1987). See also *DeSantis v. Pacific Telephone and Telegraph Co., Inc.,* 608 F.2d 327, 333 (9th Cir. 1979).

However, properly undeterred by *Bowers,* one federal district court has ruled that gays are a quasi-suspect class on a constitutional par with women, *High Tech Gays v. DISCO,* 668 F.Supp 1361, 1368–73 (N.D. Cal 1987), and one "state" supreme court—that for the District of Columbia—has held in dicta that gays are a (fully) suspect class on a constitutional par with blacks, *Gay Rights Coalition of Georgetown University Law Center v. Georgetown University,* 536 A.2d 1 (D.C. Court of Appeals 1987) (en banc). In this case, the United States Court of Appeals for the District of Columbia held that eliminating discrimination against gays is a compelling state interest, so that the D.C. Human Rights Act could compel Catholic-affiliated Georgetown University, even over Free Exercise claims, to provide gay student groups with equal access to campus facilities and all the material benefits had by officially recognized campus student groups; the court also held, however, that the University need not officially recognize the gay student groups because the D.C. statute, so the court claimed, did not require that.

While this book was in press, a brilliant opinion in a military case out of the Ninth Federal Circuit held gays a suspect class on a constitutional par with blacks. *Watkins v. United States Army,* 837 F.2d 1428 (9th Cir. 1988). Doubts have been expressed that this opinion from a divided three-judge panel—all Carter appointees—would survive an appeal to the full Ninth Circuit en banc—preponderantly Reagan appointees. See *Lesbian/Gay Law Notes* [New York], March 1988, pp. 13–14.

9. For such a failing, see the post-*Bowers* decision, *Padula v. Webster,* 822 F.2d 97, 102 (D.C. Cir. 1987) (gays have no enhanced protections under the Equal Protection Clause). See though *Watkins v. United States Army,* 837 F.2d 1428, 1436 (9th Cir. 1988), which gets just exactly right society's understanding—as it manifests itself in military regulations—of the relation between homosexual *status* and homosexual *acts:* "[T]he regulations target homosexual orientation itself. The homosexual acts and statements are *merely* relevant, and rebuttable, *indicators* of that orientation. Under the Army's regula-

familiarity with gays and a willingness to examine social realities surrounding gays. But the courts have chosen to treat gays as nonentities, unworthy of any attention. The courts simply have not been up to the task of justice when it comes to gays. Gays may be sobered to realize that the last time they won a gay case before the Supreme Court was in 1962—before gays had any public political presence at all.[10]

Worse still than the Supreme Court's abuse by willful neglect of gay issues in the last few years is the prospect that the Supreme Court will use gays as the means of abusing other groups. There is a live possibility, presaged in the sodomy and Gay Olympics cases, that the Court will find in the mechanisms which it has developed in order to avoid addressing gay issues the levers and fulcra for overturning past liberal decisions and narrowing the scope of established rights. To avoid discussing gay issues, the gay olympics case had to rake in the first and fifth amendments. In order to avoid discussing gay sex, the *Bowers* Court had to develop a test for Substantive Due Process privacy rights that would allow the mere citing of the existence of sodomy laws to justify their constitutionality. And so the Court claimed that the only activities protected by privacy rights are those that "are so rooted in the traditions and conscience of our people as to be ranked as fundamental."[11] This test, however, sets the stage for the Court to rule that its original 1973 abortion decision, *Roe v. Wade,* establishing a woman's right to abortion as part of the right to privacy, must be overturned because the

tions, 'homosexuality,' not sexual conduct, is the operative trait for disqualification" (emphasis added). So too with society as a whole. Homosexual acts are in society's eyes not defining parts of what it is to be a homosexual. Homosexual acts stand to being a homosexual as eating soul food stands to being a black person—they are rebuttable indicators of a status that is defined and despised independent of them.

10. *Manual Enterprises v. Day,* 370 U.S. 478 (1962) (held that a photo magazine of male nudes, though "dismally unpleasant, uncouth, and tawdry" and clearly appealing to prurient interest, lacked "patent offensiveness" and therefore could not be considered legally obscene and so could not be prosecuted as falling beyond the reach of the first amendment). In 1967, during the Court's most liberal period, the Court ruled in a nonconstitutional case of statutory construction that, even though Congress did not mention homosexuals in its 1952 immigration act, the exclusion for "psychopathic personality" did not, for its interpretation and application, call upon any medical, psychological, or psychiatric judgment by the courts or administrators, but was rather a term of art which necessarily entailed homosexuality, whatever the medical or psychiatric communities might say about homosexuality and psychopathology. *Boutillier v. Immigration and Naturalization Service,* 387 U.S. 118 (1967). Between 1967 and 1986 the Supreme Court issued no opinions on any gay issue.

11. See *Bowers v. Hardwick,* 106 S. Ct. 2841, 2844 (1986).

wrong constitutional standard had been used in the case and because abortion does not fulfill the requirements of the correct standard.[12] For in 1973, except for court actions, abortion was illegal in virtually every state and had been so since the end of the last century—hardly an activity rooted in the traditions and conscience of the nation. Gays may well be the axe with which the Court hews the nation's traditional commitment to civil liberties.

What are the prospects for positive judicial change? Consider two examples. In 1857 the Court in Dred Scott held that blacks could not have been considered U.S. citizens by the Founding Fathers because "that unfortunate race" was correctly "regarded as beings of an inferior order, and altogether unfit to associate with the white race, either in social or political relation; and so far inferior, that they had no rights which the white man was bound to respect; and that the negro might justly and lawfully be reduced to slavery for his own benefit."[13] Even with the passage of the Civil War amendments, it would be ninety-seven years before the Court fully reversed itself and in the 1954 school desegregation cases finally guaranteed blacks the right to "associate with the white race."[14]

Or again, take gender discrimination. In 1873 Justice Bradley, in a concurrence to a case denying women the right to be lawyers before state supreme courts, proclaimed: "The paramount mission and destiny of women are to fulfill the noble and benign offices of wife and mother. This is the law of the Creator."[15] It would take one hundred and three years before the Court would clearly have reversed the Creator's dispensation of rights to women, when in 1976, for the first time, it claimed that laws making gender-based distinctions must be substantially related to important state interests.[16]

These examples do not bode particularly well for gays, though there

12. In Roe v. Wade, 410 U.S. 113, 152–53 (1973), the Court set out as its standard for the protection of actions under the right to privacy that the actions exhibit central personally affecting values. See chapter 4, section IV.

13. Dred Scott v. Sandford, 60 U.S. (19 Howard) 393, 407 (1857) (blacks are not citizens of the United States and therefore cannot bring cases before the federal courts).

14. Brown v. Board of Education, 347 U.S. 74 (1954); Bolling v. Sharpe, 347 U.S. 497 (1954) (ruled that an Equal Protection dimension of the fifth amendment's Due Process Clause bars racial segregation in federal schools).

15. Bradwell v. Illinois, 83 U.S. (16 Wallace) 130, 141 (1873) (Bradley, J., concurring).

16. Craig v. Boren, 429 U.S. 190 (1976) (striking down gender-differentiated drinking ages).

is the rare occasion when in short order the Court has reverse‹
from the denial to the affirmation of a right. In but three years' time, in
the early 1940s, the Court changed from upholding to barring compulsory school flag salutes.[17] I will not venture a guess on whether it will
take a few years or more than a hundred years for the Court to reverse
Bowers, though already the post-*Bowers* caselaw does not look the least
bit promising for judicial reform—even without possible conservative
shifts in Court personnel.

I suggest though that to get clear on how gay politics should form
itself in the *Bowers* era requires recognizing, as my analysis of the courts'
insults to gays both in their holdings and in their procedures should now
have made clear, that business-as-usual electoral politics directed at
increasing gay happiness is not the proper means or the proper target for
gay public life. If the courts cannot be impartial in their treatment of
gays, it is hopelessly unlikely that society as a whole will give gays a fair
shake. And given the nature of the injustices laid on gays, the remedy
properly sought by gay politics is not chiefly an increase in the material
benefits of gays but the reassertion of gay dignity, which has been denied
or trampled by the very institutions which structurally are supposed to
ensure, or at least promote, justice.

It is perhaps an index of the degree to which gays have absorbed the
values of the dominant culture about their worth that gays, even politically aware gays, have tended to see social and government discrimination against them only in terms of harms rather than indignities. Gays
have shown little recognition that matters of principle are involved in
their plight—that some things are more important than happiness and
that sometimes placing happiness at risk is a way to them. What I wish
to suggest now is that gay political strategies, especially in light of the
Bowers decision, should put a premium on dignity over hoped-for, direct
practical gains.

If I am right in the belief that what is chiefly at stake in gay politics,
understood broadly, is dignity, then the gay movement primarily needs
to take the form of asserting rights by acting in a principled manner. For
proceeding in this way itself brings dignity to gays. The process of gay
politics itself should be a source of dignity and pride—and it can be. For

17. *Minersville School District v. Gobitis,* 310 U.S. 586 (1940) (upholding compulsory
public school flag salutes); *West Virginia State Board of Education v. Barnette,* 319 U.S.
624 (1943) (barring compulsory public school flag salutes).

dignity as an ideal, importantly, is something, unlike happiness, which gays can achieve to a significant degree independently of the goodwill of the dominant culture: it can be experienced in the very political procedure that gays choose. And it is so, if in asserting rights, in bringing about the conditions that make them legislatively and judicially enforceable, gays act as though they already have them, act as though they had equal respect—by respecting themselves to the degree they respect others, even in the face of certain opposition to their doing so. In this way gays put principle over practicality.

Business-as-usual gay politics does not have the proper form to achieve pride and self-respect, nor, except nominally, does it even have these as its ends. Business-as-usual politics understands dignity only in its protocol or Emily Post sense, not in the sense of principled living, not in the sense of rightful pride. To business-as-usual politics, being dignified is trying to gain respect by begging for it, by catering to the dominant culture's standards of respectability and decorum specifically, and ingratiating oneself to society's values generally. In doing so, business-as-usual politics fails to treat gay experience, feelings, and values as worthy of equal treatment, of consideration on a par with the dominant culture's. Here the hearth and home of gay dignity and self-respect is mortgaged to buy stocks in hoped-for, but improbable, practical gains. Yet it is by adhering to principles and being nurtured by them that a people gets through dark times—and these are dark times.

It is not by being subjected to repeatedly defeated expectations that a people keeps its spirits up. Gay leaders, concerned over the energies of volunteers and the wallets of patrons, have regularly wildly overestimated what they can accomplish, even with maximum solid efforts. All too often, gays have been left with both empty cups and damaged souls as the result of a naïve hope on the part of its compromising and so compromised leaders.

I recently received a fundraising flyer from one of the hard-working national gay litigative groups. It urged donations on the ground that things were certainly going to start coming up roses—and soon. It predicted imminent and eminent success in eight cases it was handling. But during the time the flyer was printed, mailed, and arrived, two of the cases described had been concluded and the organization's estimates were dead wrong: gays lost both.

Repeated wild overestimations by gay political leaders intending to drum up enthusiasm frequently simply backfire. They undercut confidence from the ranks. They kindle burn-out in leaders themselves. And they are a source of depression for everyone.

This strategy of exaggerated hope, I suggest, was really the wrong strategy for the litigative organization to be trying in the first place. For win or lose, gays should be pressing ahead in the courts. In the courts, of all places, gays assert dignity by acting as though the rights that are rightfully theirs are already theirs, by presuming their cause is just, and by charging forward in the arena of justice. For the courts in this country are structurally the chief forum for the assertion of principle and right through reasoned argument. It is there that prejudice and politics are *supposed* to be held at bay and where principle is realized in right and over practicality. Rights are trumps over general utility and social policy. Rights throw grit into the wheels of social efficiency. Only a body that structurally is beyond politics could assert such basic rights. When the Court fails in its mission, when it is swayed not by principle but by politics, the Court is to blame, not gays. Gays may get damaged by some bad decisions, but that is not a reason to be faint of spirit. The elegant Harvard heterosexual and law professor Laurence Tribe measuredly pressed a highly conservative argument for the gay side before the Supreme Court in *Bowers*—and lost. The refreshingly brash Mary Dunlap, private esquire, emanating dykeness like a supernova throwing off neutrinos, aggressively pressed gay issues before the Court in the Gay Olympics case—and lost. But in my book she offered a saintly exemplar of what gays should be doing.[18] In pressing gay cases in the forum of rights, gays do what is noble. When gays presume themselves of equal worth exactly where the labeling at least reads "EQUAL JUSTICE UNDER LAW," gays have something to be proud of—even in defeat.

Gay litigative organizations must not lick their wounds too long after *Bowers,* or act like dogs beaten into skittishness. Here especially is not the place for retrenchment. They must regroup and press on with equal protection and other sorts of cases, not taking defensive low-key stances in cases, as some have already done, and not avoiding the Supreme Court itself. The fainthearted say that lost cases establish and fix bad law, and that it is better to wait for a better court, one more politically

18. Mary Dunlap's views on Supreme Court litigation can be found in an introduction to a reprint of the Lesbian Rights Project's *amicus curiae* brief in *Bowers. New York University Review of Law and Social Change* (1986) 14: 949–52.

correct, one more politically sympathetic. To say that though is to degrade one of America's institutions, occasionally great, to the level of politics at which gay leaders themselves are operating.

The NAACP was founded in 1909. It did not have any really big wins before the Supreme Court until 1954 and only had two small wins during all the time in between, one in 1917, one in 1948.[19] But the NAACP did not give up. Neither should gays.

The gay litigative organization should not have been advancing itself like a business with product to sell—happiness. It should not have asked for a donation as a sign of confidence in its skills at social manipulation. It should have asked for the donation as a means of holding gay dignity and rights in trust.

In the legislative realm, a politics of gay dignity means brooking few compromises. Harvey Milk in his stump speech, his ya-gotta-give'm hope speech, correctly asserted: "The first gay people we elect must be strong. They must not be content to sit in the back of the bus. They must not be content to accept pablum. They must be above wheeling and dealing. They must be—for the good of all of us—independent, un-bought."[20] In particular, gay politics must avoid any legal exemptions or qualifications that reinforce antigay stereotypes. Easements from civil protections that exempt, say, fraternities from university gay protec-tions, or nonreligious church functions (like welfare efforts) from city gay rights ordinances, or teachers from state gay protections, all appeal to, project, and enhance stereotypes of gays as child molesters, sex-crazed maniacs, corruptors of the innocent, and destroyers of the family, society, and civilization. Gays must avoid enshrining these stereotypes in law. For stereotypes are not merely damaging, they assault dignity by holding that their subjects are not deserving of respect, of treatment as an equal, but are lesser forms of being, not merely failed moral agents but also not fully moral agents—wicked children at best, contagious lepers at worst. Gays cannot abide such exemptions and still pretend that they have gay pride.

19. *Buchanan v. Warley*, 245 U.S. 60 (1917) (overtly race-based zoning ordinances barred by fourteenth amendment); *Shelley v. Kramer*, 334 U.S. 1 (1948) (ruled that courts, when enforcing contracts, are acting as agents of the state and so are barred from enforcing racially based restrictive convenants).

20. Harvey Milk, "The Hope Speech," tape transcript published in Randy Shilts, *The Mayor of Castro Street: The Life and Times of Harvey Milk*, p. 362 (New York: St. Martin's Press, 1982).

Gays need as well to be especially wary of seemingly neutral rules that in fact have a radically disparate impact against gays. In the wake of the 1984 Mondale-Ferraro debacle, in which neither he nor she tendered any support for gay rights, the Democratic National Committee (DNC) nevertheless eliminated its caucus system, which included a gay caucus that guaranteed gays a voice on various committees.[21] Some gays did not object to being eliminated, because the DNC eliminated all its caucuses—including the women's, black, and hispanic caucuses. It seemed a neutral rule. But blacks, women, and hispanics were guaranteed committee representation through other means than the caucus system— means of which gays have no part. And what is more, eliminating the gay caucus eliminated a gay voice in the party's administrative workings altogether. Among the caucuses, this move had a uniquely disparate impact against gays. It was no accident that subsequently no open gays were nominated to the party's 106-member policy committee. Here a seemingly neutral rule had the effect of eliminating and silencing gays, yet silence and invisibility are gays' chief problem. The Democratic Party not only failed to remedy this problem, it indeed played upon it. The Democratic Party has insulted gays and done so in a sleazy manner through phony neutrality. Gays should not sink their energies or moneys into the Democratic Party till the Democratic Party thinks gay interests are worth hearing, and gay presence an enrichment, not an embarrassment. Till then, gays should be sinking their energies and moneys into building specifically gay institutions—they are badly needed.

More insidiously still, some neutral rules that have a wildly disparate impact against gays may in fact have a liberal or progressive sheen to them yet be all the more dangerous because of their appealing surfaces. Many conversions of gendered rules to gender-neutral rules will in fact be used against gays by the New Right, just as the New Right has successfully co-opted feminist discourse on pornography to suppress speech about and for sexuality. Congress recently made gender neutral the Mann Act, which forbids the interstate trafficking of persons for illegal or even just immoral sexual purposes. The law was originally passed to address the specific problem of the exploitation of women in

21. On gays and the Democratic Party, see "Democratic Leader Calls Gay Rights a 'Fringe' Issue," *The Advocate* [Los Angeles], May 28, 1985, no. 421, p. 18; "Frustration with Democrats Mounts," *The Advocate*, June 25, 1985, no. 423, p. 8; "Democratic Party Policy Excludes Gays—Again," *The Advocate*, October 28, 1986, no. 458, p. 16.

the white slave trade. But the law is hopelessly broad in gauge—remember that gay sex is illegal in half the states and popularly thought to be immoral everywhere. So now under the gender-neutral version of the law, if one drives into D.C., picks someone up at a "P" Street gay bar and returns with him to one's Alexandria condominium for sex, one has committed a federal offense.[22]

So called "sexual harassment" codes offer another example of gender-neutral rules with disparate impact against gays. The courts have ruled that sexual harassment is covered directly under Title VII as a form of gender discrimination. They hold this on the ground that but for the gender of one party *in its relation to* the gender of the other party involved in the harassment, the harassment (typically) would not occur. The courts, though, have turned around and inconsistently, hypocritically, yet systematically refused to use the same "but for" analysis to include gays under Title VII, even though but for one's gender in its relation to the gender of another—one's lover's—the gay person would not be losing his or her job.[23] The courts' inconsistency on this matter shows that they will go to any extreme to avoid seeing gays as having rights yet will also go to any extreme to suppress sexuality.

Though virtually all gays lack civil protections against job discrimination, invariably sexual harassment codes are now being cast in gender-neutral terms and so cover homosexual "harassment." The judicial treatment of gays exampled in "but for gender" analyses ought to give gays pause about how sexual harassment codes will be enforced—especially if gays remember that such codes typically are not limited, as they should be, to barring coercive offers directed at specific individuals, but cover any sexual speech or gesture that any "reasonable" person within hearing or vision's range might find offensive.[24] Such codes never even distinguish between speech for sex and speech about sex. Since most

22. For discussion, see Daniel Tsang, "Law Bars Interstate Transport for Illegal Sex," *Gay Community News* [Boston], December 21, 1986, pp. 3, 6.

23. For examples and discussion of the hypocrisy of the courts' "but for gender" analyses, see Rhonda R. Rivera, "Queer Law: Sexual Orientation Law in the Mid-Eighties —Part I," *University of Dayton Law Review* (1985) 10: 465–67.

24. The following is a fairly typical example of the overly broad, gender-neutral definitions of sexual harassment used in statutes and administrative law: "Sexual harassment is any unwanted sexual gesture, physical contact or statement, which a reasonable person would find offensive, humiliating, or an interference with his or her required tasks or career opportunities." *Code on Campus Affairs and Regulations Applying to All Students* (University of Illinois at Urbana–Champaign, August 1987), p. 85.

people find the existence of gays offensive, it might turn out that any recognizably gay behavior or discussion of gay sex might "reasonably" be found to be sexual harassment—"warranting" the firing of gays.

Such, seemingly neutral, sexual harassment rules are now being touted even by conservative institutions. The reason is not hard to see. Such institutions are not interested in protecting women from coercion but in suppressing sexuality and discourse about sex and in providing for themselves a pretext for getting rid of people they consider troublemakers. And they are quite willing to use feminist-sounding discourse to gloss their intentions. Gays should not, given the courts' record, expect much help in defending themselves on free speech grounds.

Shallow feminism, paired with legal formalism, is for gays a loaded gun left unattended. Gays must not allow neutral rules either insidiously to subvert their interests or to insult them by dismissing their distinctness and forcing them farther from sight.

Further, if gay activists are to hold gay pride as a political ideal, they must never—in their imagined sophistication and rush to business-as-usual, nongay politics—forget the basic truths of the coming out experience. Coming out is the fundament of gays' existence as political creatures. That experience itself offers a model for gay politics. Coming out is not chiefly a means to happiness. It is a conscious giving up of power, a subjection to discrimination, an opening up to a heightened awareness of the ways that society despises gays—these are not the materials and conditions of happiness. But no one who has gone through the experience would willingly go back into the closet. For people got something else out of the experience. They got some sense of self, a sense that, for better or worse, their life was their own, that it had a ground. This is something quite different from acquiring materials and benefits or enjoying, say, sex or a tune. Coming out is an ultimate adventure, for it is an adventure of self-discovery and of the surfacing of the person as capable of guiding her life by her own lights.

For gay politics, one chief consequence of the centrality of the coming out experience to gay existence is that nongay acquaintances, other dispossessed groups, friends, and even—or especially—blood families are not going to be very much help to the gay movement. This is what Harvey Milk said. He said: "The anger and the frustrations that some of us feel is because we are misunderstood, and friends can't feel that anger and frustration. They can sense it in us, but they can't feel it. Because a friend has never gone through what is known as coming out. I will never forget what it was like coming out and having nobody to look up to. I remember the lack of hope—and our friends can't fulfill that."[25] Friends cannot feel the indignities that gays feel. At most, family and friends can care for a gay person's happiness and that only when it does not conflict too much with their own. And so gays cannot pin too much hope on liberal nongay friends—especially in a crunch. At any point that it becomes expedient to them, liberal straight "friends" will abandon gays (need I mention the likes of former Mayors Jane Byrne and the late Harold Washington, Governors Dukakis and Cuomo)—not surprisingly, for their dignity is not at stake. Kurt Hiller said that "the liberation of homosexuals can only be the work of homosexuals themselves."[26] This is as true today as when he spoke it in 1921.

This is not to say that legislative efforts cannot be successful given that nongays will always make up social and legislative majorities. Nongays, though unable to sympathize with the essential gay experience of coming out can on occasion sufficiently empathize with issues of rights if they are cast in terms of intelligible general principles appealing to fairness and justice. There is enough garbage in everyone's lives that everyone has some sense of, some feel for injustice and the need for respite from it. At some point, everyone has at least been betrayed. And time and again city councils around the country have managed, when the argument is cast in terms of principle, to rise above the prejudices of their constituents. It was The Good doing the talking, not constituents or coalitions of the dispossessed, when in Houston and Miami and Eugene and Duluth and Wichita, city councils passed gay rights legislation, legislation which constituents would then through referendum initiatives overturn by wide margins—two to one, three to one, even five to one.

A number of national gay organizations (including one now defunct) have banked their major strategies on building coalitions with other groups—blacks, women's groups, the peace movement, liberals from the Americans for Democratic Action leftward. This is not an unprincipled thing to do. Its problem is that it will not work and is not necessary, and so is a wasteful drain on the movement. It will not work because

25. Milk, "The Hope Speech," p. 362.
26. Kurt Hiller quoted in James D. Steakley, *The Homosexual Emancipation Movement in Germany* (New York: Arno, 1975), p. 76.

these groups' fights are not gays' fights. The complete flop of mass funding solicitations to mailing lists of liberal organizations has proven this conclusively. They do not care in a way that counts for anything. Or again—the black caucus in the U.S. House of Representatives has been a fruitful source of sponsors for various proposed federal gay rights bills. Black congresspersons have risen above the prejudices of their constituents and virtually all are co-sponsors of proposed gay employment legislation, but the legislation is not a high or even middling priority for any of them. They understandably have other concerns.

What is more, one does not fight a storm by putting more orphans into it—to suppose success is to be had in this way is just a communist fantasy. The black movement achieved its political successes without coalitions of the dispossessed. And gays' repeated successes with city councils have not turned on coalitions.

Rather than bothering too much about building coalitions, gays need to develop a rhetoric of principle. They need to develop not a full scale political theory, but principled arguments—not just slogans—which the educated legislator—most of them are lawyers—can understand. The black civil rights movement was able to succeed without a ramified, articulate system of political principles. For principles the movement was able simply to tap into a cultural reserve of religious rhetoric. Right was righteousness. Gays have no such cultural religious reserve to tap into and so must develop arguments for the legislative mind. This need is all the more apparent, if it is remembered that there was no organized *argumentative* objection to the black civil rights movement,[27] while against gays a highly organized opposition claims a proprietary grip on morality. Without too much effort, gays can generate the right sort of arguments, ones that appeal to broad principle and avoid the taunt of "special interest group." This taunt is especially insidious when directed against gays since basically what gays want is simply what every one else already has—rights and privileges—the acquisition of which does not diminish those of others. Gays are not asking for a larger share of a pie of fixed size.

As an example of a principled argument that avoids the "special interest" label, consider my earlier argument on how to warrant gay job

27. See Paul Burstein, *Discrimination, Jobs and Politics: The Struggles for Equal Employment Opportunity in the United States since the New Deal* (Chicago: University of Chicago Press, 1985), p. 107.

protections.[28] Gays should not push the line that job protections are needed so that gays can get rich—that gays supposedly are rich, and selfishly so, is one of the current crop of antigay stereotypes. Rather gays should argue that jobs are one of the chief means by which people identify themselves to themselves (at least in this society) and so employment is closely linked to people's self-worth and dignity. In pitching the argument to legislators, one points out that most people worry about the indignities of retirement, even if they are wealthy, and thus one casts the argument at the proper level of generality to elicit necessary understanding and sympathy.

At a more general level of argumentation, nothing could be more important to the politics of gay dignity than for the gay movement to take a principled stand on the role of religion in public life. In 1986, Chicago politics saw gay "leaders" begging and pleading and whimpering and trying to compromise with Cardinal Bernardin for rights, but ending up without them and without dignity—another case of damaged souls and empty hands.[29] The principled stand, the right stand for gays to take toward the Catholic Church, is that its views are not legitimately to be taken into account in politics—even though of course they are taken into account. The proper scope of the separation of the private morality of religion from the public morality of law is not limited to explicit mentions of religion in law—ones that would trigger first amendment protections. The principle is larger. That in which it is singularly appropriate for one to be guided by one's own lights is singularly inappropriate as a ground to warrant burdens and benefits falling diversely upon others, burdens to those who do not agree with one's private morality, benefits to those who do—at least not through the agency of law, not through public policy. If the rationale for a law or opposition to it is solely religious or inseparable from religion, then it has no proper place in debate on the formation of law.

Now principle requires consistency here: gays cannot consistently welcome the support of California Bishops against the LaRouche AIDS referendum based on political expediency and then oppose Cardinal Bernardin's interventions into Chicago politics on the grounds of sepa-

28. See chapter 5, section II.

29. See "Gay Rights Ordinance Fails," *The Chicago Tribune*, July 30, 1986, p. 1; "Chicago City Council Defeats Gay Rights Bill," *The Advocate*, September 2, 1986, no. 454, p. 13.

rating public and private moralities. If gays think that religious justification is legitimate in the one case, they must accept it in both. Gays cannot pick and choose their religious support and this "cannot" requires drumming the gay Metropolitan Community Church out of gay politics even though it is by far the largest gay organization in the country. Gays would do well to appeal to the traditional American value that religion is not to be the fount of public policy, for it is just exactly religious opposition to gays that gives their average opponent the false appearance of being himself principled in his opposition. Here the grandeurs of Catholicism are much more dangerous than Protestant fundamentalism, Bernardin more dangerous than Falwell. Catholicism's natural law theology places God at one or two removes: "Homosexual Sex Is [Objectively] Immoral" could scream a *Chicago Tribune* frontpage headline quoting Bernardin.[30] It therefore has an air of intellectual respectability, of transferable universality, underwritten for good measure by tradition, an air that fundamentalists and their recent and revealed gods have not. It is a perfectly respectable and indeed the principled thing to do for gays to remind the nation that it is not a Catholic country; few would disagree with that. It is perfectly respectable, indeed the thing to do to remind political conservatives found bedding down with the Catholic Church on gay issues of what the National Conference of Catholic Bishops has to say about capitalism. To do that might just get them to reconsider the role of God in public policy. But in any case, it is time for gays to stop pandering to un-American religious immorality, to stop begging for rights from religious bigots and using religious do-gooders as their own front men.

In the realm of public education the keys to a principled strategy are to be open about and not to sell out gay experience and gay diversity. Better that the gay rights movement should be candid and forthright than united and accommodating. How can it be that four fifths of Americans claim they have no gay acquaintances?[31] It must be that the squeaky clean gay guys of the television docudramas all live somewhere else than the polled public. The main aim of gay public education should be gay publicity—and not by proxy. Coming out singly and in groups is still the most important thing any gay person can do politically.

Remember all those referenda that lost, where leaders in advance

30. *The Chicago Tribune*, July 17, 1986, p. 1.
31. *Newsweek*, August 12, 1985, p. 23.

seemed honestly to think that gays could win—if only gays had clean enough noses, were wholesome enough, low-profiled enough, and denied that gays were gays, denied that gays are distinctive, and instead simply claimed " 'shucks, folks, we're just people, too"? This strategy of gay denial got gays walloped in Houston by over a five-to-one margin— leaving gays devastated.[32] And since the campaign had basically denied gay experience, the strategy also left the devastated with little to fall back on. There are of course always post-mortem claims of silver linings. The gay movement is a movement of silver linings. (Gay AIDS rhetoric is thickly banded with them.) The Houston effort *really* won, so leaders held, because it was an opportunity to educate and "it helped pull us together." But it was not and it did not. There was no attempt to educate Houston about gays. There was no effort to have gays appear as gays. The campaign was not even run by gays. Gays need to get beyond the sloganeering and the vacuous platitudes of "people are just humans too." If slogans there must be, I suggest the original one, Barbara Gitting's elemental "Gay is Good."

The folks out there need to see real live breathing, justifiably angry, gay people saying "How dare you presume." Low-key campaigns simply leave the discussion of gay issues to the opposition. Conservatives cannot be appeased by denying gay experience, indeed they have capitalized on low-key campaigns and gay invisibility by claiming there really is not much, if any, antigay discrimination anyway, so (they claim) legal protections are not needed. Low-key, faceless, gay-less campaigns simply play right into this rationalization, so popular now with neoconservatives, who want to avoid sounding patently prejudicial.

Leaders in Houston and elsewhere should have honestly admitted from the beginning that the referendum had no chance of winning and used it as an opportunity instead to get some, even if just a few, gays to come out publicly and do forthright education about gays, and to get others at least to expend energies in building gay culture and institutions. When political battles are hopeless in a way that is degrading, gays should take the option of turning inward. There will always be a need to build up gay institutions. Such institutions and the fraternity and sorority they nurture are the necessary emotional bases for gay leaders. Without such bases, those working for change will utterly exhaust themselves.

32. For discussion of the Houston referendum disaster, see Stephen Kulieke, "The Houston Defeat: Why?" *The Advocate*, March 19, 1985, no. 416, pp. 10–11.

This is not to counsel gay separatism as an end but only to recognize that in the face of certain defeat nothing is to be gained by playing politics as usual. The really dark times are those for turning inward for necessary renewal. When one hides behind a vacuous nongay campaign slogan, one neither educates the public nor builds a culture.

Particularly objectionable are gay strategies that try to make gays clean up their act. Initiating gay parades in cities that do not have them or, braver still, having gay entries in nongay parades, are particularly good strategies. They show an audience which might not otherwise ever see a gay person as such and show the general population that virtually all gays look average to tedious and are completely nonthreatening even if they do not wear three-piece suits and look like young urban professionals. Such parades show that gays can be just about anyone, because gays are so diverse. The stereotypes of dizzyqueens, John Wayne Gacys and diesel dykes will not go away by keeping boas and leathers out of parades. For, as we have seen,[33] stereotypes are not inductions from skewed samples, generalizations that can be corrected and made scientific simply by unskewing the sample. Stereotypes are cultural creations and are culturally transmitted. The way to change the culture is to get it to face reality, the still largely hidden gay reality. The real dizzyqueens and diesel dykes, not the ones of culture's collective fantasy, are okay, neither requiring apologetics nor warranting grimaces from gay leaders. Take one to lunch sometime.

To "clean up" parades in hopes of immediate political expedience is to deny gay experience and culture, and to sacrifice it to and for the values of others—to be dignified without having dignity. Dignity is not buying the other guy's values just because he is in power. To have dignity is to hold that one's own values count for something, are worthy of consideration on a par with those of others. When gays try to clean up their act by nongay standards, they are denying they are worthy of equal consideration.

In going public in order to assert that gays are worthy of equal respect and to show that gays hold themselves in equal respect, it is particularly important that gays show love and affection publicly. To do so only shocks standards that should not be held to begin with, yet to do so begins to break the vicious stereotype that gays are merely pumping sex organs. And by adopting for themselves the standard that others assume

33. See chapter 1, section II.

SULLEN VOICES

for themselves, gays act with dignity and self-respect. Here is a case
where the benefits of education and the assertion of dignity overlap,
where The Good and political expediency converge. It is time for gay
love to come out—for gays to show themselves as gay, not just mention
themselves. Words are comparatively so forgettable, but men holding
hands at the museum or kissing at the train station and women cuddling
or stroking each other's hair on a park bench is indelible. If gays think
their love is as sustaining and as good as love is to be, then if they do
not assume the same prerogatives as others to express that love they are
not assuming themselves worthy of equal respect. One fails a minimum
duty to self—to do onto oneself as one in fact does onto others. At a
minimum, one has a duty to respect oneself simply because one has a
duty to respect all persons—and one is one. Closet cases perpetually fail
and so frequently deny the very existence of this simple duty-to-self. But
one cannot legitimately claim to keep one's emotions voluntarily out of
the public eye on the ground that one's "a private person" until one has
the live option to do otherwise. Here gays must not hide behind a phony
notion of privacy that says society can selectively enforce privacy conventions against gays.[34] One cannot have pride and say at the same time
"I may as well enjoy the one choice as long as I don't have the other."

When an *individual* is insulted by another *individual, expressing* indignation to the offender is the means of asserting individual dignity. Its
goal is heartfelt apology from the offender.[35] When *society* systematically assaults the dignity of a *group,* the response and remedy called for
are more severe.

The social form of asserting dignity in the face of its social denial is
nonviolent yet assertive civil disobedience. It is time for gay leaders to
put civil disobedience as an item high on their agendas. In 1985, the
United States gave America's champion and best known perpetrator of
civil disobedience the same status in the national pantheon as Abraham
Lincoln, George Washington, Christopher Columbus, and Jesus Christ.
Yet gays have learned nothing from him.

Civil disobedience is the purest principled manner in which to assert
dignity in politics, for it necessarily puts self-interest at risk for the sake
of what is right. Yet here too principle and practicality converge. Gandhi
won, King won. Civil disobedience registers in the political process an

34. See chapter 4, section II.
35. See chapter 2.

intensity of feeling which cannot be measured through the ballot box. Nonviolent civil disobedience nudges majoritarian politics without coercing it. It impels but does not compel. It appeals to and activates a latent moral sense in the general population, a sense not otherwise stirred. Its effects are catalytic. It admittedly presupposes a certain configuration of reserved forces. But a civil rights movement must suppose that such a moral sense and configuration of forces is there waiting to be tapped— if the movement is to succeed at all. Empirical study has shown that black civil disobedience did not change anyone's minds about the correctness of black civil rights legislation; rather it called forth opinion, existent but politically buried.[36] It was necessary to the movement, for only it was able to place civil rights legislation firmly on the national legislative agenda in a way that forced action on it one way or another. Currently gays are dismissable not only because politically dispossessed but especially and particularly because invisible and, in any case, thought to be wimps and pansies.

Moreover, if I have been correct in arguing that compulsory heterosexuality is not chiefly to be explained as a social custom and social choice, but rather is the lens and primary category through which society sees and structures social experience,[37] then gay experience will, if possible, simply be read out of social existence and, if not, then simply overlooked. Civil disobedience is necessary to disrupt the lens and category of compulsory heterosexuality so that gay experience will for the first time have a foreground presence. Further, civil disobedience is necessary to make society self-conscious of its otherwise unseen categories—to make that by which it sees seen.

Civil disobedience, then, is triply appropriate and necessary in addressing gays' problems with political queueing: It would put gays on the national agenda in a way likely to prompt actions one way or another. It would help overcome invisibility and stereotypes. And it would force social self-reflection—would make society aware of what it is unwittingly doing. As things are now, America thinks as little on its policy toward gays as it does on its policy toward Canada. As things are, gays are politically utterly forgettable.

If a group is subject to injustice not simply because of the sort of errors that are misapplications or local failings of a society's system of

36. See Burstein, *Discrimination*, pp. 86–96.
37. See chapter 10.

justice but also because the institutional structures of the society (including especially its judicial institutions) systematically violate justice in ways that subvert the very possibility of judicial remedy and social reform (as we now have seen to be the case for gays not only as the result of legislative acts but of the American judicial system as well), then the usual moral obligations upon the group to obey the law are considerably weakened over the range of law that affects the group as the group it is. Any compact between society and the group is then void. One cannot reasonably presume that members of a group, severally or collectively, would knowingly and willingly consent to their necessary degradation. One cannot reasonably presume that they would knowingly and willingly consent to their exile from the mechanisms of politics and of public life more generally. It is unreasonable, indeed morally incoherent, to assume that a group would contract for the suspension of the equitable administration of criminal and civil law on its behalf. And it can hardly be the case that gays ought to obey the law as a way of discharging a debt of gratitude for the many benefits they have received from society. It is right and the right time to put civil disobedience on the gay rights agenda.

Assertive civil disobedience is always a symbolic use of space. The venue of civil disobedience will therefore vary with its aims. General street disruptions have a diffused target—general civil rights legislation. Here the act is not itself an instance of what one wants. More focused civil disobedience can sometimes target and take the very form of the thing desired. Such is a sit-in at a segregated lunch counter, where the aim is, either through legislation or private moral reform, to gain access to the counter. Such imaging of aim in form has proven particularly effective where it is the government that segregates. America's great disobeyer is not Henry Thoreau but Rosa Parks, who sat at the front of a city bus in violation of law so that it would come to pass that other blacks could do so by right. As an initial target for gay civil disobedience I suggest marriage license bureaus. The gay Metropolitan Community Church might conduct its holy unions there in violation of law so that it would come to pass that other gays could marry there by right.

One of the chief cultural discoveries of the modern age is that—especially as the coarseness of criminal law gives way to the refined intrusive filaments of administrative law, be it in a dictatorship or a welfare state—dignity is most effectively erased not wholesale but in many minute steps. Dignity once compromised is not easily recovered. For dignity is required to resist degradation. Without it people prove capable of ever gradually adjusting their expectations downward to match their diminished prospects, until no depth of demeaning treatment, no amount of misery is too much to suffer. Once compromises have begun, degradation and compromise mutually reinforce each other, and so begins a spiral into degrading circumstances which would not be tolerated if coming all at once but which are tolerated when achieved piecemeal. The slide from occupational restrictions to Zyklon-B can be so smooth to the mind that does not see anything worth protesting initially, that in the end it may actually believe—even if to do so requires willful ignorance—that coffee will be served after the delousing showers.

One of the chief mechanisms of the step-by-step degradation of oppressed groups—one particularly to be avoided—is for the dominant culture to draw a distinction in the oppressed group between the good ones and the bad ones—the "good niggers" and the "bad niggers," the *Judenrat* and the resistance—and then, to get the good ones to condemn the bad ones as troublemakers—good and bad and trouble all defined by the dominant culture of course. This is the way of Uncle Tom, not Martin Luther King. And so it cannot be too soon for gays to decide what sort of people they are, Step'n Fetchit or Rosa Parks, and while deciding, remember that before the fall, pride dies.

Index

Among court decisions, only those by the U.S. Supreme Court are indexed systematically. Lower federal and state court cases are marked by a raised asterisk (*). General trends in gay law are best tracked through the field-establishing works of Rhonda R. Rivera (q.v.) —current events through Arthur S. Leonard's monthly *Lesbian/Gay Law Notes* (New York Law School).

Marriage (nongay) (*continued*)
source of privacy rights, 129–30; as institution of state, 129
Marotta, Toby, 111*n*35
Marx, Karl, 267
Masochism, 102, 288
Mason, James, 224-25
Massachusetts: solicitation law in, 55*n*20
Mass, Lawrence, 25*n*7
Mass media: and AIDS, 218-19; and black civil rights movement, 175*n*20; and gays, 174-75; *see also* First amendment
Masters and Johnson, William H. and Virginia E., 41&*n*34, 103&*n*17, 232
Masturbation: as private activity, 67
Mathy, Robin, 39*n*32
Mayer, Kenneth H., 239*n*28
Media, *see* Mass media
Meese, Edwin, 259, 271
Menstruation, 99
Merritt, Deborah Jones, 263*n*38
Metropolitan Community Churches (gay fundamentalists), 193-94, 331, 336
Meyer v. Nebraska (parental privacy rights), 91&*nn*, 127*n*5, 263*n*40
Militrary, the, *see* Armed Forces
Milk, Harvey (gay martyr), 29, 61, 187*n*44, 324, 327
Mill, John Stuart, 139-140&*nn*, 184*n*39; anti-paternalism of, 139-40; and civil rights justifications, 141-43; constitutional principle of, 139, 141; on definition of harm, 139; and libertarians, 143; on social custom as tyranny, 140; on social oppression of speech, 180; on state coercion, 140-41
Minersville School District v. Gobitis (flag salutes), 321*n*17
Mineshaft, The (gay sex club), 222*n*16
Minorities: and constitutional rights, 86-87; in democratic theory, 172; discrete and insular, 90, 169; Equal Protection rights of, 90*n*102; gays as one among, 14; *see also* Invisible minorities; *United States v. Carolene Products*
Miscegenation: and child custody, 206-9; and Equal Protection, 206-9; right to, 130; and Substantive Due Process, 78; see also *Loving; Palmore*

Mississippi: sodomy law of, 51*n*9
Missouri: sodomy law in, 49*n*1
Model Penal Code (American Law Institute), 54
Mohr, Richard D., 35*n*28, 84*n*79, 156*n*31
Molester, child, *see* Child molester
Montgomery, Alabama: civil disobedience in, 61*n*31
Moore v. City of East Cleveland (grandparents' rights), 77*n*61, 78*n*70, 92*n*111, 263*n*40
Moral agency, 59
Moral character: and sodomy laws, 56
Morality: and Civil Rights Act, 190; and gay family law, 204; and gay sex, 190; as occupational qualification, 201-4; reason in, 283-84; senses of, 31; skepticism about, 17; and sodomy laws, 204; unnaturalness in, 34
Moral Majority Report, 175-76
Moscow, 199
Murphy, Julien S., 254*n*20
Murphy, Robert, 95*n*2
Murphy, Timothy F., 26*n*9, 307*n*7
Muslims, 95
Myrdal, Gunnar *(An American Dilemma)*, 1, 3

NAACP: and the Supreme Court, 324
NAACP v. Button (associational rights), 64&*n*10
Nagel, Thomas, 100*n*15
Nalty, Bernard C., 256*n*23
National Academy of Science, 239*n*29, 257*n*25
National Association of Insurance Commissioners, 246*n*3
National Conference of Catholic Bishops, 331
National Gay and Lesbian Task Force, 27, 28*n*12
National Gay Rights Advocates, 170*n*12
National Gay Task Force v. Oklahoma City Board of Education, 171*n*15
National Endowment for the Humanities, 297
National Institute for Mental Health, 155*n*29
National security: as public good, 240